To: 나미

With my Warmest
regards + Best
wishes,

Jan. 1, 2024
Champoon C. Kim

Taming
the Tiger
Mom

Taming the Tiger Mom

Published in 2017 by Seoul Selection U.S.A., Inc.
4199 Campus Drive, Suite 550, Irvine, CA 92612

Phone: 949-509-6584 / Seoul office: 82-2-734-9567
Fax: 949-509-6599 / Seoul office: 82-2-734-9562
Email: publisher@seoulselection.com

ISBN: 978-1-62412-088-6
Library of Congress Control Number: 2017937896

Printed in the Republic of Korea

Taming the Tiger Mom

A Balanced Approach to Maximizing a **Child's Potential**

Chungsoon C. Kim

Seoul Selection

TABLE OF CONTENTS

Foreword   6
Preface   8
Acknowledgements   12

PART I. BECOMING A PARENT

Chapter 1   The Heavy Responsibilities and
             Complexities of Parenting   16
Chapter 2   What Makes Us: Genes vs. Experience   22
Chapter 3   Why the Uphill Battle?   30
Chapter 4   Gender Roles in Parenting   37
Chapter 5   Parenting Challenges of Single Mothers   42

PART II. PREGNANCY & CHILDREARING

Chapter 6   How the Prenatal Experience Shapes Our Lives   50
Chapter 7   The Growth of a Fetus   54
Chapter 8   Prenatal Use of Harmful Chemical Substances   58
Chapter 9   Weight Gain during Pregnancy   68
Chapter 10   Sex during Pregnancy   71
Chapter 11   Diet and Nutrition during Pregnancy   75
Chapter 12   Breastfeeding vs. Use of Formula   79
Chapter 13   Toilet Training   85
Chapter 14   Language Development   90
Chapter 15   Play, the First Step of Learning   100
Chapter 16   Discipline and Setting Limits   108

Chapter 17 Building Harmonious Relationships among
            Siblings   115
Chapter 18 Childhood Obesity and Its Prevention   122
Chapter 19 Challenges of Raising an Autistic Child   129
Chapter 20 Attention Deficit/Hyperactivity Disorder   134

PART III. RAISING COMPETENT AND HAPPY CHILDREN

Chapter 21 The Key to a Child's Happiness: Self-esteem   142
Chapter 22 Raising a Confident Child   152
Chapter 23 Fostering Tolerance   161
Chapter 24 Fostering Adaptability   165
Chapter 25 Choosing a Preschool or Childcare Center   171
Chapter 26 Facilitating Cognitive Development   179
Chapter 27 Fostering Creativity   193
Chapter 28 Helping Children Do Well in School   201
Chapter 29 Early Foreign Language Education: Truth
            vs. Myth   207
Chapter 30 Teaching Financial Responsibility   214
Chapter 31 Helping Children Overcome Screen Addiction   218
Chapter 32 Raising Children as an Immigrant   224

Epilogue   234
References   238
About the Author   242

Foreword

In *Taming the Tiger Mom*, Dr. Chungsoon Kim attempts to inspire and advise young parents, parents-to-be, grandparents, teachers, and professionals in the field of early childhood education.

The author asserts her position by integrating her years of experience as a scholar, esteemed professor of child and adolescent development, mother of three sons, and active grandmother of four grandchildren. Melding the vast amount of available research, prevalent academic theories, and her rich personal and professional experience, the author emphasizes the need for parents to provide their children with unconditional love and a sense of deep respect and understanding. Through genuine acceptance of children for who they are, and by providing support and the sense of security and guidance they require during their early years, adults can build the basis for trust that will help children mature to their full potential for successful adulthood.

In this book, the author describes the joy of raising children with rich memories and experiences by providing a deep pool of resources to draw upon as they emerge into young adulthood. The author further illustrates the particular importance of early childhood as a time to truly nurture the unique spirit, individual disposition, and love of learning inherent in each and every child.

When I attended my first class taught by Dr. Kim some three decades ago, I was struck by her deep understanding of the nature of children and the very unique quality of each child. Dr. Kim placed much trust and faith in children's innate abilities and ways and emphasized the need for adults to become better observers and supporters of young children. Again just a few months ago, in closing up my parents' home in Pennsylvania, I found my own letter to my mother, enthusiastically describing what I had been learning in Dr. Kim's class. I had an opportunity to pause and reflect on how she has influenced my own parenthood and professional career.

When Dr. Kim asked me to write a foreword for *Taming the Tiger Mom*, I embraced the opportunity with utmost humility and enthusiasm, for I knew this would be the opportunity for me to describe her profound influence on my own life and on countless other lives.

Beth Wise
Associate Director, Bing Nursery School
Lecturer, Department of Psychology
Stanford University

Preface

Over the past half-century, the world has undergone change at an ever-increasing rate, and parenting practices, in response, have undergone change themselves. Contemporary parents are more tech-savvy than previous generations. They are marrying later, often after establishing themselves professionally, and they are less constrained by traditional gender roles. Today's families face increasing pressure in terms of both money and time. And although families are having fewer children, the pressure on families for children to succeed is greater than ever before. Meanwhile, family structures are becoming more varied as many children grow up with single parents, same-sex parents, or stepfamilies.

Parents are raising their children in a world that is both more complicated and more flooded with information. According to Daniel Levitin, professor of psychology at McGill University, there were 30 exabytes of information in the world ten years ago, compared to 300 exabytes of information today, which is roughly 300 quintillion numerical characters' worth of information. This excess of information, not surprisingly, extends to parenting. The cross-generational passing down of parental wisdom from one's own family and neighbors is no longer common practice. Instead, parents receive overwhelming, often competing, advice from social media and Internet "experts." Books, newspapers, and magazines are replete with information on parenting. While this abundance of childrearing advice shows society's interest in parenting, it also means that there is no magic formula when it comes to raising children. More than ever, especially with the deluge of information available on parenting, parents must discern the trustworthiness of the information presented to them. Trying to sort through everyone's opinions and decide which information is reliable or which is the best to help their child can be a daunting task.

In this book, I have tried to provide young parents with some guidelines that will help them make sound parenting decisions for themselves. These are based on personal knowledge gained over forty years of teaching and widely accepted theories and reputable research. I also wrote from my own experience raising three children and four grandchildren. What was most helpful in writing this book, however, were the insights I gained from my interactions with countless children and parents at the San Jose State University Child Laboratory, where I worked as the lab director.

This book offers no secret methods for raising children, nor any success stories of exemplary parents who have raised their children to achieve greatness. I believe, however, that this book will guide young mothers and fathers to what they can do to help their children develop their full potential as unique individuals with strengths and weaknesses.

Remembering how lost I felt when my first child was born, despite being a graduate student in child development, and the countless trials and errors I experienced as a parent, I am grateful that all of my children grew up to be who they are. In retrospect, my mistakes stemmed more from trusting faddish childrearing information than from my own lack of knowledge.

For the readers who are looking for a magic formula to raise their child to be a star student or go to the best university, you will not find it in this book. I do not believe such a formula exists. I believe, however, that this book will guide parents toward the best solutions to various challenges they will encounter in rearing their children. For that reason, I have selected key topics from different phases of child development, and for each topic I have explained the important issues and how parents can help their children.

Raising a child is like tending a flower garden. Just as each plant is special and beautiful in its own way, and no two are the same, every child is born with a unique temperament and abilities. In order for flowers to bloom fully, one must water the plants in consideration of their inherent characteristics, plant them in a place with proper light levels, and fertilize the soil from time to time as needed. Tending a lily as if it were a rose will not produce the best results. Some parents do not consider their child's abilities and temperament and instead push the child to a desired goal as if putting together a stylish, high-performance automobile in a factory. As a result, the child not only has difficulty developing his or her innate potential but also suffers emotionally.

My hope is that this book will increase the chances that parents are able to provide a "safe haven" for every child, a place from which the child can draw unconditional love, encouragement, and acceptance. I also hope that it serves as a reminder that parenting practices must fit the parents as well as the child. Lastly, my hope through this book is that the readers come to see parenting as a critical responsibility of society as well as the family. Without strong families, no strong societies can exist.

Acknowledgements

I dedicate this book to the memory of my mother (1900–1990). She always accepted me for who I was with trust, encouragement, and hope. Her lifetime of devotion and unconditional love for her children was truly remarkable.

I would also like to express my deep gratitude to the late Professor Jung Il Joo, the founding President of Korean Association of Child Studies, who encouraged me to pursue graduate study in the United States and helped me get a scholarship from the Georgia Rotary International Fellowship. She was my mentor and cheerleader in all of my academic endeavors.

There are many people whose help has been invaluable in the process of completing this book, and to whom I wish to express my gratitude.

I am indebted to Ockju Noh for her suggestion for the title of this book and for her insightful and constructive suggestions. Whenever I became discouraged, her support was invaluable. Special thanks go to Amy Strage, who reviewed the entire manuscript and provided me with constructive comments and suggestions. I also appreciate the significant contributions—both in content and organization—of Jonghye Han to the Korean version of this book. I am grateful to Junesun Lee for the examples she shared from her own experience raising her daughter Sophie; they helped the text "come alive." I would also like to express my deep gratitude to Juliette B. Quinn for her careful reading and skillful editing. I also want to say a special thank-you to my grandson Stewart Kim, a high school student who read the entire book carefully and made incisive comments despite his busy schedule. Stewart's impressive editing ability and his fresh, young perspective have made this book livelier and easier to read.

Thanks also to the publishing staff at Seoul Selection for their professionalism and skill in the design and production of this book. I am grateful to Publications Manager Jin Lee for his efficient and tireless efforts to coordinate all of the different aspects of this book's production. I'd also like to thank Christine Kwon, the English manuscript editor, for a great job of editing with attentiveness to detail. She is responsible for much of the improvement to this book.

Finally, and most importantly, I extend my deep appreciation to my husband of fifty-three years, Yungho Kim. He has been my counselor and helper during difficult moments in raising our three sons and four grandchildren and also in my professional career. Without his understanding and support, I couldn't have accomplished what I have.

BECOMING A PARENT

THE HEAVY RESPONSIBILITIES AND COMPLEXITIES OF PARENTING

Becoming a parent seems rather simple. You find someone you love and care for, get married or cohabitate, and have a child, at which point you become a parent. Unlike becoming a lawyer or a physician, parenting does not require specialized education or passing a test. Nor is a higher education level or socioeconomic status a necessary part of good parenting.

Parenting is arguably one of the most common tasks we face, and yet also the most difficult. As many people who are successful otherwise will learn, things do not exactly go as planned or hoped when it comes to parenting. The founder of Samsung Group, the late Lee Byung-chul, was no exception. He was CEO of the largest company in Korea and yet considered parenting one of the most tumultuous tasks in life. Parents must adjust their parenting behavior as a child moves through different stages of development. The role of parents is especially important during a child's first few years because it is during

this period that parents essentially permeate the child's entire environment. In this phase of a child's life, the child forms an attachment to his or her parents that lays the foundation for healthy personality development, including basic trust, autonomy, and sense of initiative. During this period, the child also undergoes rapid mental and physical development.

Parenting is nothing like manufacturing a product. When a product is manufactured by a systematized process in a controlled environment, it usually comes out as intended, save for a few faulty products. Farming, by comparison, is trickier. The environment, in particular the weather, cannot be controlled, and the crops are greatly affected. Yet there is still a certain assurance that quality seeds and proper watering and fertilizing will produce a good yield most years. Parenting, though it can be likened to farming, is far more difficult. The results cannot be guaranteed. Every child is born with a unique disposition and potential, and by the age of two or three, children have already begun to have minds of their own. Even if parents have an excellent future planned for their child, the reality seldom plays out as planned. Also, as the saying goes, no two children are alike, even in the same family, even with similar genes and childhoods spent in the same family environment. If a group of parents was to follow the same method of parenting suggested in a bestselling parenting book, the results would still vary widely, because every child is different and each parent's temperament is also different.

The sound of rustling might wake up a baby very sensitive to sound while not bothering others. The trait of being extra sensitive itself is not a problem; rather, it becomes a problem when parents have a low threshold of acceptance for that trait in their baby. Sometimes just having more realistic expectations about our children can be helpful. Knowing we have a child who is of a more sensitive temperament can help us to understand that it is not our fault, that we did not make this child the way he is, and that it is not the result of "bad parenting." When parents can accept these individual differences, they can more effectively help the sensitive child successfully grow out of that stage.

For example, if a very active parent has a child who does not enjoy physical activity, this may potentially lead to conflict. Or if a parent is very social and enjoys parties and their child has a tough time feeling comfortable in a group of people, the parent may become frustrated and angry with the child. Parents must observe the needs of their children and try to meet them. Regardless of a child's disposition, a parent's sensitive and attentive care will enable healthy development to a great degree; if the parent is inattentive and does not meet the child's needs, the child will be adversely affected. A child who sometimes misbehaves is unlikely to develop a severe behavioral problem if the mother or father can provide patient, loving, and supportive care. By contrast, a mother or father who considers a child's behavior to be a serious problem and is insensitive to the child's needs has a high likelihood of affecting the child adversely. As such, there are varying levels of compatibility between parents' temperaments and a child's, similar to marital compatibility between a husband and wife. This compatibility is referred to in some literature as "goodness of fit". With more compatibility, children grow up in less stressful conditions, and parents can revel in the joys of parenthood.

There are basic principles of good parenting across generations and cultures. One is parental devotion and patience. Another is careful observation and sensitivity in identifying a child's needs and then meeting them. All parents hope their children live healthy and happy lives. Parenting methods, however, are influenced greatly by culture and environment. As such, parenting practices vary by socioeconomic status and ethnicity as well as how those parents were parented. For instance, the attitudes and practices of American parents differ from those of Korean parents, and each set of practices has its own advantages as well as its consequences. American parents generally respect the individuality of their children and are less likely to harbor unrealistic expectations for them. Also, fewer American parents expect their children to get into Harvard or become rich and famous. By contrast, Korean parents tend to have unrealistically high expectations of their children, hoping they get into a top university, or even win a Nobel Prize.

Yet not all flowers in the world have to be roses. There are thousands upon thousands of different kinds of flowers, each with a unique beauty that, in harmony with other flowers, makes the world more beautiful. This is why Chinese philosopher Zhuang Zhou said that one should neither stretch the duck's legs, which are short by nature, nor amputate the crane's legs, which are long by nature.

To care for a young, blooming tree, the gardener does needed pruning, creates shade to protect the tree from the scorching sun and erects supporting stakes to help it withstand storms. Likewise, it is the responsibility of parents to create a nurturing environment for their growing child. To this end, parents must pay close attention to their child, determine the child's needs, and take action to meet those needs. Through this process, parents can gain an understanding of their child's strengths and weaknesses and become better able to nurture the strengths and embrace the weaknesses.

Another point parents need to understand is that the child should be approached as a whole person. Parents must remember the dynamics that exist between the different domains of their child's development, including physical, socio-emotional, and intellectual aspects. For example, overweight children often find it difficult to make friends, and as a result, suffer from low self-esteem or depression. In this case, pressuring the child only to study hard will leave him or her feeling helpless; the priority should be helping the child lose weight. In a similar sense, it is difficult for a sickly child to concentrate on schoolwork. Expecting a child who often misses school due to poor health to perform well academically is unrealistic. If a child is too weak to do strenuous exercise, parents should guide the child to start with easier exercises first. The parents must first help the child get healthy, ensuring that health comes before studying hard or enjoying play and sports.

Contemporary parents face many challenges raising children in today's rapidly changing world, especially with increasing time and money pressures and the prevalence of dual-earner households. Yet I don't believe any generation of parents in human history ever considered parenting easy.

In spite of its difficulties and challenges, parenting is the most joyful and meaningful human endeavor. It is an invigorating and powerful experience where parents, together with their children, can grow.

CHAPTER 2

WHAT MAKES US: GENES VS. EXPERIENCE

Most of us at some point have asked ourselves the question of what makes us the way we are. Are we mainly a product of our genes or influences from the environment? How do we turn out the way we do? How do inherited genetic traits, parenting methods, and the setting in which a child is raised affect that child's development, and to what extent? There is an old Korean saying: "Water and children go as they are led." What does this mean in the debate of nature versus nurture? The natural flow of water from higher pressure to lower pressure can be likened to children inheriting genetic factors from their parents. At the same time, just as creating a sluice improves water flow, creating an optimal environment allows children to develop their inherent abilities and reach their full potential.

Among scholars who insist that genetic factors play a decisive role in human growth and development, some believe that intelligence level is determined at birth by the genes that a child receives from his or her parents. Well-known—albeit controversial—American psychologist Arthur Jensen claimed that 75 to 80 percent of human intelligence is determined by heredity, leaving only about 20 percent to be determined by one's environment. Recent research results on twins and adoptees offer support to this claim, suggesting that heredity has the most significant impact on one's intelligence. Research has also shown that from childhood to old age, the intelligence of identical twins tends to coincide to an increasing degree, while the intelligence of adoptees comes to resemble that of their biological parents more than that of their adoptive parents.

Facial features, complexion, height, body type, and motor skills are also known to be affected greatly by genetic factors. Even much of a person's psychological makeup, such as introversion or extroversion, aggression, and feelings of well-being, are genetically based.

Proponents of environmental determinism claim that the role of the environment in child development is greater than that of heredity. Advocates of this theory believe that children are born as the *tabula rasa*, or "blank slate," and that development occurs through training and experience. They claim that physical environment (quality of healthcare and diet), social environment (family, friends, and school), and the parenting methods used are key factors for a child's growth and development. For instance, while adoptees resemble their biological parents more than their adoptive parents in intelligence, adoption studies have also shown that children adopted into families of higher economic standing generally exhibit higher intelligence than biological siblings who were raised by their biological parents. The differences serve as the evidence that the socioeconomic status and nurturing environment of the adoptive families contribute to the intellectual development of adoptees.

In addition to family environment and parenting methods, one's social environment also affects intellectual development. Changes in environmental factors, such as enhanced educational infrastructure and improved diet, have proven to increase the intelligence of children. While the rate of increase differs by country, during the past few decades, the average IQ has reportedly been increasing by about three points every decade. There are also some instances in which environmental manipulation can deter the harmful effects of hereditary influences. One such instance is the rare hereditary disorder known as phenylketonuria (PKU), which is caused by a deficiency of an enzyme that breaks down phenylalanine. The accumulation of phenylalanine in the body causes spasms, intellectual disabilities, and psychiatric disorders. Most PKU cases are detected soon after birth through newborn screenings, with a prompt treatment that follows. Therefore, the severe signs and symptoms of classic PKU are rarely seen. Though the occurrence of PKU varies among ethnic groups and geographic regions worldwide, in the United States, PKU occurs in 1 in 10,000 to 15,000 newborns. This is a prime example of controlling hereditary influence through appropriate intervention.

According to recent neuroscience research, not only do environmental factors, such as the diet of the parents, prenatal maternal stress, and the nutrition of the fetus, influence genetic traits, but the resultant changes are also passed on to the next generation. In other words, lifestyle and environment can cause changes in genetic expression without changing the genetic code. The study of this phenomenon is called epigenetics. Research has shown that people who live in poverty for a long period of time have relatively low motivation for achievement, which influences their genes and increases the likelihood of their children having lower intelligence and less motivation to succeed.

Such findings remind us of the seriousness of the economic polarization plaguing many countries. According to a report by the United Nations Development Program, the richest 10 percent of people accounted for 23 percent of all income in Korea in 2009, while the poorest 10 percent accounted for 3 percent. The implications of economic polarization do not end with psychological and emotional scarring of the poor. The greater tragedy is that economic polarization leads to polarization in education in the next generation. According to research by the Bank of Korea and the Korean Bureau of Statistics, in 2008, households in the top 20 percent income bracket in Korea spent around seven times more on their children's education than households in the lowest 20 percent income bracket. This means that poor students are not only brought up in homes that do not have ideal environments for studying but they also receive education of poorer quality. There's a Korean proverb that says, "A dragon can sometimes rise from a small stream." In the past, it was not uncommon to hear of people overcoming difficult childhoods to save their families from hardship in Korea. Recently, however, such tales seem rare.

Is financial wealth all that parents need to be able to provide a rich educational environment for their children? Not all children of wealthy parents achieve academic success. Also, there are plenty of motivated students who, despite unfavorable family conditions, enter prestigious universities and become contributing members of society. Where I live in Northern California, more than half of high school valedictorians are of Asian descent. A significant number of them are the children of Vietnamese immigrants who sailed to the United States with few material possessions after the Vietnam War. Often, those students live with their families in small apartments, with no desks of their own, only a spot at the dining table. After supper, the TV is turned off, and the table is cleared for the children to study. On the other hand, I often see students from well-to-do families in Silicon Valley receive low grades and show little interest in studying, despite their parents hiring tutors for each subject they find challenging.

This brings to mind the American proverb that says, "You can lead a horse to water, but you cannot make him drink." In other words, even in an ideal educational environment, a child who lacks motivation cannot be forced to study.

Another theory that supports the notion that genes guide the selection of one's experience is Scarr and McCartney's model of niche picking, which suggests that humans, as active beings, seek environments that complement their heredity. A friend of mine had a kindergarten-aged daughter who begged her mom to send her to an after-school abacus program in which her friend was enrolled. Her mother, being a math education professor, was reluctant to send her. She was familiar with research findings that showed that abacus skills do not help mathematical thinking. The child pestered her mother day and night until she eventually relented and let her attend the program for a long time. Through this incident, the mother realized that her child was fascinated by the symbolic system of numbers and the regularity of arithmetic operations. Now a middle school student, the child still enjoys mathematics and communicating concisely and clearly using only numbers and symbols. She still recalls fondly the memories of the after-school abacus program, how she used to listen to the numbers her teacher called out, slide the beads, and calculate in her head. The child found an environment suited to her innate talent, all by herself.

The aforementioned heredity versus environment controversy is useful to understanding the dynamics of human development. The impacts of heredity and environment must be viewed not as opposing forces but as interacting forces. For example, the scholastic excellence of a child born to intelligent parents might be attributable to genetic factors, but it might also be due largely to a nurturing environment in which the parents encouraged the child to be intellectually curious and to pursue academic excellence. A more reasonable explanation, however, might be that the child's strengths stem from the interaction of these two factors.

Every person is born with different inherited traits into a different environment. Each child is special and precious in his or her own way. All children—those who are fragile and imperfect and those who are healthy and smart—have unique individual qualities and abilities. No two children in the world are exactly the same. Parents, therefore, must employ appropriate parenting methods and create an environment that is suited to each

child's characteristics, paying close attention to the interests of the child. It is the role and responsibility of parents and society to enable each child to develop his or her innate talents and abilities to the fullest extent.

From the modern founder of eugenics Francis Galton to the purist behaviorist John Watson, many have influenced the theory of parenting in this country in the 20th century. As we all know, psychology and child development theories swing like a pendulum. But in the 1960s, heritability studies became much easier and popular to perform, and I participated in a large-scale longitudinal twin study at Florida State University. More recently, Steven Pinker's popular book *The Blank Slate: The Modern Denial of Human Nature* (2002) brought public attention to a paradigm shift away from pure behaviorism. At about the same time, advances in genetic studies have brought more credence to the nature theory. This trend will continue for a while.

My firm belief, however, is that for a child to have a healthy, happy, well-adjusted life, parenting, not our genes, may be the predominant factor. The environment (development in the womb, nutrition, family, school, personal contacts, culture, etc.) is where we can exert our control. Also, it's important to realize that even a highly heritable trait such as the intelligence of a child correlates with the parents' intelligence by r=.80; this suggests that family environment may determine up to 36 percent of the variance. This is huge. At least, to me it is.

CHAPTER 3

WHY THE UPHILL BATTLE?

The question of how to raise children well has been a matter of concern to parents in every generation and every society. For this reason, it is natural for parents to tune in when they hear of a new, effective way to parent. But before seeking out new strategies, we must first think about the principles of parenting. Becoming a caring and devoted parent is at the base of all parenting. And parents themselves must set good examples for their children.

Children often exhibit a parent's values and behavior patterns. Selfish and prejudicial parents have a high chance of raising selfish and prejudicial children. There is no use lecturing children about being considerate of others if the parents themselves are not generous and considerate. Parents who do not obey traffic signals cannot teach their children to abide by the law. Parents who frequently fight in their home cannot expect their children to be gentle and kind. There is a Korean adage that says, "When we speak ill of others, we become like them."

A story that a friend of mine told me about a father demonstrates this very well. The father used to come home very late and drunk almost every night; he woke his children, pulling them by the ear and dragging them around. The son hated what the father did to him and said he would never do that to his own children. Surprisingly, when he grew up and became a father, he did exactly the same things his father had done. Children grow up watching their parents' good and bad behavior, and as adults, they unconsciously imitate them. That is why it is so important for parents always to be good role models—it is very hard to break the cycle.

Children learn more from their parents' actions than they do from their words, holding true to the English expression that actions speak louder than words. In my family, for example, when our children were growing up, my husband would take any chance he could get to watch football on TV, and our children would sit beside him and watch, too. Now they are in their 40s, and my children still like to pass the time watching football. Their father says, "I am an old man, but you're still young. Shouldn't you go out and exercise, not sit in front of the TV for hours?"

My children usually then jokingly retort, "When you were our age, you watched TV all the time instead of exercising." Everyone laughs at this and continues watching the game, but it's a comment that demonstrates the inconsistency between my husband's words and his actions.

Parents must always remember that it takes a long time for a person's values and behavioral patterns to change. It's very important that a child forms good habits when still young, things as simple as going to bed on time or eating healthy. As the saying goes, old habits die hard. A child who thinks nothing of breaking school rules will not turn into a model student overnight. A child who likes to hang out with friends all the time will not turn into a bookworm overnight. Helping a child change takes a long time and requires great effort and patience on the part of the parents. Moreover, values and behavioral patterns are hard to change once formed, indicating that it is most effective to teach children while they are very young, before bad habits are formed.

One of my friends once bought a set of biographies on the world's great thinkers for her preschool-aged daughter. Every night before going to bed, her daughter would pick out a book for her mom to read to her. When they finished reading, they talked about the daughter's dreams and what kind of person she wanted to become when she grew up. The child, who is now twelve years old, still remembers the accomplishments of the people in those biographies and hopes to someday become like them. Telling a child in detail about the lives of various great people is more likely to move her than merely telling the child that she should become a great person.

Many parents are disappointed when their children do not meet their expectations, and they react by scolding the children or blaming their spouse, or themselves. Unfortunately, these actions do nothing to address the underlying issue. Research in developmental psychology, genetics, and medicine suggests that the causes of various physical and psychosocial conditions such as attention-deficit disorder, hyperactivity, depression, and obesity are complex. All parents must examine their parenting methods and work toward correcting problematic areas. Having said this, we must also acknowledge that when children go astray, it is usually neither the parents' nor child's fault. As such, parents should not blame themselves. In many instances, the parents have to wait patiently until the child can come out of the situation.

Let's take the case of the family of well-known American evangelical Reverend Billy Graham. One of the Grahams' sons had a pretty tumultuous few years as a teenager, rebellious and in love with fast cars, drinking, and girls. The Grahams waited patiently, trusting that their son would realize in time what was right and wise. The same son is now doing missionary work in China. Whether children respect or think ill of their parents, they end up taking after them; children are reflections of their parents.

Close friends and neighbors as well as parents are also important in raising a child. There is a well-known African proverb that says, "It takes a village to raise a child." This proverb was much discussed when it was referenced in the title of a book written in 1996 by then-first lady Hillary Clinton. In *It Takes a Village*, she argued that in order for children to grow into capable individuals who can endure hardship, they need the warm care and love of many people around them. My close friend's son, who was born with a severe case of cerebral palsy, is a case in point. The child could hardly walk or talk until he was three years old, and no one expected that he would be able to attend a public school. Miraculously, with the help of neighbors, friends, teachers, and many others, he completed a four-year college education. He has moved out of his parents' home and, with the aid of social services, is earning his own living. He was able to achieve so much, thanks to not only his parents' dedication, love, and care but also the care of friends, neighbors, and people at his schools and his church.

Of course, a child's neighbors and social environment can sometimes have a negative influence. In the United States, it is not uncommon to find parents homeschooling their children for fear they will be picked on, face violence, or fall into bad company and pick up undesirable behavior. According to the National Center for Education Statistics, 1.5 million elementary to high school students were being educated at home as of 2010. Of course, not every parent has the qualifications and dedication to educate a child at home, nor is homeschooling the answer for every child. Parents often have no choice but to raise their children in a less-than-ideal environment. If this is the case, the parents' biggest responsibility and concern must be to shield their children from harsh winds, minimizing the negative impact from a less-than-ideal school and social environment until the child grows up to be responsible for himself.

In summary, the first reason parenting is so difficult is that the child initially needs 24/7 attention and care. For the first one or two years of a child's life, parenting is very intense and exhausting, but this constant contact with the baby and that fact alone creates a rewarding bonding experience. Also, even though each child is unique physically and temperamentally, you can meet most of a baby's physical and psychological needs based on close observation. But at three or four, children start to express their own wills. They might insist on riding the swings in the park or a tricycle on the sidewalk even though they aren't ready. When you explain to them that they need to wait until they are old enough, some children may easily give up while others continue to insist on doing it now. Every child is different, and when they start to act on their own wishes, parenting becomes more and more difficult and complicated.

Another reason parenting becomes increasingly difficult is that children learn more from how a parent acts or behaves than from what the parent says or tells them. How many parents can say they are behaving the way they want their children to behave? Many parents believe that parenting will become easier when their children can understand their verbal commands. This is not true. You have to demonstrate desired behavior, not just verbalize it.

Last, parenting poses more challenges as time passes because the child's expanded environment of friends, teachers, neighbors, the media, and the social climate starts playing a greater role. Some people think, for example, that they can minimize adverse effects from violence or bullying by homeschooling, but there is not enough evidence it works. Though it's tempting to think so, parenting does not get less demanding as your child gets older. Parenting is not easy, but it's full of love and wonder at every stage.

CHAPTER 4

GENDER ROLES IN PARENTING

Today, the roles of mother and father are not as clearly distinguished in parenting, but traditionally this was not the case. Both in the East and the West, the mother's role involved looking after the children and overseeing the provision of food, clothes, and shelter for the family, while the father's role was providing for the family financially and disciplining the children. With the shift from extended families to nuclear families and the increasing presence of women in the workforce, a growing number of couples are sharing parenting responsibilities. There remains a division of parenting responsibilities among genders—that is, mothers and fathers tending to take different roles—but the current trend towards gender equality in parenting more effectively shows that mothers and fathers are both capable caregivers. At the same time, due to the tendency of women and men to have different temperaments and characteristics, mother figures and father figures can complement each other to better facilitate a child's development. This is not a hard and fast rule. A child can be raised effectively in a household without either a mother or father. It is ideal for children's development, however, that they have both.

Although the distinction between separate spheres for men and women in American society has largely disappeared over the past century, most families remain within a fairly traditional household structure. As a result, the father often assumes the role of offering direction and advice on various difficult problems the child might face growing up. He can offer a different perspective from the mother, as he tends to have more experience in the working world. Through the process of giving advice and helping a child resolve various problems, the father can better understand and bond with his child. Boys in particular tend to learn from their fathers that there are limits to freedom and that they cannot always do as they wish in their relationships. To their children, particularly boys, the father is the model of social order and norms. Of course, this ability to model social order and norms is not exclusive to fathers, and there are many cases where the mother plays this role. Fathers also tend to engage in more aggressive play with their children. Through play, fathers encourage cooperation and competition and urge children to attempt new activities. Fathers inspire children to challenge themselves to develop new skills, stimulating cognitive and physical development.

In contrast, mothers tend to meet the physical and psychological needs of their children. In a traditional home, the mother spends more time with her children, whether it is through feeding, dressing, playing, washing, sleeping, or any of the other myriad day-to-day interactions between a mother and child. As a result, mothers tend to create a stronger psychological bond with their child than fathers. Because of this psychological bond, mothers are often more in tune with the emotions, behavioral patterns, and physical needs of their children and more able to adapt their own behavior to meet their children's needs, whether they are physical or psychological. Different genders also play different parts in the development of a child's understanding of gender roles. According to Freud's theory of child development, confirmed by various studies (Block 1983), a son identifies with his father, and in the process of emulating his father's behaviors and values, learns the male gender role. Freud emphasized that the father's role was more important than the mother's in the development of masculinity

or femininity in a son or daughter. While some of Freud's theories are no longer considered valid, others, this theory included, continue to be applicable. Well-developed gender roles lead to a healthy gender mindset, which is a prerequisite to a happy family life and social life.

Apart from Freud's theories, it has been found that the parent of the same sex as the child has a greater impact on the development of that child's understanding of gender roles than the parent of the opposite gender. In general, mothers are said to treat sons and daughters equally, while fathers treat them differently. Studies show that fathers encourage independent and constructive behaviors in their sons while they encourage dependent behaviors in daughters. Research findings indicate that a boy who grows up without a father has the potential to exhibit one of two extremes: a lack of masculinity or the tendency to show masculinity in excess. A girl who grows up without a father, by contrast, has a high likelihood of facing challenges in sexual role play and relationships with the opposite sex, and may exhibit less femininity.

Despite the tendency of men and women to take on different roles, neither gender has a monopoly on close bonding with a child. While the father's role has traditionally been limited, research shows that the involvement of fathers in childrearing has increased substantially in the past three decades. Similar studies have shown that fathers are no less capable than mothers in childrearing in spite of their historically limited involvement. Mothers, due to the phenomena known as "close contact comfort," or constant physical contact with a child through activities such as nursing and holding their children, tend to form a close bond that is crucial for a child's cognitive, emotional, and social development. Surprisingly, a similar psychological bond can be formed with fathers who are involved as a caregiver early in a child's life, with positive effects on the child's development (Lewis and Lamb 2007). The only parenting activities that remain the exclusive domain of mothers are childbirth and nursing. It becomes clear then that the father can also play a significant role in a child's cognitive, emotional, and social development.

Throughout this chapter, I have almost exclusively used the words mother and father to talk about a child's parental figures. However, an adult who is not a child's mother or father can play the role of a mother or father in a child's development. A coach, well-liked teacher, uncle, aunt, grandmother, and grandfather are all examples of these so-called "surrogate" father and mother figures. As a child, I grew up without a father, but my uncle was able to play this role of surrogate father in my life. While having both a mother and a father is a blessing, a child can grow up to be well adjusted and healthy, both mentally and physically, even if they do not have that privilege.

CHAPTER 5

PARENTING CHALLENGES
OF SINGLE MOTHERS

Growing up with the love and care of both parents is a great blessing. But many children grow up without fathers for reasons like death, divorce, or separation. A great number of other fathers are simply incapable of fulfilling their role. Even under such circumstances, there are plenty of mothers who successfully play the roles of both parents. Many people have grown up fine without a father and made great contributions to society. Abraham Lincoln, one of the greatest American presidents, grew up without a father. This doesn't mean that raising children without a spouse is by any means an easy task.

Single parenting is a difficult process. No one should underestimate it. But the reasons for single-parent households are varied and becoming more complicated. According to 1990 U.S. Census data, while about 50 percent of teenagers were living with single parents, only seven percent of them were living in a traditional single-parent household, with a widowed mother. A much higher percentage of children were living with a divorced or separated parent, or with mothers who had never been married.

When I grew up in Korea, a single-parent household meant a single-mother family. Divorce was almost nonexistent. If the wife died, the man remarried; but if the husband died, the woman remained single and raised her children alone. Confucian values were taught and observed in China and Korea for over a thousand years. At the beginning of the seventeenth century, Korean kings and the ruling class could not prevent five foreign invasions (once by Mongols, twice by the Japanese, and twice by the Chinese) and they lost face with their people. They imposed strict observance of the ethical codes of Confucianism as a means of establishing social order and maintaining the status quo. The emphasis on fidelity, which included a subject's not serving more than one king and a wife's being wholly committed to her husband, precluded divorce or remarriage. Therefore, widowed women of respected *yangban,* or members of the traditional ruling class, raised their children and maintained their households alone until their death. Because of my father's untimely death, my mother was widowed at the age of forty and left with two sons and two daughters. She dutifully fulfilled her role as a single parent until her death at the age of ninety.

I grew up with no memory of a father figure and no experience of family dissolution, marital discord, or family realignment. To me, parent meant mother. I had no awareness of what difficulties she experienced, or what sacrifices she endured. When I finally realized what her life must have been like, I was already married, now part of a new Kim family, with my own children. But one thing I know for sure is my mother never considered herself an unusually devoted mother, nor did she ever feel she had "done enough" for her children. Nowadays, however, few people uphold Confucian values as they used to. Thus, the divorce rate has been rising rapidly even in Korea.

Difficulties of single-mother families

The greatest challenges facing single-mother families are financial ones. Women earn less than men on average, and their employment opportunities are relatively limited. If a mother needs to send her child to a childcare center, hire a nanny, or work part time, her financial problems grow exponentially. In the case of divorce or separation, the father might provide child support, but the amount still tends to be lower than the average income of a two-parent family. Some divorced single mothers do not receive any child support at all. When a single-mother family has financial security, the negative impact of the father's absence is diminished considerably.

Another problem that single mothers face is the increased burden of domestic chores and parenting activities such as tak-

ing children to school and extra-curricular activities. This can increase the mother's stress level and the potential tension between mother and child, which can have a negative emotional impact on the child as well as on the mother.

Third, single mothers often face social isolation. When a spouse is lost, any social life centered on the spouse is also cut off. In particular, single mothers who are divorced or separated tend to consciously avoid social relationships linked to their former husbands, which can lead to sudden and complete social isolation.

The fourth challenge is the common misconception that single-mother families are somehow "broken" or "incomplete." Such social prejudice negatively affects growing children. Negative perceptions of children of divorced parents by acquaintances and peers can cause enormous psychological distress for both mother and child. Despite these negative attitudes, most children of single-mother families are known to adjust to school life with remarkable resiliency and develop healthy friendships. The following are some helpful parenting guidelines for single mothers:

Mothers must maintain high self-esteem. In a single-mother family, the mother's behavior has a greater impact on the child than family composition itself. If a mother considers her life to be a tragic failure, her children will have the same outlook on life.

Mothers should find father figures for their children. In a large family, grandfathers and uncles naturally become surrogate fathers in the place of the missing father. In societies of nuclear families, however, finding father figures is not always easy. Still, they can be found outside the family. For example, a teacher or coach whom the child trusts and respects can become a role model, as can a close friend of the father. Mothers should consider carefully whether these figures are reliable and respectable to determine who can help fulfill the father's role.

The child's father should be discussed in a positive light. Most children imagine or remember their fathers as ideal figures. Therefore, no matter what kind of a husband or a partner he was, the mother must respect what the child thinks of the father. That way, the mother can relieve the child of psychological conflict and ensure healthy emotional development. This is supported by a study on children who grew up with absentee fathers for many years during the Second World War. At the time, the negative effects of having absentee fathers turned out to be less significant than expected because of the children's pride in their fathers, who were fighting on behalf of their country. Needless to say, also hidden under the surface were the efforts of mothers to plant positive images of the fathers in their children's minds while carrying on the family life without interruptions.

When single mothers can maintain high self-esteem and self-confidence, establish financial security, and receive social support, their children can grow up to be confident, productive, and caring adults.

Part II

PREGNANCY & CHILDREARING

CHAPTER 6

HOW THE PRENATAL EXPERIENCE
SHAPES OUR LIVES

Most women react to their own pregnancies with fascination, concern, and anxiety. They are willing to attribute powerful and lasting effects to the prenatal experience on later development of the child. The notion that a woman's psychological and emotional state during pregnancy affects the fetus has been a persistent cultural belief in many parts of the world. For instance, Korean scholar Yi Sajudang (1739–1821) wrote in *Taegyo Singi* (New Guidelines for Prenatal Care), "Ten months of education in the mother's womb is greater than ten years of education from any teacher." Yi's words reflect the importance placed on prenatal care in traditional Korean society, a tendency that saw the fetal phase as more important than any other phase of human development. Even though some of the prenatal care advice in Yi's book delved into spiritual symbolism and superstitions, it also included information on the proper conduct of pregnant women and types of food and medicines to avoid.

Traditional Korean prenatal care has placed special emphasis on maintaining the health of the mother, with a detailed list of foods to be avoided and foods to be consumed, as well as the behavior expected of pregnant women. It was believed that eating carp during pregnancy would make the child well behaved, eating bull kidney and steamed barley would make the child strong and clever, and eating fish would make the child bright. Irregularly shaped fruit or spoiled vegetables were to be avoided. Some foods were to be avoided due to superstitious or shamanistic beliefs. Pregnant women were to maintain emotional serenity. The mother-to-be was to sit and meditate on auspicious words, memorize the wise words of sages, engage in reading poetry, practice calligraphy, and listen to beautiful songs.

Nobel laureate Amartya Sen has recently argued, while discussing the importance of in-utero experiences, that negative in-utero experiences can have a detrimental effect on health and productivity in one's life. In the 1930s, the studies of the Fels Research Institute for the Study of Human Development suggested that in-utero experiences have a considerable impact on a child's intellectual and emotional development. In England, Charles T. Baker found a high correlation between in-utero conditions and the probability of having a heart attack in one's forties. Until then, the popular belief in the fields of medicine and child development had been that experiences in the three years after birth had the most decisive effect on a child's intellectual and emotional development, but that physical health was determined by genetic factors, diet, and daily habits. After the publication of the aforementioned research findings, people came to accept the idea that factors such as the psychology and health of the expectant mother, the in-uterus experience of a child, and exposure to environmental conditions have long-term effects on a child's development after birth.

The fetus has a surprising ability to communicate with its environment through hearing. In the final phase of pregnancy, a mother can sense the fetus relaxing at the sound of her lullaby, or being startled at the slamming of a door. However, not many mothers are aware that a newborn actually remembers the sounds it heard as a fetus. An infant stops crying when his mother holds him close to her heart. This is because he is comforted by the sound he heard while in the womb— her heartbeat.

A newborn remembers his mother's voice as he heard it in the womb. In one experiment, a mother read a story out loud to her baby in utero every day. Three days after birth, the newborn was made to listen to a recording of its mother reading the story, followed by a recording of a different woman reading the story. The newborn paid attention to the recording of its mother's voice longer than to the recording of the stranger's voice. The second part of the experiment yielded even more surprising results: the infant paid attention to its mother's voice longer when she read a familiar story than when she read an unfamiliar story. These research findings show that newborns do remember the voices of their mothers heard in utero.

At one point, based on these findings, prenatal music for in-utero intellectual development became wildly popular among expectant mothers. Its effectiveness, however, was not proven scientifically, and the fad soon faded. In any case, blindly following unverified prenatal care instructions can harm rather than help. Research findings have indeed shown that high prenatal maternal stress may increase the likelihood of a child developing behavioral disabilities around school age, but we should be careful to accept too simplistic interpretations. These outcomes can result partially from the prenatal experience but also from genetics or the mother's interaction with the child after birth. Information on prenatal care endorsed by popular media or so-called experts is best taken with a grain of salt.

CHAPTER 7

THE GROWTH OF A FETUS

Human growth during pregnancy is a truly astounding transformation, from a single-cell zygote to a fully formed baby. Women are born with immature eggs, which mature with the onset of menstruation. One egg is released from the ovaries every four weeks or so, generally in the middle of the menstrual cycle (two weeks after the first day of the period). The released egg survives for approximately seventy-two hours. When the egg unites with a man's sperm, a new life is created. About eight and a half months after the meeting of the microscopic male sperm and female egg, a complete human being is formed. This is influenced by the dynamic interactions of the mother's health, habits, activities, and cultural customs, among other things, and is a truly wondrous mystery of nature.

These days, pregnancy tests can be conducted with a simple kit administered at home. Pregnancy test kits can be used any point after the day a woman is expected to start her period. Pregnancy is determined by testing the urine for the hormone human chorionic gonadotropin (HCG), which is released from the time of conception.

The duration of pregnancy is generally rounded up to nine months, but to be more specific, a baby is born around 266 days (38 weeks) after conception. The due date is generally calculated by subtracting three months from the first day of the last period and adding seven days. For example, if a woman's last period began on July 10, three months are subtracted to get April 10, then seven days are added to arrive at April 17. Delivering right on the due date is rare, though, and deliveries typically take place around two to three weeks beforehand.

Pregnancy Milestones

The terms used to describe the timing of various significant events during pregnancy can be confusing for lay people. The pregnancy is often divided into three main periods: the germinal period, the embryonic period, and the fetal period. Instead of using these terms, some simply divide pregnancy into three-month periods called trimesters. Months one, two, and three are called the first trimester; months four, five, and six the second trimester; and months seven, eight, and nine the third trimester.

Germinal Period (the first 14 days): Within hours of conception, the one-cell zygote travels slowly down the fallopian tube toward the uterus and begins the process of repeated cell division. Release of the egg to implantation takes about ten to fourteen days. Implantation is far from automatic. Approximately 58 percent of all natural conceptions and 75 percent of all in vitro conceptions fail to become properly implanted. If fertilized egg cells do not grow normally, the result is often spontaneous abortion, without the pregnant woman's awareness.

Embryonic Period (14 days to eight weeks): The period from the implantation of the fertilized egg to the eighth week is the embryonic phase. During this phase, cells differentiate and form important body organs, including the brain and respiratory organs. The heart starts beating at the end of the third week, and eyes, ears, and digestive organs are formed at the end of the fourth week. By the sixth week, circulation is established. The lungs are formed, as well as the fingers, toes, and parts of the face, such as the lips. Therefore, the expectant mother must pay extra attention to maintaining her health during this period. For instance, if a pregnant woman contracts rubella during this period, the child might be born with a congenital visual impairment, hearing impairment, or amentia.

Fetal period (nine weeks to birth): The organism is called a fetus from the ninth week after conception until it is born. After twelve weeks of pregnancy, the reproductive organs of the fetus are completely formed. The fetus begins to move, and the mother starts to feel it. By the end of the third month, the fetus has all its body parts and weighs approximately three ounces (87 grams). In the fourth, fifth, and sixth months, the heartbeat becomes stronger and the digestive and excretory systems develop more fully. The brain develops very rapidly between the fourth and sixth months of pregnancy, growing six fold during this period; it begins to react to stimuli, and the central nerves also begin to show reactions. By about the sixth month, or twenty-fourth week, the fetus develops the ability to suck and hear sounds, and weighs around 600 hundred grams. The survival rate of the baby is about 50 percent if delivered prematurely at this time. Weight is crucial to fetal viability, the ability of the fetus to life outside the womb. By thirty weeks, the typical fetus weighs about three pounds (1,300 grams), and its chances of survival have increased to more than 90 percent. At this time, the fetus can sense light and can smell. It can also suck and swallow. By thirty-seven weeks, because the lungs can function normally, babies can be born and not considered premature.

In many ways the relationship between mother and child begins during the final three months. During this time the size and movements of the fetus make the mother aware of it. The mother's sounds, smells, and behavior also become part of the in-utero experience.

CHAPTER 8

PRENATAL USE OF HARMFUL CHEMICAL SUBSTANCES

Many factors affect the development of a fetus into a healthy child, some of which are beyond our control and others of which are not. Here are some of the most common factors that can be controlled or influenced.

Smoking

Smoking is not only bad for the expectant mother but bad for the baby as well. If a fetus could talk, what would it say if the mother asked if she could smoke a cigarette? I am certain that it would immediately reply, "No, mom. It's too harmful, and I don't like it." In the United States, the harmful effects of smoking on pregnant women were recognized in 1935, and focused research on the topic began in the 1950s. In 1964, tobacco companies were required to print a warning on cigarette packages stating that smoking during pregnancy is harmful to the fetus. Cigarettes contain addictive materials, and quitting is not easy. Pregnant women, however, must quit smoking because smoking during pregnancy is related to low birthweight in babies and is known to increase the risk of miscarriage.

Cigarettes contain over 2,500 kinds of harmful chemicals. The carbon monoxide and nicotine from cigarettes are especially damaging during pregnancy. Carbon monoxide limits the supply of oxygen, which the fetus needs for growth, thus increasing the risk of the newborn having low birthweight or of premature birth. Nicotine causes the placental blood vessels to contract, interrupting the supply of oxygen and putting the fetus at higher risk of malnutrition. The fetuses of smoking mothers weigh 200–377 grams less on average than those of non-smoking mothers. Various toxins in cigarette smoke prevent the fetus from growing normally, and the effects persist after birth. If a pregnant woman smokes a pack of cigarettes a day, the oxygen supply to the fetus decreases by 20 percent. Chronic oxygen deficiency can stunt the development of the baby's central nervous system.

The rate of premature birth among women who smoke during pregnancy is 9.2 percent, three times higher than among non-smoking women. The rate of miscarriage among smoking women is one and a half times higher than among non-smoking women, and the rate of premature birth is two to three times higher. Smokers also have a higher rate of stillbirths. Smoking during pregnancy increases the rate of a woman's water breaking before the thirty-seventh week, increasing the likelihood of having a premature baby and the chance of it dying within twenty-four hours of birth.

Nicotine that enters the fetus's brain through the placenta will subsequently hinder the development of the area of the brain that controls respiration. This can increase heart rate and blood pressure, causing respiratory dysfunction. A research team at the University of Southern California found in a survey of 5,762 elementary school students that the number of asthma patients was significantly higher among children of women who smoked during pregnancy than among children of non-smoking women.

Children of women who smoke during pregnancy also have a higher chance of showing hypersensitivity and emotional instability than children of non-smoking women. Fetal oxygen deficiency caused by smoking during pregnancy not only stunts a child's physical growth but also his mental capabilities. Children of women who smoke during pregnancy have tested 3 to 4 percent lower in reading skills on average and 2 percent lower in attentiveness than children of nonsmokers.

According to the American Medical Association, the rate of sudden infant death syndrome (SIDS) among infants who are exposed to cigarette smoke within a year of birth is double the rate among unexposed infants. Research in Sweden found that, compared to the children of women who did not smoke during pregnancy, the rate of SIDS was twofold for children whose mothers smoked one to nine cigarettes a day during pregnancy and threefold for those whose mothers smoked more than ten cigarettes a day.

Women who smoke heavily are at a high risk of pregnancy complications. Habitual smoking increases the rate of placenta previa, which describes a low-lying placenta covering part or all of the opening of the uterus, and placental abruption, which refers to premature detachment of the placenta. These conditions can cause excessive bleeding and in many cases necessitate a Caesarean section. Smoking during pregnancy also causes a higher likelihood of premature rupture of the membranes (PROM), which means that the sac holding the baby inside the uterus breaks before completion of 37 weeks of pregnancy. If the rupture occurs before 37 weeks of pregnancy, it often results in a premature birth.

The immune system of the fetus is also affected and the chance of the fetus contracting diseases increases when its mother is exposed to secondhand smoke, just as when the mother smokes during pregnancy. Through the secondhand smoke, the toxins in cigarettes can enter the mother's milk and thereby be fed to the infant. Thus, the effects of smoking during pregnancy are transferred to the next generation. Gilliland and Peters (2001) surveyed 908 children, including 338 children who had been diagnosed with asthma before reaching age five, to ascertain their parents' smoking history. The results showed that a child whose mother smoked during pregnancy had a one-and-a-half times higher chance of developing asthma than a child whose mother was a non-smoker. The risk was three times higher if both the mother and the maternal grandmother were smokers. If the grandmother smoked during the mother's pregnancy, even if the mother herself was a non-smoker, the child's risk of developing asthma was double that of children with non-smoking mothers and grandmothers.

It is best that women do not smoke at all, but a smoking woman should at the very least quit after she plans to become a parent or learns of her pregnancy, so as to protect her child. Quitting smoking is the best gift an expectant mother can give to her child. Smoking spouses should also understand the harmful effects of secondhand smoke and cooperate to the best of their abilities.

Drugs

Even with today's medical advances, the effects of prescription or nonprescription (over-the-counter) drugs, illicit and/ or illegal drugs, and herbal remedies on pregnant women have not been clearly determined. Because it is unethical to conduct experimental studies on pregnant women, the effects of many of these substances on pregnancy simply aren't known. Some findings from animals such as laboratory cats, mice, monkeys, rabbits, and hamsters have been applied to pregnant women and fetuses, but questions about the validity of their applications to humans remain to be answered.

It used to be thought that the placenta—the tissue that serves as a transport system for food and wastes between the mother and her unborn child—was a barrier that protected the baby from dangerous substances and helped make the womb a safe and cozy place. But thalidomide and other substances have proved the barrier concept untrue. Therefore, in general, drugs should not be used during pregnancy unless absolutely necessary, because many can harm the fetus. Many doctors believe that drugs taken during pregnancy might be among the leading causes of the birth defects linked to environmental factors.

However, sometimes drugs are essential for the health of the mother and the fetus. In such cases, a woman should talk with her doctor about the risks and benefits of taking the drug. Depending on the type of drug, dosage, and duration of use, a drug's effects on the fetus can be temporary or permanent.

Pregnancy tests are simple these days, but women generally do not learn of their pregnancies until four to six weeks in. A woman who had taken drugs before she found out might worry about the possibility of the drugs having adverse effects on the fetus. In most cases where the drug has a significant adverse effect on an unborn child, the result is spontaneous abortion—a miscarriage that occurs before the twentieth week of pregnancy. Drugs consumed up to two weeks before the conception usually will not be transmitted to the fetus and have no particular effect on it.

Between the third and ninth weeks of pregnancy, however, the fetus begins to form its organs, and ingestion of certain drugs (i.e., thalidomide) increases the risk of the baby's becoming severely deformed or dying before birth. After the ninth week of pregnancy, even fever reducers and antibiotics should only be used after consulting with a physician. According to *TIME* magazine, around 500,000 pregnant women require treatment each year for conditions such as depression, cancer, auto-immune diseases, and influenza. In these cases, the benefits of treating these illnesses with drugs usually outweigh the risks.

Adamantly refusing to take medicine is not always the best way for the mother or the fetus. For instance, the mother's fever can be more detrimental to the fetus than taking a fever reducer. When taking medication, an expectant mother must always consult with her physician about the safety of the type of drug, dosage, and duration of use. It is also important for a pregnant woman to read the product information carefully to learn more about how the medication may affect her pregnancy and the fetus.

For your information, I am listing some of the most common drugs that can harm the fetus if taken during pregnancy. However, you should discuss with your doctor any questions or concerns you may have.

Antibiotics: Tetracycline and streptomycin, antibiotics used to treat infections, hinder the development of the fetus's tooth enamel if taken during pregnancy, increasing the chance of yellow teeth.

Aspirin: Aspirin is an over-the-counter drug commonly used to reduce fever or pain. Extended use in high doses can lengthen the duration of pain and increase bleeding during delivery. Aspirin can also cause fetal intracranial hemorrhage. In the case of Tylenol, no side effects on pregnant women have yet to be reported. Pregnancy lowers a woman's resistance to pathogens, making her more prone to catch the common cold. Pregnant women must be cautious about the drugs they use.

Vitamins: Vitamins are generally safe for pregnant women, both in water-soluble and fat-soluble form. An overdose of water-soluble vitamins is harmless to the human body because excess amounts are discharged during the metabolic process. Fat-soluble vitamin A and vitamin D should be taken with caution, however, as an overdose can cause deformities in the fetus.

Sedatives: Lithium, a treatment for bipolar disorder, can cause congenital heart defects. Antidepressants such as Prozac should also be used with precaution, for they can also harm the fetus.

Anti-nauseants: Anti-nauseants are a type of sedative that contains ingredients known to cause congenital deformities.

Frequent usage can be problematic, but taking one or two doses while traveling is not a concern.

Habitual use of sleeping pills can cause fetal addiction, and the newborn infant might show symptoms of withdrawal. Like anti-nauseants, one or two doses are not problematic.

Acne medications: Accutane is a drug prescribed for the treatment of severe cases of acne. When taken in the first trimester, the probability of the fetus developing deformities (head, face, brain, and heart) is elevated to 25 percent. The drug increases the risk of miscarriage and premature birth too. Both pregnant and fertile women should avoid taking this drug.

Weed killers, insect spray, and fungicides: Several studies indicate that it is also wise to avoid contact with weed killers, insect spray, and fungicides during pregnancy.

Alcohol

The exact correlation between the amount of alcohol consumed during pregnancy and its damage to the fetus has yet to be determined. However, alcohol has a high penetration rate through the placenta, and can cause damage or mutation of the central nervous system and the cells of the fetus. The fetus has hardly any ability to break down alcohol, and can be seriously affected by even a small amount.

The effect of alcohol on the fetus varies greatly by the amount of alcohol and the time of consumption. Research has shown that drinking three glasses of alcoholic beverages daily during pregnancy or binge drinking (about five glasses in one sitting) even once during the first trimester can result in fetal alcohol syndrome (FAS), or the less symptomatic fetal alcohol effect (FAE). FAS is a congenital condition that is linked to physical deformity and mental disability and is caused by the mother's drinking alcohol during pregnancy. FAS in a newborn is characterized by growth deficiency, facial deformities, central nervous system damage, and intellectual disability. A fetus can develop FAS at all phases of pregnancy, and many reports warn that the damage is greater in the early phase of pregnancy, when the fetus forms important organs.

In-utero exposure to alcohol between the fourth and sixth months is linked to learning disabilities. The average IQ of children whose mothers drink during this period is reported to be five points lower than that of children of non-drinking mothers. Drinking during pregnancy elevates the risk of stillbirth. After delivery, new mothers should never breastfeed after drinking. Alcohol consumed by the mother can be transmitted to the baby via breast milk. As discussed above, alcohol can do serious harm to a fetus, and it is desirable for a pregnant woman to stay away from alcoholic beverages from the moment her pregnancy is confirmed.

CHAPTER 9

WEIGHT GAIN DURING PREGNANCY

Weight management during pregnancy is crucial for the expectant mother to maintain good health, give birth to a healthy baby, and achieve healthy post-pregnancy weight loss. Eating a healthy, appropriate diet will help the baby get the nutrients it needs to grow at a healthy rate. Then how many extra calories are really necessary? Even though pregnant women do need some extra calories, they don't need to "eat for two." The recommended weight gain depends on pre-pregnancy weight and body mass index (BMI). Research has shown that a pregnant woman should eat about three hundred extra calories a day compared to her normal daily intake. This amounts to one or two light snacks, considering that a piece of bread has about one hundred calories. Eating too much during pregnancy can lead to obesity, which affects the fetus adversely and can lead to premature birth. Fat accumulation in the abdominal area and birth canal obstructs delivery and increases bleeding during delivery, which can put the mother at risk. Obesity during pregnancy also causes high blood pressure and diabetes and increases the chance of having an overweight or stillborn baby.

The amount of weight gain recommended during pregnancy by the American Medical Association has changed over the years. In the 1960s, pregnant women were warned against gaining over 22 pounds, but standards loosened in the 1970s, and any weight gain that was not sudden was considered safe. Regardless of the era, the most desirable weight gain starts with maintaining normal weight even before conception. In the United States, the recommended weight gain is about 2 to 4 pounds during the first three months, and about 1 pound per week during the rest of the pregnancy. If you are expecting twins or other multiples, you should gain 35 to 45 pounds during your pregnancy. This would be an average of one and a half pounds per week after the usual weight gain in the first three months. To maintain optimum weight during pregnan-

Table 1. Recommended pregnancy weight gain by body type

Body type	Body Mass Index (BMI)	Recommended weight gain
Underweight	less than 18. 5	28–40 lbs.
Normal weight	18. 5–24. 9	25–35 lbs.
Overweight	25–29. 9	15–25 lbs.
Obese	30 and greater	11–20 lbs.

BMI = Weight (kg) / {height (m) × height (m)}

cy, it is useful to keep a journal of the kinds and the amount of food eaten. If a pregnant woman sits around too much and does not exercise enough, she will lose her physical strength and gain weight, increasing the chance of a difficult labor. It is important to increase physical strength through moderate exercise. Generally, stretching, strolling, and other forms of light exercise are recommended until the third or fourth month of pregnancy, followed by swimming and gentle yoga from the fourth or fifth month on.

CHAPTER 10

SEX DURING PREGNANCY

Opinions and attitudes toward sex during pregnancy vary from person to person. A recent opinion poll in the United States showed that over half of pregnant women and young couples planning to have a child think that sexual intercourse is harmful during pregnancy. Fortunately, there is no scientific evidence to support this, and normal sexual activity is possible during pregnancy. However, multiple sex partners can increase the risk of STDs (Sexually Transmitted Disease), which may lead to birth and pregnancy complications such as low birthweight or premature birth. Both American and Canadian obstetrician and gynecologist associations have reported that sex during pregnancy is not harmful to the pregnant woman or the fetus. As such, there is no reason to maintain celibacy during pregnancy, and couples can enjoy a normal sex life without concern. From the seventh month of pregnancy onward, however, positions that put pressure on the belly of the expectant mother should be avoided. Experts recommend refraining from having sex during the first trimester and the last month of pregnancy. A husband and wife might have differing opinions on sex life during pregnancy and should try to reach a mutual understanding through honest conversation.

Due to fatigue and morning sickness, a woman might feel burdened by sex during the first trimester. If such a situation arises, the spouse's cooperation is necessary. A woman who has had a miscarriage should take special precautions. Four to six months into a pregnancy, morning sickness typically subsides, and the expectant mother can find peace of mind. Many couples enjoy a more active sex life during this period, but this depends entirely on each couple's thoughts and attitudes. Partners should strive to understand each other's desires after ample communication. In the last three months of pregnancy, the expectant mother's sex drive typically diminishes in preparation for delivery. During this period, positions that put pressure on the belly should be avoided. Traditionally, Korean women were told to remain celibate during this period, but there is no scientific evidence that calls for celibacy during pregnancy, save for the last month. A pregnant woman should not overexert herself, and partners should be considerate of each other when engaging in sexual activities. The figures below depict sex positions that do not put pressure on the woman's belly.

A woman's breasts become full, and her nipples grow and become sensitive during pregnancy. This adds pleasure during in-

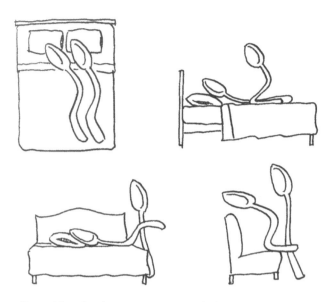

Figure. Sex positions that do not put pressure on the belly

Source: Roizen and Oz, YOU: Having a Baby, 2009, p. 185.

tercourse for some women, and pain for others; women should communicate clearly to their spouses about any discomfort experienced. If a pregnant woman's spouse suddenly stops treating her as a sexual partner, the woman should not come to a premature conclusion or be disappointed. By focusing on her femininity and behaving confidently, she can feel sexy, and her partner can see her in the same way. In some cases, the husband becomes overly cautious when the wife becomes pregnant. Unless there is a special issue, a normal sex life during pregnancy is not only harmless, but it can also bring the couple closer together. Consulting with a physician is wise if there are any questions about engaging in sexual intercourse. Keep in mind that intercourse should be avoided if the woman is showing abnormal symptoms, including placenta previa, premature contractions, vaginal bleeding, and abdominal pain, or if she has experienced a miscarriage or delivered prematurely in the past.

CHAPTER 11

DIET AND NUTRITION DURING PREGNANCY

If you are planning to get pregnant, it is important for you to have a healthy, well-balanced diet and get the nutrients you need both before getting pregnant and during your pregnancy. In the months before you become pregnant, your nutritional intake can be a key factor in the outcome of the pregnancy. The foods you eat and the vitamins and minerals you take will help ensure that both you and your baby have necessary nutrients right from the start of the pregnancy. Meals should be spaced evenly throughout the day and should consist of foods from all of the food groups. Your body depends on the food you provide to fuel system functioning, optimize your immune defenses, provide energy, and restore necessary nutrients to cells in need. Your pregnant body also has to provide the essentials your baby needs to grow and develop. You can't expect your body to be able to do all of that on a diet of fast food and soda. Eating a diet of a variety of natural and whole foods rich in vitamins and minerals will ensure your body, brain, and baby have everything necessary to be as healthy as possible during pregnancy. Since pregnant women are considered to be at higher risk of food poisoning, safe food practices are of particular importance.

A balanced diet

- Whole grains: Breads, cereals, pastas, brown rice
- Fruits: All types of fresh, frozen, or canned fruits, preferably without added sugar
- Vegetables: Eat a variety of colorful vegetables, fresh, frozen or canned, with no added salt. Raw sprouts should be avoided.
- Lean protein: Choose lean proteins, including meat, poultry, fish, eggs, beans and peas, peanut butter, soy products, and nuts. Pregnant women should avoid eating tilefish, shark, swordfish, and king mackerel, and limit white (albacore) tuna to 6 ounces per week. Deli and luncheon meats and hot dogs should be reheated if consumed.
- Low-fat or fat-free dairy: Includes milk, cheese, and yogurt. Unpasteurized milk and some soft cheeses that are made from unpasteurized milk should also be avoided.
- Healthful fats: Vegetable oils, including canola, corn, peanut, and olive oil, are good choices.

Key nutrients for a healthy pregnancy

- Folic acid: Folic acid reduces the risk of birth defects that affect the spinal cord. All women of childbearing age and pregnant women should consume at least 400 micrograms of folic acid each day. Sources include fortified foods such as cereals, pastas, and breads, supplements, and natural food sources of folate, including legumes, green leafy vegetables, and citrus fruits.

- Iron: Maternal iron deficiency is the most common nutritional deficiency during pregnancy. Pregnant women need at least 27 milligrams of iron a day. Foods with high and moderate amounts of iron include red meat, chicken and fish, fortified cereals, spinach, some leafy greens, and beans. For vegetarians and women who do not eat a lot of meat, increase iron absorption by combining plant-based sources of iron with vitamin C-rich foods. For example, try a spinach salad with mandarin oranges or cereal with strawberries.

- Calcium: During pregnancy, calcium is needed for the healthy development of a baby's teeth, bones, heart, nerves, and muscles. When a pregnant woman does not consume enough calcium, it is taken from her bones for the baby. It is important to consume adequate amounts of calcium daily before, during, and after pregnancy.

The recommended amount of calcium during pregnancy

is 1,000 milligrams per day for adolescents 14 to 18 years old and 1,300 milligrams per day for women aged 19 to 50. That means at least three daily servings of calcium-rich foods such as low-fat or fat-free milk, yogurt, or cheese, or calcium-fortified cereals and juices.

Your doctor or registered dietitian or nutritionist may recommend a prenatal vitamin/mineral supplement to help ensure that you get enough iron, folic acid, and other nutrients.

CHAPTER 12

BREASTFEEDING VS. USE OF FORMULA

Immediately after birth, an infant's daily routine involves eating, sleeping, waking and crying when hungry, suckling, and sleeping again. Newborns must be fed every two to three hours. For about a year, a newborn grows entirely on its mother's milk or infant formula (i.e., powdered infant formula). Whether a mother feeds her child breast milk or infant formula has an important impact on the infant's physical, intellectual, and emotional development.

The benefits of breastfeeding

Everyone agrees that breastfeeding is ideal for an infant's development. The American Academy of Pediatrics and the World Health Organization recommend six months of exclusive breastfeeding for all infants. Breast milk provides everything an infant needs in an optimal balance. Breast milk is especially important for a baby born prematurely or with health issues. This is because the composition of breast milk is in constant flux to suit the phase of an infant's development. Breast milk has been proven not only to be nutritionally beneficial but also superior to powdered infant formula for the emotional and intellectual development of an infant. Breast milk contains an abundance of amino acids, sugars, and fat, which are components of protein, as well as a moderate amount of vitamins, enzymes, and minerals required by the human body, making it easy to digest.

Breastfed babies rarely suffer from constipation because the milk provides substances that help with bowel movements. Unlike powdered infant formula, breast milk never causes allergic reactions and also contains antibodies that help a child build resistance to respiratory diseases such as asthma, as well as infectious diseases. It contains large quantities of beneficial cholesterol, which helps brain development. Colostrum, also known as the milk produced during the first forty-eight hours after delivery, includes immunoglobulins, which are very helpful in building a newborn's resistance to infectious diseases. A breastfed baby is reported to be less likely to become obese than a formula-fed baby. Given how securely the mother holds her baby while breastfeeding, the baby, in turn, feels emotional comfort, and the mother and child experience a strong connection—another great advantage of breastfeeding.

Breastfeeding also offers many benefits for the mother. Nursing releases oxytocin, which reduces postpartum bleeding and expedites uterine contraction. According to a report by the

American Academy of Pediatrics, the rate of breast cancer is lower in breastfeeding mothers than in mothers who do not breastfeed. In addition, mothers expend over five hundred calories a day by breastfeeding, which helps them return to their pre-pregnancy weight.

Infant formula

If the mother cannot produce enough milk or if the newborn infant cannot suck effectively, infant formula might be the only choice. In cases where the baby's exact milk intake is monitored, or breastfeeding is not an option due to the poor health of the mother or child, infant formula can be substituted for breast milk. But you should not feel guilty for not being able to breastfeed your child. I am sure that a large part of the benefit of breastfeeding comes from the mother's attitude and devotion to the baby rather than the mother's milk itself.

One of the benefits of infant formula is that it does not need to be given as often as breast milk. However, infant formula is costly, and it lacks the antibodies contained in breast milk, making formula-fed children less resistant and more likely to contract diseases than breastfed children.

If necessary, a mother can feed her infant breast milk in conjunction with infant formula. However, the American Academy of Pediatrics recommends breastfeeding until the infant is at least six months old. By feeding a combination of breast milk and formula, the mother risks a drastic decrease in her breast milk supply.

Breastfeeding: when and for how long

When a newborn baby looks around and begins to move its fist to its mouth, it is ready to be breastfed immediately. This can be anywhere from a few minutes to a few hours after delivery.

It is advisable to breastfeed a baby until it is at least twelve months old. Weaning can happen thereafter, whenever the mother and child are ready. These days, perhaps because more women are working, many women wean their babies before they are six months old. However, breast milk pumping devices are also readily available nowadays and can be used while the mother is working.

I breastfed my first child for a year and a half, the second child for ten months, and the youngest child until he was three years old. If weaning occurs before twelve months, infants should be fed iron-fortified formula.

Sometimes, the mother's nipple is inverted, making it difficult for the child to suck on the nipple. If this is the case, the husband can help by sucking on the nipple to pull it back out.

Compress the breasts to get the milk flowing, then wash the nipple with the milk. Relax and assume a comfortable position, and hold the breast to make a cup-shape so that the nipple or the breast does not press on the baby's nose, and the baby can feed comfortably. Rather than scheduling breastfeeding times, it is better to feed the child when it wants.

Do not breastfeed if the child is crying or has just finished crying. While breastfeeding, gently pat the baby and lock eyes, and when it pauses, talk to the baby tenderly. When the baby is finished, try not to rock your body because the baby could throw up.

Finally, mothers should do their best to avoid alcohol, cigarettes, and coffee while breastfeeding.

Feeling the mother's warm body and listening to her heart beat while being breastfed helps the emotional stability of the infant, offering a sense of warmth to both mother and child. The mother feels emotional fulfillment as she watches the lips of her nursing baby and its peaceful and satisfied expression. This is a joy and blessing that only nursing mothers can enjoy.

COMMON PROBLEMS IN BREASTFEEDING

Clogged milk ducts: A red lump may appear on the breast if the milk ducts are clogged by dried milk. This can be very painful. The most effective remedy to relieve soreness is to offer the baby the breast with the lump, and to feed as often as possible. If the baby cannot drain the milk completely, milk should be expressed from that breast after feeding. Massaging and applying warm towels to the affected area and taking warm showers are also helpful. If the lump remains unchanged, it could lead to more serious issues such as milk duct infection, so make an appointment to see your doctor immediately.

Irritated nipples: The most effective remedy for tender nipples is exposing them to air as often as possible. It is helpful to dry the affected area after feeding with a hair dryer on a low setting. Nipples should be cleaned only with water. Lanolin cream with no chemical additives can be helpful.

CHAPTER 13

TOILET TRAINING

When children develop the muscles and reflexes to control their excretions and learn that excrement is dirty, they have to be taught go to the bathroom on their own. When a child understands enough language and shows interest in using the toilet as adults do, the child is ready for potty training. Between two and two and a half years old is usually a good time to start potty training. In general, children stop dirtying diapers before they stop wetting diapers, and girls are trained earlier than boys.

SIGNS THAT A CHILD IS READY FOR TOILET TRAINING

· The child gives presents to make others happy and likes to receive compliments.

· The child wants to try everything without help and shows pride in completing a task.

· The child likes to imitate adults and other children.

· The child can use enough speech to express his needs,

and understands all of the words necessary for toilet training.
· The child soils his diaper at regular times.
· The child imitates other family members using the toilet.
· The child expresses through words or facial expressions when he needs to relieve himself.

The best time for toilet training is when the above behaviors are observed. Toilet training can be easy and fun, with fewer mistakes, which will boost the child's confidence, when the child is ready. Summer is a better time for toilet training because light clothing makes it easy to get in and out of undergarments. If the child is undergoing a stressful situation, such as a move to a new home or the arrival of a new sibling, training should wait for a later time.

Toilet training should be a fun activity, like a game. A good child-sized toilet is one that the child likes and can sit comfortably in. Children generally like toilets that look similar to an adult toilet. To help the child get used to the child-toilet, sit the child on the toilet and let the child go with clothes on. Allowing the child to read picture books or play with toys on the toilet is another effective technique.

Help the child understands that "pooping" is a natural bodily function that everyone has. A popular picture book among children, *Everyone Poops!* (Gomi 1993) was useful when my grandson was first introduced to the toilet. We read the book together many, many times and had him follow along with the actions in the book. He had fun and was proud of himself, as though toilet training had made him a "big boy."

Mothers can usually tell by the child's facial expression if the child needs to poop. Place the child-toilet next to the regular toilet. Sit the child on his toilet and sit yourself on the toilet, and call out, "Poo-poo!" to encourage the child to defecate. Having friendly conversations with the child about the subject and using a common vocabulary like "poo poo" and "pee pee" is helpful.

In the past, it was common practice to train children by emphasizing that urine and feces are dirty and unsanitary. According to more recent research, however, this method is not necessarily desirable; if the mother or other people hold their noses, frown, or make a big fuss about something that has come out of his body, a toddler might feel rejected. This reminds me of a funny incident that happened many years ago when one of my children was being toilet-trained.

I came home from work one day, and my son asked, "Mom, you love my poop, don't you?"

"Of course," I quickly responded.

"Nanny doesn't!" he said. I explained that I loved him more than anyone else, so everything about him was precious to me, but someone who was not his mother might think that his "poo poo" was smelly and dirty. And that's okay.

When the child is using the toilet, the parents should not rush the child or act impatient. Encourage the child, saying, "You can do it. Let's keep trying," and wait as long as is needed. After the child is finished, praise the child for his accomplishment. If the child makes a mistake, rather than scolding him, tell the child "it's okay" and assure the child that everyone makes mistakes. If mistakes persist, however, it is best to put off toilet training for a while. Mistakes are common when the child is tired, has had too much liquid, or is feeling tense, even if the child is familiar with using the toilet. Toilet mistakes can also be part of a regressive pattern shown by a child when a new sibling has arrived.

According to Freud's theory, overstressing the filth of human excrement can often manifest in mysophobia or the fear of uncleanliness. Erik Erikson argued that a child's experience of toilet training has a significant effect on character development, especially on the development of a sense of autonomy. A child feels pleasure from discharging when and where he wants, and gains self-confidence from learning to manage and control his own body. In fact, children with mysophobia are often found to have had overly strict toilet training. If toilet training is too strict or coercive, or if the child is punished or teased for making a mistake, the child will feel shame and doubt. Parents must remain relaxed and reassuring and approach potty training as if playing a fun game to help children gain confidence. Bear in mind that toilet training is a milestone in your child's development.

Toilet training generally takes from three to six months. Some children, however, will wet their pants at night until they are around five years old. Other children refuse to be trained or show regressive behaviors. Parents must have patience and continue to encourage their children. If the child continues to resist toilet training, it is a good idea to wait a month or two before beginning again. Most importantly, parents should ensure that the child does not feel shame or a sense of doubt.

If a child feels pressure during toilet training, he might begin to hold it in so as to escape the situation. The child may then develop constipation and even feel pain when passing stool. Should such a situation arise, keep in mind that a child should never be given a laxative without instruction from a pediatrician; parents must consult a doctor for proper treatment. Parents should also consult a pediatrician if a child over three years old shows no interest in toilet training. A child refusing to use the toilet could be a sign of constipation or fear of being in the bathroom alone. Or it could just mean that the child is not familiar with the toilet or does not want to sit still, wanting to return to his games. A child might act distracted simply to get his parents' attention. Parents should find out the exact reason and respond accordingly.

CHAPTER 14

LANGUAGE DEVELOPMENT

Language competence refers to one's ability to clearly understand words and speech and express one's thoughts accurately
and effectively. We cannot emphasize enough the importance
of having language ability in our lives. Language is necessary for
higher forms of thought process. Barack Obama's election as the
forty-fourth U.S. President is largely attributed to his strength as
a public speaker. He has a superior ability to listen carefully to
other people and express his thoughts and opinions effectively.

Because language often serves as a building block of thought,
many scholars claim that thinking ability and language ability are
closely related. Some scholars go further, asserting that a man's
thinking is no richer than the language he knows. They explain
that Native American languages have few words to describe colors. Thus Native Americans have not developed a keen ability
to distinguish colors. By contrast, the Inuit people, who have
over twenty words to describe the various textures and states of
snow, have a well-developed concept of sub-zero precipitation

and ability to distinguish the different types of snow.

Jean Piaget set forth a contrasting argument, saying that while language is necessary for intellectual development, a lack of language does not prohibit a man from thinking. In any case, language is the basis for acquiring knowledge and thinking, and thus, it is certain that language development is closely related to thinking ability. Applicants who apply for graduate school, including law school and medical school, are required to submit scores from standardized tests that measure verbal ability (among other things), such as the GRE, LSAT, and MCAT. They are required because language ability is one of the measures that can predict the success of students in their studies.

Early stages of language learning

Some research has shown that the earliest language learning begins in utero when the fetus begins recognizing the sounds and speech patterns of its mother's voice. However, many writers believe the child's language development begins at birth. Philosophers like Kant have suggested that the newborn's cry expresses "wrath at the catastrophe of birth." Some psychologists, however, would deny that the newborn baby has enough ability to express a particular emotion. A child's language ability develops most rapidly during the first five years after birth, a period considered critical for language development. Some psycholinguists call children in this stage "linguistic geniuses."

After children turn five years old, acquiring a new language becomes more difficult. In general, girls develop faster than boys in their language development.

Learning language is a complex process. However, it is worth noting that the ordinary healthy child learns to talk with no formal teaching if he hears plenty of speech. But how does the baby master such complex language so early and so easily? According to Noam Chomsky and his followers, the reason that children can learn such a complex language so efficiently is because the human brain is equipped with a structure that facilitates language development. Chomsky labeled this facilitator the Language Acquisition Device (LAD), one of the unique abilities of a human. However, research in recent years has suggested that Chomsky's theory has some validity but overlooks the social context in which the language learning occurs. The adult's sensitivity and appropriate guidance in the language learning process as well as the child's innate learning ability together play a significant role in language learning.

Newborns have been found to block out all other sounds immediately after birth to concentrate on listening to their own mother's voices rather than to the voices of other adults. Before learning to speak, an infant expresses himself with cries and facial expressions, including mouth movements. He wriggles all over with delight when he is happy. He vocalizes and blows bubbles. A baby's cry of pain and cry of hunger sound different in intensity and pitch. A mother has to listen and observe her baby carefully in order to learn his physical and psychological needs and try to meet them. Singing, reading, and talking with non-verbal babies are all very helpful activities for a baby's language development. A mother should make eye contact with her crying baby as she satisfies his needs, and talk with him while doing simple tasks such as changing diapers, saying, for example, "You are wet. You will feel better after we change your diaper." This will help her baby's language development.

There is great individual variability in language learning. According to one study, about 10 percent of 24-month-olds have a vocabulary of more than 550 words, but another 10 percent speak fewer than 100 words. It's more than a fivefold difference. However, parents should be reminded of the fact that learning words or speaking early does not necessarily mean intellectual superiority. Likewise, a child who is slow to speak does not necessarily have a problem with language development. Some children are always talking as they play. They sing or talk to themselves. Other children use few words, going quietly about the business of play although they show that they understand and are listening to what is being said. They practice speech less.

Most babies begin babbling by six or seven months of age and begin to enunciate words starting at around ten months. At around 20 months, they combine words to express thoughts and begin to acquire words rapidly. When a baby begins babbling, the parents should pay close attention to the sounds, even if they are unintelligible, and encourage the baby to continue babbling. The more time the child spends babbling, the more he can practice speaking. When the child begins to talk, the parents should listen and react even more attentively. Rather than correcting the child's pronunciation or usage, the parents can simply model the words correctly. For a child to learn to speak, he should have many opportunities to try. Modeling language for the child is important, but it is more important to listen to the child and give him ample opportunities to talk.

For most people of all ages, it comes naturally to talk to babies using "baby talk"—in a higher-pitch voice, with more low-to-high fluctuation, using simpler, more concrete, and shorter sentences. But research findings support the opposite notion that when communicating with babies, grammatically correct and complete sentences are more helpful to the baby's language development. For instance, if the child says, "Water!" demanding water, the parent can say back to the child, "Do you want water? Then say, 'Water please!'" Personally, I've used both styles of talking in moderation with my children and grandchildren and found no harm done.

In the early stages, a word often stands for a whole object or an experience. For example, "hot" may mean the stove as well as the heat it gives off and the warning given to control action. In this early stage, nothing takes the place of a wide variety of appropriate first-hand experiences. The child needs to see, touch, taste, and do something with the object if he is to understand the full nature and meaning of the label attached to it. New knowledge and words should come from firsthand experiences, not from the printed page. If he can roll a ball, sit on it, bounce it, throw it, watch it float in the water, and play with several different kinds of balls, he stores up impressions that create a complete concept of "ball."

Observing honeybees buzzing busily about, collecting honey, or a snail moving slowly, carrying its heavy load on its back, is a meaningful experience for a child. Listening carefully to the sounds of cicadas, the rain, and crickets, having a conversation about stars and constellations while watching the night sky, walking barefoot across the wet sand at the beach, listening to the sound of the waves, and building a sandcastle are all activities parents can do with their child that can greatly enhance the child's language and intellectual development. To broaden a child's experiences, parents can take their children to a market, a department store, the zoo, a botanical garden, or a bakery to stimulate the child's interest and talk about the shared experience.

When the child grows older and begins to ask questions about the world around him, the parents have to give answers that the child can understand and that will encourage the child to seek more knowledge and ask more questions. When the child is talking, the parents should focus and listen patiently and express clearly that the child has been understood. It is desirable for the parents to lower their bodies to the child's eye level and look into the child's face during conversation.

Developing a good reading habit from a young age is also very helpful for a child's language development. Rather than reading many books, it is helpful to read a few books repeatedly that the child likes until the child becomes familiar with those stories. For preschoolers (two to five years old), books about daily happenings or other familiar topics, with many repeating words and sentences, are recommended.

With my grandchildren, I read the same books I had read to my children forty years earlier. I had stored them safely, and despite their age, they were almost as good as new. When I told my grandson that these were the books I had read to his dad when he was young, he showed greater interest in them and handled them more carefully. In order to hand down books through generations, it is important to buy well-crafted books with quality content. Until the child can read on his own, presenting the child with too many books can confuse him. For children to enjoy reading, it is important for them to see that the parents also enjoy reading books.

In summary, the following guidelines can help parents stimulate their child's language development:

Parents should model grammatically correct speech. They must use complete sentences and explicit words. "Please put this empty can in the recycle bin!" is more preferable to "Please put this in that!" The child hears and learns a pattern of exact speech in the first sentence but not in the second.

Parents should ask open-ended questions rather than yes-or-no questions. "What do you think will happen if we are late going to school?" "What should we do if our car doesn't start?"

Parents should listen carefully to what the child says, try to understand what the child is expressing, and respond accordingly. Children need to feel that their parents value their words and feelings. It is discouraging to anyone to have their words met with indifference or only a half-hearted attempt to listen.

Parents should encourage talking. Children gain speech competence by having many opportunities to speak and talk about things that interest them with an interested and sympathetic listener.

Parents should provide activities that promote language use. Excursions to places of interest stimulate conversation, as does asking children to tell stories about their day before falling asleep. Puppet play also encourages preschoolers' language development, as simple role playing does for older children.

The guidelines above apply to children with normal language development. If there is any doubt about a child's language development, parents should consult with a pediatrician to take appropriate measures. If necessary, parents can seek a more accurate diagnosis and get assistance from a speech therapist. Consulting with an expert can minimize damage and help the child develop normally.

SIGNS OF LINGUISTIC DISABILITY (AROUND THE AGE OF TWO)
· The child avoids eye contact.
· After eighteen months, the child cannot understand or

repeat any words.

- The child has difficulty learning simple children's songs.
- The child does not know the names or the functions of objects around the house.
- The child has a significantly shorter attention span than other children when reading a book or watching TV.
- The child cannot enunciate clearly, and people cannot understand much of the child's speech.

CHAPTER 15

PLAY, THE FIRST STEP OF LEARNING

The fervor for early education has taken playtime away from children. Children are always pressed for time, and on the rare occasions when they have free time, they watch TV or play computer games instead of playing with friends and/or play materials such as mud, sand, building blocks, etc. Play, however, is something all healthy children should enjoy, and a primary vehicle for their learning. In addition to its role in cognitive development, it integrates children's physical, emotional, and social development.

All animal offspring learn the techniques and skills they need to adapt to their environments through play. Affection between a mother and her offspring, food-finding techniques, and most other functions necessary for survival are learned through play. Humans are no exceptions. If play for adults means a break from the weight of daily life, refreshment, and repose, for children it is life itself. Children spend almost all of their waking moments playing. In other words, play is a child's main occupation. Play arouses a child's innate curiosity, helping him understand new objects and phenomena, and facilitates his intellectual development. Friedrich Fröbel argued that play should be a focal point of early educational activities.

Activities and forms of play change with the times, as well as with social and cultural changes. Play is self-initiated, with motivation for involvement coming from the child, and it is usually spontaneous. A play activity naturally draws a child's attention, allows freedom, and is enjoyable and fun.

Piaget categorized play into sensory motor play, imaginary play, symbolic play, and cooperative play. The play in infancy constitutes sensory motor play and appears when the baby starts to be aware of people and objects. He begins to play with his fingers, sucking or touching them, and using them to drop, throw, or knock on toys. Later on, he begins to use his toes. The physical modes begin in the games parents play with infants, such as peek-a-boo. Turning a light switch on and off may also be a good play activity for a child. They stop these games once they figure out how it works, but in the process, children learn to distinguish between the different textures, smells, shapes, sizes, colors, and functions of various objects.

Around age three, children may begin role playing, pretending to be an astronaut preparing for an adventure in space, putting out a fire, making roads in the dirt or sandbox for cars, carrying on telephone conversations using a pretend cell

phone, going to doctors, or disciplining imaginary children. Through this kind of play, a child expresses ideas, thoughts, and feelings. Children also use play to try to make sense of what they see and hear and master feelings of fear and anxiety. In this kind of play, the child focuses on active participation. Usually the child is in control of the action. By play-acting in the role of mother, father, doctor, nurse, or pilot, a child imitates and identifies with adults.

Children around four to five years of age engage in symbolic play. For example, a stick becomes a rifle, and a large cardboard box becomes a house. In the late preschool years between the ages of 4 and 6, children begin to engage in cooperative play, requiring an evolved set of organizational skills and a higher degree of social maturity. Through this form of play, children learn the necessary skills for social and group interactions. Let us examine in more detail how play can help children develop.

Play increases abstract thinking and problem-solving abilities

In the process of playing with objects, children come to understand their physical properties. For example, after repeatedly playing on steel playground equipment in the sun, a child learns that metal is hard and becomes hot quickly in the sun. A child playing with building blocks naturally learns formal concepts as he thinks about how to construct the three-dimensional form he has in mind. In this way, abstract concepts are learned through hands-on experience. According to the developmental psychologist Lawrence Frank, play allows children to learn by themselves what no one can teach them. Because play does not trigger any psychological conflict, a child can explore his thoughts freely and experiment during play. Through this process, a child naturally acquires problem-solving skills and develops various other life skills.

Play aids physical development

Play that requires whole-body movements aids a child's physical development. For example, activities such as building with blocks help a child's eye–hand coordination. Activities that involve exploration, such as hiking, motivate a child to be physically active and provide opportunities to learn survival skills. They are especially useful if childhood obesity is a concern.

Play teaches social skills

While playing with friends, a child learns the meaning of cooperation, patience, and respect for rules. He learns to understand and consider others' feelings. For instance, while playing with a friend, a child learns that he cannot take away a friend's toy, no matter how much he wants to have it, and that he cannot do everything he wishes. The child learns this naturally, and no one has to teach the child. By imitating and identifying with adults through role play, children learn to understand others and little by little come to understand the social order of living together.

Play helps healthy emotional development

Erikson asserted that play functions to relieve or control a child's psychological conflicts, fears, fantasies, stress, and aggression. Because of limited language ability, children cannot effectively express feelings of defeat, frustration, jealousy, and anxiety from daily life. Play, then, provides children with an outlet for these negative emotions. For example, a child might release the jealousy he feels toward his newborn sister or brother by hitting or harassing a doll. Play can be a means of treating children with psychological problems. Play therapy uses activities including puppet play, role playing, drawing, and blocks to treat autism, dependency, aggressive tendencies, and various other mental conditions in children. Play is also a way for children to handle the problem of being "little" in a world of big people. In play, they can identify themselves with "big" roles and lessen the helpless feeling of being "little."

Play boosts imagination and fulfills a child's wishes.
According to Lev Vygotsky, play is a means of wish fulfillment. Through imaginary play, a child can become anyone or anything he wishes to be: an astronaut, a soldier, a firefighter, or a mom or a dad. As a result, the child's imagination expands and becomes richer.

TIP GUIDING CHILDREN'S PLAY ACTIVITY

1 SHOW INTEREST, OBSERVE THE PLAY, AND GIVE SUPPORT WHEN NEEDED

When children play, parents should act as interested adults rather than guides who direct their play activity. By observing their children at play, parents can gain greater insight into how their children see the world. Parents should understand the frustration of the physical world in which the child lives, the right of the child to explore, and possible aggressive impulses in relationships with siblings and playmates. Parents should accept those undesirable feelings and allow children to be truthful about their resentment, aggressiveness, and negativity. Through play, a child often expresses inner conflicts and fears. Parents, then, have an opportunity to help the child do something positive about such feelings. However, parents should also lay the groundwork by letting the child know that it's alright to kick a ball, but not a sibling.

2 ELIMINATE "HURRY!"

Children need time to think, plan, and carry out their play. Therefore, it is important for parents not to hurry their children and give them enough time to play in a relaxed environment without pressure. As much as is possible, children should be given uninterrupted time to finish playing to their satisfaction.

3 PROVIDE MATERIALS THAT CAN SERVE MULTIPLE PURPOSES (E.G., BLOCKS, BOXES, BOARDS)

Ordinary objects can be used by imaginative children in many different ways. Cardboard cartons can be modified in endless ways, and empty cereal boxes, butter cartons, cans with smooth edges, tapes, paper, and string can transform a house into a grocery store. Organize supplies neatly in a clearly labeled container so that the child can find them when he wants to play with them. When children know where materials are kept and can find them in their place, it reduces needless frustration.

4 ▼ KEEP THE CHILD FROM PLAYING WITH TOO MANY TOYS OR OBJECTS AT ONCE

Children need to develop the capacity to pick out familiar elements in a given situation, relate the known to the unknown, and accept the differences. In the process of developing this ability, it can be confusing for young children if they are given too many toys at once. It is best to allow the child to spend plenty of time with one or a few toys. If the child receives many toys for a birthday or holiday, give the child a few at a time instead of all at once. Put the rest of the toys away until new ones are needed. If the child spends a long time with the same toy, he has more chances to creatively incorporate it into many different activities.

CHAPTER 16

DISCIPLINE AND SETTING LIMITS

Normal, healthy children misbehave at times. Therefore, their behavior must be controlled for their own good as well as for the good of those around them. The term discipline is often used synonymously with punishment, but it is better understood as actions adults take to help a child change his unacceptable behavior into acceptable behavior. Adults need to identify for children what kinds of behaviors are acceptable and help them understand the possible consequences of their behavior for themselves and others. Punishment, on the other hand, describes actions adults take to stop unacceptable behavior by making a child suffer physically or mentally. Young children are often unaware of why they are being punished. When a young child is punished often, he perceives himself as a bad child. You can imagine yourself how it would feel to grow up thinking you are a "bad person."

Discipline helps children develop self-control over their impulsive behaviors. It does not mean forcing a child to fit the ideal image the parents have of him. Many parents lose their tempers when their children act against their wishes, bursting out in anger, raising their voices, and punishing the children. Such reactions might stop the unacceptable behavior momentarily, but they don't help children to learn acceptable behavior. When children do not understand why their parents are angry with them or why they are being punished, they simply try to avoid trouble for the moment out of fear.

Methods of discipline and the degree of control must change with the child's maturity. For a very young child, discipline should be centered on physical safety. As a child grows a little older, the parents should also focus on helping children to be considerate of other's needs and to value other's rights as well as their own.

The single most common reason that parents fail to discipline a child is that they focus on the child's behavior without understanding the reason for that behavior. This can be likened

to treating only the symptoms and not the disease causing the symptoms, like treating a fever without dealing with the infection causing it. For example, if a four-year-old boy constantly bumps into his two-year-old sister on purpose, it is necessary to stop the behavior right away, but your attitude toward discipline will likely be more important than the methods you use. If you try to understand the reason for the older brother's actions, you will be less surprised by them and find it easier to respond in helpful ways. Perhaps his behavior is a result of his feeling that his little sister is getting more attention. Or perhaps he is being bullied at school, and feeling stressed as a result. What good is it to scold him for being mean to his younger sibling, when the root of the problem lies elsewhere? The job of parents is to understand the situations their child is facing, in this case ostracism, and prioritize solving the issue at hand.

1 ▼ PROVIDING UNCONDITIONAL LOVE IS THE ESSENTIAL FOUNDATION OF DISCIPLINE

All parents love their children, but not many parents love their children as they are. When a child misbehaves and refuses to do what he is told, it is easier said than done to wait patiently for the child to change, all the while staying positive and trying to understand the reason for the child's behavior. That does not mean that parents should accept unacceptable behavior. Unconditional love helps parents develop the ability to empathize—to see, feel, and think from the child's perspective. Unconditional love builds a strong emotional bond between parents and children. Children who have a strong emotional bond with their parents want to make them happy. Thus, they behave in ways that please their parents, not because they fear the consequences but because it is their joy to please the ones they love.

2 ▼ ALLOW CHILDREN TO ASSERT THEMSELVES

Children want to be independent. In the process of becoming independent, they feel the urge to assert themselves so that they can prove their independence. Sometimes, they will assert themselves by not doing what they are told. Satisfying a child's desire to assert his opinions is important and also essential to healthy emotional development. For instance, a young child may close his mouth tightly when his parent tries to brush his teeth. Instead of interpreting this behavior as defiance, the wise parent waits, giving him space and time to assert his independence, having faith that the child will soon cooperate.

3 ▼ LIMITS SHOULD BE REASONABLE

Unless the safety or the rights of the child or the rights of others are endangered, prohibitions limiting a child's behavior should be minimal. At the same time, rules about unacceptable behavior should be clearly defined and consistently maintained. When a child can clearly distinguish acceptable and unacceptable behaviors, he can act with confidence and self-control. Parents often believe that they have a clear idea of which behaviors they allow or forbid, but this is not actually the case for a surprising number of them. Being busy, tired, or happy is not an excuse for parents to allow unacceptable behaviors. Parents should not prohibit a child's behavior in some instances and then allow the same behavior at other times. In addition, a behavior that the father prohibits should not be allowed by others—for example, the grandmother—and rules should apply equally to all siblings.

4 ▼ STATE DIRECTIONS IN A POSITIVE RATHER THAN A NEGATIVE FORM

It has been demonstrated that directions stated in a positive form are more effective than those given negatively. Prohibitive, negative language triggers defiance and other negative emotions in children. On the other hand, positive language that proposes specific actions is met with less resistance. Let's say your child has a habit of biting people when he is excited or grouchy. Rather than saying "Don't bite your brother," it is better to give the child a piece of cloth and suggest "Bite this instead! It hurts your brother when you bite him." Parents can also try to have the child bite his own finger or another part of his body to explain why he should not bite people. Instead of saying "Don't run inside the house," say "If you want to run around, go outside and run." Instead of saying "Don't throw the ball at the window," say "Throw the ball into the yard." Instead of saying "Don't shout in the house," say "Talk quietly inside the house."

5 ▼ AVOID TRYING TO CHANGE BEHAVIOR BY SHAMING

No children are likely to develop desirable behavior as the result of shame. Parents should discard the gestures, the tone of voice, and the words that may convey the impression that the child should feel ashamed. Children do not change their behaviors without feeling self-respect. Labeling behavior as hyperactive or aggressive is damaging to the child's sense of self-respect. Parents can help their child if they accept him as he is and try to make it possible for him to succeed, rather than reproving him because he does not meet their expectations. In order for a child to change his behavior, he needs to feel that he is respected by others. Parents also need to be reminded that it takes time for a child to learn acceptable behavior. Just as it is more desirable to defrost frozen foods at room temperature rather than in a microwave oven, parents should wait patiently for changes in their children's behavior;

6 ▼ GIVE GUIDANCE OR SUGGESTIONS AT THE MOST EFFECTIVE TIME

There is a right moment for stepping into a situation if guidance and redirection are to be effective. Instructions given too soon may deprive the child of a chance to work things out for himself. A suggestion made too late may have lost any chance of being successful. Therefore, the timing of guidance or suggestions can be as important as the instruction itself.

7 ▼ MODEL ACCEPTABLE BEHAVIOR

Children learn more from the actions of their parents than from their words. The word discipline is derived from the word disciple, meaning a student or follower. Children want to be like their parents, both consciously and unconsciously; if parents maintain self-control and act properly in difficult situations, their children learn to control their emotions in similar situations. When parents are considerate of others rather than thinking only about their own interests, their children learn to be considerate of others as well. Of course, parents, being human, make mistakes and are sometimes imperfect. When parents accept and apologize for their mistakes—thus taking responsibility for their own actions and not attempting to preserve a veneer of perfection—their children learn independence and tolerance in the truest sense.

CHAPTER 17

BUILDING HARMONIOUS
RELATIONSHIPS AMONG SIBLINGS

Siblings spend most of their lives together from birth and grow up with the same parents, forming a strong psychological bond that is unlike those found in any other human relationships. Sibling relationships are the longest-lasting family ties we have, and they are the most likely to bring happiness and support. But they can also be the most complex and difficult relationships to maintain well. Siblings learn much from each other and can provide mutual emotional consolation, but they may also experience competition, jealousy, and conflict. Sibling rivalry occurs in almost every house with more than one child, and at all ages.

The effects of birth order on personality have been the subject of research for decades. In addition to birth order, parents' expectations, the total number of siblings, the age difference between siblings, and the gender of siblings also have a significant impact on a child's development. The first child is born amidst

great interest and expectation from the parents and relatives, but the second child and any subsequent children rarely receive the same interest and benefits the first child enjoyed, even if the parents make a conscious effort to treat them equally. Telling evidence can be found in family photo albums. Often the number of photos of the first child is greater than that of the second child, which is greater than that of the third child.

Parents generally put more effort and care into raising the first child and are stricter in disciplining the first child. The first child, who grows up an object of high expectations and affection from his parents, may be burdened with a sense of responsibility for younger siblings. If there is a large age difference with the next child, the first child sometimes takes on the role of another parental figure, leading the family in his own way. The youngest child, on the other hand, usually grows up with much love and affection from his older siblings as well as his parents, and is often optimistic and dependent. Middle children, having both younger and older siblings, often believe they lack uniqueness and receive less attention from their parents, and even feel neglected, but broader experiences and ample stimulation can lead them to grow up to be independent and self-sufficient.

In general, siblings of the same gender and siblings with a small age difference are more likely to experience conflict because the younger child is reluctant to accept the authority of the older sibling, and the older sibling feels his or her privileges being taken away by the younger sibling. This, however, is only a general theory, and healthy sibling relationships can be achieved through wise parenting. Below are some tips that parents should keep in mind to ensure good relationships between their children.

TIP TO PROMOTE HEALTHY SIBLING RELATIONSHIPS

1 PREPARE YOUR CHILD FOR THE ARRIVAL OF A NEW SIBLING

When a new sibling is born, the older child might feel that no one is paying attention to him and that everyone cares only about the new baby. For a child, thinking that his parents do not love him as they did before can be shocking, and sharing his parents' attention and affection with another sibling is a very difficult thing to do. As an old Korean adage puts it, the jealousy a child can feel toward a younger sibling is similar to what a wife might feel if her husband brought home a younger, more attractive woman and asked that his wife "share" him. Children want their parents always to be by their side and are anxious about losing their parents' love.

Therefore, parents should prepare a child emotionally for the arrival of a new sibling, in order to reduce the child's fear and negative attitude toward the younger child. As soon as the child recognizes the changes in the mother's body, the parents should explain that a younger sibling will be born soon. It is a good idea to elicit the older sibling's opinions, asking questions such as "Do you think the baby would like a blue blanket, or a yellow blanket?" After the baby is born, compliment the older child often for things that he can do but the baby cannot. For example, say "You can pour water into the cup. The baby can't do that, can he?" It is important to make sure that the older child understands clearly that feeling jealous of the baby is understandable, but harming or hurting the baby is unacceptable.

Even if looking after the newborn is a lot of work, the parents should also spend daily quality time with the older child. If possible, it is desirable to give the older child tasks to help take care of his younger sibling. Even if the task is a trivial one, it can help the child build a relationship with his sibling. The parents should also make sure that the child understands sufficiently that they have to spend more time with the baby because the baby needs more help, not because they love the baby more.

2 ▶ NURTURE THE STRENGTH AND INDIVIDUALITY OF EACH CHILD

Parents should respect and encourage their children, nurturing each child's unique strengths and helping their individuality blossom. Parents must help children understand that their particular strengths and individuality cannot be compared, just as an apple, a peach, and a pear are all different in taste and fragrance. If a child shows exceptional talent in a particular area, the parents must take precaution so that his siblings do not feel overshadowed by the child. Some competition and envy are inevitable between siblings, and arguments and fights are natural, but these conflicts should be kept to a minimum. One way is to encourage siblings to play different sports or play different instruments, so as to eliminate chances for comparison or competition.

3 ▶ DO NOT COMPARE

Avoid comparing one child to another. Some parents say, "Your brother does his homework without being told. Why do you have to be reminded to do your homework?" Or "Can't you take your empty plate to the sink like your sister?" Such words cause bad blood between siblings. Moreover, the child being unfavorably compared perceives favoritism. If a child's behavior is undesirable, the parents should focus on the behavior. They should clearly point out the fault. But there is no need to compare the child to his siblings. This goes for paying compliments, too. Do not say, "Your older sister always forgets something when she runs errands, but you always remember everything. You're great!" Say instead, "You're great! You're so good at running errands."

4 ▼ DO NOT FAVOR ONE CHILD OVER ANOTHER

All children are precious and lovely to a parent no matter how many children they have, but it is possible for parents to feel more affection for one child than another. Still, the parents must make a conscious effort to abstain from favoritism. We all know the stories that have appeared in mythology and works of art throughout the ages, all over the world, about competition between siblings for a parent's love. Conflict between siblings is a serious issue in family relationships. If parents favor one child over the others, this will breed jealousy and discord, and the less favored children might harbor resentment toward the parents.

It doesn't matter if parents are actually showing favoritism or not. If a child feels his parents have showed favoritism, this becomes his reality. Therefore, parents should communicate with their children as often as they can to ensure that they feel loved. Childhood memories of such experiences sometimes leave deep scars. Parents must make every effort to treat their children fairly. Treating children fairly does not necessarily mean treating them the same way all the time. Saying "I played with your sister for an hour, so now I will spend an hour with you" is not the way to be fair. Rather, parents should assess each child's needs and situation, saying, for example, "I have to help your sister with her homework now. When we are finished, I will help you with what you need." Treating children fairly involves following a fair principle that the children can sufficiently understand and accept.

5 ▼ AVOID LABELING YOUR CHILDREN

Parents often carelessly use labels that characterize their children. When parents use negative labels such as "piggy," "troublemaker," or "stubborn bull" for a child, he subconsciously accepts those labels as his identity and tends to act accordingly. A negative self-image is fossilized in this way and hurts a child's self-esteem, but positive labeling is equally problematic, as children have a strong tendency to act according to their parents' expectations. Labeling can act as a kind of psychological pressure on a child. Statements such as "my child is a top student" or "my child is nice" can limit and suppress a child's thoughts and behaviors. A child whose parents always call him a top student may feel obligated to be one, and when he finds himself falling short, doing poorly on an exam, for example, or letting his grades fall, he might feel discouraged and criticize himself harshly.

Labels used by parents to characterize their children can also trigger jealousy and conflict among siblings. A "troublemaker" might envy and resent his "model student" older brother. The child who does not have musical talent might think that because she is not a "musical genius" like her sister, she can never be a good musician, no matter how hard she tries. Parents must recognize that carelessly uttered labels can have a decisive impact on a child's identity and should thus make constant efforts to refine their language.

CHAPTER 18

CHILDHOOD OBESITY AND ITS
PREVENTION

Childhood obesity is emerging as a global social issue. It is not a problem limited to the United States alone. It is a problem in many countries around the world, both developed and developing. Moreover, the obesity epidemic is accelerating, even among babies and toddlers. A plump child was once considered a healthy child. Excess weight was thought to be something children would outgrow. But now it is recognized as an indicator of lifelong troubles and one of the most serious modern public health problems. Nearly one in three children (ages 2–19) in the United States is overweight or obese. The 2009 Health Examination of School Children, conducted by the South Korean Ministry of Education, Science, and Technology, reported 13.2 percent of elementary to high school students in South Korea to be obese.

Childhood obesity increases cholesterol level and causes high blood pressure, asthma, and type 2 diabetes. In short, it's a serious problem that commonly leads to adult obesity. Childhood obesity also leads to excessive hormone secretion, which causes early sexual maturation, which is characterized by early puberty, an interruption of normal growth and physical development in children. In addition, obese children are often teased and ostracized at school, leaving potentially serious scars in the form of low self-esteem, possible depression, and other psychological disorders.

Childhood obesity is the result of many factors working in concert with one another. While excessive intake of high-calorie foods and a lack of exercise are the major culprits, physical environment, parental influence, food advertisements, heredity, and other factors are also at play.

Parents, especially mothers, are a child's first teachers and role models, as well as those who decide what food to provide the child. For this reason, mothers can be said to play the most significant role in prevention and treatment of childhood obesity. First of all, how the child is fed during the infant phase—that is, whether a child is fed breast milk or infant formula, and if formula, what kind—is of significant concern. Research has shown that breastfeeding helps prevent a child from becoming obese, namely due to a breastfeeding baby's tendency to stop feeding when it is satisfied. A baby on infant formula, on the other hand, does not get the chance to learn to control its intake, as the mother determines the amount she feeds her baby.

Such babies will occasionally consume excessive calories because their mothers feed them more than the recommended amount of formula, or they introduce baby food early without reducing the baby's formula intake.

In many cases, the mother fails to observe the child's condition objectively. Even if a child's obesity is obvious to others, the mother might think her child is just a little bit chubby. There are also common unfounded beliefs, for example that plump children are cuter, or that fat helps young children grow taller; these ideas only push up the rate of childhood obesity. If you are unsure whether or not your child is obese, comparing his measurements to objective standards is necessary.

Body mass index (BMI) is a measure used to determine childhood overweight and obesity. Overweight is defined as a BMI at or above the 85th percentile and below the 95th percentile for children and teens of the same age and sex. Obesity is defined as a BMI at or above the 95th percentile for children and teens of the same age and sex. A child's BMI score can be obtained through a simple internet search for "BMI calculator." Enter your child's height and weight and the calculator will give you your child's BMI. Or you can calculate BMI by dividing your child's weight in kilograms by the square of his height in meters. For children and teens, BMI is age and sex specific and is often referred to as BMI-for-age. A child's weight status is determined using age- and sex-specific percentile for BMI rather than the BMI categories used for adults. This is because children's body composition varies as they age and varies between boys and girls. Therefore, BMI levels among children and teens need to be expressed relative to other children of the same age and sex. The CDC (Centers for Disease Control and Prevention) Growth Charts are the most commonly used indicator to measure the size and growth patterns of children and teens in the United States.

It is true that childhood obesity is also genetically influenced. According to one study, the rate of childhood obesity is 75 percent if both parents are obese and 25–50 percent if only one parent is obese. If both parents are normal weight, the probability of their children becoming obese is less than 10 percent.

There has been heated debate in the United States since research results were published showing that food advertisements increase the rate of obesity. This is particularly relevant because the average American child reportedly watches over forty thousand food commercials a year on television. This figure doubled from twenty thousand in 1970. Over 50 percent of food commercials on television are for candy, fast food, and drinks and cereal with high sugar content. These foods are high in calories and fat and low in fiber, which is necessary for good health. According to research done through the 1970s and 1980s, children under eight years old have a high tendency to understand advertisements as facts, and have a strong preference for foods that they recognize from commercials.

What is the right way for parents to prevent obesity?
Although parents influence what their children eat and will do the best job they can to prevent childhood obesity, they are constantly battling a myriad of societal and biological influences on their children's eating behavior. The following are recommendations for parents based on research findings and expert advice:

· Breastfeed the child for at least six months, up to a year if possible.

· Be sure every member of the family cultivates healthy eating habits. Reduce the frequency of eating out. Change the family diet to include many high-fiber foods, which give a sense of fullness and have fewer calories. To this end, the meal plan should include many fruits and vegetables, and a reduced amount of fatty foods. Foster a habit of drinking water instead of fruit juice from a young age.

· Encourage the child to eat a balanced diet from a young age. Food cannot be forced on children; they learn best if their parents and others around them are good eaters and enjoy eating everything. Give the child smaller portions than you think they should have. Children eat better when the food is cut into small pieces and arranged attractively. Drinks should also be given in small amounts in small cups so that the child can finish and ask for more. However, some research findings suggest that restricting children's access too rigidly to certain foods makes them like and want these foods even more over time. Bear in mind the importance of moderation in all parenting practices.

· Don't keep junk food, including sodas and other sugary drinks, in the house. If it's not there, they can't eat it and neither can you.

· Give the child three meals a day, at regular times, and be sure not to skip breakfast.

· Make sure that the child gets daily physical exercise or stays active at home or outside. Schedule frequent occasions for the whole family to exercise together, encouraging the child to perceive exercise as a fun activity.

· Make sure that the child gets plenty of sleep. According to research, lack of sleep has an adverse effect on children's academic performance and increases the risk of becoming overweight. Help the child develop a habit of going to bed at a regular time.

· Avoid putting the child on a diet if possible. A diet program can cause the child to become overly sensitive to eating and can lead to anorexia or bulimia in adolescence.

Changing daily habits is challenging even for adults. Changing your child's eating and exercise habits means changing your own as well. You are a role model. If you exercise and eat healthily, your child will see that and follow suit. Constant attention, patience, and love from the parents are required for a child to change his daily habits. Some people say that parents are to blame for childhood obesity. According to research by Sarah Anderson at Ohio State University, an infant who has an insecure relationship with its mother is at a 30 percent higher risk than other infants of becoming obese at the age of four or over. In other words, parental neglect is causing children to become overweight. In order to build a secure, affectionate relationship, it is important for parents to observe their child closely to detect warning signs and react appropriately. "Chubbiness" is neither endearing nor a sign of being healthy. Parents must recognize obesity as a serious disorder that harms a child's physical and mental health. There is a growing body of research that documents discrimination against fat children by their peers and teachers, even from their parents. Parents should realize that it is their responsibility to prevent and treat childhood obesity. Healthy eating and exercise should be part of a regular lifestyle.

In addition, parents need to teach their children to take individual action and personal responsibility. They need to learn about nutrition and the necessity to exercise more and be aware of the lure of advertising. Teaching children about healthy eating choices and encouraging physical activity is a worthwhile effort. However, adults also need to take responsibility for the environment in which children live so that children do not have to be experts on all things related to healthy eating and exercise. In many cases, children suffer from the effects of adults' poor choices.

CHAPTER 19

CHALLENGES OF RAISING AN AUTISTIC CHILD

I am not an expert on special education, but I cover autism in this book because more than a few helpless parents have come to me asking for advice, saying that their child is showing signs of autism. As it turned out, most of these children were not out of the ordinary; they were simply a little bit slow in their language development, or preferred to play alone. I once met a father who was convinced that his child was autistic because the child's mother was cold and showed little affection for the child. Parents should never diagnose their children so wantonly, nor should they treat a perfectly normal child as if he or she were autistic. It is heartbreaking to think about children being made to suffer for their parents' mistakes. For parents who are in doubt, below is a brief explanation of symptoms and causes of autism and ways to help autistic children.

There are many different types of autism, with varying symptoms and levels of severity. While children with severe autism exhibit a stark difference in growth and development from normal children, mild autism might easily go unnoticed. The majority of autistic children (about 70 percent) have lower-than-average IQ, but some show exceptional skills in specific areas, such as remembering numbers, solving puzzles, playing or composing music, and creating intricate works of art. The special kind of individual with autism who demonstrates profound skill in a specific area is called an autistic savant.

A person with Asperger's syndrome has difficulty forming personal relationships; shows stereotypic symptoms, including repetitive patterns of behavior; and has restricted behaviors, interests, and activities. Asperger's syndrome is a pervasive developmental disorder without noticeable delay of language development, which differentiates it from other autism spectrum disorders in that early language delay is insignificant. People with Asperger's syndrome who have normal linguistic development might still have difficulty communicating with others because of their tendency to use pedantic or indirect language.

According to a report by the Center for Disease Control, one out of five hundred children has autism, and one out of one hundred children has an autism spectrum disorder. Autism is more than twice as frequent in boys than girls.

Major symptoms of autism include a lack of social and communication skills, linguistic disability, and restricted and repetitive behaviors. Autistic children live in their worlds and have

difficulty forming relationships with other people. They do not make eye contact with or react to other people, and lack the ability to understand other people's emotions. Their language is often characterized by echolalia or automatic repetition of words spoken by someone else. If they can speak intelligibly, they have severe trouble starting or continuing conversations with other people. Repeatedly rocking back and forth, moving one's fingers, and spinning a toy are typical behaviors.

Autistic children have a tendency to focus on specific aspects of a thing. They are reluctant to accept changes or new things, and a small change in their surroundings can make them feel extremely anxious. Compulsive behaviors, an extremely low ability to learn and adjust, and heightened sensitivity to sounds and textures are some other characteristics commonly observed in autistic children. Unlike other children, autistic children do not engage in imaginary play. Children with severe autism might show self-injurious behaviors. The symptoms of autism differ by child, but parents should seek a diagnosis from a professional if their child does not start to babble close to his first birthday, has not learned to speak by eighteen months old, or does not make eye contact and is expressionless.

There are countless causes of autism, but mutation of the SHANK3 gene has been found to be the single most common cause. Genetic mutations cause 90 percent of the condition, while environmental factors—that is, all risk factors that can have a negative impact on the fetus during the phase of brain development—cause the remaining 10 percent. Maternal stress, nutritional deficiency, pharmaceutical side effects, and bacterial and viral infection can all contribute to autism. Emotional shock and deprivation of affection were once thought to be factors in autism, but this was disproved in the 1960s.

How can parents help autistic children?

The most effective ways to help autistic children are early diagnosis and integrative treatment. Symptoms of autism can be observed before the child is three years old. It is best to recognize the symptoms and begin treatment as early as possible because early treatment can greatly improve a child's linguistic and social abilities. Speech therapy is most urgent, for it influences a child's intellectual development, though treatment of linguistic behavior and social skills should be accompanied by proper medication. If possible, the parents should consult with multiple specialists to get an accurate diagnosis, and then begin treatment with a specialist with whom they and the child feel most comfortable. Exchanging information with other parents of autistic children and seeking their advice is also advisable. The parents must gain an accurate understanding of the specific treatment their child needs and what they can expect from the treatment. They must also take precautions to ensure they do not employ unverified treatments.

Some parents carry an enormous psychological burden and feelings of guilt, believing that they are somehow to blame for their child's autism. They are tormented, suspecting their child's condition to have been caused by flaws in their parenting methods or a lack of affection. As explained above, the causes of autism have no correlation to psychological disorders or lack of affection. Any such guilt is entirely misplaced.

CHAPTER 20

ATTENTION DEFICIT/ HYPERACTIVITY DISORDER

Characterized by an inability to sustain attention, distractibility, hyperactivity, and impulsive behaviors, attention deficit/ hyperactivity disorder (ADHD) is a condition that is often diagnosed in childhood. Until the 1970s, it was widely believed that ADHD occurred in childhood and persisted until the adolescent period, but research has shown that ADHD can continue into adulthood if left untreated.

Not all children who are hyperactive or easily distracted are diagnosed with ADHD, but it can be damaging to dismiss a child's symptoms as an issue that time will cure. Having said that, it is also true that diagnosing a child with a true clinical disorder is not a simple task. The condition is often misdiagnosed, so it is important to seek the opinions of specialists who can diagnose the child accurately and provide appropriate treatment.

According to statistics compiled by the American Academy

of Pediatrics, the prevalence rate of ADHD among school-aged children is 3–8 percent and reported three times more often in boys than in girls. ADHD begins early in childhood and lasts for an extended period. It is also found in adults, but many adults live their entire lives unaware of their condition. The severity of ADHD ranges from showing minor symptoms to being serious enough to require treatment from a specialist.

General Symptoms of ADHD

The child lacks the capability of selective attention. His attention does not improve from pointing this out. The child might be listening to his teacher, but as soon as he hears another sound, his gaze moves toward the sound. The child often gets wrong answers on exams because he does not finish reading the questions. He has difficulty focusing on one thing for an extended period. The child is easily distracted and loses his pos-

sessions often.

The child shows hyperactivity, getting up from his seat without permission and running around the classroom, or moving his arms and legs continuously. He tends to act before thinking, and talks and moves around excessively.

Even if the child knows and understands the rules, he cannot resist urges to act hastily, and shows impulsive behaviors such as answering before another person finishes asking a question, or interjecting while another person is talking. Hyperactivity symptoms diminish through adolescence and as the patient reaches adulthood, but tendencies toward impulsive behaviors often persist into adulthood.

Causes

The exact cause of ADHD has not yet been discovered. Based on adoption studies and twin studies, the predominant view is that ADHD is caused by hereditary factors. However, many children showing ADHD symptoms are born to parents with no symptoms. Various environmental factors, such as environmental pollution, smoking or drinking during pregnancy, premature birth, underweight birth, and head injury during childhood, have been discussed as possible causes of this disorder, but without definitive evidence, there is still much room for debate.

Treatment

The effects of ADHD are long term, and this condition is not easy to cure completely. Therefore, treatment must prioritize reducing symptoms and minimizing disruptions in daily life caused by the condition. There are three main forms of treatment for ADHD: medication, psychotherapy, and special education. Integrating all three forms of treatment is often the most effective strategy.

Medications commonly used to treat ADHD include Ritalin and Adderall. These drugs might help a child by calming his or her mind and increasing concentration, but they do not provide a fundamental cure and can cause side effects, including hypersensitivity, loss of appetite, and insomnia. A child's condition and constitution should be considered carefully before deciding on a medication and dosage. Physical activity is also helpful in treating ADHD, as it increases the levels of dopamine, norepinephrine, and serotonin in the brain. Learning individual sports that require concentration on body movements, such as dance, gymnastics, and skateboarding, is recommended, as is playing team sports with friends. Sessions with a cognitive-behavioral therapist or a special education expert are another treatment option. Before beginning such sessions, the parents should research the therapist or expert's qualifications and experience in treating ADHD.

Advice for Parents

· **Consistent parenting is a very important component of raising a child with ADHD.** The child needs an organized environment where everything has a place. It is important for the parents to instruct the child to set a schedule for meals, homework and study, play, and bedtime, and follow it consistently. It is recommended that clocks be placed in various parts of the house so that the child can view them easily. In particular, the schedule should allow sufficient time for doing homework and getting ready for school in the morning, so that the child has plenty of time to finish these tasks. Parents must be aware of the time and place of the child's activities.

· **The parents should create a comfortable sleeping environment for the child.** Regular, sufficient sleep is very helpful in treating ADHD, as the condition is accompanied by sleep disorders and a child might suffer insomnia as a side effect of medication. In response, the parents should encourage a sleep schedule in which the child wakes and sleeps at regular times. The parents should make sure the child turns off all electronic devices (TV, computer, video games, smartphone) an hour before going to bed and avoids intense physical activity during the time leading up to bedtime. Playing ambient sounds (e.g., rain, waves, or a clock pendulum) can also be an effective means of inducing sleep.

· **The simpler the child's daily schedule, the better.** The child should neither be idle with nothing to do nor should they have too many extracurricular activities that might further distract or excite them.

· **At home, the parents should provide the child with a private space where the child can feel relaxed and at ease.**

Although ADD and ADHD are relatively common, its symptoms closely correlate with that of a normal child's behavior. Therefore, it is important to recognize that any number of these symptoms may not necessarily indicate that your child has ADD or ADHD. Labeling a child with ADHD when in fact they do not meet the criteria can be incredibly damaging to that child. A child without the disorder who is nonetheless labeled as having ADD or ADHD can internalize the stigma attached to the conditions, resulting in poor self-esteem. Also, misdiagnosis of ADD or ADHD and administering of unneeded medications can have serious negative side effects on a child. Therefore, it is necessary to get the opinions of multiple specialists before you conclude your child has ADD or ADHD.

PART III

RAISING COMPETENT AND HAPPY CHILDREN

Chapter 21

The Key to a Child's Happiness: Self-esteem

A child's self-esteem and self-concept are closely related. Children with high self-esteem believe that they are capable and valuable, and that they are precious to the people around him. Such children are generally satisfied with themselves, have hopes for the future, and are not easily discouraged by difficulties they may face. A child with high self-esteem feels that the people surrounding him accept him as he is, and trusts that they will protect and help him. He knows that if something bad happens to him his mother and father will be sad, and if he goes far away, they will miss him. By contrast, a child with low self-esteem feels that people do not accept him as he is, are not interested in him, or do not care what happens to him.

One's self-esteem is not developed in just one phase of life; someone who had positive self-esteem during his childhood can begin to harbor negative self-esteem during adolescence. Someone who had poor self-esteem during early childhood can develop more positive self-esteem later on. Factors such as household income and the education level and social status of the parents, which can affect other aspects of a child's development, do not have a major effect on the formation of a child's self-esteem. On the other hand, the child's relationships with his parents, friends, and relatives are known to have a significant impact. In particular, the level of affection that parents have towards their child before he enters school becomes the basis of the child's self-esteem.

Experts in child development and early childhood education assert that the primary objective of good parenting and preschool education should be helping children develop high self-esteem. High self-esteem is regarded as a key mental quality that plays a significant role in facilitating one's mental health, building positive interpersonal relationships, and ensuring academic achievement. The emphasis on high self-es-

teem in the United States, especially among early childhood educators, stems from historical and social trends during the mid-twentieth century.

In the 1960s, the United States underwent an economic boom as well as social turmoil surrounding human rights issues and anti-war protests. The country was fighting the Cold War; it had survived the Cuban Missile Crisis without catastrophe, but the dark cloud of the Vietnam War covered every corner of society. After President John F. Kennedy was assassinated and succeeded by Lyndon B. Johnson, the Civil Rights Acts was passed in 1964. In the United States, education had traditionally been under the jurisdiction of the state and local governments, but following the enactment of the Civil Rights Act, the federal government provided a fund for the education of children from low-income families, to prevent their entering school unprepared and thus break the vicious cycle of low school achievement. This led to the initiation of the Head Start Program to improve early childhood education in low-income families. In the process of evaluating the efficacy of federal educational support, it came to light that children from low-income families not only received lower grades on average but also had a strong tendency to believe their low achievements were determined by some external force rather than by the lack of their individual effort. This triggered a series of studies to find out about the relationship between self-esteem and academic achievement as well as its connection with various psychological and behavioral problems.

When we synthesize the results of the various studies over the past fifty years, surprisingly, self-esteem did not have a significant relation to academic achievement. Yet students with low self-esteem had a higher probability of showing problem behaviors (drinking, violence, running away from home) and higher levels of depression. My own studies with Korean-American adolescents living in the United States have revealed similar results. Korean-American youths with low self-esteem are more likely to skip school, run away from home, attempt suicide, be promiscuous, abuse alcohol, and use drugs than their Korean-American adolescent peers with high self-esteem.

In spite of past research that shows no significant relationships between self-esteem and school achievement, I believe, as do most experts in child development and early childhood education, that high self-esteem plays a key role in student academic achievement. Children who view themselves as competent, have hope for the future, and are resilient, will inevitably try harder to achieve their goals, whether those are academic goals or goals in other fields.

1 ▼ THE SENSITIVE CARE AND AFFECTION OF PARENTS ARE THE FOUNDATIONS OF A CHILD'S SELF-ESTEEM

Imagine yourself in the place of a baby who spends many hours in a mother's or caregiver's tender arms, is breastfed on cue, and whose cries are sensitively responded to. For example, the baby cries to be fed or comforted and receives an affectionate and timely response. As a result, the baby feels loved and valued. Affectionate responses to a baby's verbal and nonverbal cues are the key to an infant's self-value.

Psychologist Stanley Coopersmith (1967) stated that children are their mother's emotional mirror. If the mother is relaxed and responsive to the cues the baby gives, the baby will learn that his or her cues will elicit positive responses in the future. On the other hand, if the baby's needs are not met, and his or her cues go unanswered, the baby will feel that his or her signals will receive no response. Thus, the baby feels worthless and concludes something along the lines of "I am at the mercy of others, and there's nothing I can do to reach them." There is no magic here. The child, in tune with his or her mother's emotions, will read into the mother's body language and respond accordingly.

For example, one mother when bathing her child responds to the baby in a tender voice, and proudly gazes at the baby's body submerged in water, her eyes full of love. When the baby squeals with joy, the mother answers back, and when the baby splashes water, the mother joins in the game. After such bathing, the baby falls asleep easily and sleeps longer. Another mother focuses only on bathing her child and hurries through the task as though it is a cumbersome chore. The baby becomes restless, uncooperative, and stressed. In response, the mother becomes more stressed herself and continues to treat the time as an unpleasant chore, and the child continues to resist and feel stressed whenever he is bathed. Mothers who are relaxed while interacting with their children will, in turn, elicit a relaxed response, and will continue to treat spending time with their children as relaxing. Mothers who are stressed and inattentive when interacting with their children will elicit fussy and uncooperative responses and will grow to see spending time with their children as stressful.

While breastfeeding, one mother tries to make it easier for her baby to suckle, continuously talking to and making eye contact with the baby. Another mother lets her baby feed while using her free hand to flip the pages of a book, or concentrating on a TV show. The second mother is not concerned whether her baby is being fed comfortably or well. She ignores the baby when it babbles, and when the baby pulls on her clothes, she shakes off the baby's hand, not even looking her baby in the face. How will an infant with such experiences come to feel that he or she is precious to anyone? Parents who are responsive will help their child to develop positive self-esteem, while parents who ignore their children or are non-responsive may cause the child to develop low self-esteem.

How a mother treats her infant influences how the child regards himself. Of course, you must remember that self-esteem is not formed overnight. Constant and responsive parental care and affection for an infant over time are of the utmost importance.

2 ▼ LOVE YOUR CHILDREN AS THEY ARE

Parents must accept their child as he or she is and be interested and take part in what the child is doing. Feeling loved is the most important factor in the development of a child's positive self-esteem. A child can sense when the mother accepts him for who he is. When parents accept their child and reflect back to their child the positive image they have of him, he learns to think well of himself.

For example, a mother takes her son to an amusement park. He chooses not to try any of the scarier rides there. In a situation like this, the mother can perceive the child's actions in one of two ways. The first is to conclude that he is adverse to new experiences. Another, more positive way to look at his behavior is to understand that the child is simply cautious and needs to feel more comfortable before he tries any of the rides. In other words, if a parent is quick to see a child's actions as indicative of negative character traits, the child will read into his or her parent's response and will have a hard time developing a positive self-esteem.

3 ▼ NURTURE A SENSE OF BELONGING

It is important for a child to feel a sense of belonging as he or she grows up. If a child feels that he or she is being respected within the family, he or she will find it easier to make friends outside the family.

As the child matures, his or her sense of belonging should expand beyond the immediate family to relatives and friends. Parents should encourage their child to take pride in his family, especially in particular members of the family or in the family history. To this end, parents can show their child photographs or articles left by a deceased family member, tell the family history or stories about ancestors, and bring the child along to family reunions. This pride and sense of belonging are not dependent upon the family's achievements or prestige. The family need not be rich and famous or possess a royal pedigree. Instead, help your child to be proud of your family because of the way you genuinely care for one another and maintain a strong familial bond.

4 ▼ BE RESPECTFUL WHEN CONVERSING WITH YOUR CHILD

Parents should respect the child's point of view and opinions and give practical and appropriate responses. For instance, if the parents feel that the child is spending too much time watching TV or playing video games, they should discuss the issue with the child, share their opinions, and respect the child's point of view when finding a resolution. Parents should not command their child to turn off the TV right away, or raise their voices without understanding the situation. It is essential to handle the child's point of view respectfully.

Rather than stressing and expecting that a child succeed all the time, teach the child how to react when things do not go well. When a child's self-esteem is diminished from disappointment or crisis, the parents' continued support and love can help him rebound. Encouraging the child to think about what went wrong after a crisis is over can help the child draw on his or her experience and overcome future crises more effectively.

5 ▼ KNOW THE POWER OF A FEW KIND WORDS

Parents who accept and respect their child as he is would never talk carelessly to him. Parents must keep in mind that a few comforting words can be a great encouragement in times when a child seems dispirited. Telling them "you always keep your promises," "you are very responsible," or "I always believe in you" makes a child proud. If the parent believes that the child is smart, the child who knows this will continue to study hard through challenges; if the parent regards the child as an honest person, the child will make every effort to live honestly. As I stated earlier, parents should never compare a child to his siblings or friends. Careless statements like "Why can't you be like your brother and do something right?" can be detrimental to a child's self-esteem. Keep in mind that a few hurtful words from parents can leave children with lifelong scars.

6 ▶ BECOME YOUR CHILD'S PSYCHOLOGICAL MEDIATOR

It is important for a child to establish a firm basis for high self-esteem before he enters kindergarten. In kindergarten, a child comes in contact with a wider range of people, including classmates, friends, and teachers. Each of these people has a significant influence on the development of the child's self-esteem. Outside the home, academic performance, athletic ability, popularity among friends, physical appearance, and other attributes become criteria for judgment. Parents should not deny this fact, for closing their eyes will not change the situation. When a child begins going to school, the parents should do their best to negate the negative effects of the outside world on the child.

No child can possess all of the characteristics that society holds up as desirable. Therefore, parents should highlight a child's strengths while embracing his weaknesses. Compared with Korean society, for instance, American society places a higher value on being good at sports and getting along with other children than on being a top student academically. There is a clear tendency for children with well-rounded personalities to have higher self-esteem than children who only get good grades. But not every child can be popular, good at sports, and well rounded. Parents should act as a windbreak between the child and the expectations of the child's social circles. They should play the role of psychological mediator and emotional protector for the child in the child's new and ever-expanding environment.

CHAPTER 22

RAISING A CONFIDENT CHILD

If our primary parenting goal is to raise a competent and happy child, we should help our children develop self-confidence. Confidence helps our children deal with the challenges they face in life. A confident child believes in his or her abilities. He or she is also more willing to try new things, which in turn helps the child to learn. Having confidence also means the child is more likely to feel comfortable with himself or herself as well as with others. Such children also feel they have something worthwhile to give to others.

A child's belief in his or her own ability to do things is important for their motivation, perseverance, and success in life. As the classic picture book *The Little Engine That Could* has taught in an accessible and appealing way since 1930, a positive outlook and belief in oneself is essential in the face of adversity. Children's self-belief or self-efficacy can motivate them more than their actual skill level. For example, if a child truly believes he can pass a test or ride a bike, the child may be more likely to actually achieve it than another child who has better ability but lacks confidence.

Confidence requires a positive outlook on life. Being positive is looking on the bright side or seeing the glass as half full as opposed to half empty. There is an old Korean story that describes this well. There were two mothers: One mother was always happy while the other was always sad. The mothers both had two sons. Each mother had one son who made a living by selling umbrellas for rainy days and another who made a living by selling straw sandals for sunny days. On sunny days the happy mother was happy thinking of her son who sold straw sandals, and on rainy days she felt happy thinking of her son who sold umbrellas. In contrast, on sunny days the pessimistic mother worried about her son who sold umbrellas, and on rainy days she worried about her son who sold straw sandals. People may have a natural tendency either to be more optimistic or more pessimistic, but these mindsets are not fixed and can be changed through experience.

A confident child is also more willing to try new things and this helps him to learn. Furthermore, confidence helps the child interact with other children, which makes it easier for him to form friendships. We live in a social world, so our relationships with others are of significant importance to our wellbeing.

Some children have confidence from a young age, while other children do not. Therefore, many people believe that confident children are born naturally confident, but this is not true. To an extent, these differences are due to the child's innate temperament, but they are largely the result of how the child has been brought up and raised. Consequently, parents have an important role to play in helping children be more confident. The following are some useful guidelines.

Meet your child's needs

It is important that parents try to meet their child's fundamental needs. Some mothers do not meet their child's needs because they fear spoiling the child. They do not feed their babies unless it is feeding time, even if the child is crying from hunger. Or they do not take the child in their arms when the child reaches for them, even when the child is crying to be held because he is not feeling well. If a child has many such experiences, he is likely to grow up distrustful of other people and of his own ability to communicate.

Abraham Maslow claimed that if children are to be motivated to reach the highest level of their potential, their fundamental needs—biological and physiological needs, safety needs, belongingness and love needs—must be met. Early childhood education scholar K. Read asserted that satisfying the basic needs of a child during preschool years does not spoil a child. Rather, children get spoiled when parents, trying to give children what they think they should have, end up giving them too much of what they do not actually need. If a young child wants to try something, the parents should allow him to try it, even if it is inconvenient or worrisome. For example, a mother might be cooking in the kitchen when her child says he wants to help her cut something with a knife. This might concern the mother for safety reasons or because it would be more time-consuming on her part, but the mother should make a provision for her child to have the experience of cutting with a smaller, safer knife under close supervision. If a child wants to help his or her mom with baking cookies, the mother should allow her child to measure, pour, etc. The mother would do well to help the child feel like he is able to help his mother and gain confidence in accomplishing a task. To do this, though, the mother has to have patience.

Trust in your children

If parents trust their child's ability and his choices, the child will gain confidence in his ability and judgment and eventually mature enough to act responsibly. In general, a child behaves according to how he is seen by the people around him, especially that child's parents. If parents want the child to accomplish something, they should allow the child to try. Even if they are not convinced that the child can accomplish the task, it is important that they respect and trust the child's choice and will.

My ten-year-old grandson wanted to refit a toy gun he had

been playing with, so I took him to a store to get the parts. He had written down the sizes and numbers of the exact parts that he needed so as not to forget anything. Refitting the toy gun with his own hands made him proud, and he favored the refitted gun over his other, more expensive toy guns.

When I visited my son's house later, I noticed that a hinge on the kitchen cupboard had come loose. When I mentioned that it should be fixed, my son told the same ten-year-old grandson from my previous story to bring the right tool and fix the hinge. Feeling proud that his father trusted his ability and had assigned him a task, my grandson ran to get the screwdriver and fixed the cupboard door right away. It was a relatively simple task, but through this experience, my grandson probably was able to gain the sort of confidence that will help him accomplish other, greater tasks in the future.

Help your child to build successful experiences

Accumulating successful experiences is the best way to build confidence. Prepare opportunities for your child to feel a sense of accomplishment; it does not matter if the task is small and trivial. Parents must learn through close observation what their child is capable of doing and what he is not. For example, trying to teach a child to read when he is not prepared, or forcing potty training on a child who is not ready, is setting the child up for failure, and repeated failures cause a child to lose confidence.

Suppose that a six- or seven-month-old toddler is trying hard to reach a rattle. Rather than putting the rattle in the child's hand, the parents might put the rattle close to the child, so that it's easier to reach. After reaching the rattle, the toddler will experience a sense of achievement at having done it all on his own.

Wanting to do everything well is a basic human desire, but when parents insist that children perform tasks they cannot handle, it subjects them to the experience of repeated failure. Such failures disrupt the formation of confidence in the child. Instead, parents should give their child every opportunity to succeed, and should be unsparing in giving heartfelt praise and encouragement when the child accomplishes a task. If the child, to his dismay, fails, the parents should not fail to applaud the child's effort.

Have realistic expectations of your child

There is a saying about parents who teach their child to run before he learns to crawl. Such excessive expectations from parents can often diminish a child's self-confidence. A child who learns that he is not meeting his parents' expectations feels dejected and inferior. Carelessly uttered criticisms, such as "Why would you ever do something so foolish?" or "You can't do anything right!" are negative comments that can crush a child's confidence. Remember that everyone has positive and negative qualities, strengths and weaknesses. A child cannot easily develop confidence when the people who are important to him, especially his parents, do not accept him as he is.

Support your children through difficult times

When a child comes out from under his parents' wings and starts going to school, he is exposed to external influences that his parents cannot control. Teachers take over the parents' role of trying to understand a child's characteristics and helping him resolve conflicts, but there are certainly limits. Eventually, a child will naturally compare himself to his classmates and might feel intimidated by children who excel in their studies, at art, or at sports. His feelings might be hurt from time to time by conflict among friends. As a result, for a child who has just started school, the parents have to become reliable psychological supporters. Parents should talk with their child about his or her day-to-day experiences at school. They should console him if he is displeased, and share in his joy if he had an exciting experience, or even offer discreet advice. Overall, the role of the parents remains crucial after a child starts going to school. Parents must always be attuned to how their child is adjusting to school and what is going on with his friends while also giving a helping hand when necessary, so that the child, still vulnerable to external influences, does not lose confidence.

A friend of mine told me that her daughter had been selected to go to a math competition as her school's representative but

looked depressed. When she talked to her, her daughter told her two of her friends who were not selected had said hurtful things to her. My friend suggested her daughter talk with the school counselor. The counselor intervened, and the coach had a conversation with the other children. As it turned out, those children, who were proud of being gifted in math, had misbehaved out of jealousy when they were not selected. In this case, not only the child who was selected but also the other children were hurt, and they all needed the care of adults. In such cases, the parents must assure the child that asking for help from parents, teachers, or counselors is not the same as "telling" on other children and thus nothing to be ashamed of.

Teach your child how to fail

Parents have an innate desire to protect their children. A parent naturally desires to prevent their child from experiencing sadness, disappointment, and failure. It might seem nice at the moment to prod a child's sports coach to give them more playing time. However, this is counterproductive to ensuring that your child gains confidence in the face of difficulties and failure. A child needs to learn that failure is both inevitable and acceptable. What is important is not failure or success, but the maturation that takes place through these experiences. It is important to let children know that failure is in fact necessary to personal growth. For example, do not praise your child only for winning a baseball game. Instead, praise them for their hard work and any improvements they have made. In addition, show your children that failure is something that all people experience, for instance, by explaining some of your failures and mistakes, and how you overcame them. In this way, a child can learn to not be discouraged by failures and disappointment.

CHAPTER 23

FOSTERING TOLERANCE

Tolerance is the willingness to be open to and accept different viewpoints, cultures, ethnicities, and religions—among other things—that are not ours. To put it into different terms, it is an extension of the golden rule in that if we desire that others respect and accept us for who we are and what we believe, we must extend that same courtesy to others. The virtue of tolerance is exemplified in our Constitution—the Bill of Rights is almost exclusively concerned with it—and in some of our greatest national leaders. Abraham Lincoln, for example, was a figure who demonstrated the virtue of tolerance. Lincoln acknowledged the strengths of Edwin Stanton, his longtime political opponent and critic, and asked Stanton to work by his side. As a result, Stanton is remembered in American history as particularly effective Secretary of War.

In her 2007 bestseller, *Day of Empire*, Yale University professor Amy Chua analyzed and compared historical global superpowers, including Persia, Rome, Mongolia, China, Great Britain, and the present-day United States. The author points out that these historic superpowers were all ethnically and culturally diverse and characterized by tolerance among their people. The Achaemenid Persian Empire employed vanquished people in high government offices and embraced the languages, cultures, and religions of such people. The reason that the Roman Empire flourished was that it accepted vanquished people as Roman citizens, allowed them merit-based ascension in status, and acknowledged their religions. At the end of the Roman Empire, however, the enforcement of extremely unfair policies led to an insurgency of the Germanic peoples, which ultimately caused the empire's demise. Chua cites discrimination against ethnic and cultural minorities and these groups' persecution under the pretense of racial, religious, and ethnic purity as the reason for the demise of empires. In her examination of U.S. history, Professor Chua also argues that the acceptance of a great number of immigrants from Europe and Central and South America before and after the two World Wars, as well as the pursuit of a tolerant policy to provide fair compensation for their labor and efforts, is what made the United States a global superpower.

The reason that I mention the tolerant policies of historical empires is to point out that tolerant national policies are ultimately derived from the tolerance of each individual member of society. For any country to achieve economic development and play an important role in international affairs, its children must be taught to mingle with children of different ethnicities, philosophies, and cultural spheres. Childhood experiences play an especially important role in fostering a person's tolerance. Children aged two to five already recognize people who are different from them and observe how such people are treated by the adults around them.

The best way to teach a child the virtue of tolerance is to give the child frequent opportunities to interact with a broad range of people. It is also a good idea to encourage the habit of considering issues from another person's perspective, perhaps through role playing. For example, parents can have their child walk down the street blindfolded for a time to see what it is like to be blind, or spend time in a wheelchair. If there is a news report on TV or an article in the newspaper about people who are persecuted or treated unfairly because they are different from others, parents can discuss the position of the persecuted people with their child. Rather than shielding children from the intolerance of others, which can be detrimental, it is better to help children understand what tolerance means and why it is important; to do so, they must learn the immense cost of intolerance. In this way, seeking to educate your children about both the importance of tolerance and the cost of intolerance, in addition to personally modeling tolerance for them in your daily life, is vital.

For example, parents can teach their children, within reason, about the horrid atrocities committed during the Second World War because of intolerant mindsets. For example, because the Japanese viewed themselves as superior and were entirely intolerant of those who were not part of their race, they were able to justify horrible crimes such as sexual slavery against non-Japanese groups that they occupied. Similarly, white Americans justified slavery and the denial of the basic human rights of blacks in America because of their belief in the superiority of white people over black people.

However, if the parents do not show tolerance of others in their own lives, all of this effort will be in vain. It would be irrational for parents to be hostile or resentful toward people who have different ideas from them yet talk of tolerance with their child. Children take after their parents. If the parents demonstrate tolerance, their children will learn to be tolerant in turn. Children of intolerant parents are highly likely to develop a similarly intolerant mindset.

Tolerance is a fundamental quality that every citizen of the global village must seek to live out. The ability to accept and acknowledge different people and cooperate with them is as important as a child's ability to acquire knowledge or play sports. Fostering tolerance in children is an important responsibility that today's parents must fulfill in order to help their children become better human beings and more equipped global citizens.

CHAPTER 24

FOSTERING ADAPTABILITY

In today's diverse and rapidly changing society, in a world in which we are challenged to compete with one another, having enough mental flexibility to adapt to change is crucial. Only a generation ago, most people dedicated themselves to one profession all their lives. In modern times, however, people change jobs frequently, whether by their own decisions or because they are forced to do so. Even if a person stays in one job, the knowledge and skills required in the workplace today are in constant flux and always evolving. Charles Darwin argued, "It is not the strongest of the species that survives, nor the most intelligent that survives. It is the one that is most adaptable to change." These words not only apply to the evolution and survival of organisms but also describe the reality of the world that humans live in. We must help our children to develop flexibility and adaptability, two traits that will enable them to react appropriately to their rapidly changing world.

Confidence begets adaptability

Often, a child who lacks confidence in his ability and judgment fears change. The child avoids trying new things and might have difficulty making friends. Fear of change is the biggest stumbling block to a child's adaptability. In order to remove this stumbling block, parents must first raise their child's self-confidence. To this end, parents must create frequent opportunities for their child to experience a sense of success and accomplishment. Parents can set their children up for success at all stages of life; if a two-year-old child wants to put his clothes on by himself, the parents might do little things for the child, aligning his sleeves, for example, or putting his shoes on the correct side, so that the child can accumulate successes. The more successes the child experiences, the more confidence he gains, and the more he learns to adapt to change. On the other hand, repeated failure can cause a child to lose confidence and be timid in the face of change. For this reason, parents must not expect or force their child to complete an overwhelming task. Determining to what degree a child can be aided to experience success and to what point a child should be permitted to do the tasks on his own is a key parental skill.

Encourage exploration

Parents must stimulate their child's curiosity and encourage him to explore his surroundings. Communing with nature is an

effective way to elicit a child's interest in change and help him gain insight. By observing and exploring nature, a child faces unexpected situations and naturally acquires problem-solving skills as he looks for answers. If the family lives in a large city or if both parents work, it might be difficult to find opportunities for the child to commune with nature. In such a situation, the parents can grow potted plants on their balcony, have the child sow seeds in containers to grow vegetables or flowering plants, or take the child to a nearby park to observe trees, touch plants, or listen to the chirping of cicadas. When a child asks a question, it is important that the parents answer promptly and in language that the child can understand easily. Giving a scientifically accurate answer is of secondary importance; try to give an answer that makes sense to your child. Elicit your child's interest in various natural phenomena by asking questions, and encourage him to think about the phenomena from various angles. Asking questions such as "why is this flower fresh looking while that one looks wilted?" or "why did the cicada suddenly stop making a sound?" stimulates a child's curiosity and imagination.

Foster a sense of stability in your child

Stable children exhibit high adaptability to new environments and flexibility in their thinking. In other words, stability is the basis of confidence, and confidence is the basis of a child's adaptability and flexibility of behavior and thinking.

Stability is achieved when a child grows up in a familiar and stable environment and his psychological and physical needs are met. To be stable, a child's eating and sleeping times must be consistent, to a degree. If the parents get help from a nanny or grandparents to care for the child, they must communicate clearly with the helper so that the environment does not change too drastically. When hiring a nanny, parents must ensure that their child develops a good, stable, trusting relationship with the person.

Overprotection is poison

Without the experience of trying new things and succeeding, a child cannot develop flexibility or adaptability. If parents allow their child to do only the things that they know that the child can do safely, out of fear that the child will hurt himself or fail, they are depriving the child of new and unexpected experiences and thus weakening the child's tolerance for change. Encourage your child to attempt new things, as adventure matures children.

In general, children adapt to change more quickly than adults because, unlike adults, they are better equipped to think flexibly without being hung up on fixed ideas. Parents should not try to direct their child's behavior and thoughts according to what they think is the ideal direction. Creativity and the ability to think flexibly only emerge when a child feels and experiences something for himself.

Help your child to develop a wider range of relationships

Create opportunities for your child to make new friends. By socializing with children from various environments and cultures, a child will become more open-minded and generous. Make an effort to give your child opportunities to meet and socialize with children of diverse backgrounds. Signing up for a local sports team or joining an orchestra is a good way for a child to meet people outside of school. One child I know trained on a swim team after school and went to a music school on Saturdays, gradually observing that the two groups of children had starkly different characteristics. Still, the child formed friendships in both groups of children, bonds that became stronger year after year. Under such circumstances, parents must respect and welcome all of their child's friends without prejudice. From parents' open-mindedness, a child acquires flexibility of thinking and healthier human relationships.

CHAPTER 25.

CHOOSING A PRESCHOOL OR CHILDCARE CENTER

Choosing the right preschool and childcare center for your child is not an easy task for most parents, who have little time, knowledge, or support for making satisfactory choices. Preschools and childcare centers are provided in a variety of settings in reflection of the diverse needs of today's families. Programs range from private to public, including federally funded programs and those affiliated with religious institutions or universities.

Regardless of the type of center you are looking for, it is important to start researching and applying to a few programs as early as you can, because space is often limited. Also, because so much is riding on your choice, you should invest time and energy in making the right decision. Proximity to home or work, good facilities, and low costs shouldn't be the primary criteria for selecting a program for your child, even though these are important factors to be considered.

First, considering that the child will spend a large part of his waking hours there, parents should consider the impact this experience might have on the child. An abundance of research findings support the conclusion that children who attend high-quality preschool and child-care facilities benefit in the areas of intellectual and language development, as well as in learning sociability and considerateness. This experience also affects future academic performance, economic outcomes, and even health. In addition, support offered to families by high-quality programs works to decrease parental stress, improve mother–child relationships, and increase the stability of care and parent satisfaction, and thus contributes to the enhanced well-being of children attending such a program.

Parents should also be reminded of the fact that the best school for another child might not be the best match for yours. Your child's intellectual, emotional, and physical needs, as well as his temperament, age, and health, should be the basis for the decision. You can seek advice from neighbors and friends with children who went to a certain childcare center, or use the Internet to find an active network of parents with preschool-age children in your community.

You can also go online to search for names of schools and childcare centers with any red flags, like records of complaints by parents, health or safety violations, or other noteworthy issues. The Child Care Aware website makes it easy to search for preschools by zip code. The National Association for the Education of Young Children (NAEYC) website allows users to research preschools in their area that have NAEYC accreditation.

The main point is that if you have a child who needs to go to a preschool or childcare center, you need to be proactive. Do not wait until the time comes for your child to go to school. It is best to search for a school at least a year ahead of enrollment time.

After you narrow down the schools, you should make an arrangement to visit the ones you are considering. If possible, visit the program a few times at different times of a day, to get a better sense of how the program is run. When you visit the program you are considering, observe about how it measures up with regard to the following key indicators of quality.

The program's philosophy and goals

Early childhood education programs should be well rounded, with a balanced focus on developing physical, social, emotional, and intellectual abilities. A good preschool supports the optimal development of each child. Children develop a sense of self-worth when they are individually valued for who they are and their strengths are recognized. For instance, the late founding director of Stanford University's Bing Nursery School, Edith Dowley, explained the core of the school's philosophy as the effort to treat every child as an honored guest at the school. As this statement suggests, if children are to develop well, they need to feel that people like and value them. Good schools use play as a major vehicle for children's learning and enjoyment. Children learn through play using all of their senses, through doing things with materials, representing concepts, and rehearsing roles, thus clarifying them, so it is important that preschool programs value child-initiated and teacher-supported play activities. The program should also help children with their language development, which is the building block of thinking ability, and equip them to learn to value their own rights as well as the rights of others. A good program should increase the participation and involvement of the parents and the community.

The teachers

There is plenty of evidence that the teacher is the most important single factor in determining the quality of children's experiences in a school. It's not only the teacher's skill and professional qualification but also attitudes and feelings that influence what that teacher does with the children and for the children. The teacher needs to be in good physical health and emotionally stable. A good teacher must be flexible, empathic, and responsive to children's needs. It is of utmost importance that the teacher has faith and hope that every child can learn and change.

Teacher stability is a significant factor in predicting optimal outcomes for children. Unfortunately, wages for the childcare

workforce are relatively low, and consequently, teacher turn-over rates are high. High staff turnover rates have been found to be a predictor of less desirable caregiving and a lower level of attachment with children. Centers where pay is lower also have much higher staff turnovers. Parents concerned about stability of care should inquire, if possible, about the wage structure of the center they are considering as well as the training of the teachers and caregivers.

The size of the group and the staff–child ratio

If parents are to make optimal choices for their children, they will need to become more aware of factors in the facility they are considering that may affect how well their child does in that environment. Generally, preschoolers who are enrolled in smaller classes attain higher scores on kindergarten and first-grade readiness tests. In smaller classes, teachers and caregivers tend to be more sensitive to the children's needs, and children are more involved and interested in activities. The teacher-child ratio should be considered in relation to the group size. The ratio recommended by the National Association for the Education of Young Children (NAEYC) is one to three for infants in a group of six, one to five for toddlers (21 to 36 months) in a group of ten, and one to six for preschool children (30 to 48 months) in a group of twelve.

A focus on developmentally appropriate firsthand experiences

Learning through experience is very important for preschoolers. Cognitive psychologist Jean Piaget posited that the thinking process of preschoolers is different from that of adults. Children understand objects through sensory experiences rather than by what adults teach them.

Children are born with an intrinsic motivation to explore unknown worlds rather than absorb knowledge through reading, writing, and arithmetic exercises. It is important to help preschoolers to take an interest in their surroundings and arouse their curiosity. For instance, when new grass sprouts after a few days of rain, a child should be encouraged to observe the changes carefully. A teacher should elicit a child's interest by asking questions: "Was there grass before?" "What made the grass grow?" "Does this grass look different from that grass?"

Adequate indoor and outdoor space

The NAEYC suggests a minimum of 35 square feet of indoor playroom floor space per child and a minimum of 75 square feet of outdoor play space per child. Southern exposure is desirable for the playrooms. Rooms facing south are sunny and bright with plenty of light coming through low windows. The physical environment affects the behavior and development of children and adults who live and work in it. It affects the level of involvement by the children and the quality of their interaction with adults.

Indoor play spaces should include areas for dramatic play, manipulative play such as blocks, a quiet reading area, and other areas designated for various individual and group activities.

There should be sufficient outdoor space for the children to run around freely and safely, as well as adequate and well-maintained equipment for gross motor activities. Spaces should be free of hazards such as broken equipment, sharp corners, and steep stairs without handrails. Teachers should encourage children to play outdoors and allow sufficient time for outdoor play.

Attention to health and safety

Clean kitchens and bathrooms are very important. Toilets and facilities for washing and drying hands and faces should be near the play area and should be easily supervised. Snacks and meals should be planned and prepared with nutrition and health in mind.

Beauty

In addition to being safe and functional, a school should be an attractive place. Attention should be given to color and pleasing lines and shapes, in the form of framed children's artwork, for example, or a graceful flower arrangement, or an interesting mobile. Children are very perceptive and responsive to beauty in their surroundings.

In summary, empowering parents to make wise choices and to demand options for quality childcare will take concerted efforts from parents, families, volunteer organizations, employers, communities, and all levels of government. Most of all, parents should keep in mind that it takes time to find a good preschool and childcare center for their child. For many children, preschool is their first life experience outside of their home and family, so parents will want to make sure this critical transition from home and family to school life is as positive, safe, and cognitively stimulating as possible. It is worthwhile to spend adequate time and resources on deciding on the right preschool and childcare center for your child.

CHAPTER 26

FACILITATING COGNITIVE
DEVELOPMENT

Cognitive development is the process by which a child acquires the ability to process information, learn language, grasp
concepts, and master skills. The biological underpinning of
this process is the miraculous growth and development of
the child's brain. While it is true that many critical events in
brain development occur in utero, from the moment the child
is born, he is active in constructing his own knowledge of the
world and interacting dynamically with it. This is why infancy
and the preschool years are a period of such remarkably rapid
and complex cognitive development. While a two-year-old's
body weight is only about 20 percent of an adult's, the weight of
his brain is about 75 percent of an adult's (Shore 1997). At the
structural level, the number and complexity of neural connections (as measured by the density of dendrites in the cerebral
cortex) increases exponentially from birth to about age two,
with many areas of the brain having more neural connections

at that point than at any other age (Diamond 1990). While the rate of growth of neural connections slows, there is an amazing "pruning" process; reinforced connections are strengthened while unused connections weaken and disappear. Therefore, the motto for rich neural connections is "Use it or lose it!" This period of high neural "plasticity," which roughly corresponds to the preschool and early school years, is a critical window of cognitive development. Indeed, there is abundant evidence from the study of child development that intellectual development appears to be fastest in the first four to five years of life.

Furthermore, Jean Piaget, the pioneer of cognitive development research, emphasized that a child's thinking is qualitatively different from that of an adult. He suggested a developmental sequence to intellectual development: the sensorimotor stage (birth to age 2), the preoperational stage (ages 2 to 7), the concrete operational stage (ages 7 to 11 or 12) and the formal operational stage (ages 11 to 12 and beyond). All children progress through these stages in this order, and according to Piaget, there is no skipping of stages because each successive stage builds on the previous stage.

In this chapter, I will focus on cognitive development during the first seven years of life (the sensorimotor stage and the preoperational stage), as this is the most critical time for children's cognitive development.

During the sensorimotor stage (birth to age 2), the child

perceives the world using his sensory organs and motor skills alone. In other words, for the first two years of a child's life, his knowing and thinking consists of information acquired through the activities of seeing, hearing, and feeling.

During the preoperational stage, children become increasingly proficient at constructing and using mental symbols (words and images) to think about the world around them. Despite this advancement in symbolic reasoning, a child of this stage still has limitations in thinking. The child is egocentric, lacking the ability to think from another person's perspective, and is incapable of logical thinking. If a child is cold, he thinks everyone else in the world must be cold, and if a candy is delicious to him, he thinks everyone will like it.

A good example of illogical thinking can be illustrated by this episode with my grandson Spencer. When he was around four years old, he used to come to our home to stay with us until his mother came to pick him up after work. Whenever he had to leave, I would tell him how sad I was because I couldn't see him until he came back the next day. One day, he told me excitedly, "Grandma! I have an idea. How about we go to Mexico, find some bones on the beach, put them together, blow in some blood and make another me. Then you can keep one of me here, and I can go home with my mom." I didn't know how to respond to him for a minute. Then I said, "It sounds like a great idea! But do you really think we can make another one of you like that?" I wanted him to think about it himself, rather than telling him that it wouldn't work.

Another example of egocentric thinking can be seen in my four-year old grandson Nathan when I take him to the barbershop. They give him a lollipop when he is finished, and he eats most of it but then gives the rest to me when his hands gets sticky. He insists that I finish it up. When I tell him that I don't like lollipops, he simply can't understand why I don't like what he loves so much. I try to explain to him with no success that just because it tastes good to him doesn't mean it tastes good to everyone.

Many American psychologists, however, claim that Piaget underestimated the intellectual capacity of young children. They believe that young children can understand abstract concepts before six or seven years old. For instance, psychologist Jerome Bruner argues that, with proper guidance, there is no limit to what a child can learn, regardless of age. Disagreement among scholars has given rise to varying theories on early childhood education and cognitive development, leading to a wide range of teaching methods and educational content. What is generally agreed upon is that children who reach three or four years of age are capable of learning important facts and developing important concepts. They can observe and examine, make comparisons and infer relationships, make simple predictions, use numbers and measure, classify things, solve simple problems, and carry out simple investigations.

An important factor in the learning that children do at this stage is proper support and guidance that is suited to their level of developmental maturity. The following are some helpful strategies to foster the cognitive development of young children.

Help your child learn from experience

In infancy, direct sensory experience is very important to a child's cognitive development. Hearing or reading repeatedly that the sky is blue and the grass is green does little to increase a child's intellectual capacity. A child flawlessly memorizing and reciting the contents of a book is no different than a parrot repeating someone's words. How often can a child living in a large, polluted city see a blue sky nowadays? Teaching a child that the grass is green is not as meaningful to the child's cognitive development as allowing the child to see and touch the color and texture of grass as it changes from season to season and helping him learn why this happens.

The point I am making here is that in infancy, children understand the world around them through the five senses—seeing, hearing, tasting, smelling, and feeling—along with the sense of muscular movement. The greater the input of sensory impressions and sensory experiences they receive through play, the more they can improve their tools for understanding the world. An infant experiences an object as completely as possible by touching it, rolling it, pulling it, twisting it, sucking on it, looking at it from all angles, and dropping it to make sounds. Parents play a critical role in their child's cognitive development by providing a wide variety of sensory experiences and encouraging their use as a means for the child to understand the world.

Parents should also be alert to the possibility of visual and hearing impairments in their children, because problems with the visual and auditory senses impede learning in the young child, whose learning takes place largely through sensory experiences. Sometimes, parents misjudge the cause of their child's misbehavior. A child with poor vision may get easily distracted or may act clumsily.

Preschool-age children continue to learn by looking at, feeling, and playing with the objects around them. The richer their sensory experiences, the better equipped they are to understand objects. Fewer sensory experiences means fewer physical impressions, which discourages a child's curiosity and his urge to explore. A healthy child enjoys practicing until a skill is mastered. You might have observed a toddler go up and down stairs or climb over objects until he can do it easily. For example, the preschool-age child tries many different methods of riding a tricycle.

Nathan, our four-year-old grandson, after mastering the art of riding and backing the tricycle into a narrow driveway, has experimented with cutting corners, taking curved paths, and riding over objects. He even seems to enjoy puncturing the tires by riding into a sharp object and then having to go to the bicycle shop with his grandfather for repairs. He feels good about his ability to explain the problem to the employee in the store in order to get the tire fixed. His grandpa usually lets him talk to the employee directly, and he enjoys that he can do things by himself. It gives him confidence.

Another activity Nathan enjoyed in the past is trying to understand what garbage collectors do. He used to love watching garbage truck drivers go about their work. He would smell the garbage and observe the procedure, sometimes talking to the drivers. As busy as they were, some of them kindly took the time to say hello and exchange a few words with Nathan. One day, Nathan decided to follow the garbage truck with his grandfather and ran from house to house chasing it until he got very tired and could no longer keep up. A few other activities he loved to do were pulling a loaded wagon or using a wheelbarrow to carry objects, digging with a shovel, raking leaves, and hammering nails under his grandpa's supervision.

Running, sometimes barefoot, on sand or grass, doing rhythmic activities to music, playing with manipulative toys like trucks, cars, interlocking blocks, and puzzles, creating art with a paint brush or large crayons or a felt pen, or cutting with scissors are all examples of experiences that provide ample opportunities to think and learn. Sometimes it may be scary for parents to watch a three- or four-year-old child use tools or tumble down a hill, but it is important to give the child a chance to try new things under your supervision. Whether physical or mental, taking reasonable risks is essential to a child's development.

Help your child develop cognitive skills through the mastery of language

Certain cognitive skills are developed because of the child's need to master language. For many words, it is enough for a child to use his senses to understand their meaning, but when he comes across words that cannot be understood using physical senses, like "when," "how," and "why," he must deal with them in other ways. That's why the preoperational child keeps asking the "why" and "how" questions. From the answers he receives from his parents and teachers, he starts to attach meaning to abstract words about relationships or purposes.

The questions that the child asks thus give clues to the child's level of thinking. How you answer his questions is also an important matter that deserves much thought and attention. Lately, Nathan has been very interested in Christmas and wants to buy a Christmas tree to decorate by himself. So he keeps asking, "When are we going to buy a Christmas tree?" His question shows that he is paying more attention these days to the matter of time. When he noticed the neighbors' Christmas lights lit up, he seemed to realize that Christmas was nearing. I told him that we would have to wait a little longer to buy the tree if we wanted it to be fresh on Christmas. That answer was correct but probably inadequate. So he kept asking "When?" "Today is November 25," I told him, "so let's wait for two more weeks." Then he wanted to know exactly where November 25 was on the calendar. When I showed him, he counted two weeks ahead to December 9 and made a mark there. He knows a week means seven days. "Let's buy it sooner," he said. "It's too long to wait. This led to a discussion on the number of days in a week and in a month, and I taught him the phrase "wait longer." Until children have asked questions, tested out the answers, and corrected and refined their understanding of them, they cannot appreciate the meaning of concepts like weeks or waiting longer.

Provide concrete experiential learning opportunities

Parents should encourage their child to think, reason, question, and experiment. Young children are explorers. They are curious and they investigate. The parental role is not to teach but to foster the child's urge to discover. Children store up impressions of amounts and relationships that are essential for later stages in understanding. For instance, they can learn mathematical concepts through play activities. "These are too big. I need smaller blocks to build the garage for my cars." Nathan says this to his grandfather as he shows him the garage where he wants to park his cars. Learning that some blocks are big, others small, and some in between provides the child with important information that will serve as a foundation for understanding mathematical principles and conceptions of space. Blocks, Legos, and puzzles are the best toys for fostering cognitive development. The use of expressions such as "different," "the same as," "high," "low," "heavy," and "light" help the child to understand volumes and weight.

Early childhood education specialists make it clear that a child's learning to just count does not mean that the child understands the numbers; in fact, counting has very little value in terms of developing the concept of quantification. This is why it is more advisable that parents help a child to construct mathematical concepts through concrete experiences. He "learns" two from having had many experiences with two. He has two hands, two eyes, two ears, and two feet, or one big block and two small blocks. He can see how two small blocks can be used in place of one large block. At the table, there is a chair for him and one for his sister. Here the child has direct experiences with the very basis of numbers, that is, one to one correspondence.

Serve as a guide, not as a dispenser of information
Children are innately interested in the objects and phenomena of the world in which they live, and eager to explore them. In order to capitalize on a child's natural urge to observe, explore,

experiment with, and manipulate the things around them, parents should guide them to interact with various objects and pay attention to the outcomes. For example, you might provide a number of magnets of different sizes and shapes, together with a miscellaneous assortment of items such as rubber bands, pieces of string, bits of wood, paper clips, and nails. After the child has played with the materials for a while, you might say, "You seem to be having fun playing with the magnets. What have you observed or discovered?" Your child might show you the nails and paper clips clinging to the magnets, saying, "Look, magnets pick up nails." "Do your magnets pick up everything?" you might ask then. In this way, through proper questioning and seemingly casual suggestions, you can guide your child to systematize his exploration. Without his realizing it, you can guide him to understand that magnets attract some things but not others.

Encourage problem solving by not stepping in immediately when a problem occurs

When a child is trying to put together a puzzle and is having difficulty finding a piece, parents might help the child by covertly moving the piece to a place where the child is likely to notice it, rather than just giving the piece to the child. A child gains confidence and a sense of accomplishment when he completes a task for himself. Also, parents should realize that completing real puzzles made of wood or cardboard pieces is a completely different learning experience for a child compared to completing puzzles on a computer, tablet, or mobile phone.

Rather than instruct your child, allow him to think and experiment

In the process of amassing various impressions through sensory experience, children learn to group and distinguish those impressions in their own ways. They learn to understand that not all furry animals are cats; some furry animals might be dogs. They understand that objects can be distinguished by their color, weight, size, and form. The parents' role during this phase is not to instruct their child but to facilitate and protect his impulse to investigate. It is helpful to ask questions appropriate to a child's intellectual level so that the child can naturally learn the functions of the objects around him. Parents can also encourage their child to think about daily activities such as eating and sleeping in connection with the concept of time, or ask questions about the functions of familiar objects, such as water, trees, and grass. The most important thing is to help the child feel the joy of discovering and learning new facts for himself, as in the following example.

A four-year-old discovered a boat at the bottom of a water bucket. Puzzled at the sunken boat, which had been floating the previous day, the child soon found out that a boat sinks when it fills with water. His mother asked, "How can you place the boat on the water so that water doesn't get in?" The boy thought about it, playing around with the boat until it finally made sense. Through this experience, he not only came to understand how a boat floats but also learned firsthand the pleasure of discovery through asking, thinking, and experimenting.

New experiences should be amongst familiar ones

Parents should keep in mind that children learn most when there are familiar elements in the experience and when they can relate the unfamiliar to something they know. A child is more likely to enjoy watching a cement mixer and men at work putting in his neighbor's new driveway more than a trip to a factory with a lot of big pieces of machinery that he does not recognize.

For those looking to teach their child new things, it is not necessary to always take him to new places or to buy many different kinds of toys. If anything, it is more important to allow the child to repeat an experience multiple times. In the words of Marcel Proust, "The real voyage of discovery consists not in seeking new landscapes but in having new eyes." Too many new and unfamiliar experiences can easily confuse a child; instead, the familiarity developed from repeating an experience allows a child to see what he has not noticed before. In this way, a child can derive pleasure from seeing and learning more because a new experience is only meaningful if a child can connect it to his past experiences or current interests.

Provide materials and experiences in which children are interested

Children are most absorbed when they are most interested. They concentrate and persist when their interest level is high. We can thus facilitate their learning by making interesting materials and experiences available to them, and linking what they experience to things they already like. For example, a few years ago, a San Francisco art museum held a Van Gogh exhibition. Many parents drove for hours to the museum to show their children the paintings of the world-renowned artist. I read an interesting news article, though, that described one child who had taken a serious interest in the contents of a nearby garbage can while waiting in line to enter the museum, but showed indifference to the actual paintings on display inside the museum. This shows clearly that what parents think will interest their child might be completely different from what actually interests the child.

Parents should encourage children to devote effort to pursuing their interests. Rather than being overseers who determine and control their child's activities, parents should become unassuming facilitators who help their child be proactive and experience success.

CHAPTER 27

FOSTERING CREATIVITY

Every child is born with the innate ability to be creative. It is one of the major attributes that differentiates humans from other animals. It is also one of the most important mental abilities for children to develop if they want to be happy, competent, and well-adjusted adults. Creative people are flexible, confident, and better at problem solving because they are better able to adapt to technical advances and deal with change, as well as take advantage of new opportunities. But why do so many people feel their creativity is stifled before they reach adulthood? Is it because of inappropriate parenting or our early childhood educational practices?

Mathematician and philosopher Alfred North Whitehead (1978) defined creativity as the ability to produce new and valuable products or thoughts in the fields of literature, science, and art. In the early 1950s, psychologist J. P. Guilford (1975) broke down the elements of creativity as fluency, originality, and elaboration of ideas, and devised tools to measure these elements. Following Guilford's work, Ellis Paul Torrance (1962) developed a measure of creativity that was used widely in research on creativity. The concept of creativity has recently expanded to include new ideas and methods that increase the efficiency of business management, making the definition of creativity broader. In general, however, creativity can be defined as the flexibility of thought that enables one to look at a subject from a new perspective and find better solutions. Intellect and creativity often overlap and go hand and hand, but they do not refer to the same ability. Especially among people with an IQ of 120 or higher, an individual's IQ does not necessarily correlate with his or her level of creativity. That is, a highly intellectual person does not necessarily have high creativity.

Creativity develops the most in early childhood. How parents and teachers guide their child during this early stage of life makes a great impact on the development of creativity. The following are some specific guidelines for how parents can help foster creativity in their children.

Nature is the greatest source of inspiration

A child's world is full of wonder and excitement. Following a rainbow in a wide open field or walking in the woods on a rainy day can inspire delight and awe. Children enjoy discovering the wonders of nature, but we often deny them this pleasure because such activities can be inconvenient, interfere with bedtime, or involve wet clothing that has to be changed, or mud that has to be cleaned off. Yet frequent encounters with nature can deepen the affinity a child feels with nature and cultivate a desire to explore. A sense of wonder springs forth in all of us when we commune with nature. Parents should help their children preserve this sense of wonder so that it lasts them a lifetime and serves as an antidote against boredom and disenchantment in later years.

Bolton and Wilson (1975) argued that nature provides the most important inspiration, enabling creative expression throughout one's life, and that childhood experiences in particular create vivid memories that last a lifetime. These words encapsulate the significance of communing with nature during infancy and early childhood. Looking at beautiful flowers blooming close to home and exploring their colors, shapes, fragrances, and textures is enough to awaken a sense of wonder about nature and life. With your child, observe the clouds, the moon, and the stars, and feel the changing of the weather and seasons. Encourage your child to smell the briny air by the ocean, hear the crash of waves and the whisper of smaller ripples of water, and feel the ocean water tickling the bottoms of their feet. Learning about the ocean as a concept in a book or a scene from a documentary does not compare to experiencing the real thing. Invite your child also to listen to the insect orchestras in August, watch birds soar through the sky, and recognize cumulus clouds in the distance. Let him go out into the yard after an afternoon shower and notice the beautiful leaves glittering in the sun and fluttering in the breeze. Let him spend time observing an ant carrying a load many times heavier than its own weight, and a spider busy mending a web damaged by a shower. Experiencing nature with one's own senses nourishes a child's sense of wonder, and through these experiences, creativity blossoms.

Sensory experience is important

Parents should provide ample opportunities for their children to use their five senses (sight, hearing, smell, taste, and touch) to notice and closely observe surrounding objects. Parents and teachers often try to teach concepts to a child by rote memorization or repetition. For example, they try to teach that the sun rises in the east and sets in the west by stating this as fact, not realizing it is more important for a child to have the opportunity to observe this for himself, perhaps by watching where the sun rises in relation to the house where he lives. A child can observe how the colors of the sky and the clouds change when the sun rises and sets, and how the temperature changes during these times of the day, all by seeing, hearing, and touching with his or her own senses. As I've said before, a young child understands objects through sensory experiences, and accumulating numerous strong sensory impressions is thus helpful to his creative development. Before memorizing the names of flowers

and animals or learning that a species of tortoise lives for over a hundred years, a child should be given the opportunity to compare various flowers in terms of color, fragrance, shape, and texture. Sensory experiences accumulated at a young age remain for a long time; these impressions broaden a child's thinking and provide new food for thought.

Child-initiated, parent-supported activities are important

My grandson, as I mentioned in an earlier chapter, developed an interest in making air rifles at the age of ten. He refitted rifles with new attachments. He considered the activity an intriguing challenge, and it gave him a great sense of accomplishment. He purchased the materials he needed, like adhesive tape, plastic pipes, and rubber bands, with pocket money that he had saved by helping his mother with household chores. For several years, he was happily absorbed in the activity.

From his parents' perspective, it seemed like another chore to take him to the hardware store to buy materials, and clean up after he finished assembling a toy. But when an idea captures a child's interest, it is advisable for the parents to help the child follow through with his idea. I reminded the other members of the family to leave things the way he had left them until he was finished, and not to touch anything, even when cleaning the room. His grandfather supported his effort by asking about the things he needed for the project and taking him to get parts when necessary. Producing a high-functioning toy gun was not the point of the activity. What was important was that the child initiated an activity with his own idea and developed confidence in his ability to carry out his plan with an adult's support.

Parents should remember that their child needs uninterrupted time and space to finish an activity to his satisfaction. As my grandson grew older, his interest in tinkering with toy firearms waned, but he developed an interest in a tinkering of a different sort: experimenting in a lab to understand the workings of telomerase in muscular regeneration. While his area of interest changed, his positive experiences early on in taking initiative and carrying out his ideas led to confidence and a desire to continue in a different sort of creative endeavor.

Provide raw materials from which the child can make his own world

I often hear fathers complain about building an elaborate playhouse for their children only to find that the children don't use it very much, preferring to play in a space of their own choosing. Parents need to realize that children are interested in almost everything, except possibly the things they are expected to be interested in; instead of choosing for them, it's a good idea to lay our world open to them.

Children can discover junk heaps and use what they find to create their own worlds. What a child needs is the raw material from which he can make what he wants. If you provide sand, water, mud, clay, finger paints, blocks, paints, papers, scissors, and tape, he can transform it into anything he wishes.

Remember to provide materials and supplies that spark imagination, and present them in an inviting and eye-catching manner. Using attractive baskets to present materials such as tissue papers, crayons, and scissors will draw a children's attention. Children may choose to play with the items you give them, or they may not, but keep in mind that it's okay for the items to be fashioned or discarded as fits the inner life of individual children. Never force children to produce what you think they should. For example, understand that when children paint, it's often their feelings, and not the objects in their environment, that they are putting on paper.

Share feelings and communicate from your child's viewpoint

Rachel Carson wrote in her 1965 book *The Sense of Wonder*, "If a child is to keep alive his inborn sense of wonder . . . he needs the companionship of at least one adult who can share it, rediscovering with him the joy, excitement and mystery of the world he lives in." For a child to be creative, the parents must be creative. Keen sensitivity is necessary for parents to see the world and nature through the eyes of their child. When parents attempt to share in their child's emotions from his or her viewpoint, the child's imagination will grow strong and healthy. A parent's willingness to look, listen, and learn about a child's way of doing things is vital. Children can communicate much better if parents are receptive in their words, nonverbal responses, and actions.

Encourage children to be flexible in their thinking

Encourage children to think about many different ways to solve a problem and consider more than one solution to a problem. When they successfully solve a problem, ask them whether they can solve it again, but find a new way to do it. It is also important for them to remember that everyone makes mistakes and fails. Children who are afraid of failure and taking risks will curb their creative thinking. Sharing with them about mistakes you have made recently can help them feel it's acceptable and inevitable to make mistakes. Everyone should be entitled to make mistakes. Children should be taught that what you learn from the mistake has a much greater impact than the mistake itself.

CHAPTER 28

HELPING CHILDREN DO WELL
IN SCHOOL

For parents, gaining an accurate understanding of their child's learning abilities and study habits is not always an easy task, especially when trying to help the child do well in school. It is difficult enough to get a child to stop sleeping in or shed simple bad habits, let alone become a better learner. A child's learning ability can be said to encompass vocabulary, math skills, reasoning skills, and spatial perception, along with other attributes that influence learning, such as memory, concentration, motivation for learning, and emotional stability. Parents should learn where their child's strengths and weaknesses lie as soon as possible. It is their responsibility to understand a child's learning ability and characteristics in order to help the child reach his inherent potential.

In 2011, the parenting style of the aforementioned professor Amy Chua, author of *The Battle Hymn of the Tiger Mother*, became a sensation in South Korea. In the book, Professor Chua

documented her experience raising two "perfect" daughters—girls who were never allowed to watch TV, were required to be the top student in every subject, and had to spend two to three hours a day practicing music. An excerpt from the book was published in the Wall Street Journal under the title of "Why Chinese Mothers Are Superior," triggering heated debate over Chua's parenting methods. In the segment, Chua explained that her book was written for American parents who give too much freedom to their children.

Despite what she argues, parents should note that Chua's strict parenting methods worked with her first daughter, but not with her second. Chua went so far as to record her younger child Lulu protesting, saying to her, "You're a terrible mother. You're selfish. You don't care about anyone but yourself." Chua confessed that, after such exchanges, she realized that she had to change her parenting approach so as not to lose her daughter: She allowed Lulu more freedom but did not give up her parenting style completely. She negotiated with her daughter and reached a compromise through discussion. Even Amy Chua, the most famous "tiger mom" of them all, learned through the course of raising her second child the necessity of accommodating her methods to her children's unique needs. Parents need to strive to have the sensitivity and flexibility to understand the uniqueness of each child and adapt their parenting approaches to fit the child instead of trying to mold the child to a set expectation of success. The following are some suggestions for parents seeking to help children do well in school:

Instill a mindset of "I can do it" in your child

Carol Dweck, author of *Mindset: The New Psychology of Success*, argues that mindset plays an important role in maximizing potential and reaching personal goals. Drawing on twenty years of research on mindset, Dweck says what determines whether you accomplish your goals is whether you have a "fixed" mindset or a "growth" mindset. When a student with a fixed mindset does poorly on his midterms, he gets discouraged and feels ready to give up, blaming his low scores on his own incompetence. A student with a growth mindset, however, thinks of ways to change his strategy in studying and tries to do better on the next test. The student with the growth mindset doesn't easily get discouraged by the current results, but instead focuses on making steady progress. When a child does poorly at school, the parents should encourage and instill in the child a growth mindset so that, rather than falling prey to a sense of defeat, the child buckles down and tries harder for the next test, believing he can do better.

Make sure your child get enough sleep on school nights

Parents should make sure that their child goes to sleep early on school nights. It is very important for a child to develop the habit of getting plenty of sleep because, in the end, old habits die hard. Parents need to make it a routine for their child to go to bed early from a young age and make as few exceptions as possible. If the habit is formed young, the child will continue to go to bed voluntarily and at an appropriate time when he is older. Plenty of research has proven that lack of sleep hinders learning.

Foster your child's ability to ask questions

When instructing your child, it is important to teach him what kind of questions to ask, as well as how to ask them. In this connection, cognitive psychologists have revealed that how one thinks is more important than what one thinks. Parents, then, should teach their child to ask questions that can give rise to interesting, new ways of thinking, rather than focus on simply getting the right answer. Patterns and structures in which parents and teachers are always the ones asking questions and children are the ones giving answers should be avoided.

Encourage your child to take on new challenges

Parents should discourage their child from backing down from challenging tasks and instead promote the idea of striving to reach a goal. Every task is accompanied by a certain degree of risk, and one cannot achieve anything without taking risks. Help your child to learn that it is important to make small progress each day to reach a goal. Remind your child that "Rome wasn't built in a day." At the same time, be careful to propose challenges that realistically suit the child's abilities so that, with effort, he can succeed.

Encourage your child to study with a clear purpose

Help your child to set goals with a clear purpose and work toward them without parental intervention. As some people say, "Knowing your purpose in life gives you tenacity of life." This is a principle that applies equally to adults and children. A child who knows the reason he is studying will spend his time at his desk much more effectively. Parents should stay calm and wait patiently until their child finds his purpose.

Help your child set realistic goals

Help your child set goals for learning. Help the child identify concrete activities that can be achieved with effort and that contribute to realistic goals, and provide encouragement along the way. Parents who set unrealistic goals for their child will cause the child to become discouraged and lose confidence. Parents should not be greedy.

Have your child make a detailed schedule for studying

Make a weekly schedule with a list of daily study materials and activities, and check off finished tasks as they are completed. To be effective, a list should consist of fewer than ten items. This way, the parents can easily check on the child's progress and the child can use his time effectively. It is best that this habit is formed while the child is still in primary school because the parents will play a diminishing role in the child's studies as the child moves up in years. To become great coaches when they can, parents should carefully consider their child's characteristics when fostering the habit of planning. That said, a coach cannot, and should not, get on the field in place of the athlete. Much to my chagrin, some parents think they are helping their children by doing their assignments for them, but they are not helping anything.

CHAPTER 29

EARLY FOREIGN LANGUAGE EDUCATION: TRUTH VS. MYTH

In today's globalized world, the ability to speak, read, and write in multiple languages is a great asset. An increasing number of parents are recognizing the necessity of learning foreign languages and are teaching their children Latin, Spanish, German, French, and Chinese from a young age. Since the benefits of immersion education have become widely known, language immersion kindergartens and elementary school programs, where foreign teachers run classes only in their native languages, have risen in popularity.

While there might be personal differences, anyone can achieve some level of fluidity in a foreign language if he or she studies from a young age. Recent studies on language development indicate that before two or three years old, acquiring two or more languages does not require more effort and time than acquiring one language, and does not interrupt the acquisition of the mother tongue. A newborn baby can distinguish almost all sounds, but this ability begins to deteriorate beginning around one year from birth. In the process of acquiring a single language, the human brain learns to ignore unnecessary sounds. A child who grows up in a bilingual environment develops distinct neural circuits for the two languages. Linguists claim that the best time to acquire a new language is before entering school, when children can absorb language like sponges. This ability begins to deteriorate after around six years old and then drops rapidly from adolescence onward.

My sons, who were born and raised in the United States, are a case in point. When my older son was in the third grade and my second son was two years and eight months old, my family moved to South Korea for about two years. My older son's Korean was so poor that he had to enroll in an international school, but my second son became fluent in Korean shortly after we arrived in Korea. After three or four months in Korea, he could speak like native Korean children. There may be many reasons for this difference, but I suspect the difference in the ages of the two children was the key factor.

I am not arguing that foreign languages must be learned before entering school, but there is a critical period in a child's language development that can be taken advantage of by parents who want their child to speak a foreign language fluently. It should also be noted, however, that it is possible for children

RAISING COMPETENT AND HAPPY CHILDREN

to learn foreign languages well despite not starting young. Another point to keep in mind is that children who learn a foreign language at a very young age tend to forget the language easily if they do not continue to use it over time. Therefore, it is necessary to provide a child with an environment where he or she can continue using the foreign language consistently outside of class time.

The pros and cons of early foreign language education

There is no doubt that children living in a globalized era will benefit from learning a globally used foreign language, such as Spanish or Chinese, in addition to their mother tongue. As discussed above, acquisition of a new language is most effective before entering school, so early foreign language education is certainly helpful in increasing a child's foreign language proficiency. However, parents need to consider the pros and cons of early foreign language education and decide objectively whether it will truly help their child's development, or if there's a possibility for harm. Parents should not be moved by mindless fads perpetuated by the media or by the obsession others have with early education. In the United States and South Korea, foreign language is part of most school curricula from junior high school, meaning that children will eventually have the opportunity to learn a foreign language.

From the perspective of the government and the private

sector, early foreign language education is desirable because the more citizens who are proficient in a foreign language, the easier it becomes to secure the human resources required by government and the private sector in the globalized era. For parents raising a child, however, the issue is not so clear cut. They must consider the financial feasibility of paying for foreign language instruction and also appraise the degree of their child's motivation. Parents and societies that obsess over early foreign language education risk overestimating its importance.

Korean parents similarly tend to think that English must be taught at an early childhood education institution. Both Korean and American parents overwhelmingly believe that native teachers and immersion programs are essential, and that classes in such an environment should start at a young age. These beliefs, however, are misguided. If a child has a strong desire to learn a foreign language, he or she will have no problem learning from a non-native teacher with good pronunciation and sound teaching methods.

Another point to keep in mind is that superb foreign language instruction by a native teacher alone will not help a child learn the language effectively. For a native teacher to teach effectively, classes must be based on the teacher's solid understanding of the characteristics of his native language and culture. Professional teacher training is essential, and parents should decide on a program only after acquiring sufficient information about the teacher's qualifications and skills. Utilizing the quality multimedia learning materials available today, children can acquire accurate pronunciation of a foreign language without the guidance of a native speaker. Parents should keep in mind that the most important factor is whether their child is motivated to learn.

Another important consideration is how well an institution suits the individual's purpose for learning a foreign language, whether it is simply improving conversation skills or increasing overall proficiency, which encompasses reading, writing, listening, and conversation skills. Much more time is required to cultivate reading and writing skills than to learn daily conversation. The most important foreign language education should begin when a child is mentally prepared, that is, interested and motivated, to take on such a task. Forcing a child who is unprepared can have damaging consequences; for example, it has been observed that some children who are forced by their parents to learn two languages before the age of five will develop a stutter.

Acquiring a foreign language is different from acquiring one's mother tongue. Given the right opportunity, and with some effort, anyone can learn a foreign language, but not all children are born with the ability to achieve fluency or are given the chance to grow up in an environment where they can pick up a foreign language naturally. Excessive expectations from the parents can create unnecessary psychological pressure, causing the child to feel frustration and a sense of defeat. Parents should not forget that foreign language proficiency is only one of the many skills one needs to acquire in life.

Investment in foreign language education and its effectiveness

When it comes to foreign language proficiency, Americans are generally behind Europeans, who grow up surrounded by many different languages. When I was in graduate school, I witnessed many fellow PhD Candidates repeatedly fail their foreign language examinations (French or German), one of the degree requirements. In retrospect, this is not so surprising. Acquiring a foreign language requires a great deal of effort and a pressing need. As citizens of a wealthy country, my colleagues were not inconvenienced or threatened in their social lives or careers because of their lack of foreign language proficiency, so they did not need to pour their hearts into the task.

Parents must remember that learning a foreign language includes speaking and writing in the language of another country. For all ethnicities and cultures, speech came before text. Parents must think about the purpose of teaching a child a foreign language, whether it is facilitating conversation while traveling, attending social functions, or understanding and adopting the skills and knowledge accumulated by that culture.

While vocabulary and listening are important elements in evaluating a student's language proficiency, reading comprehension is the core of evaluation for any language. This is because the ultimate purpose of foreign language acquisition is not acquiring the ability to carry on simple day-to-day conversations but gaining a key to the cultural heritages of foreign civilizations.

If a child has a basic aptitude for learning languages, beginning during the middle school years should be sufficient for the child to learn a foreign language. Aside from vocabulary, English reading comprehension and writing skills are largely transferable to French or Chinese language learning. However, if fluency in speaking is the goal, early education is highly recommended.

CHAPTER 30

TEACHING FINANCIAL RESPONSIBILITY

All parents want their children to have financial stability when they grow up and achieve independence. Yet parents often do not teach their children the skills and attitudes necessary to ensure financial stability. As such, it is important to teach children the value of money and how to budget wisely. Such a financial education is best initiated early, preferably when the child is still in grade school. In today's world, a plethora of attractive and fancy new products come out daily, and everybody wants to own better products than what they already have. Learning self-restraint is not easy under these circumstances. When parents themselves have a hard time not overspending, it is a challenge to teach their children the same skill. I do not mean to say that parents should not buy new products for their child, but rather that, while the child is still young, the parents should teach him or her to determine the difference between needs and wants.

TIP WAYS TO TEACH YOUR CHILDREN FINANCIAL RESPONSIBILITY

1 TEACH YOUR CHILD HOW TO EARN MONEY

"Give a man a fish and he will eat for a day; teach him how to fish and he will eat for the rest of his days." John D. Rockefeller mentioned this old saying when asked about the financial education of his children. Dubbed the Oil King of the early twentieth century, Rockefeller was the richest man of all time. He preached that parents should provide their children with opportunities and methods for making money rather than giving them money to spend. Children, he explained, should be taught from a young age that they must work to earn money for their own spending. Give your child an allowance, but be tight with it, so that if he needs more, he can earn some extra in return for helping around the house. Pay the child an agreed amount for each task: for example, five dollars for organizing and taking out the trash on recycling day, or two dollars for watering the plants. Payment should not be given to children for tasks that would be their responsibility even if they were not paid. For example, cleaning their room or completing homework should not be tasks that children are be compensated for.

2 ENCOURAGE YOUR CHILD TO RECORD HIS OR HER ALLOWANCE SPENDING

By recording daily income and expenses in a notebook, a child can reflect on his or her finances. Encourage the habit of keeping receipts. This will be helpful when the child becomes an adult. If your child begins to keep track of his or her spending, they will begin to differentiate needed spending from superfluous spending as well as develop the skills of budgeting. In addition, exchanges and returns are made simpler with a receipt.

3 ▶ ENCOURAGE YOUR CHILD TO CONSIDER PEOPLE IN DIFFICULT SITUATIONS

In the United States, it is fairly common to find places that provide free meals for the needy. When your child enters middle school, have him or her volunteer at a soup kitchen, visit poor neighborhoods, and read literature that addresses destitution so that he understands that there are many people who have difficult lives because of a lack of financial stability. Through these experiences, the child will understand the importance of financial responsibility and naturally learn the differences between his own desires and the demands of reality.

4 ▶ FOSTER THE HABIT OF FRUGALITY

"Waste not, want not." This simple phrase offers a path towards a frugal mindset. As the phrase states, if a child adopts a mindset of not wasting, then he or she will likely avoid the pitfall of greed. Frugality and economy are not only about saving money but also about reducing the waste of the earth's limited natural resources. As members of the global community, a frugal lifestyle is both virtuous and responsible, with an increasing number of people advocating the "Three Rs"—reduce, reuse, recycle—as the lynchpin of modern financial education.

A late professor at the university where I once taught was a model of frugality and economy. She lived alone all of her life and, having lived through the Great Depression in the 1930s, knew what scarcity was like. Being of a generation that had experienced real hunger, she was economical as a way of life. Her life spanned three centuries, from her birth in 1897 to her passing in 2001. After retirement, she volunteered at various organizations until she was close to ninety years old. She set a good example for everyone around her, for instance, cutting napkins into halves to get the most use out of each piece, and reusing paper for notetaking. Rather than being focused on saving money, she was motivated by habits of conservation and moderation. She never owned a car in her life; she considered driving when she could use public transportation selfish and wasteful. In her will, she asked to be cremated and her ashes to be sprinkled in the ocean, expressing her wish that precious land not be used to bury her body. Her mind was sharp until she died, and she donated all of her assets and possessions to local charities and the needy. She lived a life of frugality and economy and derived pleasure from helping the less fortunate and donating to social welfare organizations.

As this professor's life demonstrated, a frugal and economic lifestyle is not only beneficial to oneself but also to one's neighbors and society as a whole. Reducing wasteful use of the earth's limited resources so that future generations can enjoy the same privileges we have today is the least we can do. In the end, frugality and economy are connected to living in harmony with others. This is the reason why we must instill habits of frugality and economy in our children.

CHAPTER 31

HELPING CHILDREN OVERCOME
SCREEN ADDICTION

"My child is wasting too much time watching TV and playing computer games!" is a complaint I have often heard from American mothers. Research has clearly shown that the content of TV programs and computer games has short-term effects on children, but whether they have long-term effects remains to be seen. Nevertheless, the problem is that children who spend too much time watching TV, playing video games lose time they would have otherwise used to exercise or study. If a child looks for every opportunity to play computer games and plays for five or six hours without leaving the room, treatment for addiction is necessary. According to experts, children who have game addiction are likely to lose creativity, develop emotional instability, and become antisocial.

The American Academy of Pediatrics recommends that parents not expose children under two years old to any television and restrict children over two years old to no more than one to

two hours a day of quality early childhood programming. At two years old, children find everything new and wondrous, and they have a strong desire to explore their surroundings using their five senses. Brain development occurs most rapidly in the first two years of human life. According to recent brain development research, the number of synapses created in a twenty-four-month-old toddler's brain is double that created in an adult brain. Unless this period is followed by vigorous brain activity, unused neurons begin to deteriorate from age six to seven. Therefore, during this period, it is important for a child to gain rich experiences through play and various activities, and develop thinking skills instead of watching TV. When a child spends too much time watching TV, he or she misses out on forming emotional connections and developing social skills through interactions with his parents and the people around him.

Smartphone addiction among youths is also emerging as

a social and emotional issue. A recent study shows that 75 percent of U.S. youths use smartphones. As with TV and game addiction, the side effects of smartphone addiction are formidable. The "smartphone generation" is now infamous for its lack of face-to-face communication, lower capacity for real-life social interaction, and the excessive amount of time it spends attached to phones and social media. Teenagers carry around smartphones all day long and exchange text messages with friends to the extent that they disrupt classes at school, dinners, family time, and even time with friends. When I see a child grow anxious and uneasy after being pulled away from his smartphone momentarily, it is hard to know whether smartphones exist for people or people exist for smartphones.

TIP

GUIDELINES FOR PREVENTING TV, COMPUTER GAME, AND SMARTPHONE ADDICTION

1 ▼ PLACE THE TELEVISION AND COMPUTER IN THE LIVING ROOM OR SOME OTHER OPEN AREA OF THE HOME

Putting a TV in a child's bedroom is less than ideal. When a preschooler plays computer games, the parents should take part and engage the child in conversation.

2 ▼ LIMIT TIME SPENT WATCHING TV AND PLAYING COMPUTER GAMES

Adjust a child's total allowed weekly screen time based on the child's age, level of maturity, and the degree to which the screen time that he or she receives disrupts his or her ability to function. For example, there is less need to regulate the screen time of a child who already shows little interest in television. Conversely, a child who is obsessed with watching their favorite programs and refuses to turn off the television while that program is on should have their screen time more severely restricted. The way in which you allocate screen time should be based on the child's interests. If a child is interested in SpongeBob more so than other cartoons, adjust the amount of time they get to watch SpongeBob to accommodate for their interest. In addition, turn off the TV during meals to make time for conversation. Make sure that your child watches TV or plays computer games after he has completed his homework. A child should never do homework while watching TV.

3 ▼ SELECT TV PROGRAMS SUITABLE FOR EVERYONE IN THE FAMILY AND WATCH AS A GROUP

If all members of the family happen to enjoy television, seek to watch television programs that everyone in the family enjoys together. Take time to ask your child's opinions about what he or she has watched and have discussions about what they have watched. This serves to build common ground and a stronger family bond.

4 SET A GOOD EXAMPLE

Parents must set an example of responsible TV and computer usage for their children. If parents want to teach their children to turn off the television during dinner, they should themselves actively seek to turn off the television before meals. For example, my husband often watched sports on the television during dinner. As a result, my son picked up the bad habit of watching sports through dinner. In turn, he taught those habits to his children, despite his wife's best efforts to break the habit. Even having just one parent occasionally forget to turn off the TV before dinner may set a poor precedent for a child. The child may become confused as to when it is permissible to watch TV during dinner and when it is not. This may cause conflict if the child, from watching his parents' behavior, believes he should be able to watch TV in specific circumstances, while the parents, unaware of the behavior they have modeled, do not permit it. It is much easier to simply set a clear and consistent example of turning off the TV before dinner from the outset.

5 PAY ATTENTION TO YOUR CHILD'S SMARTPHONE USAGE TO PREVENT ADDICTION

For the "smartphone generation," spending hours a day staring at a small handheld screen seems to be the norm. Part of this is the new youth culture; young people's lives are far more intertwined with cell phones than ever before, and so it makes sense that they would spend more time with their phones. However, it is important to help minimize a child's dependency on cell phones. Having no-cell-phone periods, when cell communication is not necessary, can be beneficial in ensuring that a child learns healthy alternatives to cell phone usage. Removing a child's phone, while uncomfortable for the child, helps break patterns of dependency on the phone. A child who is used to always having a phone with them becomes trained to look to their phone for entertainment when bored, instead of engaging in conversation or seeking other means of entertainment. A child who is used to not having a cell phone around will seek these healthier alternatives first.

In a similar way, opting not to give a child a smartphone at the earliest opportunity may also be beneficial. Giving a young child easy access to instant gratification through cell phones teaches early dependence on cell phones. Instead, opt to allow a cell phone only after the child has learned to survive without one. There is no magic age at which to give a child a cell phone, as this is dependent on the child's maturity and addictive tendencies towards other electronics, although most recommend sometime in middle school. Teaching children educational and effective usage of cell phones is also helpful. Show them how to use cell phones to improve their lives through faster communication, easier access to a great mass of information, and usage of apps helpful in day-to-day activities, rather than simply as a means to stave off boredom.

CHAPTER 32

RAISING CHILDREN AS AN IMMIGRANT

Currently, the best estimate is that about 20 percent of children under the age of 18 in the United States are immigrants or children of an immigrant. Parenting is a difficult challenge for anyone, but immigrant parents face even more stress. Parenting becomes more difficult if the parent and their children are moved to a socially, ethnically, and/or linguistically different country. Until the 1960s, the vast majority of immigrants to the United States were Europeans. Therefore, their acculturation in the United States was relatively easy for immigrants and their children. The situation has changed greatly for immigrants of the past half century, who are mostly Latinos and Asians.

Acculturation is the modification of a person as a result of contact with a different culture. In most cases, it requires learning a new language and new customs. But as might be expected, when an ethnically different person must acculturate to a new society, the task becomes much more difficult. To illustrate this, one can compare an Irish immigrant to the United States and a Korean immigrant to the United States. It quickly becomes clear how much similarities of language and ethnicity can help the Irish immigrant's acculturation process, as compared with that of the Korean immigrant.

Since the 1960s, a large number of Asians and Latinos have immigrated to the United States for predominantly economic reasons. The task of acculturating has been more difficult for such immigrants compared to the European immigrants of the past, and as parents, they face great pressure.

Parenting issues facing Asian immigrant parents

The speed of acculturation differs by individuals, but children who immigrate at an early age (1.5 generation) and children who are born in the United States but raised by immigrant parents (2nd generation) acculturate much faster than their parents, especially in acquiring English-speaking ability. As a result, in many cases, a child, especially the oldest one, plays the role of a parent (role reversal). The child assumes the role of interpreter for their parent at school, the hospital, or a social services agency. In most cases, the child outgrows this role reversal situation, but family dynamics are still changed. Parents should know that this can be a heavy burden to the child.

The societies and family structures of many Asian countries are hierarchical and characterized by collectivism, compared to the more individualistic American culture. In the United States, families tend towards less authoritarian family dynamics, but Asian parents can interpret this as disobedience and losing control of their children.

While immigrant children are learning English faster than their parents, they are also losing their native languages. Many children are not proficient enough in their native tongue to communicate well with their parents who are not proficient in English. Also, parent-child communication between immigrant children and their parents becomes more difficult because the parents do not sufficiently understand the society of the country they immigrated to, and have not experienced school life in the United States.

Parents may immigrate for economic reasons, but many immigrant families experience, at least in the beginning of their new lives, economic hardship. Both parents may have to work, and parents may not be able to find a job in the field they have been trained for. Despite working hard, they may not make enough money to support the family as desired. Not realizing this situation, children may resent the fact that their parents do not have money to buy things for them that their friends enjoy.

With adolescent children, things usually get worse. Immigrant parents have usually left a society that they knew and were comfortable with in order to provide better opportunities for their children. The parents want to help their child to do well in school and be happy in life. But how much can a parent do to help their child when their child is going to a school in an environment that the parents never experienced in their own childhood?

However, Asian-American children are doing amazingly well in one area, that is, academic success in school. We don't know the reason for this. It may be a byproduct of the United States immigration policy, according to which the United States admitted well-educated, middle-class immigrants from East Asia (China, Japan, and Korea). As a result, their children ended up doing very well in school. Another explanation for the academic success of Asian-American children is the effectiveness of Asian parenting practices.

Parents of any ethnicity want to see their children do well in school. But Asian parents, in their home countries as well as in the United States, are almost obsessed with the academic success of their children. This puts psychological pressure on their children. Asian immigrant parents should know that American society places high importance on children being well rounded children and not just academically successful. Moreover, your child is growing up with peers who value friends who are popular or good at sports as much as academic high-achievers.

I will attempt to summarize helpful suggestions for immigrant parents in raising their children. These suggestions are not all based on sound research findings, but they are not simply my personal opinions either. Professionals working in the field have long found them useful.

1 ▼ TALK OFTEN WITH YOUR CHILDREN

Regardless of how frustrating or difficult it is to communicate with your children, you have to talk often with them to find out what is going on in their lives. There may not be very much you can do but you have to know what's going on.

2 ▼ LET YOUR CHILDREN MAKE THEIR OWN DECISIONS

Don't be afraid to disagree with your children, but do not insist on your opinion on issues such as how to dress or who to spend time with. It is best to let your child decide. You must understand that children want to fit in with their peers.

3 ▼ BE CONFIDENT ABOUT HOW YOU RAISE YOUR CHILDREN

Not all of the problems you face with your children are unique to your situation as an immigrant parent. For instance, immigrant parents tend to think they have an excessive amount of conflict with their children because they are immigrants. To address this question, I did a study comparing the incidence of conflict in families with Korean immigrant teens and families with Caucasian teens. It turned out that Korean teens had conflicts with their parents more often, but not necessarily at a greater intensity when compared with Caucasian families. Some people doing research on family conflicts believe that looking at intensity and frequency of parent-child conflict separately produces more meaningful implications.

4 FOCUS ON CREATING A CARING ENVIRONMENT

A caring and cohesive family is the backbone for healthy development of children, especially in the teenage years. There has been enough research evidence to support that this is true in the case of immigrant teens, too. High-risk behaviors (e.g., gang involvement, alcohol and drug use, suicidal ideation) are much lower among teens growing in a caring and cohesive family.

5 MAKE THE RULES, ALSO MAKE SPACE FOR DISAGREEMENT

Regardless of whether a child is a 1.5-generation immigrant, who moved to their new country at an early age, or a second-generation immigrant, born in their home country but raised by immigrant parents, the child is growing up in two cultures. In the case of a Korean child in the United States, Korean culture is learned at home and American culture is learned at school. Despite these cultural differences, it is important to establish to your children that you are their parents. They should be expected to respect you and follow the rules you set in your home. At the same time, you should allow them to express their disagreement when they feel it is necessary, instead of expecting unquestioning obedience.

6 ▸ KNOW THE FACTS ABOUT ASIAN PARENTING METHODS

An immigrant parent should know what is fact and what is speculation regarding Asian parenting and its impact on the academic success of children. My personal view is that the East Asians who have immigrated to the United States are not a representative sample of the general East Asian population but rather a particularly highly motivated and educated segment of the same. Consequently, their children are not different from children of the American middle and upper-middle class, and it's no surprise that Asian-American children are doing well in school. If the question is whether immigrant East Asian children do better academically than other ethnic groups in the United States, there isn't enough data to prove that. The data we do have shows that, compared with national population statistics, a higher percentage of East Asian children are enrolled in competitive colleges in the United States. But this could be due to any number of factors independent of parenting.

The following are some of the parenting practices found to positively impact Asian-American children to do well in school:

Research findings so far show that Asian parents, as well as their children, believe that effort counts more than inborn ability (e.g., IQ) in academic success. As parents, we can apply this principle in our childrearing.

Research findings show that Asian parents avoid teaching anything (sports, academic subjects, music, etc.) until their child is ready both physically and mentally. This is another point Asian parents can use in parenting to avoid "burnout" as well as help a child have "sustained interest." It would be very unwise for the parents to cause burnout by introducing a physical or mental activity prematurely, and we must keep in mind that a child cannot maintain a "sustained interest" in something unless the child is good at it. It is hard to be good at something if a child starts too early.

Alternately, one thing that Asian parents often do that is detrimental is micromanage their children's lives. In general, give your child time to develop skills to self-manage his activities and schedule. Leave your child alone without constant checking. Try to avoid distracting them from their own routine as much as possible. Too much distraction is as harmful as helicopter parenting.

Every society or ethnic group has a parenting method it believes to be especially effective for promoting academic excellence in children. As I explained, the parenting methods mentioned above have been found to be helpful. But I don't believe it's a particular parenting technique that has enabled the academic success of Asian American children. From a broader perspective, academic excellence is a deeply embedded cultural value among people in the East Asian countries. It is probably related to Confucian teachings that equate academic excellence with enlightenment. For this reason, East Asians and Asians of other regions uphold academic achievement with an almost religious conviction. Yet it is important to realize that while most people seek academic excellence, only a few can accomplish it. Particularly in the United States, where the education system and society in general seek to cultivate children into well-rounded individuals and not just academic achievers, it is not as easy for Asian parents to make academic success a priority of life for their child. So if academic excellence is your goal for your child, you have to convince your child of it first, then help him structure his life to minimize distractions from this pursuit.

7 ▼ PAY ATTENTION TO YOUR CHILD'S NEEDS

As stated earlier, Asian immigrant children in the United States live within two disparate cultures. Outside their home, they are immersed in the culture of their American peers, while at home they are surrounded by the culture of their ethnic homeland. Researchers divide the personalities that appear among people who straddle two distinct cultures into four types (Berry, 1980). These types, as applied to Asian immigrants in the United States, are as follows:

Type I (Integration)	A person who accepts both his or her own heritage and American culture, including language, values, and behavior patterns, and can apply them selectively as needed
Type 2 (Assimilation)	A person who abandons his or her own heritage and culture and assimilates him or herself into mainstream American culture
Type 3 (Separation)	A person who rejects American culture and adheres to his or her own heritage and culture
Type 4 (Marginalization)	A person who refuses to or is unable to adapt to either culture

Type 2 is perhaps ideal from the perspective of mainstream American society, but from the perspective of the Asian American minority, Type 1 is the most desirable. Most Asians in the United States typically want their children to be accustomed to both Asian and American culture and speak both languages fluently.

Raising a child in the United States to be bilingual and bicultural, however, is easier said than done. It is a task that requires extreme care and consistency on the part of the parents as well as adaptability and desire on the part of the child. Forcing a child to accept both cultures without consideration for the child's disposition and adaptability will likely backfire. It will put the child at risk of developing a Type 4 personality. Therefore, rather than obsessing over their own desires, parents should always pay close attention to their child's concerns and wishes. Otherwise, they risk the possibility that the child might feel no affinity to any culture at all, and identify himself as neither American nor connected to his native culture. It would be truly unfortunate if children grew into marginalized adults as a result of their parents' preoccupation with making them perfectly bicultural and bilingual.

Epilogue

Upon my retirement almost ten years ago, my sons and their families gave me a great amount of encouragement and support to write this book. At first, I was hesitant to undertake this project, as I hadn't done any writing other than textbook writing and scholarly papers, and I didn't think I could write for a more general audience. However, after giving it some thought, I concluded that writing this book might be the best gift I could leave for my beloved family, in particular my three sons, my daughters-in-law, and my grandchildren. Time flows like a river, and at my age, the old saying "With empty hands we come, emptyhanded we go" is especially close to my heart. I hope this book serves a number of purposes.

First, I hope that through this book I have managed to convey my very deepest admiration for the mothers and fathers of my own parents' generation, for the sacrifices they made and the unwavering devotion they showed to their children, albeit in ways that might be difficult for children of this generation to appreciate. The people of my parents' generation in Korea endured horrendous fetters, living through Japanese colonization, World War II, and the Korean War. Even as they fled to shantytowns during the war, they sent their children to makeshift schools. With no refrigeration, food spoiled quickly in the summer. Our mothers washed and boiled the spoiled rice for themselves, but for their children they lovingly packed lunchboxes of fresh rice topped with a fried egg. Now, in the twenty-first century, when I tell my grandchildren stories from that time, they say, "Grandma, you're telling the old stories again."

Why do I repeat the same stories? To never forget my heartfelt gratitude for my mother's generation and the valuable lessons they left for us. They made food, clothing, and education available to their children, even though they did not have enough themselves. Because of the devotion and sacrifice of their generation, our generation was able to remain strong through the turbulence of our own time.

Second, I hope that the generations of my children and grandchildren find this book useful and inspiring as they set out to raise their own children. As I have described the developmental tasks for each age and stage and phase of childhood, I have tried to illustrate what children themselves bring to the table, and how the environment, both broadly and narrowly defined, shapes their developmental journey. The countless situations and decisions that arise in the everyday life of parents are complex and nuanced. Sometimes, we have time to reflect on the best course of action or thoughtfully discuss how to proceed, but often, we must respond in the moment.

And so, I have tried to convey some of the general principles that both research and personal experience have led me to conclude will lead to the best outcomes.

And finally, in closing, I share a most heartfelt wish. Shortly after my retirement, as I had just started this writing project, a terrible accident befell my youngest son. He sustained a traumatic brain injury that left him near death. As he has battled to recover his abilities, I have been inspired by his perseverance. Before his accident, he had brought me books to help me with my writing. One of his first questions to me as he began to recover his language abilities was about how the book was progressing. Needless to say, I will be elated when I can hand him a copy of this book, printed and bound. And I will be even more thrilled when the day comes when he regains enough functioning that he can read it on his own.

Good parenting is to have patience and faith in your children that they will change for the better. There is no magic formula for successful parenting. Devotion, patience, love, and waiting are the extent of a parent's lot.

Throughout this book, there are hints of my own experiences and endeavors. I am delighted to have finally written a book that reflects my life and thinking, rather than a textbook for a class. Although my mother passed away a long time ago, every joyous occasion and difficult time I have experienced makes me think of her. Every time I recall her face, peace and warmth wash over me. I hope that my children remember me one day as I remember my mother.

Spring 2017
Chungsoon C. Kim

References

Berry, J. W. (1980). Acculturation as varieties of adaptation. In A. M. Padilla (Ed.) *Acculturation: Theory, models and some new findings*. Boulder, CO: Westview

Block, J. H. (1983). Differential premises arising from differential socialization of the sexes: Some conjectures. *Child Development, 54*, 1335-1354.

Bolton, J., & Wilson, Y. (1975). *To discover, to delight*. San Jose, CA: 1476 Phantom.

Carson, R. (1965). *The sense of wonder*. New York: Harper & Row Publishes, Inc.

Center for Disease Control and Prevention (2005). *Preventing obesity and chronic diseases through good nutrition and physical activity*. Retrieved June 15, 2016 the World Wide Web: http://www.cdc.gov/nccdphp/pefactsheets/pepa.html

Chua, A. (2009). *Day of empire: How hyperpowers rise to global dominance- and why they fall*. New York: Doubleday.

Chua, A. (2011). *Battle hymn of the tiger mother*. New York: Penguin Press.

Clinton, H. R. (1996). *It takes a village: And other lessons children teach us*. New York: Simon & Schuster.

Coopersmith, S. (1967). *The antecedents of self-esteem*. San Francisco: W. H. Freeman & Co.

Diamond, A. (1990). Neuropsychological insights into the

meaning of object concept development. In S. Carey & R. Gelman (Eds.), *The epigenesis of mind: Essays on biology and cognition.* Hillsdale, NJ: Erlbaum.

Dweck, C. S. (2006). *Mindset: The new psychology of success.* New York: Random House.

Erikson, E. H. (1963). *Childhood and society.* New York: Norton.

Ferber, R. (1985). *Solve your child's sleep problems.* New York: Simon and Schuster.

Freud, S. (1935). *A general introduction to psychoanalysis.* (J. Riviare, Trans.). New York: Modern Library.

Freud, S. (1938). *The basic writings of Sigmund Freud.* (A. A. Brill, Ed. & Trans.). New York: Modern Library.

Galinsky, E., & Friedman, D. (1993). *Education before school: Investing in quality childcare.* New York: Scholastic Paperbacks.

Gilliland, F. D., Li, Y., & Peters, J. M. (2001). Effects of maternal smoking during pregnancy and environmental tobacco smoke on asthma and wheezing in children. *Am. J. Respir. Crit. Care Med., 163*, 429-436.

Gomi, T. (1993). *Everyone poops.* Brooklyn, NY : Kane/Miller Book Publisher.

Guilford, J. P. (1975). Creativity: A quarter century of progress. In I. A. Taylor & J. W. Getzels (Eds). *Perspectives in creativity* (pp. 37-59). Chicago: Aldine.

Institute of Medicine (2009). *Weight gain during pregnancy: Reexamining the guidelines.* Washington, D. C.: National Academies Press,

Jensen, A. R. (1969). How much can we boost I.Q. and scholastic achievement? Harvard Educational Review, 33, 1-123.

John, J. (2015). Top tips for eating right during pregnancy. *Academy of nutrition and dietetics.* Retrieved April 15, 2016 from the World Wide Web: http://www.eatright.org/resource/health/pregnancy/what-to-eat-when-expecting/eating-right-during-pregnancy.

Kim, C. C., Miura, I. T., & Love, R. L. (2000). Adolescent-parent conflicts in immigrant Korean and mainstream American families. *Abstract, XVIth Biennial ISSBD (International Society for the Study of Behavioral Development) meetings,* No. 350.

Lewis, E., & Lamb, M. E. (2007). *Understanding fatherhood: Review of recent research.* London: Joseph Rowntree Foundation.

Piaget, J. (1983). Piaget's theory. In P. H. Mussen (Ed.). (1983). *Handbook of child psychology* (4th ed.). W. Kessen (Ed.). Vol. I: *History, theory, and methods.* New York: John Wiley & Sons.

Pinker, S. (2002). *The blank slate: The modern denial of human nature.* New York: Viking

Piper, W., & Bragg, M. C. (1961). *The little engine that could.* New York: Platt & Munk.

Roizen, M. F., & Oz, M. C. (2009). *You having a baby.* New York: Free Press.

Scarr, S., & McCartney, K. (1983). How people make their own environments: A Theory of Genotype $\rightarrow$ Environment Effects. *Child Development, 54,* 424-435.

Shore, R. (1997). *Rethinking the brain: New insights into early de-*

velopment. New York: Oxford University Press.

Torrance, E. P. (1962). *Guiding creative talent.* Englewood Cliffs, NJ: Prentice-Hall.

Whitehead, A. N. (1978). *Process and reality: An essay in cosmology.* New York: Free Press.

About the Author

Chungsoon C. Kim received her undergraduate education in Home Economics at Seoul National University in Seoul, Korea. She earned her MA in child development from the University of Georgia and her PhD in the same field at Florida State University. She taught at San Jose State University for forty-two years (from 1965 to her retirement in 2007), with the exception of a two-year stint at Seoul National University as an associate professor and as chair of the Child and Consumer Studies Department. She was the chair of the Child and Adolescent Development Department at San Jose State University, where she is now an emeritus professor.

Dr. Kim is the author of several books, including *Child Development and Guidance*. She has also published twenty-six research papers in peer-reviewed scholarly journals. Her research has explored the effects of child-rearing attitudes and practices on the development of children, the parenting practices of American versus Korean mothers, the effects of language on children's development of number concepts, and sources of the adolescent-parent conflicts in Korean-American and American families.

She is the recipient of many awards, including the Best Home Economics Professor Award and the Outstanding Advisor Award from San Jose State University, as well as the American Educational Research Association's Outstanding Study of the Year Award.

Credits

Author   Chungsoon C. Kim
Translator   Ma Eun-ji

Publisher   Kim Hyunggeun
Editors   Christine Kwon, Lee Jin-hyuk
Copy Editor   Eileen Cahill
Designer   Cynthia Fernández, Jung Hyun-young

Science
of Coercion

Science
of Coercion

*Communication Research
and Psychological Warfare
1945–1960*

CHRISTOPHER SIMPSON

New York   Oxford
OXFORD UNIVERSITY PRESS
1994

Oxford University Press

Oxford   New York   Toronto
Delhi   Bombaby   Calcutta   Madras   Karachi
Kuala Lumpur   Singapore   Hong Kong   Tokyo
Nairobi   Dar es Salaam   Cape Town
Melbourne   Auckland   Madrid

and associated companies in
Berlin   Ibadan

Published by Oxford University Press, Inc.,
200 Madison Avenue, New York, New York 10016

Oxford is a registered trademark of Oxford University Press

Library of Congress Cataloging-in-Publication Data
Simpson, Christopher.
Science of coercion : communication research and psychological
warfare, 1945–1960 / Christopher Simpson.
p.   cm. Includes bibliographical references and index.
ISBN 0-19-507193-X
1. Psychological warfare.
2. Communication–Research–United States.
3. United States–Military policy.
4. Cold War.
I. Title.
UB276.S56   1994
355.3'434'0973—dc20
93-3661

The author gratefully acknowledges permission to reprint excerpts from:
Public Opinion, by Walter Lippman. © 1965, Macmillan Publishing Company.
Public Opinion Quarterly, one figure from Stuart Dodd, p. 551, Winter 1958, University of
Chicago Press.
Unmastered Past: The Autobiographical Reflections of Leo Lowenthal, edited and translated by
Martin Jay. © 1987, The Regents of the University of California.
Survey Research in the United States: Roots and Emergence, 1890–1960.
© 1987, The Regents of the University of California.
Encyclopaedia of Social Science, Harold Lasswell, vol. 11, p. 524, © 1933, 1961 by Macmillan
Publishing Company.
The Necessity for Social Scientists Doing Research for Governments, Ithiel de Sola Pool, from
International Studies Quarterly, vol. 10 (2), paragraph 1. Reprinted courtesy of Blackwell
Publishers.

9 8 7 6 5 4 3 2 1

Printed in the United States of America
on acid-free paper

For Tom, Burney, and Bruce

Acknowledgments

I owe special thanks to Michael Gurevitch, Jay G. Blumler, and Mark Levy of the University of Maryland, as well as to Susan Coyle, for their many insights and patience throughout this project. Many thanks are also due to Bernd Greiner and the Hamburg Institut für Sozialforschung; Noam Chomsky; K. C. Lee; Marsha Siefert of the *Journal of Communication*; Bill Solomon and Bob McChesney; Allan Hunter and the Havens Center at the University of Wisconsin; Sandy Ungar and Pat Aufderheide at American University; David Roll of Oxford University Press; Bruce and Caroline Simpson; and, of course, to Gail Ross, who encouraged me to pursue this project along the way. Thanks to Robert Speigelman, John Kelly, Craig Nelson of Johns Hopkins University, Sriramesh, Krishnamurthy of the University of Washington Archives, and Martin Manning of the U.S. Information Agency Library, all of whom were kind enough to share out-of-print psychological warfare texts that proved essential to this study; L. John Martin, W. Phillips Davison, and John Prados for sharing their recollections and insights with me; Charles O'Connell for access to his study on Harvard's Russian Research Center and Brett Gary for access to his work concerning the Rockefeller Archive Center; Lauren Brown of the University of Maryland Libraries Historical Manuscripts and Archives Department for his help with the Bureau of Social Science Research archives; George Arnold and Mark Saxon of American University's archives; Edward Reece and John Taylor of the U.S. National Archives; Dennis Bilger of the Truman Presidential Library; David Marwell of the Berlin Document Center; and to the Interlibrary Loan and reference specialists of the

McKeldin Library at the University of Maryland at College Park, whose assistance with my endless requests for obscure materials went above and beyond the call of duty. Special thanks to Meiling Wang, Wendy Babbitt, Mark Raskin, Mark Solovey, Mark Pavlick, and Nancy Bernhard, all of whom read early drafts of this book and offered ideas and criticism.

Washington, D.C.   C.S.
April 1993

Contents

1. Defining Psychological War, *3*
2. World War and Early Modern Communication Research, *15*
3. "The Social Scientists Make Huge Contribution," *31*
4. Academic Advocates, *42*
5. Outposts of the Government, *52*
6. "Barrack and Trench Mates," *63*
7. Internationalization and Enforcement of the Paradigm of Domination, *94*
8. The Legacy of Psychological Warfare, *107*

Appendix: Dr. Stuart Dodd's List of "Revere-Connected Papers" (1958), *118*

Bibliographic Essay, *123*

Notes, *133*

Index, *195*

Science
of Coercion

1

Defining Psychological War

Communication research is a small but intriguing field in the social sciences. This relatively new specialty crystallized into a distinct discipline within sociology—complete with colleges, curricula, the authority to grant doctorates, and so forth—between about 1950 and 1955. Today it underlies most college- and graduate-level training for print and broadcast journalists, public relations and advertising personnel, and the related craftspeople who might be called the "ideological workers" of contemporary U.S. society.[1]

Government psychological warfare programs helped shape mass communication research into a distinct scholarly field, strongly influencing the choice of leaders and determining which of the competing scientific paradigms of communication would be funded, elaborated, and encouraged to prosper. The state usually did not directly determine what scientists could or could not say, but it did significantly influence the selection of who would do the "authoritative" talking in the field.

This book takes up three tasks. First, it outlines the history of U.S. psychological warfare between 1945 and 1960, discussing the basic theories, activities, and administrative structure of this type of communication enterprise. Second, it looks at the contributions made by prominent mass communication researchers and institutions to that enterprise. Third, it examines the impact of psychological warfare programs on widely held preconceptions about communication and science within the field of communication research itself.

Since World War II, the U.S. government's national security campaigns have usually overlapped with the commercial ambitions of major advertisers and media companies, and with the aspirations of an enterprising stratum of university administrators and professors. Military, intelligence, and propaganda agencies such as the Department of Defense and the Central Intelligence Agency helped bankroll substantially all of the post–World War II generation's research into techniques of persuasion, opinion measurement, interrogation, political and military mobilization, propagation of ideology, and related questions. The persuasion studies, in particular, provided much of the scientific underpinning for modern advertising and motivational techniques. This government-financed communication research went well beyond what would have been possible with private sector money alone and often exploited military recruits, who comprised a unique pool of test subjects.[2]

At least six of the most important U.S. centers of postwar communication studies grew up as de facto adjuncts of government psychological warfare programs. For years, government money—frequently with no public acknowledgment—made up more than 75 percent of the annual budgets of Paul Lazarsfeld's Bureau of Applied Social Research (BASR) at Columbia University, Hadley Cantril's Institute for International Social Research (IISR) at Princeton, Ithiel de Sola Pool's Center for International Studies (CENIS) program at the Massachusetts Institute of Technology, and similar institutions.[3] The U.S. State Department secretly (and apparently illegally) financed studies by the National Opinion Research Center (NORC) of U.S. popular opinion as part of the department's cold war lobbying campaigns on Capitol Hill, thus making NORC's ostensibly private, independent surveys financially viable for the first time.[4] In another case the CIA clandestinely underwrote the Bureau of Social Science Research (BSSR) studies of torture—there is no other word for it—of prisoners of war, reasoning that interrogation of captives could be understood as simply another application of the social-psychological principles articulated in communication studies.[5] Taken as a whole, it is unlikely that communication research could have emerged in anything like its present form without regular transfusions of money for the leading lights in the field from U.S. military, intelligence, and propaganda agencies.

This book is, in part, a study of the sociology of knowledge. It looks at the relationship between the production of "knowledge"—in this case preconceptions about communication and coercion—and the social and political conditions of a particular era. In this instance, leading scholars identified the cramped, often brutal attributes of mass communication characteristic of one stage of advanced industrial societies, then substituted *that* conception of communication for communication *as such* through a process detailed in the pages that follow. Put slightly differently, the idea of communication became something like a Rorschach test through which favored academics spoke about the world as they believed it to be, and thereby helped institutionalize that vision at the expense of its rivals.

I focus on the role of U.S. government psychological warfare programs in that process, partly because the story of their impact on this aspect of academe has been largely forgotten or suppressed. But this book is not intended to be a complete history of mass communication research or of the forces that have shaped it; it is simply an opportunity to look at the field in a new way. At least two other important formative forces, in addition to psychological warfare projects, have been highly influential in the evolution of modern communication research. These are strictly academic or scholarly developments, on the one hand, and commercial studies for private companies, on the other. University scholars have written extensively about the academic history of the field and will undoubtedly continue to do so.[6] Most authors, however, have sidestepped any substantive discussion of the role of commercial research in the intellectual evolution of communication research, this despite comments from both Paul Lazarsfeld and Robert Merton asserting that commercial projects were crucial to the development of the field.[7]

Tracing the links between federal research sponsorship and the evolution of academic preconceptions about communication and mass media presents particularly knotty questions. The evidence shows that psychological warfare projects became a major, and at times the central, focus of U.S. mass communication studies between 1945 and at least 1960. But to what extent did the intense attention to this topic shape the broader structure of assumptions and "received knowledge" of the field?

Research funding cannot by itself create a sustainable academic zeitgeist, of course.[8] Sponsorship can, however, underwrite the articulation, elaboration, and development of a favored set or preconceptions, and in that way improve its competitive position in ongoing rivalries with alternative constructions of academic reality.

U.S. military, propaganda, and intelligence agencies favored an approach to the study of mass communication that offered both an explanation of what communication "is" (at least insofar as those agencies' missions were concerned) and a box of tools for examining it. Put most simply, they saw mass communication as an instrument for persuading or dominating targeted groups. They understood "communication" as little more than a form of transmission into which virtually any type of message could be plugged (once one had mastered the appropriate techniques) to achieve ideological, political, or military goals. Academic contractors convinced their clients that scientific dissection and measurement of the constituent elements of mass communication would lead to the development of powerful new tools for social management, in somewhat the same way earlier science had paved the way for penicillin, electric lights, and the atom bomb. Federal patrons meanwhile believed that analysis of audiences and communication effects could improve ongoing propaganda and intelligence programs.[9]

Entrepreneurial academics modeled the scientific tools needed for development of practical applications of communication-as-domination on those that had seemed so successful in the physical sciences: a positivist reduction of complex phenomena to discrete components; an emphasis on quantitative description of change; and a claimed perspective of "objectivity" toward scientific "truth." With few exceptions, they assumed that mass communication was "appropriately viewed from [the perspective of] the top or power center," as Steven Chaffee and John Hochheimer put it, "rather than from the bottom or periphery of the system."[10]

Effective persuasion and propaganda were (and are) widely viewed as a relatively rational alternative to the extraordinary brutality and expense of conventional war. Persuasive mass communication can improve military operations without increasing casualties, its advocates contend, especially when encouraging a cornered enemy to surrender rather than fight to the death. Similarly, by supporting the morale and improving the command and control of their own forces, those who can exploit these techniques reap clear military advantages. More fundamentally, U.S. security agencies see propaganda and psychological warfare as a means to extend the influence of the U.S. government far beyond the territories that can be directly controlled by U.S. soldiers, and at a relatively modest cost. The CIA's radio broadcasting into Eastern Europe, for example, became "one of the cheapest, safest, most effective tools of [U.S] foreign policy,'' as Jeane Kirkpatrick—long a vocal proponent of U.S. psychological operations—argued.[11]

Psychological warfare's role in the evolution of communication research must be examined in the context of political developments of the 1940s and 1950s. In truth, the primary object of U.S. psychological operations during this period was to frustrate the ambitions of radical movements in resource-rich developing countries seeking solutions to the problems of poverty, dependency, and entrenched corruption. The events in Iran, Egypt, Korea, the Philippines, Guatemala, Vietnam, and other countries discussed in upcoming chapters bear this out.

But that was not at all how things seemed at the time to many U.S. social scientists. To them the "real" enemy seemed to be Josef Stalin, not Iranian nationalists or Philippine Huk guerrillas. Stalin ruled the Soviet Union with extraordinary brutality up to his death in 1953, and many in the West regarded the terror of the Stalin years to be the defining feature of every communist society. The United States and the Soviet Union clashed repeatedly over geopolitical hot spots around the world, and the Soviets conducted a large and reasonably sophisticated psychological warfare campaign against the United States. Many observers in the West reasoned that the Marxist-Leninist doctrinal commitment to world revolution and the fact that communists were active in various labor and anticolonial movements proved that Moscow controlled a well-oiled, worldwide revolutionary conspiracy. The Soviet detonation of an atomic bomb in 1949, Mao Zedong's victory in China, and the outbreak of war in Korea were seen by many as warnings that the Soviet Union was bent on literally "taking over the world."

The Soviet view of the international competition, in contrast, was that the United States was an expansionist empire. The United States had already absorbed much of western Europe and the former European colonies into a postwar international economic order built around the dollar. The United States had isolated the Soviet Union internationally, severely restricted trade, and embarked on a clandestine campaign to overthrow the governments of the Soviet Union and several of its satellite states. It had openly intervened in Korea and secretly sponsored coups in a growing list of developing countries. The United States had twice used atomic bombs on civilian populations, the Soviets pointed out, and had on several occasions threatened nuclear attacks on the USSR, China, Korea, and Vietnam.

Given this situation, many leading U.S. social scientists regarded U.S. psychological warfare programs as an enlightened and relatively peaceful means of managing international conflicts through measures short of all-out war. As Ithiel de Sola Pool argued, social scientists' active participation in U.S. foreign policy initiatives was necessary because the "mandarins of the future"—Pool's term of praise for the decision-making elite—need a "way of perceiving the consequences of what they do if [their] actions are not to be brutal, stupid and bureaucratic but rather intelligent and humane. The only hope for humane government in the future," he continued, "is through extensive use of the social sciences by the government."[12]

In reality, though, U.S. and Soviet psychological warfare programs each fed its rival's appetite for escalated conflicts, particularly in contested countries in the Third World. Scientific research programs on either side that claimed to be a defensive reaction to foreign intrigues were easily interpreted in the rival's camp as aggressive preparations for war.

At heart modern psychological warfare has been a tool for managing empire, not for settling conflicts in any fundamental sense. It has operated largely as a means to ensure that indigenous democratic initiatives in the Third World and Europe did not go "too far" from the standpoint of U.S. security agencies. Its primary utility has been its ability to suppress or distort unauthorized communication among subject peoples, including domestic U.S. dissenters who challenged the wisdom or morality of imperial policies. In practice modern psychological warfare and propaganda have only rarely offered "alternatives" to violence over the medium-to-long term. Instead, they have been an integral part of a strategy and culture whose premise the rule of the strong at the expense of the weak, where coercion and manipulation pose as "communication" and close off opportunities for other, more genuine, forms of understanding. The problem with psychological warfare is not so much the content of individual messages: It is instead its consistent role as an instrument for maintaining grossly abusive social structures, notably in global North/South relations.

In the end, U.S. military and intelligence agencies became instrumental in the systematic elaboration of an interlocking series of concepts about communication that have defined much of post–World War II communication research. True, some academic and commercial roots of

U.S. communication studies can be traced back as far as the eighteenth century. Even so, cold war–era psychological warfare studies provided extensive, selective funding for large-scale projects designed to elaborate, test, and publicize the possibilities of communication-as-domination. They helped create networks of sympathetic insiders who enjoyed control over many aspects of scholarly publishing, rank and tenure decisions, and similar levers of power within academe. In doing so, these programs contributed significantly to the triumph of what is today regarded as mainstream communication research over its rivals in U.S. universities.

Federal agencies such as the Department of Defense, U.S. Information Agency, and Central Intelligence Agency and their forerunners provided the substantial majority of funds for all large-scale communication research projects by U.S. scholars between 1945 and 1960.[13] Despite the heavy secrecy that still surrounds some aspects of U.S. psychological warfare, it is clear that the federal government spent as much as $1 billion annually on these activities during the early 1950s.[14] As is discussed in later chapters, the government allocated between $7 million and $13 million annually for university and think-tank studies of communication-related social psychology, communication effect studies, anthropological studies of foreign communication systems, overseas audience and foreign public opinion surveys, and similar projects that contributed directly and indirectly to the emergence of mass communication research as a distinct discipline.[15] The major foundations such as the Carnegie Corporation and the Ford Foundation, which were the principal secondary source of large-scale communication research funding of the day, usually operated in close coordination with government propaganda and intelligence programs in allocation of money for mass communication research.[16]

Psychological warfare projects demanded scientific accuracy and academic integrity, to be sure, but they were at their heart applied research tailored to achieve narrowly defined political or military goals. Government agencies sought scientific data on the means to manipulate targeted populations at home and abroad, and they were willing to pay well for it at a time when there was very little other funding available for large-scale communication studies.

Further, some powerful factions of the government, notably the FBI and other domestic security agencies, aggressively repressed rival scientific concepts concerning communication, particularly those trends of critical thought they regarded as subversive. Because of the bitterness of the cold war, the influence of McCarthyism, and the strength of clandestinely funded ideological campaigns then under way among U.S. scholars (each of which is discussed in more detail in later chapters), unorthodox analysis of the relationships between communication and ideology could lead to professional ostracism, hostile FBI investigations, attacks in the press, and even violence.[17] Sociological research that could be interpreted as critical of U.S. institutions usually entailed serious professional risks during the 1940s and 1950s, and it sometimes carries similar risks today.

In time psychological warfare projects became essential to the survival of important centers of what are today regarded as mainstream mass communication studies in the United States. They were central to the professional careers of many of the men usually presented as the "founding fathers" of the fields; in fact, the process of selecting and anointing founding fathers has often consisted of attributing enduring scientific value to projects that were initiated as applied studies in psychological warfare. Thus Daniel Lerner's *Passing of Traditional Society*—today widely recognized as the foundation of the development theory school of communication studies—is usually remembered as a politically neutral scientific enterprise. In reality, Lerner's work was conceived and carried out for the specific purpose of advancing U.S. propaganda programs in the Middle East.[18]

U.S. psychological warfare programs between 1945 and 1960 provide a case study of how the priorities and values of powerful social groups can be transformed into the "received knowledge" of the scientific community and, to a certain extent, of society as a whole. It is a twofold story, first of the successes and failures of the government's effort to achieve the engineering of consent of targeted populations at home and abroad, and, contained within that, the story of the mechanisms by which consent was achieved among the scientists who had been hired to help with the job. Intriguingly, the latter effort was apparently more successful than the former, at least for a time. Study of psychological warfare is in part a look at how powerful groups manage change, reconstitute themselves in new forms, and struggle—not always successfully—to shape the consciousness of audiences that they claim as their own.

What, then, is "psychological warfare"? According to William Daugherty, the term first appeared in English in a 1941 text on the Nazis' use of propaganda, fifth column activities, and terror in the early stages of the European war.[19] U.S. military and intelligence organizations stretched the definition during World War II to cover a broader range of applications of psychology and social psychology to wartime problems, including battlefront propaganda, ideological training of friendly forces, and ensuring morale and discipline on the home front.[20]

Since World War II, U.S. military and NATO manuals have typically defined "psychological warfare" or "psychological operations" as tactics as varied as propaganda, covert operations, guerrilla warfare, and, more recently, public diplomacy.[21] Communist theoreticians have often referred to somewhat similar activities as "agitation and propaganda" and regarded them as a component of the related, yet broader concepts known as class struggle and peoples' war.[22] British and Nazi German strategies and tactics in the field have historically been termed "political warfare"[23] and *Weltanschauungskrieg* ("worldview warfare"),[24] respectively. Each of these conceptualizations of psychological warfare explicitly links mass communication with selective application of violence (murder, sabotage, assassination, insurrection, counterinsurrection, etc.) as a means of achieving ideological, political, or military goals. These overlapping conceptual systems often contributed to one another's development, while retaining characteristics of the political and cultural assumptions of the social system that generated it.

Within the present context, psychological warfare can best be understood as a group of strategies and tactics designed to achieve the ideological, political, or military objectives of the sponsoring organization (typically a government or political movement) through exploitation of a target audience's cultural-psychological attributes and its communication system. Put another way, psychological warfare is the application of mass communication to modern social conflict: it focus on the combined use of violence and more conventional forms of communication to achieve politicomilitary goals.

A more complete illustration of the U.S. government's view of psychological warfare can be found in the definition used by the U.S. Army in war planning during the early cold war years. The army's definition was classified as top secret at the time it was promulgated (early 1948) and remained officially secret until the late 1980s, when I obtained a collection of early psychological warfare planning records through a Freedom of Information Act request. One of these documents reads:

> Psychological warfare employs all moral and physical means, other than orthodox military operations, which tend to:
> a. destroy the will and the ability of the enemy to fight.
> b. deprive him of the support of his allies and neutrals.
> c. increase in our own troops and allies the will to victory.
> Psychological warfare employs *any* weapon to influence the mind of the enemy. The weapons are psychological only in the *effect* they produce and not because of the nature of the weapons themselves. In this light, overt (white), covert (black), and gray propaganda; subversion; sabotage; special operations; guerrilla warfare; espionage; political, cultural, economic, and racial pressures are all effective weapons. They are effective because they produce dissension, distrust, fear and hopelessness in the minds of the enemy, not because they originate in the psyche of propaganda or psychological warfare agencies.

The phrase "special operations," as used here, is defined in a second document as

> those activities against the enemy which are conducted by allied or friendly forces behind enemy lines. . . . [They] include psychological warfare (black), clandestine warfare, subversion, sabotage, and miscellaneous operations such as assassination, target capture and rescue of downed airmen.[26]

The army study goes on to summarize several of the tactics of persuasion just outlined, the three most basic of which are known as "white," "black," and "gray" propaganda. "White propaganda," the army states, "stress[es] simplicity, clarity and repetition." It is designed to be perceived by its audience as truthful, balanced, and factual, and the United States publicly acknowledged its promotion of this type of information through outlets such as the Voice of America. "Black" propaganda, in contrast, "stresses *trouble, confusion,* . . . and *terror*."[27] A variation of black propaganda tactics involves forging enemy documents and distributing them to target audiences as a means of discrediting rival powers. The U.S. government officially denies that it employs black propaganda, but in fact it has long been an integral aspect of U.S. foreign and domestic policy. "Gray" propaganda, as its name suggests, exists somewhere between "white" and "black" and typically involves planting false information about rivals in news outlets that claim to be independent of the U.S. government.[28]

Other U.S. Army and National Security Council documents from the same period stress three additional attributes of the U.S. psychological warfare strategy of the day: the use of "plausible deniability" to permit the government to deny responsibility for "black" operations that were in truth originated by the United States;[29] a conscious policy of polarizing neutral nations into either "pro-" or "anti-U.S." camps;[30] and the clandestine targeting of the U.S. population, in addition to that of foreign countries, for psychological operations.[31]

Throughout this book, psychological warfare and psychological operations encompass this range of activities, as specified by the Army and the National Security Council. Several points should be underlined. First, psychological warfare in the U.S. conception has consistently made use of a wide range of violence, including guerrilla warfare, assassination, sabotage, and, more fundamentally, the maintenance of manifestly brutal regimes in client states abroad. Second, it also has involved a variety of propaganda or media work, ranging from overt (white) newscasting to covert (black) propaganda. Third, the targets of U.S. psychological warfare were not only the "enemy," but also the people of the United States and its allies.

In the pages that follow I first discuss U.S. psychological warfare prior to 1945, stressing the early work of noted communication theorists Harold Lasswell and Walter Lippmann and the pioneer studies underwritten by the Rockefeller Foundation. I then describe the emergence of informal social networks among communication researchers employed in psychological warfare projects during World War II.

Turning to the postwar period, I next trace the interdependent evolution of psychological warfare and communication research during the cold war. I pay special attention to *Public Opinion Quarterly (POQ)*— long regarded as among the most prestigious mainstream academic journals of communication research—as a barometer of the impact of psychological warfare programs on academic concepts of what communication "is," what it could be, and how best to study it.

In the final chapters I review the scientific legacy of U.S. government psychological warfare contracting between 1945 and 1960 and summarize some insights into how these programs have affected preconceptions about communication, ideology, and responsible scholarship in the United States.

2

World War and Early Modern Communication Research

Psychological warfare is not new, of course. It is a modern coalescence and development of very old methods. Some of the earliest human civilizations used symbols, masks, and totems as instruments of power,[1] and the ancient Chinese military philosopher Sun Tzu documented the use of relatively sophisticated "psychological" tactics in both warfare and civil administration as early as the fifth century B.C.E.[2] Closer to home, the native peoples of North America have a strong tradition of using symbols and ceremony to cement tribal morale and (more rarely) to terrify rivals that was established well before the European invasion.[3] Similarly, European settlers in American made extensive use of propaganda tailored to various audiences, guerrilla warfare, and terror during the revolt against England,[4] the Mexican War,[5] the U.S. Civil War,[6] and the long campaign to wrest control of the continent from indigenous peoples.

But it was not until World War I that the U.S. government institutionalized and employed psychological warfare in its modern sense. In 1917, President Woodrow Wilson appointed George Creel to lead an elite Committee of Public Information made up of the U.S. secretaries of war, navy, and state. As Harold Lasswell wrote, Creel's new office was "the equivalent of appointing a separate cabinet minister for propaganda . . . responsible for every aspect of propaganda work, both at home and abroad."[7] President Wilson played a surprisingly strong personal role in devising U.S. psychological operations of his day, reviewing Creel's proposals for operations and even revising the galley proofs of propaganda pamphlets prior to their distribution.[8] The U.S. War Department meanwhile established a small psychological warfare subsection within the intelligence division of the War Department General Staff, and a parallel propaganda section under the general headquarters of the U.S. Expeditionary Forces in Europe.[9]

Much of the bureaucratic momentum for psychological warfare dissipated in the wake of the war, however. The War Department disbanded its psychological and propaganda sections in 1918, shortly after the Allied victory. The Creel committee dissolved in 1919, ending virtually all formal coordination of U.S. overseas propaganda efforts for the next twenty years. By the time the United States entered World War II in 1941, there was only one officer in the U.S. War Department General Staff who had had psychological warfare experience.[10]

In the United States, the psychological warfare projects of World War I left their strongest legacy in academic circles, particularly in the then embryonic field of communication research. Harold Lasswell's 1926 dissertation entitled *"Propaganda Technique in the World War"* examined the belligerents' propaganda programs as case studies in persuasive communication, exploring wide-ranging concepts such as political communication strategies, audience psychology, and manipulation of symbols. Similarly, Walter Lippmann based his two keystone texts, *Public Opinion* (1922)[12] and *The Phantom Public* (1925),[13] largely on his wartime experiences as chief leaflet writer and editor of a U.S. propaganda unit with the American Expeditionary Forces, and as secretary of The Inquiry, a prototypical U.S. intelligence agency organized by President Wilson to support the U.S. negotiating team in Paris.[14]

Both works investigated the impact of the new phenomenon of genuinely mass communication on Western industrial society. Both revealed the complex and often paradoxical relationship between mass communication and the professed values of democracies. Lasswell and Lippmann argued that new technologies for communication and transportation had awakened millions of disenfranchised people to a world outside their factories and villages, but that the traditional economic, political, and social structures that had shaped life during the nineteenth century remained in place. This led to potential explosions, as Lasswell and Lippmann saw things, including the Bolshevik revolution of 1917 and the wave of labor rebellions that swept through Europe and the United States in the wake of World War I.

Lippmann's career during these years illustrates a phenomenon that was to become much more common in the aftermath of World War II: He was an intellectual who shaped psychological strategy during the war itself, and then helped integrate that experience into the social sciences once most of the shooting was over. Lippmann's highly influential concept of the "stereotype," for example, contended that new communication and transportation technologies had created a "world that we have to deal with politically [that is] out of reach, out of sight, out of mind." The "pictures in our heads" of this world—the stereotypes—"are acted upon by groups of people, or by individuals acting in the name of groups."[15] The complexity and pace of the new world that Lippmann envisaged, together with the seeming ease with which stereotypes could be manipulated for political ends, led him to conclude that "representative government . . . cannot be worked successfully, no matter what the basis of election, unless there is an independent, expert organization for making the unseen facts [of the new world] intelligible to those who have to make the decisions."[16] The converse of that proposition was that decision makers had a responsibility to repair the "defective organization of public opinion," as Lippmann put it, in the interests of social efficiency and the greater good. These concepts, first introduced in *Public Opinion,* are illustrated throughout that text with references to Lippmann's wartime experiences as a propagandist and intelligence specialist.

Persuasive communication aimed at largely disenfranchised masses became central to Lippmann's strategy for domestic government and international relations. He saw mass communication as a major source of the modern crisis and as a necessary instrument for any managing elite. The social sciences offered tools that could make administration of what would otherwise be highly unstable social structures relatively rational and effective, he contended. In an era when methods of social supervision in industrial societies still mainly consisted of guns and policemen's clubs, many academics and intellectuals hailed Lippmann's insights as enlightened and humane.[17]

Lasswell extended the idea, giving it a Machiavellian twist. He emphasized employing persuasive media and selectively using assassinations, violence, and other coercion as means of "communicating" with and managing disenfranchised people. He advocated what he regarded as "scientific" application of persuasion and precise violence, in contrast to bludgeon tactics. "Propaganda [has attained] eminence as the one means of mass mobilization which is cheaper than violence, bribery and other possible control techniques," he wrote in 1933, adding that "successful social and political management often depends on proper coordination of propaganda with coercion, violent or non-violent; economic inducement (including bribery); diplomatic negotiation; and other techniques."[18] "Propaganda must be coordinated with information and espionage services which can supply material to the propagandists and report progress of propaganda work. That propaganda can be effectively correlated with diplomatic, military and economic pressures was abundantly demonstrated during the [First] World War."[19]

Lasswell understood that communication is intimately bound up with social order. Looked at dialectically, human communication and various forms of social order seem to define one another, to establish one another's boundaries; they probably cannot exist in isolation from one another. In this sense, communication might be understood as both the conduit for and the actual substance of human culture and consciousness.

Both the concept and the term "communication" had evolved from a far richer tradition than the cramped model offered by Lippmann and Lasswell. Etymologists say the word entered the English language around the fourteenth century, derived from the Latin *com* (literally "together") and *munia* ("duties"), meaning "the sharing of burdens."[20] In this traditional vision, communication, to the extent it was articulated, was seen as a process of sharing with others (through cultural interchange, ceremony, commerce, etc.) within any particular social context, as distinct from existing primarily as a medium for giving directions. That understanding of communication's root meaning can also be seen in related terms—community, commune, communion, and so on. Any society's distribution of its "burdens" may vary greatly from another's, of course, and there is little assurance that "sharing" is necessarily equitable. But the dialectical link between the collective, interactive attributes of communication and the attributes of any given social order seems to remain steady, even in very different societies.

Lippmann and Lasswell articulated a very narrow vision that substituted, for communication as such, one manifestation of communication that is particularly pronounced in hierarchical industrial states. Put most bluntly, they contended that communication's essence was its utility as an instrument for imposing one's will on others, and preferably on masses of others. This instrumentalist conception of communication was consistent with their experience of war and with emerging mass communication technologies of the day, which in turn reflected and to an extent embodied the existing social order.

For Lasswell, the study of all social communication could be reduced to "*who* says *what* to *whom* with *what effect*"—a dictum that is practically inscribed in stone over the portals of those U.S. colleges offering communication as a field of study. This was a seemingly simple, logical approach to analysis of communication, but it carried with it sweeping implications. Lippmann and Lasswell's articulation of communication-as-domination permitted a significant step forward in applying a positivist scientific method to the study of social communication. Positivism has traditionally been based in part on taking complex, unmeasurable phenomena and breaking them up into discrete parts, measuring those parts, and bit by bit building up a purportedly objective understanding of the phenomenon as a whole. Its early applications in the social sciences in the United States had been pioneered at the University of Chicago, Columbia University, and other academic centers.

New measurement techniques of this sort often have substantial impact on society outside of academe, however. In this case, Lasswell's formulation dovetailed so closely with emerging commercial and political forces in the United States that his slogan became the common wisdom among U.S. social scientists almost overnight. By reducing communication to the Lasswellian model of *who* says *what*, et cetera, it became possible for the first time to systematically isolate and measure those aspects of communication that were of greatest relevance to powerful groups in U.S. society.

The power of Lasswell's model (and its many derivatives) began with its ability to help create commercially viable products and services. It went beyond that, however, to permit supplanting and often suppressing rival visions of what social communication is or could be. Here's how: For mass consumer societies to establish and maintain themselves, it seems to be necessary for media to have the capacity to sell the attention of mass audiences to advertisers, who use that attention to promote their goods and services. To do that successfully, media organizations must have some means for measuring "popular attention" (and similar indices) in order to effectively market their services to potential advertisers. Lasswell's model and the various methodological innovations associated with it—which were introduced by Frank Stanton, Paul Lazarsfeld, Hadley Cantril, and others[21]—provided the necessary conceptual foundation for measurement of the services media sell to their customers.

From the advertisers' point of view, however, the simple sale of products and services is not enough. Their commercial success in a mass market depends to an important degree on their ability to substitute their values and worldview for those previously held by their audience, typically through seduction and deflection of rival worldviews. Automobile marketers, for example, do not simply tout their products for their usefulness as transportation; they seek to convince their customers to define their personal goals, self-esteem, and values in terms of owning or using the product. In mass consumer societies many customers do not simply purchase commodities; they instead eventually *become* them, literally and figuratively.

Put another way, early modern communication research often presented the de facto voicelessness of ordinary people—voicelessness in all fields *other* than selection of commodities, that is—as though it was communication itself. Terms like "Pepsi Generation," "Heartbeat of America," and "I Love What You Do for Me" (to cite modern examples) have always been more than simple advertising slogans. They have been successful from the advertisers' point of view only to the extent they have defined a way of life.

Thus the (professed) ability to measure mass media messages and the responses they trigger became one necessary prerequisite to a much broader social shift, a shift in which modern consumer culture displaced existing social forms. That process, moreover, consistently has been marked by great violence, frequently including genocide, as the "modern" world overwhelms indigenous cultures and peoples.

The mainstream paradigm of communication studies in the United States—its techniques, body of knowledge, institutional structure, and so on—evolved symbiotically with modern consumer society generally, and particularly with media industries and those segments of the economy most dependent on mass markets.[22] Communication research in America has historically proved itself by going beyond simply observing media behavior to finding ways to grease the skids for absorption and suppression of rival visions of communication and social order.

Clearly, social communication necessarily involves a balancing of conflicting forces. A "community," after all, cannot exist without some form of social order; or, put another way, order defines the possible means of sharing burdens. Lasswell and Lippmann, however, advocated not just order in an abstract sense, but rather a particular social order in the United States and the world in which forceful elites necessarily ruled in the interests of their vision of the greater good. U.S.-style consumer democracy was simply a relatively benign system for engineering mass consent for the elites' authority; it could be dispensed with when ordinary people reached the "wrong" conclusions. Lasswell writes that the spread of literacy

> did not release the masses from ignorance and superstition but altered the nature of both and compelled the development of a whole new technique of control, largely through propaganda. . . . [A propagandist's] regard for men rests on no democratic dogmatisms about men being the best judges of their own interests. The modern propagandist, like the modern psychologist, recognizes that men are often poor judges of their own interests. . . . [Those with power must cultivate] sensitiveness to those concentrations of motive which are implicit and available for rapid mobilization when the appropriate symbol is offered. . . . [The propagandist is] no phrasemonger but a promoter of overt acts.[23]

Lasswell and Lippmann favored relatively tolerant, pluralistic societies in which elite rule protected democracies from their own weaknesses—a modern form of noblesse oblige, so to speak. But the potential applications of the communication-as-domination zeitgeist extended far beyond the purposes that they would have personally approved. Nazi intellectuals in Germany proved to be instrumental in many aspects of communication studies throughout the 1930s, both as innovators of successful techniques and as spurs to communication studies outside of Germany intended to counteract the Nazi party's apparent success with propaganda. Josef Goebbels' work in social manipulation via radio, film, and other media is well known.[24] On a more academic plane, a bright young security service agent, Otto Ohlendorf, established a German research center known as the Deutsche Lebensgebiete in 1939 to apply new tools such as opinion surveys to the problem of determining *who* said *what* to *whom* with *what effect* inside Hitler's Germany. He was successful, on the whole, and his performance at the Deutsche Lebensgebiete laid the foundation for his later career as commandant of SS Einsatzgruppe D in the Caucasus, where he organized the murder of ninety thousand people, most of them Jewish women and children.[25] Ohlendorf's principal sponsor and mentor was a leading SS intellectual, Dr. Reinhard Hoehn of the Institute for State Research at the University of Berlin, who emerged after the war as one of Germany's most prominent experts on question of public opinion and the state.[26] Several other leading German mass communication and public opinion specialists contributed their skills to Nazi publicity and opinion-monitoring projects. Notable among them was Elisabeth Noelle-Neumann, who began her career at the Goebbels intellectual journal *Das Reich* and eventually emerged as one of Europe's most celebrated communication theorists.[27]

"Worldview Warfare" and World War II

During the second half of the 1930s, the Rockefeller Foundation underwrote much of the most innovative communication research then under way in the United States. There was virtually no federal support for the social sciences at the time, and corporate backing for the field usually remained limited to proprietary marketing studies. The foundation's administrators believed, however, that mass media constituted a uniquely powerful force in modern society, reports Brett Gary,[28] and financed a new project on content analysis for Harold Lasswell at the Library of Congress, Hadley Cantril's Public Opinion Research Project at Princeton University, the establishment of *Public Opinion Quarterly* at Princeton, Douglas Waples' newspaper and reading studies at the University of Chicago, Paul Lazarsfeld's Office of Radio Research at Columbia University, and other important programs.

As war approached, the Rockefeller Foundation clearly favored efforts designed to find a "democratic prophylaxis" that could immunize the United States' large immigrant population from the effects of Soviet and Axis propaganda. In 1939, the foundation organized a series of secret seminars with men it regarded as leading communication scholars to enlist them in an effort to consolidate public opinion in the United States in favor of war against Nazi Germany—a controversial proposition opposed by many conservatives, religious leaders, and liberals at the time—and to articulate a reasonably clear-cut set of ideological and methodological preconceptions for the emerging field of communication research.[29]

Harold Lasswell, who had the ear of foundation administrator John

Marshall at these gatherings, over the next two years won support for a theory that seemed to resolve the conflict between the democratic values that are said to guide U.S. society, on the one hand, and the manipulation and deceit that often lay at the heart of projects intended to engineer mass consent, on the other. Briefly, the elite of U.S. society ("those who have money to support research," as Lasswell bluntly put it) should systematically manipulate mass sentiment in order to preserve democracy from threats posed by authoritarian societies such as Nazi Germany or the Soviet Union.

One Rockefeller seminar participant, Donald Slesinger (former dean of the social science at the University of Chicago), blasted Lasswell's claims as using a democratic guise to tacitly accept the objectives and methods of a new form of authoritarianism. "We [the Rockefeller seminar] have been willing, without thought, to sacrifice both truth and human individuality in order to bring about given mass responses to war stimuli," Slesinger contended. "We have thought in terms of fighting dictatorships-by-force through the establishment of dictatorship-by-manipulation."[30] Slesinger's view enjoyed some support from other participants and from Rockefeller Foundation officers such as Joseph Willits, who criticized what he described as authoritarian or even fascist aspects of Lasswell's arguments. Despite this resistance, the social polarization created by the approaching war strongly favored Lasswell, and in the end he enjoyed substantial new funding and an expanded staff courtesy of the foundation. Slesinger, on the other hand, drifted away from the Rockefeller seminars and appears to have rapidly lost influence within the community of academic communication specialists.

World War II spurred the emergence of psychological warfare as a particularly promising new form of applied communication research. The personal, social, and scientific networks established in U.S. social sciences during World War II, particularly among communication researchers and social psychologists, later played a central role in the evolution (or "social construction") of U.S. sociology after the war. A detailed discussion of U.S. psychological operations during World War II is of course outside the scope of this book. There is a large literature on the subject, which is discussed briefly in the Bibliographic Essay at the end of this text. A few points are worth mentioning, however, to introduce some of the personalities and concepts that would later play a prominent role in psychological operations and communication studies after 1945.

The phrase "psychological warfare" is reported to have first entered English in 1941 as a translated mutation of the Nazi term *Weltanschauungskrieg* (literally, worldview warfare), meaning the purportedly scientific application of propaganda, terror, and state pressure as a means of securing an ideological victory over one's enemies.[31] William "Wild Bill" Donovan, then director of the newly established U.S. intelligence agency Office of Strategic Services (OSS), viewed an understanding of Nazi psychological tactics as a vital source of ideas for "Americanized" versions of many of the same stratagems. Use of the new term quickly became widespread throughout the U.S. intelligence community. For Donovan psychological warfare was destined to become a full arm of the U.S. military, equal in status to the army, navy, and air force.[32]

Donovan was among the first in the United States to articulate a more or less unified theory of psychological warfare. As he saw it, the "engineering of consent" techniques used in peacetime propaganda campaigns could be quite effectively adapted to open warfare. Pro-Allied propaganda was essential to reorganizing the U.S. economy for war and for creating public support at home for intervention in Europe, Donovan believed. Fifth-column movements could be employed abroad as sources of intelligence and as morale-builders for populations under Axis control. He saw "special operations"—meaning sabotage, subversion, commando raids, and guerrilla movements—as useful for softening up targets prior to conventional military assaults. "Donovan's concept of psychological warfare was all-encompassing," writes Colonel Alfred Paddock, who has specialized in this subject for the U.S. Army War College. "Donovan's visionary dream was to unify these functions in support of conventional (military) unit operations, thereby forging a 'new instrument of war.'"[33]

Donovan, a prominent Wall Street lawyer and personal friend of Franklin Roosevelt, convinced FDR to establish a central, civilian intelligence agency that would gather foreign intelligence, coordinate analysis of information relevant to the war, and conduct propaganda and covert operations both at home and abroad. In July 1941 FDR created the aptly named Office of the Coordinator of Information, placing Donovan in charge.[34]

But that ambitious plan soon foundered on the rocks of Washington's bureaucratic rivalries. By early 1942 the White House split the "white" (official) propaganda functions into a new agency, which eventually became the Office of War Information (OWI), while Donovan reorganized the intelligence, covert action, and "black" (unacknowledgeable) propaganda functions under deeper secrecy as the OSS. Officially, the new OSS was subordinate to the military leadership of the Joint Chiefs of Staff, but the relationship between the military and the civilian OSS was never smooth. Donovan frequently used his personal relationship with FDR to sidestep the military's efforts to restrict the OSS's growing influence.[35]

Similar innovations soon spread through other military branches, usually initiated by creative outsiders from the worlds of journalism or commerce who saw "psychological" techniques as a means to sidestep entrenched military bureaucracies and enhance military performance. Assistant Secretary of War John J. McCloy, a longtime Wall Street colleague of Donovan, established a small, highly secret Psychologic Branch within the War Department General Staff G-2 (Intelligence) organization. (McCloy is probably better known today for his later work as U.S. high commissioner of Germany, chairman of the Chase Bank, member of the Warren Commission, and related posts).[36] McCloy's Psychologic Branch was reorganized several times, briefly folded in the OSS, shifted back to military control, and renamed at least twice. The Joint Chiefs meanwhile established a series of high-level interagency committees intended to coordinate U.S. psychological operations in the field, including those of the relatively small Psychological Warfare Branches attached to the headquarters staffs of U.S. military commanders in each theater of war. If this administrative structure was not confusing enough, the psychological warfare branch attached to Eisenhower's command in Europe soon grew into a Psychological Warfare Division totaling about 460 men and women.[37]

These projects helped define U.S. social science and mass communication studies long after the war had drawn to a close. Virtually all of the scientific community that was to emerge during the 1950s as leaders in the field of mass communication research spent the war years performing applied studies on U.S. and foreign propaganda, Allied troop morale, public opinion (both domestically and internationally), clandestine OSS operations, or the then emerging technique of deriving useful intelligence from analysis of newspapers, magazines, radio broadcasts, and postal censorship intercepts.

The day-to-day war work of U.S. psychological warfare specialists varied considerably. DeWitt Poole—a State Department expert in anticommunist propaganda who had founded *Public Opinion Quarterly* while on sabbatical at Princeton before the war—became the chief of the Foreign Nationalities Branch of the OSS. There he led OSS efforts to recruit suitable agents from immigrant communities inside the United States, to monitor civilian morale, and to analyze foreign-language publications for nuggets of intelligence. Sociologists and Anthropologists such as Alexander Leighton and Margaret Mead concentrated on identifying schisms in Japanese culture suitable for exploitation in U.S. radio broadcasts in Asia, while Samuel Stouffer's Research Branch of the U.S. Army specialized in ideological indoctrination of U.S. troops. Hadley Cantril meanwhile adapted survey research techniques to the task of clandestine intelligence collection, including preparations for the U.S. landing in North Africa.[38]

There were six main U.S. centers of psychological warfare and related studies during the conflict. Several of these centers went through name changes and reorganizations in the course of the war, but they can be summarized as follows: (1) Samuel Stouffer's Research Branch of the U.S. Army's Division of Morale; (2) the Office of War Information (OWI) led by Elmer Davis and its surveys division under Elmo Wilson; (3) the Psychological Warfare Division (PWD) of the U.S. Army, commanded by Brigadier General Robert McClure; (4) the Office of Strategic Services (OSS) led by William Donovan; (5) Rensis Likert's Division of Program Surveys at the Department of Agriculture, which provided field research personnel in the United States for the army, OWI, Treasury Department, and other government agencies; and (6) Harold Lasswell's War Communication Division at the Library of Congress.

Dozens of prominent social scientists participated in the war through these organizations, in some cases serving in two or more groups in the course of the conflict. The OWI, for example, employed Elmo Roper (of the Roper survey organization), Leonard Doob (Yale), Wilbur Schramm (University of Illinois and Stanford), Alexander Leighton (Cornell), Leo Lowenthal (Institut für Sozialforschung and University of California), Hans Speier (RAND Corp.), Nathan Leites (RAND), Edward Barrett (Columbia), and Clyde Kluckhohn (Harvard), among others.[39] (The institutions in parentheses simply indicate the affiliations for which these scholars may be best known.) OWI simultaneously extended contracts for communications research and consulting to Paul Lazarsfeld, Hadley Cantril, Frank Stanton, George Gallup, and to Rensis Likert's team at the Agriculture Department.[40] OWI contracting also provided much of the financial backbone for the then newly founded National Opinion Research Center.[41]

In addition to his OWI work, Nathan Leites also served as Lasswell's senior research assistant at the Library of Congress project, as did Heinz Eulau (Stanford).[42] Other prominent contributors to the Lasswell project included Irving Janis (Yale) and the young Ithiel de Sola Pool (MIT), who, with Leites, had already begun systematic content analysis of communist publications long before the war was over.[43] Lasswell's Library of Congress project is widely remembered today as the foundation of genuinely systematic content analysis in the United States.[44]

At the Army's Psychological Warfare Division, some prominent staffers were William S. Paley (CBS), C. D. Jackson (Time/Life), W. Phillips Davison (RAND and Columbia), Saul Padover (New School for Social Research), John W. Riley (Rutgers), Morris Janowitz (Institut für Sozialforschung and University of Michigan), Daniel Lerner (MIT and Stanford), Edward Shils (University of Chicago), and New York attorney Murray Gurfein (later co-author with Janowitz), among others.[45] Of these, Davison, Padover, Janowitz, and Gurfein were OSS officers assigned to the Psychological Warfare Division to make use of their expertise in communication and German social psychology.[46] Other prominent OSS officers who later contributed to the social sciences include Howard Becker (University of Wisconsin), Alex Inkeles (Harvard), Walter Langer (University of Wisconsin), Douglas Cater (Aspen Institute), and of course Herbert Marcuse (Institut für Sozialforschung and New School).[47] OSS wartime contracting outside the government included arrangements for paid social science research by Stanford, the University of California at Berkeley, Columbia, Princeton, Yale's Institute of Human Relations, and the National Opinion Research Center, which was then at the University of Denver.[48] Roughly similar lists of social scientists and scholarly contractors can be discovered at each of the government's centers of wartime communications and public opinion research.[49]

The practical significance of these social linkages has been explored by social psychologist John A. Clausen, who is a veteran of Samuel Stouffer's Research Branch. Clausen made a systematic study during the early 1980s of the postwar careers of his former colleagues who had gone into the fields of public opinion research, sociology, and psychology.[50] Some twenty-five of twenty-seven veterans who could be located responded to his questionnaire; of these, twenty-four reported that their wartime work had had "lasting implications" and "a major influence on [their] subsequent career." Clausen quotes the reply of psychologist Nathan Maccoby (Stanford): "The Research Branch not

only established one of the best old-boy (or girl) networks ever, but an
alumnus of the Branch had an open door to most relevant jobs and
career lines. We were a lucky bunch.'' Nearly three-fifths of the respondents indicated that the Research Branch experience ''had a major
influence on the direction or character of their work in the decade after
the war,'' Clausen continues, ''and all but three of the remainder indicated a substantial influence. . . . [F]ully three-fourths reported the
Branch experience to have been a very important influence on their
careers as a whole.''[51]

Respondents stressed two reasons for this enduring impact. First, the
wartime experience permitted young scholars to closely work with recognized leaders in the field—Samuel Stouffer, Leonard Cottrell, Carl
Hovland, and others—as well as with civilian consultants such as Paul
Lazarsfeld, Louis Guttman, and Robert Merton. In effect, the Army's
Research Branch created an extraordinary postgraduate school with obvious scholarly benefits for both ''students'' and the seasoned ''professors.''

Second, the common experience created a network of professional
contacts that almost all respondents to the survey found to be very
valuable in their subsequent careers. They tapped these contacts later
for professional opportunities and for project funding, according to
Clausen. ''Perhaps most intriguing'' in this regard, Clausen writes,

> was the number of our members who became foundation executives.
> Charles Dollard became president of Carnegie. Donald Young shifted
> from the presidency of SSRC [Social Science Research Council] to that
> of Russell Sage, where he ultimately recruited Leonard Cottrell. Leland
> DeVinney went from Harvard to the Rockefeller Foundation. William
> McPeak . . . helped set up the Ford Foundation and became its vice
> president. W. Parker Mauldin became vice president of the Population
> Council. The late Lyle Spencer [of Science Research Associates] . . .
> endowed a foundation that currently supports a substantial body of social
> science research.[52]

There was a somewhat similar sociometric effect among veterans of
OWI propaganda projects. OWI's overseas director Edward Barrett
points out that old-boy networks rooted in common wartime experiences
in psychological warfare extended well beyond the social sciences.
''Among OWI alumni,'' he wrote in 1953, are

the publishers of *Time, Look, Fortune,* and several dailies; editors of such magazines as *Holiday, Coronet, Parade,* and the *Saturday Review,* editors of the *Denver Post.* New Orleans *Times-Picayune,* and others; the heads of the Viking Press, Harper & Brothers, and Farrar, Straus and Young; two Hollywood Oscar winners; a two-time Pulitzer prizewinner; the board chairman of CBS and a dozen key network executives; President Eisenhower's chief speech writer; the editor of *Reader's Digest* international editions; at least six partners of large advertising agencies; and a dozen noted social scientists. [53]

Barrett himself went on to become chief of the U.S. government's overt psychological warfare effort from 1950 to 1952 and later dean of the Columbia Graduate School of Journalism and founder of the *Columbia Journalism Review.* [54]

It is wise to be cautious in evaluating the political significance of these networks, of course. Obviously Herbert Marcuse drew quite different political conclusions from his experience than did, say, Harold Lasswell, and it is well known that even some of the once closely knit staff of the Institut für Sozialforschung who emigrated to the United States eventually clashed bitterly over political issues during the cold war. [55] Nevertheless, the common experience of wartime psychological warfare work became one step in a process through which various leaders in the social sciences engaged one another in tacit alliances to promote their particular interpretations of society. Their wartime experiences contributed substantially to the construction of a remarkably tight circle of men and women who shared several important conceptions about mass communication research. They regarded mass communication as a tool for social management and as a weapon in social conflict, and they expressed common assumptions concerning the usefulness of quantitative research—particularly experimental and quasi-experimental effects research, opinion surveys, and quantitative content analysis—as a means of illuminating what communication "is" and improving its application to social management. They also demonstrated common attitudes toward at least some of the ethical questions intrinsic to performing applied social research on behalf of a government. The Clausen study strongly suggests that at Stouffer's Research Branch, at least, World War II psychological warfare work established social networks that opened doors to crucial postwar contacts inside the government, funding agencies, and professional circles. Barrett's comments concerning the Psychological Warfare Division suggest a similar pattern there. As will be discussed in more depth in the next chapter, the various studies prepared by these scientists during the war—always at government expense and frequently involving unprecedented access to human research subjects—also created vast new data bases of social information that would become the raw material from which a number of influential postwar social science careers would be built.

3

"The Social Scientists Make a Huge Contribution"

Following World War I the U.S. government had shut down its propaganda and foreign intelligence agencies within months after signing the Treaty of Versailles. After World War II, by contrast, the Truman and Eisenhower administrations institutionalized these agencies and encouraged them to acquire sweeping powers. This policy had considerable implications for the social sciences in the United States, because the leaders of these agencies frequently considered the social sciences essential to their missions.

At the same time, the meaning of the term "psychological warfare" evolved in important ways that are outlined in this chapter. During World War II, the United States had been unambiguously committed to a declared war against a clear enemy, and psychological warfare had contributed to that struggle. Postwar conflicts were considerably different: war had not been "declared" in any traditional form, even in the long battles in Korea and Vietnam; the front lines, disputed territories, and even the enemy were almost always hazy; and each major international faction regularly deceived its own population and the world at large concerning how and why the contests were fought.

Within that context, concepts like "psychological warfare" and "psychological operations" acquired new layers of euphemistic explanations and cover stories. As will be seen, these myths permitted national governments to pursue covert political operations abroad, and even fight medium-scale wars, while at the same time evading virtually all oversight and accountability for what they were doing. Most U.S. social scientists, like most Americans generally, were kept well out of the loop when the national security apparatchiks made decisions.

But there were exceptions. For those scientists with the connections and insights necessary to refine U.S. government tactics for pursuing purported American interests abroad, the ambiguity of the cold war offered significant professional opportunities. For the first time in peacetime, the U.S. government was an eager customer for some types of social science expertise, particularly concerning foreign countries. This was especially true of the rapidly growing U.S. intelligence community.

"In all of the intelligence that enters into waging of war soundly and the waging of peace soundly, it is the social scientists who make a huge contribution," Brigadier General John Magruder of the OSS testified during Senate hearings in early November 1945.[1] Political, economic, geographic, and psychological factors were of "extraordinary importance" to the overall postwar intelligence effort, he insisted, adding that

the government of the United States would be well advised to do all in its power to promote the development of knowledge in the field of social sciences. . . . Were we to develop a dearth of social scientists, all national intelligence agencies servicing policy makers in peace or war would be directly handicapped. . . . [R]esearch of social scientists [is] indispensable to the sound development of national intelligence in peace and war.[2]

Magruder introduced a chart into the Senate record illustrating the OSS leadership's perspective, which is revealing on at least two counts (see Figure 1). In the OSS leadership's view, wartime and peacetime operations formed a clear continuum. While different tactics could be employed as situations changed, the intelligence community's fundamental perspective remained that U.S. interests could be best achieved by dominating rival powers, regardless of whether the United States was technically at peace or at war at any given time.[3] Magruder saw peaceful engineering of consent for U.S. aims as desirable when it worked, but the option of using violence to achieve national goals remained essential. Moreover, as Figure 1 illustrates, the OSS also believed that virtually every aspect of postwar intelligence operations should employ sociology, social psychology, or both.

Despite the OSS leadership's ambitions, however, the shift from hot

USE OF SOCIAL SCIENCES IN OSS INTELLIGENCE

DESCRIPTIVE INTELLIGENCE : Detailed and Inclusive background information

BASIC SOCIAL SCIENCES

POLITICAL SCIENCE ◆ ■

ECONOMICS ■

STATISTICS ◀

HISTORY ●

SOCIAL PSYCHOLOGY ◆

SOCIOLOGY ■

ANTHROPOLOGY ◀

GEOGRAPHY ●

STRATEGIC SURVEY

Governmental structure and authority
Political institutions
International relations

Social structure
Social institutions
Social ethics and customs
Geographical data
Population statistics
Health and sanitation

Nature of economy
Natural resources
Manufacturing and industry
Trade and commerce
Finance
Agriculture
National expenditure
Public morale

Terrain and climate
Utilities
Transportation

INTELLIGENCE FOR POLICY & OPERATIONS

e.g.

WAR
Character of invasion beaches
Strategic dependants of imports
Morale stamina of public

PEACE
Pressure groups
Trade and currency controls
Potential government leadership

33

war to cold war—and the institutionalization of communication studies that came in its wake—proceeded in fits and starts after 1945. OSS chief Donovan had long been a favorite of Franklin Roosevelt, but he was mistrusted by Roosevelt's successor, Harry S Truman, and by many in the U.S. Congress. Truman ordered the OSS dissolved in late 1945 and transferred most of its intelligence collection and psychological warfare staff to the Department of State.[4]

A second important World War II psychological warfare agency, the OWI, had already been dismantled by Republicans in Congress, who had concluded that OWI's propaganda in the United States had provided de facto support for Roosevelt's 1944 reelection drive by praising his leadership in the war. A number of southern Democrats on Capitol Hill had also been offended by OWI's promotion of racial integration in the army and in war plants—an example of the progressive agenda of many government propaganda programs during the Roosevelt era—and they too had voted to break up the agency.[5] Stouffer's Research Branch in the army did carry over into the postwar era, but under different leadership and with greatly reduced funding.[6]

Despite these shifts, the trend toward institutionalization and expansion of postwar psychological operations asserted itself at least as early as January 1946. That month, Truman established the Central Intelligence Group (CIG), the immediate predecessor to the Central Intelligence Agency (CIA), under the leadership of a political ally of the administration, General Hoyt Vandenberg of the Army Air Corps.[7] The CIG's charter limited the agency's work to intelligence analysis; nonetheless, its offices provided an institutional umbrella for a number of OSS veterans with psychological warfare experience who might otherwise have returned to civilian life. Less than two years after that, Truman replaced the CIG with the CIA, the bulk of whose budget for the next decade was to be dedicated to covert warfare, "black" propaganda, and other psychological operations.[8]

A pronounced drift emerged throughout the U.S. intelligence community toward U.S. intervention abroad to reintegrate failing European empires, confront the Soviets, and link domestic dissent with communist movements overseas. In January 1946 Major General W. G. Wyman, chief of intelligence of the U.S. Army Ground Forces, prepared a lengthy analysis reflecting his view of the ideological threats facing the U.S. government and the measures he believed necessary to meet them. American soldiers, occupation forces in Germany, and civilians at home

were all suffering from a serious "confusion of mind" when it came
to Marxism, he said.

> Where is the mental penicillin that can be applied to our loose thinking
> to insure the wholesome thought that is so urgently needed in our country
> today? . . . Our troubles of the day—labor, demobilization, the discon-
> tented soldier—these are the sores on which the vultures of Communism
> will feed and fatten.

Wyman then proposed his solution:

> There must be some agency, some group either within or outside our
> national security forces, which can interest itself in these matters. There
> must be some weapon by which we can defend ourselves from the secret
> thing that is working at our vitals—this cancer of modern civilization.
> . . . A new government policy is desperately needed to implement [this]
> psychological effort. . . . We must combat this creeping shadow which is
> in our midst.[9]

Wyman's proposals were never openly adopted in the United States,
in part because cultural barriers in this country militate against a major
military role in civilian politics. But the U.S. Army did undertake
Wyman's ideological campaigns within the armed forces and among
civilian populations in areas then under U.S. military occupation such
as western Germany, Japan, and parts of Austria. There the army's
former Psychological Warfare Division (now reincarnated as part of the
Army's Civil Affairs Division) began a massive campaign for strengthening ideological unity among U.S. forces and for remolding attitudes
among the former enemy population.
　　Their effort must be ranked as one of the single largest campaigns
of purposive communication ever undertaken by a democratic society.
Brigadier General Robert McClure, the wartime chief of the Psychological Warfare Division, offered an inventory of the propaganda assets
the army brought to bear on international audiences and on U.S. soldiers.
McClure's list began with RIAS radio in Berlin broadcasting into eastern
Europe; the *Stars and Stripes* daily newspaper; more worldwide radio
broadcasts than the Voice of America; troop education programs (a
legacy of Stouffer's work) in both Europe and the Far East; fifty to
seventy-five new documentary films produced each year; up-to-the-
minute newsreels in three languages produced each week; control of all

U.S. commercial films shown in occupied regions; control of postal censorship and publication licensing of all newspaper, magazine, and book publishers in the U.S. zones; operation of cultural centers in sixty cities; publication of five glossy foreign-language magazines designed for distribution to foreign audiences (the U.S. State Department was producing but one such magazine, McClure noted with satisfaction); printing of literally hundreds of millions of educational pamphlets and leaflets; publication of daily U.S. military government newspapers in three countries; and much more.[10] Not on McClure's list, but noteworthy in the present context, were large public opinion survey operations under the leadership of polling specialists Frederick W. Williams and Leo Crespi (in Germany) and anthropologists Herbert Passin and John W. Bennett (in Japan). Both became important centers for development of U.S. overseas and foreign-language polling techniques.[11]

The United States often adopted propaganda and psychological operations as one substitute for U.S. soldiers abroad as America demobilized much of its wartime army after 1945. By the end of the decade of the 1940s, many U.S. policymakers regarded these efforts as having been largely successful, though not yet completed. Determining the effectiveness of these programs is probably impossible today, considering the passage of time and the difficulties inherent in any attempt to disentangle communication effects from other social factors. The point here, however, is that important factions in the U.S. security establishment believed propaganda and psychological warfare campaigns on this scale to be essential to U.S. national security, and they were willing to pour tens of millions of dollars into these programs. The perceived success of these campaigns reinforced arguments within the government in favor of expanded psychological operations against restless populations in Europe and the developing world, as well as against the Soviet Union and its satellites.

Similar developments were under way in the fields of "black" and "gray" propaganda, covert warfare, and other sensitive aspects of psychological warfare. Between 1946 and 1950, the Truman administration created a multimillion-dollar secret bureaucracy for conducting clandestine warfare. For nearly the next thirty years, the very existence of this bureaucracy was denied repeatedly.

Much of the story of U.S. covert operations in postwar Europe and Asia remains buried in classified files and is in fact protected by statute from disclosure through the Freedom of Information Act or routine declassification.[12] The basic structure of this bureaucracy was revealed for the first time during the congressional investigations following the Watergate break-in, however. It is known, for example, that in the summer of 1946 Secretary of War Robert Patterson ordered the army to lay the administrative groundwork for the establishment of new Airborne Reconnaissance Units similar to the OSS teams that had assisted guerrilla struggles in Nazi-occupied France and Yugoslavia during the war.[13] (Despite the name, these groups specialized in sabotage and paramilitary operations and had little to do with "reconnaissance" in its usual sense.) The following spring, the State-Army-Navy-Air Force Coordinating Committee (SANACC)—the highest level U.S. political-military coordinating body of the day—created an elite interagency subcommittee euphemistically titled the Special Studies and Evaluation Subcommittee to "take those steps that are necessary to keep alive the arts of psychological warfare . . . [and to ensure] that there should be a nucleus of personnel capable of handling these arts in case an emergency arises."[14]

That summer, Congress passed the National Security Act, a sweeping reform of U.S. security agencies. This law created the CIA out of the earlier CIG, established the National Security Council (NSC) to advise the president on management of political-military strategy both at home and abroad, and reorganized the armed services.[15] Among the first questions faced by the new CIA was that of the constitutionality of clandestine psychological operations. Within weeks of the founding of the agency, the CIA's first director, Admiral Roscoe Hillenkoetter, asked the agency's counsel for a formal legal opinion concerning whether the 1947 law had authorized "secret propaganda and paramilitary operations" in peacetime.

The CIA's general counsel, Lawrence Houston, replied that it had not. The agency's charter authorized intelligence gathering and analysis, Houston said, which meant the collection and review of facts. Covert warfare and secret propaganda operations had not been approved by Congress, and the CIA's expenditure of taxpayer money on unauthorized activities would be against the law. Even if the president directly ordered covert operations, Houston continued, it would be necessary for Congress to specifically authorize the funds for them before they could be carried out legally.[16]

Houston's concerns led to two National Security Council actions on December 9, 1947, that became the first formal foundation for U.S.

covert warfare in peacetime. These decisions illustrate the extent to which U.S. psychological warfare has had, from its inception, multiple, overlapping layers of cover stories, deceits, and euphemistic explanations even within the secret councils of government. In this case the NSC created two such layers simultaneously, each contradicting the other.

First, the NSC approved a relatively innocuous policy document known as "NSC 4", entitled "Coordination of Foreign Information Measures." This assigned the assistant secretary of state for public affairs responsibility to lead "the immediate strengthening and coordination of all foreign information measures of the U.S. Government . . . to counteract effects of anti-U.S. propaganda."[17] Importantly, NSC 4 was classified as confidential, the lowest category of government secret. Tens of thousands of government employees are permitted access to confidential information, and the existence and nature of confidential policies can be publicly discussed with members of the press, although it is illegal to pass a confidential document to a person without a security clearance. As a practical matter, this meant that word of this confidential action would likely be publicized in the news media as an NSC "secret decision" within days, perhaps within hours.

That is precisely what took place. In time, a series of public decisions grew up around NSC 4 authorizing funding for the Voice of America, scholarly exchange programs, operation of "America House" cultural centers abroad, and similar overt propaganda programs. Officially, the policy of the U.S. government on such measures was that "truth is our weapon," as Edward Barrett—who was soon to be put in charge of the effort—put it. Barrett's widely promoted policy asserted that the United States openly presented its views on international controversies and frankly discussed the flaws and the advantages of U.S. society in a bid to win credibility for its point of view. This was not "propaganda" (in the negative sense of that word), Barrett insisted; it was "truth."[18]

In reality, however, only minutes after completing action on NSC 4, the NSC took up a second measure: NSC 4-A. This was classified as "top secret," a considerably stricter security rating. Legal circulation of top-secret papers is limited to authorized persons with a need to know of their contents; disclosure of even the existence of a top-secret decision to any person outside that circle is barred. In NSC 4-A, the NSC directed that the newly approved overt propaganda programs "must be supplemented by covert psychological operations." The National Security

Council's resolution secretly authorized the CIA to conduct these officially nonexistent programs and to administer them through channels different from the "confidential" program (i.e., the public program) authorized under NSC 4.[19]

The NSC's action removed the U.S. Congress and public from any debate over whether to undertake psychological warfare abroad. The NSC ordered that the operations themselves be designed to be "deniable," meaning "planned and executed [so] that any U.S. Government responsibility for them is not evident to unauthorized persons and that if uncovered the U.S. Government can plausibly disclaim any responsibility."[20]

This seemingly self-contradictory, multilayer approach helped construct a euphemistic, bureaucratic sublanguage of terms that permitted those who had been initiated into the arcana of national security to discuss psychological operations and clandestine warfare in varying degrees of specificity depending upon the audience, while simultaneously denying the very existence of these projects when it was politically convenient to do so—a phenomenon that is crucial to understanding the later role of U.S. social scientists in these enterprises. In an added twist, NSC 4 established an officially confidential (but in reality public) program concerning "Foreign Information Measures," which were sometimes referred to as "psychological measures" or "psychological warfare" in public discussions. This paradoxical structure helped to preserve the myth that the United States was dealing with the world in a straightforward manner consistent with the ideals of democracy, while the Soviets were waging a different sort of cold war, one that relied on deceit, propaganda, and clandestine violence.[21]

Less than six months later, the National Security Council replaced NSC 4-A with a second, more sweeping policy decision known as NSC 10/2, which granted the CIA still greater authority for clandestine warfare. NSC 10/2 created an entirely new government branch under the CIA whose budget, personnel, and very existence was a state secret: the Office of Policy Coordination (OPC). In its first weeks of existence, the new group was named the Office for Special Projects, but this title was thought to be too revealing because the euphemism "special projects" had become associated with clandestine OSS activities during the war. The name was therefore changed to Office of Policy Coordination, although the organization was an operational group that had nothing to do with policy or its coordination.[22] Frank Wisner, a brilliant, driven

Wall Street lawyer who had played a prominent role in the OSS, became its chief.[23]

Administratively, the OPC was a division of the CIA, but it was funded through the State Department and answered to that department's policy planning chief George F. Kennan on policy matters.[24] In practice, that meant that the dynamic Wisner enjoyed considerable autonomy for his division. By 1952 Wisner's "office" employed about six thousand personnel in forty-seven field stations in the United States and around the world. The OPC's annual budget has never been officially made public and so remains disputed among historians, with estimates running from about $82 million annually in 1950 dollars to three times that amount.[25] Virtually all of these funds were spent on "black" psychological warfare.

The NSC termed the OPC the United States' "Psychological Warfare Organization." Thus the phrase "psychological warfare"—with its connotation of media and persuasion, albeit of a hard-hitting sort—*itself* became a euphemism to conceal covert activities that most governments consider to be acts of war. As the OPC's charter put it, the agency's tasks included "propaganda, economic warfare; preventative direct action, including sabotage, anti-sabotage, demolition and evacuation measures; subversion against hostile states, including assistance to underground resistance movements, guerrillas and refugee liberations [sic] groups, and support of indigenous anti-communist elements in threatened countries of the free world."[26] OPC simultaneously created a specific branch for managing assassinations and kidnapping of "persons whose interests were inimical" to the United States, as well as for murdering double agents suspected of betraying U.S. intelligence agencies.[27]

William Corson, a career intelligence officer who investigated the origins of the OPC for a 1976 U.S. Senate inquiry, captured the same concepts in more informal—but perhaps more enlightening—terms:

> The intelligence community's reaction to the NSC's apparently unanimous endorsement and support of the "dirty tricks" authorizations was swift. In their view no holds were barred. The NSC 10/2 decision was broadly interpreted to mean that not only the President but *all* the guys on the top had said to put on the brass knuckles and go to work. As word of NSC 10/2 trickled down to the working staffs in the intelligence

community, it was translated to mean that a declaration of war had been issued with equal if not more force than if the Congress had so decided.[28]

In this context the phrase "psychological warfare" enjoyed multi-layered, often contradictory meanings, depending upon the degree to which the people using the phrase and their audience had been initiated into this officially nonexistent aspect of U.S. policy. For the public, the term seems to have implied basically overt, hard-hitting propaganda and other mass media activities. For the national security cognoscenti and for psychological warfare contractors, the same phrase extended to selected use of violence—but defining exactly how much violence was often sidestepped, even in top-secret records. Meanwhile, the U.S. government systematically denied responsibility for any specific act of violence, typically denouncing news reports of U.S.-sponsored clandestine operations as fabrications of communist propagandists.[29] In this way, the Truman and Eisenhower administrations mobilized broad constituencies to support U.S. psychological warfare programs—including constituencies among social scientists and other academics—while at the same time evading accountability for what was actually taking place.

4

Academic Advocates

Looked at with the benefit of hindsight and what came to light during
the Watergate-related investigations, the pages of *Public Opinion Quarterly* during the first decade after World War II illustrate several important features of the alliance that emerged after 1945 between a select
group of academic entrepreneurs and the government's psychological
warfare agencies. *POQ* had been founded in 1937 at Princeton University by DeWitt Poole, who was at that time on sabbatical from the
U.S. State Department division responsible for eastern European affairs.

POQ's work during the postwar years reflects Poole's concerns, revealing at least three characteristics of U.S. propaganda and covert
operations. First, many of the journal's articles explicitly discussed
American experience in psychological warfare, presented relevant research results, or advocated expanded U.S. programs of this type. *POQ*
articles exhibiting this relatively unambiguous characteristic were often
indexed under "psychological warfare" or "propaganda," or both, in
POQ's annual index.[1]

Second and usually more subtly, a substantial number of articles
targeted *POQ*'s own audience for persuasion concerning the appropriateness of U.S. intervention abroad, the emerging cold war, and the
proper role of mass communication research professionals in those efforts. Such articles frequently took the form of extended reviews of
books concerning foreign affairs.[2]

Finally, a number of the journal's editors and contributors maintained
unusually close relations with the clandestine or "denied" side of the
U.S. government's psychological warfare effort at the Department of

State, CIA, and the armed services. In fact, at least one-third of *POQ*'s editorial board can be identified today as financially dependent upon psychological warfare contracting.[3]

POQ's explicit articles concerning psychological warfare can be readily identified by their language and their themes. For example, during 1945 *POQ* published a report on the use of polling techniques to obtain military intelligence on the island of Saipan,[4] a review of the work of the principal U.S. domestic propaganda agency, the OWI;[5] a discussion of the use of opinion polls among Japanese nationals to determine effective propaganda themes;[6] and an argument in favor of intensifying U.S. propaganda against communism in Latin America.[7] A similar pattern continued for the remainder of the decade. A complete list of *POQ*'s explicit articles concerning psychological warfare would become tedious, but representative examples published between 1945 and 1949 include two further studies of the OWI,[8] seven reports on the dynamics of German civilian and military morale during World War II and on Allied attempts to influence it,[9] three case studies of the use of leaflets and postcards as propaganda vehicles,[10] six essays concerning morale and training programs among U.S. troops,[11] at least twelve reviews of books on wartime propaganda and psychological warfare,[12] and more than fifteen studies on various aspects of U.S. and Soviet propaganda and psychological warfare campaigns.[13]

Despite the volume of this material, and the frequent use of the terms "propaganda" and "psychological warfare" in *POQ*'s headlines and texts, the journal's authors were unable to arrive at any clear definition of exactly what was meant by those words. Terms like communication, propaganda, and psychological warfare meant quite different things to different people, even among experts in the field.

This was illustrated in Leo Crespi's 1946 review of *Propaganda, Communication and Public Opinion: A Comprehensive Reference Guide,* by Bruce Lannes Smith, Harold Lasswell, and Ralph Casey. Crespi took Lasswell to task for arguing that "propaganda is language aimed at large masses . . . to influence mass attitudes on controversial issues," whereas "education," in the Lasswellian view, is "primarily concerned with transmitting skill or insight, not attitude." As Crespi saw it, in contrast, any "socially enlightened educator" would agree that "a particular concern of education is to 'influence mass attitudes on controversial topics.' . . . [Lasswell's] attempt at a distinction fails."[14] Thus, while propaganda and psychological warfare were frequent topics of discussion, there remained considerable dispute among leaders in the field over exactly what those terms meant and how they might be distinguished from any other form of communication.

To carry the conundrum a step further, a few issues later a second leading expert, Hans Speier of the RAND Corporation, presented an extended discussion of "The Future of Psychological Warfare" in which he used the terms "propaganda" and "psychological warfare" interchangeably throughout.[15] Similarly, in *POQ*'s published annual index, the titles listed under index entry terms "propaganda" and "psychological warfare" overlap in such idiosyncratic ways as to offer few meaningful guidelines for distinguishing one from the other.[16]

Despite the journal's avoidance of a clear-cut definition, it is possible to identify the dominant arguments put forward concerning psychological warfare during the first five years after World War II. These can be most conveniently summarized through review of two theoretical articles on the topic by Donald McGranahan and Hans Speier, respectively. McGranahan's "U.S. Psychological Warfare Policy," published in the form of an extended letter to the editor in the fall 1946 issue,[17] focused on how best to use what was known about the social-psychological and anthropological characteristics of a given population when choosing coercive tactics for use against that population. This was the "relation of our psychological intelligence to our psychological warfare policy," as McGranahan put it. Briefly, he argued that U.S. psychological warfare tactics up to that time had suffered from an "advertising complex." Too much stress had been put on the principles of commercial advertising and public relations, where an advocate was said to be "careful not to offend the public or any important segment of it. [His] interest is in the broadest mass audience and the lowest common denominator." Even during World War II, the United States had been too reluctant to directly criticize Hitler in its broadcasts to Germany, he contended, because once having learned that many German soldiers remained loyal to Hitler, the United States was concerned that offending their faith might encourage them to fight all the harder.[18]

McGranahan contended that a "frontal attack" on rival ideologies would be more effective. "Evangelical propaganda" involving direct attacks on paganism had effectively spread Christianity, he argued, and the Soviet technique of "violent attacks [on rival] leadership, as well as on [its] political system," had mobilized internal discontent in the populations the Soviets had targeted. The United States should exploit these insights through propaganda and other psychological warfare techniques "adapted to [its] own particular objectives and based upon our democratic philosophy of life." In sum, U.S. psychological warfare should be campaigns of active subversion against targeted states. If U.S. programs were to be effective, they should be aimed primarily at indigenous, discontented groups who could be convinced to risk everything to attack a rival's government; they should only secondarily appeal to the "lowest common denominator" of the target's populations.[19]

McGranahan's argument resonated well with some American traditions and would seem to be easily applicable to wartime situations in which the United States was unambiguously dedicated to the defeat of a rival regime. But it begged the more difficult questions raised by postwar psychological warfare operations: Are these "revolutionary" tactics appropriate for use against governments with which the United States is officially at peace? And, considering that the sponsorship of subversion campaigns must frequently be secret in order for them to be successful, how exactly is a democratic society to determine which campaigns are appropriate and how far they are to be carried?

Hans Speier's article on "The Future of Psychological Warfare" appeared as the lead article in the spring 1948 issue. The historical context is important here. President Truman had "drawn the line" against popular revolutions in Greece and Turkey a year previously, and U.S.–U.S.S.R. relations were headed for—but had not yet reached—the watershed symbolized by the Berlin crisis of 1948. Inside the U.S. government, the National Security Council had in December 1947 secretly passed NSC 4 and NSC 4-A, the official authorization for campaigns of clandestine propaganda, sabotage, and subversion. Among the most important sponsors of NSC 4 and NSC 4-A within the government was Frank Wisner, who was in December 1947 chief of the Occupied Areas Division at the State Department, and who would a few months later be appointed chief of OPC, the clandestine warfare agency. Wisner's second in command at State during his effort to secure passage of NSC 4-A was Hans Speier.[20]

By the time Speier's article appeared that spring, he had left the government and had taken a temporary roost at the New School for Social Research in New York. *POQ* presented his essay to its readers as that of a private scholar rather than that of a government official. Nevertheless, Speier's commentary clearly was born at least in part out of his government work, where he had specialized in the sociology and social psychology of reeducating populations in the U.S. occupation zone of Germany and Austria. In his *POQ* article, Speier argued that the United States had permitted its psychological warfare weapons to "fall into desuetude" since 1945 and should now refurbish them. Specialists in the field had never received the support within the government that they deserved, he contended, in large part because their previous efforts had been put together on an ad hoc basis after World War II had already begun. This time around, however, "the United States cannot afford to persist in its indifference toward political and psychological warfare," nor would it be possible to "rely on improvisation once more if it should be impossible to avoid war."[21] As Speier saw it, U.S. clandestine subversion campaigns against the Soviet Union and rebel nationalist groups in developing countries should be extended and escalated.

He contended that the U.S. government should prepare immediately to "impos[e] martial law [in the United States] to guard against defeatism, demoralization and disorder," if that proved necessary. More urgent in Speier's mind, however, was activation of a strong "offensive" program designed to overthrow rival regimes. "Subversion [is the] aim of strategic propaganda," Speier wrote. "The United States . . . can wage sincere political subversion propaganda against the dictatorial Soviet regime, particularly in the political realm. . . . Planning and preparation for strategic propaganda in a future war must begin now."[22]

Thus by the end of the 1940s Speier, McGranahan, and other prominent communication research specialists used the pages of *POQ* to call on U.S. security agencies to employ state-of-the-art techniques to facilitate the overthrow of governments of selected foreign countries in a "future" war—the preparations for which should begin immediately. Speier's program included coercive measures, even the imposition of martial law, to ensure that the U.S. population cooperated. Although Speier presented his argument in the form of a proposal, it is today known from the declassified records of the National Security Council that many of the measures he recommended were in fact actually under way at the time his article appeared.[23]

Turning to the second and more subtle manifestation of psychological warfare themes in *Public Opinion Quarterly*, many *POQ* articles targeted the journal's own audience for persuasion concerning U.S. policy on cold war operations in contested countries worldwide and on the proper role of mass communication research professionals in that effort. These texts did not usually advocate psychological warfare campaigns in the sense that McGranahan and Speier did, but instead framed their discussion in such a way as to reinforce the foreign policy initiatives and propaganda themes of the powerful "internationalist" faction within the U.S. government. As I noted earlier, this phenomenon can be seen in the extensive play *POQ* gave to reviews of books on various aspects of foreign affairs that strongly demonstrated the reviewer's (and presumably the editors') support for the foreign policy initiatives of the Truman administration—even when the books had little meaningful relationship to the study of public opinion. Between the winters of 1946 and 1947, for example, *POQ* published twenty-seven book reviews. Of these, six (22 percent) concerned books on the Soviet Union, each of which was a general-interest work. All of them were reviewed by a single author, Warren Walsh, who used each of his commentaries to conclude that cold war between East and West was necessary, and that the conflict had been instigated by the Soviets.[24] None of Walsh's reviews dealt with public opinion or communication research, other than in the banal sense that any political writing involves public opinion in some fashion.

The point here is not the merit of Walsh's opinions. Rather, it is the journal's willingness to propagate a monochromatic picture of issues that were among the most controversial of the day. The use of the single author and the single point of view suggests that the magazine did indeed have an editorial "line" on East–West relations, and that it did not welcome contrary points of view.

The journal's reporting on other international issues shows a similar trend. *POQ*'s coverage of public opinion polling in Italy, for example, was initiated in spring 1947 with a study by P. Luzzatto Fegiz, "Italian Public Opinion,"[25] which focused on the possible electoral strength of Italy's Communist party (CPI). Fegiz outlined a method he had developed that purportedly could determine the degree of communist sympathy among Italian voters and concluded that Italy might soon "become an integrant [*sic*] part of Russian-dominated Eastern Europe." This concern was followed up in a second feature article in winter 1947, "The Prospects of Italian Democracy" by Felix Oppenheim, who expressed many of the same themes,[26] and in two later *POQ* articles on Italian public opinion published in 1949 and 1950 that reported on the propaganda techniques used during the 1948 election campaign.[27]

Again, some historical background is appropriate. The CPI was during the late 1940s probably the most powerful communist organization in western Europe. The Truman administration's National Security Council was deeply concerned that Italian voters might democratically elect a socialist–communist coalition government, a move that the NSC regarded as putting Italy behind the Iron Curtain. NSC 4 and NSC 4-A's first clandestine psychological warfare project became a no-holds-barred campaign to ensure the CPI's defeat in the 1948 election, including multimillion-dollar, "deniable" propaganda projects aimed at both Italian and American audiences.[28]

In reporting on Italy, POQ's authors consistently articulated the main psychological warfare themes of the U.S. government in articles that were ostensibly about Italy, rather than about psychological warfare as such. The point once again is not the merit of POQ's position, nor is it necessary to assume that POQ was a willing participant in the government's effort to mold U.S. public opinion on the Italian elections. What is apparent on its face, however, is that the academic journal promoted a single point of view on these political issues, and that it did not air contrary views.

Opposition to this "propagandistic" aspect (as some might call it) of POQ's content was rare, but it did take place. One protest came from Alfred McClung Lee, who wrote to the editors of the journal in the spring of 1947 criticizing George Counts' 1946 article, "Soviet Version of American History."[29] Lee contended that Counts' work had one-sidedly indicted Soviet writers for distorting U.S. history in their magazines, without recognizing that many U.S. authors also twisted Soviet history when they considered it useful. Lee's note was to be the last published protest to the politicization of POQ for more than a decade. There appears to have been passive resistance among some POQ readers to the stress the journal placed on ideologically charged foreign political news, however. Intriguingly, a 1948 survey of POQ readers found that 20 percent of the respondents preferred that "less attention [in the journal] be given to descriptions of popular attitudes abroad," and that POQ should instead place greater emphasis on scientific methodology, case histories of publicity campaigns, and research into the effects of publicity.[30]

The third expression of psychological warfare themes in POQ and similar academic literature during the first years after World War II can be seen in the unusually close liaison that some of the journal's authors and editors maintained with clandestine psychological warfare projects at the CIA, the armed services, and the Department of State. This can be found in both manifest and veiled form in many articles appearing in the journal, and in the composition of *POQ*'s editorial board. Hans Speier's emergence as a prominent "private" advocate of expanded psychological warfare shortly after his work with Frank Wisner at the Occupied Areas Division at the State Department, discussed previously, is one example of an informal link between a prominent *POQ* author and the government's clandestine warfare programs.

This phenomenon became considerably more widespread, however, though rarely easy to identify. A good example of latent linkages can be seen in Frederick W. Williams' 1945 article "Regional Attitudes on International Cooperation."[31] On a manifest level, Williams' study simply reports data gathered by the American Institute of Public Opinion and the Office of Public Opinion Research at Princeton during the winter of 1944–45 concerning popular attitudes on the U.S. role in international affairs, broken out by geographic region of the country. Williams uses the data to strongly advocate "making the United States more international-minded," as *POQ* described it.[32]

In the decades since the article first appeared, it has become clear that Williams' data had been collected in an ongoing clandestine intelligence program underwritten by Listerine heir Gerard Lambert on behalf of the Roosevelt administration. The U.S. Congress had in those years barred the expenditure of government funds on most types of attitude surveys of U.S. voters, arguing that it was the Congress' job under the Constitution to represent "public opinion." Congress' concern was in part political, because FDR used rival sources of information on public opinion to advance controversial policies, not least of which was the president's drive toward an "internationalist" foreign policy. Despite the congressional strictures, the White House hired Hadley Cantril and Lloyd Free for "government intelligence work," as Jean Converse puts it, including clandestine intelligence collection abroad and public opinion surveys in the United States. Cantril and Free in turn engaged Frederick Williams and the American Institute of Public Opinion as field staff for research on behalf of the administration.[33]

Meanwhile, *Public Opinion Quarterly*'s board of editors included a substantial number of men who were deeply involved in U.S. government psychological warfare research or operations, several of whom were largely dependent on government funding for their livelihood. The journal's editorial advisory board during the late 1940s, for example, was made up of twenty-five to thirty individuals noted for their contributions to public opinion studies and mass communication research. Among those on the board with readily identifiable dependencies on government psychological warfare contracting were Hadley Cantril, Harold Lasswell, Paul Lazarsfeld, and Rensis Likert, whose role as government contractors are documented in Chapters 5, 6, 7, and 8 of this study. They were joined on the *POQ* board by DeWitt Poole, who later became president of the CIA's largest single propaganda effort of the era, the National Committee for a Free Europe.[34] Another prominent board member was CBS executive Frank Stanton, also a longtime director of both Radio Free Europe and the Free Europe Fund, a CIA-financed organization established to conduct political advertising campaigns in the United States and to launder CIA funds destined for Poole's National Committee for a Free Europe.[35] The journal's editor during 1946 and 1947 was Lloyd Free, a wartime secret agent on behalf of the Roosevelt administration who some years later was destined to share a million-dollar CIA research grant with Hadley Cantril.[36]

This pattern appears to have been repeated at several other important academic journals of sociology and social psychology of the era, although quantitative studies of their content remain to be done. The *American Sociological Review* (*ASR*), published by the American Sociological Society, overlapped so frequently in its officers and editorial panels with those of *Public Opinion Quarterly* and its publisher, the American Association for Public Opinion Research, that board members sometimes joked that they were unsure which meetings they were attending.[37] While *ASR* published articles about a considerably broader range of sociological subjects than did *POQ*, the *ASR* articles and book reviews concerning communication remained confined to a group of fewer than a dozen authors who were simultaneously the dominant voices in *POQ*. The range of views concerning communication and its role in society remained similarly circumscribed.

Further, an informal comparison of articles published during the 1950s concerning mass communication and public opinion in *POQ* and the prestigious *American Journal of Sociology* (*AJS*) shows that its articles in this field were just as rooted in psychological warfare contracts as were those appearing in *POQ*. The 1949–50 volume of *AJS,* for example, featured eight articles on various aspects of mass communication and public opinion. At least four of these stemmed directly or indirectly from ongoing psychological warfare projects, including work by Hans Speier and Herbert Goldhamer (both of RAND Corp.), Samuel Stouffer (from the *American Soldier* project), and Leo Lowenthal (then the director of research for the Voice of America, whose political odyssey is discussed in Chapter 6).[38]

In sum, the data show that *Public Opinion Quarterly*—and perhaps other contemporary academic journals as well—exhibited at least three important characteristics that linked the publication with the U.S. government's psychological warfare effort during the first decade after World War II. First, *POQ* became an important advocate for U.S. propaganda and psychological warfare projects of the period, frequently publishing case studies, research reports, and polemics in favor of expanded psychological operations. Second and more subtly, many *POQ* articles articulated U.S. propaganda themes on topics *other* than psychological warfare itself. Examples include the magazine's editorial line on U.S.–Soviet relations and on the Italian election of 1948.

Finally, data suggest that some members of the journal's editorial board and certain of the authors maintained an unusually close liaison with the clandestine propaganda and intelligence operations of the day. The traces of these relationships can be found in several articles mentioned in this chapter and in the composition of *POQ*'s editorial board, at least one member of which—*POQ*'s founder DeWitt Poole—was a full-time executive of a major propaganda project organized and financed by the CIA.

This influence over the editorial board and editorial content of the field's most prestigious academic journal was only a symptom of a deeper and more organic bond that is discussed in the next chapter. Money became one of the most important links between the emerging field of mass communication studies and U.S. military, intelligence, and propaganda agencies. Precise economic figures cannot be determined because of the lack of consistent reporting from the government, the continued classification of some projects, and the loss of data over the years. Even so, the overall trend is clear.

"The primary nexus between government and social science is an economic one," write Albert Biderman and Elisabeth Crawford of the Bureau of Social Science Research. It is "so pervasive as to make any crisis of relations with the government a crisis for social science as a whole."[39]

5

Outposts of the Government

For the first decade after 1945—which is to say, the decade in which communication studies crystallized into a distinct academic field, complete with colleges, graduate degrees, and so on—U.S. military, propaganda, and intelligence agencies provided the large majority of all project funding for the field. The earliest cumulative data concerning government funding of social science is provided by the National Science Foundation (NSF) in 1952; that report shows that over 96 percent of all reported federal funding for social science at that time was drawn from the U.S. military. The remaining 4 percent of government funding was divided about equally between conventional civilian agencies (Department of Labor, Department of the Interior) and civilian agencies with clear national security missions (such as the Federal Civil Defense Administration and the Office of Intelligence and Research at the State Department). Social science funding rooted in national security missions totaled $12.27 million that year, the NSF reported, while comparable "civilian" funding totaled only $280,000.[1]

This extreme skew in favor of national security–oriented social science studies appears to have attenuated during the course of the 1950s, even as overall academic dependency on the federal government increased. Directly comparable funding data for the late 1950s are not available due to changes in the National Science Foundation's data collection and reporting, but the available data indicate that annual research obligations by national security agencies (i.e., Department of Defense, civil defense, U.S. Information Agency [USIA]) for the social sciences increased slightly over the decade, to $13.9 million in 1959.

Meanwhile, civilian funding (principally from the departments of Agriculture and Health, Education and Welfare) grew quite sharply over the same time to $41.4 million. The apparent military–civilian balance in the 1959 figures cannot be taken at face value, however, because a significant amount of security-oriented social science contracting took place under the aegis of the National Advisory Commission on Aeronautics in the wake of the Soviet *Sputnik* launch. This very large research budget—totaling more than twice as much as all other social science funding combined—is not broken out into categories that permit direct comparison to the 1952 data.[2]

Be that as it may, to the extent that social science was supported by the U.S. government during the 1950s, that support was usually tied to national security missions, especially during the first years of the decade. This was particularly true of mass communication studies. A close review of *Public Opinion Quarterly,* the *American Journal of Sociology, American Psychologist,* and other academic literature published between 1945 and 1955 reveals several dozen medium- to large-scale projects funded by the Office of Naval Research, Air Force, Army, CIA, and USIA. The only comparable "civilian" study appears to have been a 1950 Department of Agriculture survey of the effects of television on dressmakers—one of the earliest such studies of television effects—that was apparently never written up for academic journals. The Agriculture Department, Tennessee Valley Authority, and other civilian agencies also supported a limited number of consumer preference opinion surveys, Harry Alpert reported in 1952.[3] But the National Science Foundation data show that the scale of such projects was quite small compared to the ongoing military, intelligence, and propaganda research.

At least a half-dozen of the most important centers of U.S. communication research depended for their survival on funding from a handful of national security agencies. Their reliance on psychological wafare money was so extensive as to suggest that the crystallization of mass communications studies into a distinct scholarly field might not have come about during the 1950s without substantial military, CIA, and USIA intervention.

Major beneficiaries included the Bureau of Applied Social Research, the Institute for Social Research at the University of Michigan, the National Opinion Research Center, the Bureau of Social Science Research, the RAND Corporation, and the Center for International Studies at MIT. Moreover, this list must be regarded as preliminary at this time. Several of the more important academics engaged in mass communication studies became activist supporters of U.S. psychological warfare projects and derived part of their income from participation in such efforts over a period of at least two decades. This was particularly true of Wilbur Schramm, who is widely credited as the single most important definer of U.S. mass communication studies of his day. These scholars and the organizations they were affiliated with became central to the elaboration and to the practical social power of what has come to be known as the dominant paradigm of U.S. mass communication research during the 1950s.

The Survey Research Center (SRC) at the University of Michigan (today known as the Institute for Social Research [ISR]), for example, was established by Rensis Likert in the summer of 1946 using a number of the personnel who had served under Likert in the Program Surveys operation during the war. The "SRC functioned during its first year as something of an outpost of the federal government," writes Jean Converse in *Survey Research in the United States*.[4] Major early contracts included a ten-year grant from the Office of Naval Research for studies of the psychological aspects of morale, leadership, and control of large organizations, and a series of contracts for surveys of Americans' attitudes on economics for the Federal Reserve Board, which was in those early postwar days deeply concerned about the potential for a renewed 1930s-style depression and social upheaval as veterans returned to the civilian work force.[5] Early SRC/ISR research with strategic intelligence applications included U.S. Air Force–funded interview studies of Soviet defectors and refugees. The object of that study was twofold: first, identification of social-psychological attributes of the Soviet population that could be exploited in U.S. propaganda, and second, collection of intelligence on military and economic centers inside the Soviet Union to target for atomic attack in the event of war.[6]

SRC archival records show that federal contracts contributed 99 percent of SRC revenues during the organization's first full year (1947) and well over 50 percent of SRC/ISR revenues during its first five years of operation. Angus Campbell, who later became director of the institution, has reflected that had the federal funding been canceled during this period, the SRC/ISR "probably would not have survived."[7]

At the National Opinion Research Center, perhaps the most liberal and reform-minded of the early centers of survey research, about 90 percent of the organization's work during the war years was made up of contracts from the Office of War Information, the government's principal monitor of civilian morale. This backing was "probably critical in making [NORC's] national capacity [for conducting surveys] viable," Converse writes.[8] Congress canceled the OWI project in 1944, but the NORC field studies of civilian morale and attitudes were continued under a series of secret, "emergency" contracts with the Department of State. That arrangement became institutionalized, and it provided a survey vehicle onto which NORC later marketed "piggyback" questions for commercial customers.

It was probably illegal for the State Department (though not for NORC) to enter these contracts, and that led to an unpleasant scandal when Congress uncovered the continuing "emergency" surveys fourteen years later in 1958.[9] The State Department is prohibited by statute from spending funds to influence Congress, and the NORC surveys had indeed been put to that use by the department. NORC's archives indicate that without the State Department contract during the institution's first decade, the organization would probably have found it impossible to maintain a national field survey staff, which was essential to NORC's academic and commercial work and for the group's economic survival.[10]

A second noteworthy NORC contract during the center's first decade was a study for the U.S. Army Chemical Corps of individual and group responses to "community disasters," in which natural disasters such as earthquakes and tornadoes were used as analogues to model responses to attacks with chemical weapons.[11] In time, NORC undertook a related series of disaster studies that became the U.S. government's main data base for evaluating the psychological effects of nuclear war.[12]

Funding for the Bureau of Applied Social Research at Columbia University appears to have been more diversified. BASR records from its first years are sketchy, but Converse concludes that approximately 50 percent of BASR's budget from 1941 to 1946 stemmed from commercial work such as readership studies for *Time* and *Life* magazines and a variety of public opinion surveys for nonprofit organizations. Other funds stemmed from a major Rockefeller Foundation grant and, to a much lesser degree, from Columbia University.[13]

By 1949, the BASR was deeply in debt to Columbia University and lacked a cushion of operating funds with which to cover project expenses while waiting for clients to make payments. The cash flow problem was sufficiently severe that Lazarsfeld speculated in fundraising appeals that BASR would be forced to close its doors if help was not forthcoming.

By the end of that year, however, BASR's Kingsley Davis won new military and intelligence contracts that substantially improved BASR's finances. By fiscal year 1950–51, BASR's annual budget had reached a new high, some 75 percent of which consisted of contracts with U.S. military and propaganda agencies.[14] Major federally funded BASR projects of the period included two U.S. Air Force studies for intelligence gathering about urban social dynamics abroad, a large project for the Office of Naval Research, and a multiyear contract with the Voice of America for public opinion surveys in the Middle East.[15] BASR's dependence on federal money may in fact have been even higher, because some ostensibly "private" studies were actually subcontracts from private institutions of projects that had originated in the federal government. One example of this is technical consultation on interviewing and survey techniques by BASR's Lee Wiggins and Dean Manheimer for surveys of Soviet émigrés in Europe. Harvard's Russian Research Center was the prime contractor; funding for that project was drawn primarily from the U.S. Air Force and the CIA.[16]

The Voice of America project began in September 1950 with BASR as the prime contractor; Charles Glock organized the day-to-day work. Extensive, methodologically ambitious surveys were conducted in Iran, Turkey, Egypt, and four other Middle Eastern countries, each of which was a major target of U.S. psychological warfare efforts of the period.[17] At least two of the countries, Iran and Egypt, experienced CIA-supported coups d'état while the study was under way.[18]

Lazarsfeld helped compose the survey questions, which were eventually asked by native-language researchers in the field. These included inquiries such as:

97a. How do you feel about the behavior of Russia in world affairs? How about its behavior towards [your] country? (Probe also for changes.) How long have you felt that way?

42. If you were put in charge of a radio station, what kinds of programs would you like to put on? (Probe here.)[19]

BASR arranged for translation, tabulation, and analysis of about two thousand interviews and eventually delivered a confidential report to the Voice of America designed to guide U.S. propaganda broadcasts in the region. Nonclassified studies of some of the same data were publicized through *Sociometry, Public Opinion Quarterly,* and other academic journals. These included reports on purported "Political Extremists in Iran" by Benjamin Ringer and David Sills and a comparative report on communications and public opinion in four Arab countries by Elihu Katz and Patricia Kendall.[20]

Military and Foundation Networks

This dependency of three of the United States' most important centers of communication and public opinion research on contracts with military and propaganda agencies became but one skein in a broader, more complex, and more enveloping web of relationships. The flow of money to favored federal contractors moved through networks of personal contacts, friends, and colleagues such as those documented in the Clausen study of academic networks discussed earlier. These informal associations provided an important new dimension to the social and scientific impact of government funding patterns.

Their impact can be demonstrated in the interservice Committee on Human Resources, which the Department of Defense established in 1947 to coordinate all U.S. military spending on social psychology, sociology, and the social sciences, including communication studies.[21]

The Defense Department and a narrow group of influential academic entrepreneurs employed the committee as a confidential contact point for government–academic networking. In 1949, its chairman was Donald Marquis (University of Michigan and president of the American Psychological Association). He was aided by committee members William C. Menninger (Menninger Foundation, a major military contractor for studies of "combat fatigue" and related forms of psychological collapse), Carroll Shartle (then at Ohio State University and later chief of the Psychology and Social Science Division of the Office of the Secretary of Defense), and Samuel Stouffer (Harvard). Civilian deputies included Henry Brosin (University of Chicago), Walter Hunter (Brown University), and Frederick Stephan (Princeton), while professional Staff included committee executive director Raymond Bowers (later chief of the Bureau of Social Science Research [BSSR]), and his aides Dwight

Chapman and Henry Odbert. Psychologist Lyle Lanier (New York University) succeeded Bowers as exective director later that year.[22]

The committee did not allocate funds, but it was responsible for oversight of the social science portion of the military budget, recommended projects, and signed off on major research initiatives. The budget, papers, and meeting notes of the group were classified. In 1949, the committee was responsible for oversight of about $7.5 million in social science research funds—by far the largest single source of funding of the day for this field of inquiry.[23]

The Committee on Human Resources was divided into four panels, each of which specialized in a particular aspect of social science. The panel on Human Relations and Morale is of most interest here; it oversaw most U.S. military psychological warfare research and had the most direct impact on funding for communication studies. Other panels were Psychophysiology (studying primarily human engineering of high-technology weapons, motor skill development, etc.), Personnel and Training (developing psychological testing of recruits, examining the sociology of leadership and groups, etc.), and Manpower (research into the personnel requirements and mobilization of the armed forces).[24]

The composition of the panel on Human Relations and Morale illustrates the continuing pattern of tight, inbred relationships in psychological warfare matters among a handful of academic specialists in communication and the military establishment. It also raises a distinct possibility of conflict of interest among the scholars responsible for oversight of government programs, because the U.S. government was dependent on expert advice on communication research from scholars who were themselves among the primary beneficiaries of the programs they were overseeing. The Human Relations panel chair was psychologist Charles Dollard, who was president of the Carnegie Corporation, trustee of the RAND Corporation, and a veteran of Stouffer's World War II Research Branch team. Panel members included Hans Speier (who by then was based at the RAND Corporation, where he eventually became director of social science research.[25] Alexander Leighton (of Cornell and later Harvard, whose work during the late 1940s depended largely on the records of the U.S. Strategic Bombing Survey in Japan,[26] and Carl Hovland (of Yale, whose most influential work, *Experiments in Mass Communications* [1949], required exclusive access to the wartime records of Stouffer's Research Branch of the army).[27]

A list of the panel's paid consultants reads like a who's who of mainstream U.S. communication studies of the period. According to a December 1948 report in the *American Psychologist,* "special consultants for expert advice"[28] included Harry Alpert (of Yale and BASR), Kingsley Davis (newly appointed director of BASR, whose role in obtaining government contracts to rescue BASR was discussed earlier), John Gardner (Carnegie Corporation and later secretary of health, education and welfare during the Johnson administration), Harold Lasswell (Yale), Rensis Likert (director of the Institute for Social Research), and Elmo Wilson (of International Research Associates, a major contractor of U.S. government overseas public opinion research).[29]

The roles of panel chair Charles Dollard and consultant John Gardner reveal the complexity of the web of financial and personal relationships among selected communication scholars and the federal government. Dollard was the president of the Carnegie Corporation; Gardner was a senior Carnegie executive. Both were personally involved in the funding and oversight of the ostensibly private *American Soldier* studies by Samuel Stouffer, Carl Hovland, Leonard Cottrell, and others, and in the sponsorship of the Russian Research Project at Harvard, which was a joint Carnegie–U.S. Air Force–CIA enterprise that employed Raymond Bauer, Alex Inkeles, and others in communication studies focusing on the Soviet Union.[30] (The Harvard project was the contractor for the ISR and BASR consultancies on studies of Soviet refugees discussed a moment ago.)

Thus Carnegie's Dollard was chairing and Carnegie's Gardner was advising the Department of Defense's primary committee on the scientific aspects of psychological warfare at a time when two of Carnegie's most important projects were dependent upon Department of Defense cooperation for funding, for exclusive access to data, and for research subjects. At least two of the senior academics on the same committee (Stouffer and Hovland) meanwhile depended in some degree on Dollard and Gardner's goodwill and money for their privileged position in the world of scholarship, for it was the Carnegie executives who controlled the purse strings of the funds on which Stouffer and Hovland relied.

At a minimum, this establishes that the social science programs at Carnegie and the Department of Defense were not conducted in isolation from one another. The substantial overlap of key personnel, funding priorities, and data sources strongly suggests that the two programs were in reality coordinated and complementary to one another, at least insofar as the two organizations shared similar conceptions concerning the role of the social sciences in national security research. Between them, the Carnegie Corporation and the overlapping government oversight committee exercised control (or substantial influence) over the large majority of both public and private funds for academic mass communication studies in the United States during the late 1940s and early 1950s, particularly over funding for the large, higher-profile projects that often make or break academic careers in the United States.

This informal network of scholars and managers was quite conscious of its role as an economic and political power broker within the academic community. Carnegie's John Gardner discussed this in a 1987 interview with Charles O'Connell, who was studying the origins of Harvard's Russian Research Center. Asked about the sociometry of post–World War II social science, Gardner replied that he was involved in at least four important "networks" that interacted in making decisions concerning major social science initiatives.

> First of all, there was what I would call the behavior science network. It was [Charles] Dollard and [Clyde] Kluckhohn and [Pendleton] Herring and myself and Sam Stouffer and John Dollard [brother of Charles] at Yale and Alex Leighton . . . who were deeply interested in the behavior sciences and what they might do to illuminate some of the issues that we were all interested in. . . . The second network would be kind of a Harvard network which would certainly be [James B.] Conant and [Devereux] Josephs [treasurer of the Council on Foreign Relations]. . . . A third network is kind of an international affairs network that grew out of the war. . . . [A]ll of us folks came back [from the war] deeply committed to think about international affairs and we met in various forums, worked together, Ford, Rockefeller, ourselves, State Department. . . . [31]

The fourth network, Gardner continued, was built around Stouffer's Research Branch in the army and included Charles Dollard, Frank Keppel, Frederick Osborn (Stouffer's military superior during the war and an active Carnegie trustee), and, of course, Stouffer himself.

Building on that point for a moment, it is useful to look briefly at two other other important sources of social science funding during the cold war years, the Rockefeller Foundation and the Russell Sage Foundation. At the Rockefeller Foundation, social science funding was headed for most of the 1950s by Leland DeVinney, Stouffer's coauthor in the *American Soldier* series.[32] During his service, the Rockefeller organization appears to have been used as a public front to conceal the source of at least $1 million in CIA funds for Hadley Cantril's Institute for International Social Research, for reasons discussed in more detail in a later chapter.[33] Nelson Rockefeller was himself among the most prominent promoters of psychological operations, serving as Eisenhower's principal adviser and strategist on the subject during 1954–55.[34]

At Russell Sage, Leonard Cottrell served as the chief social psychologist from 1951 to 1967; he was frequently a public spokesman for the group and enjoyed substantial influence in the Sage Foundation's decision making.[35] Cottrell simultaneously became chairman of the Defense Department's advisory group on psychological and unconventional warfare (1952–53), member of the scientific advisory panel of the U.S. Air Force (1954–58) and of the U.S. Army scientific advisory panel (1956–58), and a longtime director of the Social Science Research Council.[36] Cottrell was among the most enthusiastic boosters within the social science community for psychological warfare operations, repeatedly calling for "a new club [among social scientists] dedicated to the task of bringing the full capability of our disciplines to bear on this field."[37]

Taken as a whole, the evidence thus far shows that a very substantial fraction of the funding for academic U.S. research into social psychology and into many aspects of mass communication behavior during the first fifteen years of the cold war was directly controlled or strongly influenced by a small group of men who had enthusiastically supported elite psychological operations as an instrument of foreign and domestic policy since World War II. They exercised power through a series of interlocking committees and commissions that linked the world of mainstream academia with that of the U.S. military and intelligence communities. Their networks were for the most part closed to outsiders; their records and decision-making processes were often classified; and in some instances the very existence of the coordinating bodies was a state secret.[38]

This was not a "conspiracy," in the hackneyed sense of that word. It was rather precisely the type of "reference group" or informal network that is so well known to sociologists. The informal authority exercised by these networks reveals a distinctly centrist ideological bent: Projects that advanced their conception of scientific progress and national security enjoyed a chance to gain the financial support that is often a prerequisite to academic success. As is discussed more fully in later chapters, projects that did not meet these criteria were often relegated to obscurity, and in some cases actively suppressed. One result of this selective financing has been a detailed elaboration of those aspects of scientific truth that tend to support the preconceptions of the agencies that were paying the bill.

That the funding agencies and interlocking committees described here helped underwrite the articulation of a particular paradigm of mass communication studies of the period is self-evident; the elaboration of paradigms is after all what research *is*. The more important question is how great a contribution the government's psychological warfare projects made to the construction of the Zeitgeist of U.S. communication studies. Clearly, other forces also made contributions, particularly the commercially oriented projects stressed by Merton and Lazarsfeld and the academic developments discussed by Delia and others.[39]

The precise weight to be given to each of these factors in the evolution of communication research will no doubt continue to be debated, because the surviving data are simply too sketchy to permit final answers. Nevertheless, it is clear that the government's national security agencies underwrote the economic survival of key communication research centers, funded large-scale research projects, and sustained networks of sympathetic scholars who enjoyed decision-making power over the substantial majority of research funds for the field. The impact of these elements on the "received knowledge" of the field of communication research is explored in the next chapter.

As will become apparent, the "dominant paradigm" of the period proved to be in substantial part a *paradigm of dominance,* in which the appropriateness and inevitability of elite control of communication was taken as a given. As a practical matter, the key academic journals of the day demonstrated only a secondary interest in what communication "is." Instead, they concentrated on how modern technology could be used by elites to manage social change, extract political concessions, or win purchasing decisions from targeted audiences. Their studies emphasized those aspects of communication that were of greatest practical interest to the public and private agencies that were underwriting most of the research. This orientation reduced the extraordinarily complex, inherently communal social process of communication to simple models based on the dynamics of transmission of persuasive—and, in the final analysis, coercive—messages.

6

"Barrack and Trench Mates"

The threefold pattern of academic participation in psychological operations discussed earlier reached a new peak during the Korean War. Prior to 1950, much of the discussion of psychological warfare in academic journals had concerned World War II experiences or had focused on what should be done to implement a "psychological" strategy in the emerging cold war. From 1950 on, however, reports began to focus on ongoing psychological operations and on new, military-financed research into the effects of communication.

Many of the Korean War–era studies were presented by men who would come to be remembered as among the most prominent mass communication researchers of the day. In the end, it is they who wrote the textbooks, enjoyed substantial government and private contracts, served on the editorial boards of the key journals, and became the deans and emeritus professors of the most influential schools of journalism and mass communication in the United States. What can be seen here is the process of construction of social networks whose specialty became production of what was claimed to be "knowledge" about a particular topic—in this case, "knowledge" about communication.

Shortly after the opening of the Korean War in 1950, the air force sent Wilbur Schramm, John W. Riley, and Frederick Williams to Korea to interview anticommunist refugees and to study U.S. psychological operations. They prepared a classified study for the Air Force, a declassified, academic version for publication in *POQ,* and a mass market booklet titled *The Reds Take a City.*[1] The popular *Reds* text provided war and atrocity stories tailored to support the United Nations police action in Korea. It was eventually translated into several Asian and European languages at U.S. government expense, and it became a mainstay of "authoritative" accounts of the Korean conflict.

Meanwhile, summaries and interim reports concerning BASR's research in the Middle East for the Voice of America appeared in *POQ* on at least six occasions, one of which was a glowing review of Daniel Lerner's book on the project, which was published in a *POQ* issue edited by Lerner himself.[2] Methodological reports drawn from U.S. Air Force, Army, and Navy research projects proliferated in the academic literature in the wake of the Korean conflict,[3] as did studies of Eastern European and Soviet communications behavior, at least one of which was almost certainly produced under contract with the CIA.[4]

The field of overt or "white" propaganda had evolved prior to Korea in somewhat the same way as had "black" propaganda and clandestine operations. Congress passed the Smith-Mundt Act authorizing a permanent U.S. Office of International Information (OII) less than three months after the National Security Council adopted NSC 4 and NSC 4-A in late 1947. This office evolved into the agency known today as the U.S. Information Agency (USIA) and its overseas arm, the U.S. Information Service (USIS). The Voice of America (VOA) was folded into this operation and its budget was sharply increased in the wake of the late 1940s crises in Czechoslovakia, Berlin, and China.[5]

At first, journalists and public relations executives seem to have enjoyed more influence than social scientists in U.S. overt propaganda operations. Doctrinal statements issued by the OII and the early USIA reflect the working theories of journalists and "commonsense" theories of lay observers (to use Denis McQuail's media theory terminology,)[6] rather than social science theories. They made only a vague distinction between elite and mass audiences for most U.S. propaganda, for example, although even the earliest academic exchange programs attempted to focus on foreign elites and young professionals likely to become members of elites. True, U.S. radio broadcasting to western Europe became fairly sophisticated, with audience research in the region contracted out to private survey specialists employing native interviewers. (The government used private cover for these surveys, it said, because acknowledgment of the U.S. sponsorship of the survey was seen as likely to influence respondents.) The costly and politically sensitive broadcasting to "closed" societies in eastern Europe and Communist China, on the other hand, was done on a wing and a prayer, with very little real knowledge of the extent to which U.S. radio signals were penetrating local jamming and no hard information at all as to how many people might be listening to the signals that did get through.[7] U.S. intelligence and propaganda agencies knew very little of the effects of the U.S. program. Was it winning friends for the United States? Was harsher rhetoric effective—or should it be avoided? Did "information" programs really make any difference?

The government sought out social scientists who had cooperated during World War II to answer these questions in the wake of political attacks on the Voice of America and the U.S. information program by Senator Joseph McCarthy and his allies. The renewed relationship between the federal agencies and these scholars soon became symbiotic. Many social scientists regarded mass communication research as a promising, but seriously underfunded field, and they competed eagerly to land the new contracts. The government rewarded those who appeared to be most reliable and best able to make contributions to its ongoing propaganda, intelligence, and military training programs. As will be seen, one practical result of the competition for contracts was that much of the pressure for ideological conformity was not imposed from without but came from *within* the social science community.

"The Push-Button Millennium"

First, should communication studies undertaken for "white" propaganda outlets such as the Voice of America or the U.S. Information Agency properly be considered participation in U.S. psychological warfare? Study of *Public Opinion Quarterly,* the *American Journal of Sociology,* and other leading academic journals of the period shows clearly that many academic authors considered their work to be a form of psychological warfare and undertook their projects with that end in mind, particularly during the Korean War.

In the summer of 1951, for example, the annual meeting of the American Association for Public Opinion Research (AAPOR) offered three major sessions focusing on psychological warfare that featured most of the prominent communication researchers of the era. In each session, the reported consensus of opinion was that U.S. international communication research could be best understood as a contribution to U.S. psychological operations. The Monday, June 25, session was chaired by W. Phillips Davison and titled "The Contributions of Public Opinion Research to Psychological Warfare." Featured speakers included Elmo Wilson (of International Public Opinion Research), Leo Lowenthal (research director at the Voice of America), Daniel Lerner (Stanford University), and Joseph Stycos (BASR specialist in developing areas). Davison represented the RAND Corporation, which in those years was entirely dependent on U.S. Air Force and CIA contracts. The overall tone of the session was perhaps best captured by the ancedote Davison used when introducing Wilson, who had recently completed an ostensibly private, whirlwind public opinion study of five West European countries. The central question of Wilson's surveys, " 'Who is on our [i.e., the U.S. government's] side?' was measured in terms of the willingness of people to do something about their feelings," Davison said. But Wilson's studies had been so demanding that the "Soviet agents tailing him had to be replaced for nervous exhaustion."[8]

Lowenthal's presentation summed up the Voice of America's vision for communication studies with a bit of fancy: The Voice was seeking the "ultimate miracle," namely, "the push-button millennium in the use of opinion research in psychological warfare. On that distant day," Lowenthal continued, "the warrior would tell the research technician the elements of content, audience, medium and effect desired. The researcher would simply work out the mathematics and solve the algebraic formula" and the war would be won.[9] In the later, published version of that paper (which Lowenthal coauthored with Joseph Klapper, who was then also at the VOA), Lowenthal termed the VOA's international broadcasting "one type of psychological warfare" and said that communication studies and public opinion surveys were "barrack and trench mates in the present campaigns."[10]

Joseph Stycos, who was at that time chief of the BASR project for the Voice of America in the Middle East, cited psychological warfare as the central rationale for the VOA project. He presented his survey of nomadic populations as primarily "important for the long-term study of psychological warfare"—not as scientifically valuable in its own right, or even as useful for facilitating "communication" in the sense of a two-way exchange of ideas between the nomads and the U.S. government.[11]

These sentiments were by no means confined to the Voice of America. A second AAPOR session, chaired by John MacMillan of the Office of Naval Research, focused on "Opinion and Communications Research in National Defense.'' The U.S. Air Force's presentation stressed several key areas of air force psychological interest, including "measurement of the 'Panic Potential' of a public, effectiveness of leaflet dropping as a means of communication, and the whole problem of psychological warfare.''[12] Meanwhile, the AAPOR Presidential Session, chaired by Paul Lazarsfeld, featured as its keynote speaker Foy Kohler, chief of the International Broadcasting Division at the State Department. Kohler's theme was "the role of public opinion in . . . the on-going world struggle for power between the United States and the Soviet Union.''[13]

A special *POQ* issue on International Communications Research published in winter 1952 marked a new high point in the integration of psychological warfare projects into academic communication studies. Guest-edited by Leo Lowenthal, who was at that time research director of the Voice of America, the special issue was the first formal compilation of state-of-the-art research and theory on international communication of the cold war. The project deserves special mention because it demonstrates the close interaction between "private" communication scholars and the government's psychological warfare campaigns, as well as some aspects of a system of euphemistic language that served as a cover for that relationship.

Leo Lowenthal's work on the *POQ* project and at the Voice of America exemplifies the complex, often contradictory pressures that whipsawed intellectuals and scientists during the early cold war years. Lowenthal—a Jewish refugee from Nazi Germany, a self-described Marxist working for the U.S. government during a decidedly anticommunist era of U.S. history, and a culturally oriented critic of communication theory in the heyday of functionalism—was nothing if not a survivor and an iconoclast.[14] Nevertheless, the trajectory of Lowenthal's published ideas and of his career during the late 1940s and 1950s parallels—with one important exception to be discussed in a moment—those of a number of well known anticommunist liberals such as James Burnham, Jay Lovestone, Sidney Hook, and Max Eastman, all of whom spent years as Marxist theoreticians and activists prior to taking up cudgels against Stalin's government. The widespread disillusionment with the "God that failed"[15] as a hugely popular text of the period put it was driven along by a sense of betrayal generated by the Hitler-Stalin pact of 1939, the increasingly obvious brutality and antisemitism of Stalin's regime, the stultifying intellectual life inside many communist political organizations, and, not least, a highly effective propaganda campaign in the West tailored to discredit and undermine support for revolution among intellectuals and labor leaders.[16]

By the late 1940s a number of the more important advisers to CIA and State Department psychological warfare campaigns had trained as Marxists at one point or another during their careers, and were now applying dialectics and other Marxian insights to the task of psychological warfare against the Soviet Union, China, and Third World nationalism. So too with Leo Lowenthal, whose principal critical writings and editorial work for *Public Opinion Quarterly* and other academic journals of the early 1950s are unambiguously dedicated to applying critical (Marxist or post-Marxist) insights to the task of improving U.S. international propaganda.[17]

Lowenthal's modern recollections concerning his VOA years still reflect the ambivalence of many intellectuals of his day. "I'm not interested in posing as an ardent critic of American foreign policy," Lowenthal commented years later during an interview concerning his government work.[18]

> I looked at it from the vantage point of my specific function [at VOA]; after all, I was only the director of a certain department within the American propaganda apparatus that didn't make political decisions itself. ... The governmental activity didn't compromise either [Herbert] Marcuse [who had worked in German propaganda analysis for the OSS during World War II] or me. ... I'd have to say that neither during the war, when I worked for the Office of War Information, nor in the postwar period [at VOA] did I ever have the feeling that I was working for an imperialist power. ... After all, there were two superpowers opposing each other, and it's difficult to make out just who—the United States or the Soviet Union—engaged in the more imperialistic politics right after the war.

As things turned out, Lowenthal was *not* like Burnham, Lovestone et al., in that he refused to become a professional anticommunist activist as the cold war deepened. He preferred instead to enter academe as a professor at Stanford and the University of California after being bounced out of his government job by the new Republican administration in 1952.[19] In the end, Lowenthal may have succeeded during later years where many other academics have failed: He managed to adapt Marxist, functionalist, symbolic interactionism and other often mutually hostile intellectual traditions to one another, and he lived long enough to become something of a grand old man in the social sciences.[20] But Lowenthal's work in psychological warfare at the Voice of America was not an anomaly, in the final analysis; it was instead consistent in most respects with that of other reform-minded communication research scientists. Lowenthal's experience at VOA points up the ambiguity and paradoxical character of the U.S. intelligentsia's response to U.S. psychological warfare, and the extent to which otherwise iconoclastic scholars felt compelled to take sides in the superpower confrontations of the early cold war.

Lowenthal's 1952 *Public Opinion Quarterly* text on international communication research provided a vehicle for articles that had in fact been prepared under government contract—though not publicly acknowledged as such—to be propagated within the sociological and social-psychological communities as advanced thinking on the subject of international communication. One example is Charles Glock's "The Comparative Study of Communications and Opinion Formation,"[21] a relatively detailed presentation on the concept of a national communication system, its relationship to mass audiences and opinion leaders in any given country, and an outline of methods for study of such systems. Lowenthal presented Glock's work to *POQ* readers as simply a product of the Bureau of Applied Social Research, without further reference to the social and political context in which Glock's concept had emerged. However, the recently opened archives of the Bureau of Social Science Research indicate that Glock's work had in fact been underwritten by the Department of State as part of a joint BASR-BSSR project to improve techniques of manipulating public opinion in Italy and the Near East, both of which were major targets of U.S. psychological operations of the day.[22]

Political considerations clearly shaped Glock's research agenda. "We would like to know to what extent the nationalistic awakening among former colonial peoples in the East has led to a general distrust of anything which comes from the 'imperialist' West," Glock stressed. "In Egypt, there is some evidence that among intellectuals, news from America is viewed somewhat ambivalently. . . . What needs to be studied, then, in the area of opinion formation is the different ways in which information about the world is absorbed . . . under varying social, political and economic systems."[23]

Whatever the scientific merit of Glock's analysis, it is evident that his project was applied political research designed to support a particular aim, namely, the advancement among the populations of Italy and the Near East of the U.S. government's conceptions of its national interest. The adoption of Glock's insights by other mass communication scientists of the period was also carried out within the same ideological framework. Glock's work did not become, as some might have it, simply a neutral scientific advance that would be taken up by others without the political baggage that had been imposed by its original sponsors. Instead, as a practical matter, virtually all U.S. research into "national communication systems" during the decade that followed Glock was underwritten by the Department of State and the U.S. Army as a means of achieving the same political and ideological ends that had motivated the initial sponsorship of Glock's project. The BSSR archives make that point clearly: Glock's writings provided the foundation for a successful 1953 contract bid by the BSSR to develop further studies along the same line for Lowenthal's office at the Department of State,[24] for a series of studies concerning the "national communications systems" of the Eastern European satellite countries[25] and of the Philippines[26] and, later, for similar studies on behalf of the U.S. Army concerning communication systems in the Asian republics of the Soviet Union.[27]

Several other articles in the same special issue of *POQ* have similar characteristics. Benjamin Ringer and David Sills' "Political Extremists in Iran: A Secondary Analysis of Communications Data" presented itself as simply a BASR study of opinion data concerning an unstable Middle Eastern country. In reality, it was a product of a State Department–sponsored study of political trends in a country that was at that moment in the midst of a CIA-sponsored coup d'état to remove the nationalist government of Mohammed Mossadegh, whose supporters made up many of the purported "political extremists" of the article's title.[28] Roughly similar attributes can be found in the special issue's reporting on Soviet communications behavior[29] and communist radio broadcasting to Italy[30] and in a methodological discussion of the value of interviews with refugees from Eastern Europe as a barometer of the effectiveness of U.S. propaganda.[31]

Daniel Lerner provided ideological guidance for readers of the special issue. Lerner's contention, which was presented at length and without reply from opposing views, was that scholars who failed to embrace U.S. foreign policy initiatives "represent a total loss to the Free World." As Lerner saw it—and presumably as the editors saw it as well, for they endorsed Lerner's stand—campaigns against purportedly "neutralist'' sentiments such as "peace, safety [and] relaxation [of tensions]" were the "responsibility of everyone able and willing to improve the coverage, depth and relevance of communications research."[32]

The "private" context created by publication in *POQ* also helped advance the system of euphemism that insulated scholars from the actual uses to which their work was put. Lowenthal's work provides an example. In the summer of 1952, Lowenthal wrote frankly in *Public Opinion Quarterly* that "research in the field of psychological warfare" was a major aspect of the Voice of America work he was supervising.[33] But less than six months later, the special issue he edited dedicated to "International Communications Research" contains no explicit articles on psychological warfare qua psychological warfare at all[34]—a fact that was illustrated in *POQ*'s index for 1952, which listed only two published articles on "propaganda" and none at all on "psychological warfare."

This insulation proved effective. Four of the major articles from the Lowenthal issue, including Glock's, were recycled for university audiences for the next twenty years in Wilbur Schramm's college text *The Process and Effects of Mass Communication,* which is widely regarded as a founding text of graduate mass communication studies in the United States.[35] This work challenged the popular preconception that media audiences behave as an undifferentiated mass, which is also sometimes known as the "magic bullet" approach to propaganda. Schramm went on to present theories and research results tailored to exploit what was then known of audience behavior—the "opinion leader" phenomenon, the tendency to create "reference groups," and so on—as tactical elements in designing more successful campaigns to manipulate groups of people.

Schramm portrayed the reports as "communication research" rather than as, say, "psychological warfare studies." Either description is accurate; the distinction between the two is that the former term tends to downplay the social context that gave birth to the work in the first place. Similarly, Schramm presented the source of these texts as being *Public Opinion Quarterly,* not government contracts, thus adding a gloss of academic recognition to the articles and further confounding an average reader's ability to accurately interpret the context in which the original work was performed.[36] Given this tacit deceit, the audience's favored interpretation of the Schramm presentation is not likely to have been that Doctor Glock chose to make his living by offering advice on a particular type of communication behavior (international political propaganda), because that information had been stripped from the text that the audience saw. What the audience saw, rather, was an implicit claim, backed up by *Public Opinion Quarterly* credits, that the apparent consensus of scientific opinion is that international communication studies are largely an elaboration of methods for imposing one's national will abroad.

The work of the Bureau of Social Science Research illustrates the interwoven relationship between federal programs and U.S. mass communication studies beginning during the Korean War and continuing throughout the 1950s. The BSSR was established at American University in 1950, and much of its archives are today held at American University and by the University of Maryland Libraries at College Park. During the 1950s BSSR employed prominent social scientists such as Robert Bower, Kurt Back, Albert Biderman, Elisabeth Crawford, Ray Fink, Louis Gottschalk, and Ivor Wayne.[37]

The BSSR contract data that have survived show that the U.S. Air Force funded BSSR studies on "targets and vulnerabilities in psychological warfare" of people in Eastern Europe and Soviet Kazakhstan; a project "directed toward understanding of various social, political and psychological aspects of violence . . . as it bears on control and exploitation of military power"; a report on "captivity behavior" and psychological collapse among prisoners of war; and a series of studies on the relative usefulness of drugs, electroshock, violence, and other coercive techniques during interrogation of prisoners.[38] The Human Ecology Fund, which was later revealed to have been a conduit for CIA monies, underwrote BSSR's studies of Africa and of prisoner interrogation methods.[39] BSSR meanwhile enjoyed USIA contracts for training the South Vietnamese government in the collection of statistically sound data on its population, training USIA personnel in mass communication research techniques, collecting of intelligence on USIA audiences abroad, and performing a variety of data analysis functions.[40] These contracts certainly contributed 50 percent, and perhaps as much as 85 percent, of BSSR's budget during the 1950s.[41]

Beginning at least as early as 1951, the USIA hired BSSR (along with BASR and others) for a high-priority program to inculcate a state-of-the-art understanding of communication dynamics into the USIA's overseas propaganda programs. The surviving archival record shows that the BSSR succeeded on at least three counts: it introduced modern audience survey methods,[42] introduced the concept of "opinion leaders" and the distinction between "elite" and "mass" audiences for propaganda and psychological operations,[43] and introduced the concept of a "national communication system" (as that phrase was used by Paul Lazarsfeld and Charles Glock)[44] as a target for penetration by U.S. government propaganda.[45]

The BSSR studies for the State Department establish that, contrary to common wisdom, the widely recognized "personal influence" or "two-step" model of communication dynamics had become the backbone of USIA mass communication research at least four years before the publication of Elihu Katz and Paul Lazarsfeld's watershed text on the topic, *Personal Influence* (1955).[46] As early as 1951, Stanley Bigman of Lazarsfeld's Bureau of Applied Social Research prepared a confidential manual on survey research entitled *Are We Hitting the Target?* for the U.S. International Information and Educational Exchange Program (USIE), the immediate predecessor of the USIA.[47] (The BASR was at that time testing some aspects of "personal influence" models of communication behavior in a major project in the Middle East sponsored by the Voice of America).[48] Shortly after completing the manual, Bigman transferred to BSSR, where he continued the *Target* project and undertook a follow-on contract in 1953 for study of public opinion and communication behavior in the Philippines.[49] The *Target* manual stressed a number of concepts that were at the cutting edge of communication studies of the day, describing methods for using surveys to track the impact of "personal influence" networks on popular attitudes, tips on identifying local "opinion leaders" suitable for special cultivation, relatively sophisticated questionnaire design techniques, methods of compensating for interviewer bias, and similar state-of-the-art techniques that were well ahead of most academic opinion studies of the day.[49] Bigman's project taught the USIA how to use native Filipino interviewers to identify local opinion leaders; obtain detailed data on respondents' sources of information on the United States; compile statistics on local attitudes toward democracy, nationalism, communism, and U.S.–Philippines relations; and secure feedback on the effectiveness of particular USIA propaganda efforts in the Philippines.

Bigman's modest 1951 manual illustrates that the evolution of the "personal influence" concept was more complex and considerably more dependent upon government sponsorship than is generally recognized today. The most common version of this concept's evolution traces it exclusively to New York State voting studies between 1945 and 1948 by Lazarsfeld, Berelson, and McPhee, then abruptly jumps forward to the publication of the New York data in *Voting* (1954)[50] and more fully in *Personal Influence* (1955).[51] In reality, however, BSSR and BASR work in propaganda and covert warfare in the Philippines and the Middle East accounts for most of the six years of development between the germination of the personal influence concept and its publication in book form.

The BSSR's Philippines project of the early 1950s also demonstrated the ease with which ostensibly pluralistic, democratic conceptions of communication behavior and communication studies could be put to use in U.S.-sponsored counterinsurgency campaigns and in the management of authoritarian client regimes. Paul Linebarger, a leading U.S. psychological warfare expert specializing in Southeast Asia, bragged that the CIA had "invented" the Philippines' president Raymon Magsaysay and installed him in office.[52] Once there, "the CIA wrote [Magsaysay's] speeches, carefully guided his foreign policy and used its press assets (paid editors and journalists) to provide him with a constant claque of support," according to historian and CIA critic William Blum.[53]

The CIA's idea at the time was to transform the Philippines into a "showplace of democracy" in Asia, recalled CIA operative Joseph B. Smith, who was active in the campaign.[54] In reality, though, Magsaysay's U.S.-financed counterinsurgency war against the Huk guerrillas became a bloody proving ground for a series of psychological warfare techniques developed by the CIA's Edward Landsdale, not least of which was the exploitation of the USIA's intelligence on Filipino culture and native superstitions. Tactics (and rhetoric) such as "search-and-destroy" and "pacification" that were later to become familiar during the failed U.S. invasion of Vietnam were first elaborated under Landsdale's tutelage in the Philippines.[55]

The relationship between the USIA and the CIA in the Philippines can be best understood as a division of labor. The two groups are separate agencies, and the USIA insists that it does not provide cover to the CIA's officers abroad.[56] But intelligence gathered by the USIA, such as that obtained through Bigman's surveys of Filipino "opinion leaders," is regularly provided to the CIA, according to a report by the House Committee on Foreign Affairs.[57] USIA and CIA work was first coordinated through "country plans" monitored by area specialists at

President Truman's secretive Psychological Strategy Board (established in 1951) and, later, at the National Security Council under President Eisenhower.[58] By the time the Philippines project was in high gear during the mid-1950s, Eisenhower had placed policy oversight of combined CIA-USIA-U.S. military country plans in the hands of senior aides with direct presidential access—C. D. Jackson and later Nelson Rockefeller—who personally monitored developments and formulated strategy.[59]

At the time, the implicit claim of BSSR's work for the government was that application of "scientific" psychological warfare and counterinsurgency techniques in the Philippines would lead to more democracy and less violence overall than had, say, the crude massacres of 1898–1902, when a U.S. expeditionary force suppressed an earlier rebellion by Philippine nationalist leader Emilio Aguinaldo.

But looking back today, there is little evidence that such claims ever were true. More than forty years has passed since BSSR and the USIA's work in the Philippines began. The Huks were defeated; a relatively stable, pro-Western government was established in the country; and a handful of Filipinos have prospered. Yet by almost every indicator— infant mortality, life expectancy, nutrition, land ownership, education, venereal disease rates, even the right to publish or to vote—life for the substantial majority of Filipinos has remained static or gotten worse over those four decades.

BSSR's academics did not set U.S. policy in the Philippines, of course. But they did provide U.S. military and intelligence agencies with detailed knowledge of the social structure, psychology, and mood of the Philippines population, upon which modern antiguerrilla tactics depend. Despite its claims, U.S. psychological warfare campaigns in the Philippines and throughout the developing world have generally *increased* the prevailing levels of violence and misery, not reduced them.

Military Sponsorship of "Diffusion" Research

While the USIA and Voice of America's psychological warfare projects were usually more or less overt and the CIA's covert, those of the U.S. armed services generally fell somewhere between the extremes. The military agencies underwrote several of the best known and most influential communication research projects performed during the 1950s, though their contribution was not always publicly acknowledged at the time.

A telling example of this can be found in Project Revere, a series of costly, U.S. Air Force–financed message diffusion studies conducted by Stuart Dodd, Melvin DeFleur, and other sociologists at the University of Washington. Lowery and DeFleur's later textbook history of communication studies calls Revere one of several major "milestones" in the emerging field.[60] Briefly, Project Revere scientists dropped millions of leaflets containing civil defense propaganda or commercial advertising from U.S. Air Force planes over selected cities and towns in Washington state, Idaho, Montana, Utah, and Alabama. They then surveyed the target populations to create a relatively detailed record of the diffusion of the sample message among residents. The air force sponsorship of the program was regarded as classified at the time and was not acknowledged in Dodd's early report on the project in *Public Opinion Quarterly*.[61] Later accounts by Dodd, DeFleur, and others were more frank, however.[62] The air force invested about a "third of a million 1950s dollars" in the effort, Lowery and DeFleur later pointed out,[63] making it one of the largest single investments in communication studies from the end of World War II through the mid-1950s.

Project Revere embodied the complex dilemmas and compromises inherent in the psychological warfare studies of the era. For Dodd and his colleagues, the money represented "an almost unprecedented opportunity" for "research into basic problems of communications."[64] The catch, however, was that the studies had to focus on air-dropped leaflets as a means of communication. This medium was an important part of U.S. Air Force propaganda efforts in the Korean conflict, in CIA propaganda in Eastern Europe, and in U.S. nuclear war–fighting strategy during the 1950s, but it had no substantial "civilian" application whatever.[65]

Dodd and his team contended that the leaflets could be employed as an experimental stimulus to study properties of communication that were believed to be common to many media, not leaflets alone. They developed elaborate mathematical models describing the impact of a new stimulus, its spread, then the leveling off of knowledge of the stimulus. They stressed the data that were of most interest to the contracting agency: the optimum leaflet-to-population ratio, effects of repeated leaflet drops on audience recall of a message, effect of variations in timing

Figure 2

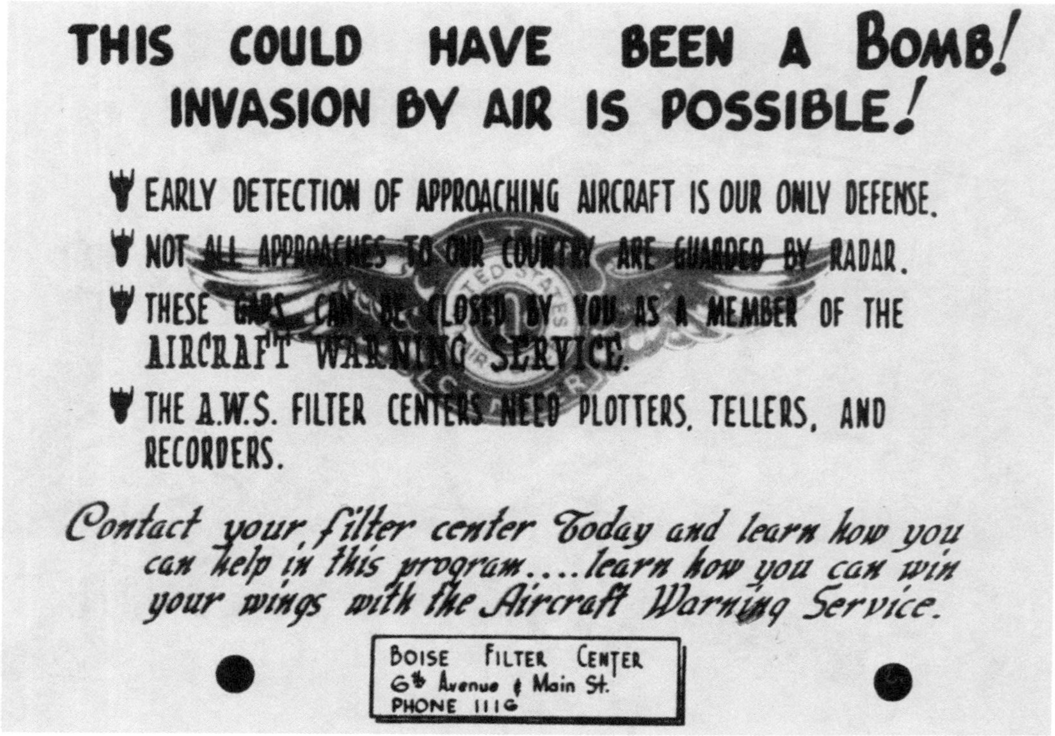

THIS COULD HAVE BEEN A BOMB!
INVASION BY AIR IS POSSIBLE!

♥ EARLY DETECTION OF APPROACHING AIRCRAFT IS OUR ONLY DEFENSE.

♥ NOT ALL APPROACHES TO OUR COUNTRY ARE GUARDED BY RADAR.

♥ THESE GAPS CAN BE CLOSED BY YOU AS A MEMBER OF THE AIRCRAFT WARNING SERVICE.

♥ THE A.W.S. FILTER CENTERS NEED PLOTTERS, TELLERS, AND RECORDERS.

Contact your filter center today and learn how you can help in this program....learn how you can win your wings with the Aircraft Warning Service.

BOISE FILTER CENTER
6th Avenue & Main St.
PHONE 1116

Figure 3

78

of drops, and so on. Perhaps the most important lesson of general applicability derived from the project, according to De Fleur, was that diffusion of any given message from person to person—which is to say, through the second step of "two-step" social networks—necessarily involves great distortion of even very simple messages.[66]

The project generated dozens of articles for scholarly journals, books, and theses. De Fleur, Otto Larsen, Ørjar Øyen, John G. Shaw, Richard Hill, and William Catton based dissertations on Revere data.[67] In 1958, *Public Opinion Quarterly* published a chart Dodd had prepared of what he termed "Revere-connected papers" (see Appendix). A glance at the titles and journals on Dodd's list vividly illustrates the manner in which work performed under classified government contracts entered the mainstream of the mass communication studies and the extent of penetration that it achieved.

Dodd's project was both a study of propaganda and a propaganda project in its own right. The sample messages clearly served to stimulate popular fear of atomic attacks by Soviet bombers at the height of the famous (and contrived) "bomber gap" war scare of the 1950s (see Figure 2). In reality, many of the communities targeted in Dodd's study were at that time inaccessible to American commercial airliners, much less Soviet bombers. Most historians today agree that the U.S. Air Force manufactured the purported bomber gap to shore up its position in internal Eisenhower administration debates over strategic nuclear policy.[68]

No opposition among Dodd's team of academics to the actual or potential applications of their studies has come to light thus far. It is worth noting, however, that the CIA abruptly canceled its European air-dropped leaflet program in 1956 following a fatal crash by a Czech civilian airliner whose controls became entangled in a flight of the balloons used to carry the leaflets into Czech airspace. The U.S. government publicly disclaimed any responsibility for the crash or for the officially nonexistent leaflet propaganda program.[69]

The CIA and the Founding Fathers of Communication Studies

Turning to a consideration of CIA-sponsored psychological warfare studies, one finds a wealth of evidence showing that projects secretly funded by the CIA played a prominent role in U.S. mass communication studies during the middle and late 1950s. The secrecy that surrounds any CIA operation makes complete documentation impossible, but the fragmentary information that is now available permits identification of several important examples.

The first is the work of Albert Hadley Cantril (better known as Hadley Cantril), a noted "founding father" of modern mass communication studies. Cantril was associate director of the famous Princeton Radio Project from 1937 to 1939, a founder and longtime director of Princeton's Office of Public Opinion Research, and a founder of the Princeton Listening Center, which eventually evolved into the CIA-financed Foreign Broadcast Information Service. Cantril's work at Princeton is widely recognized as "the first time that academic social science took survey research seriously, and it was the first attempt to collect and collate systematically survey findings."[70] Cantril's *The Psychology of Radio,* written with Gordon Allport, is often cited as a seminal study in mass communication theory and research, and his surveys of public opinion in European and Third World countries defined the subfield of international public opinion studies for more than two decades.

Cantril's work during the first decade after World War II focused on elaborating Lippmann's concept of the stereotype—the "pictures in our heads," as Lippmann put it, through which people are said to deal with the world outside their immediate experience. Cantril specialized in international surveys intended to determine how factors such as class, nationalism, and ethnicity affected the stereotypes present in a given population, and how those stereotypes in turn affected national behavior in various countries, particularly toward the United States.[71] Cantril's work, while often revealing the "human face" of disaffected groups, began with the premise that the United States' goals and actions abroad were fundamentally good for the world at large. If U.S. acts were not viewed in that light by foreign audiences, the problem was that they had misunderstood our good intentions, not that Western behavior might be fundamentally flawed.

Cantril's career had been closely bound up with U.S. intelligence and clandestine psychological operations since at least the late 1930s. The Office of Public Opinion Research, for example, enjoyed confidential contracts from the Roosevelt administration for research into U.S. public opinion on the eve of World War II. Cantril went on to serve as the senior public opinion specialist of the Office of the Coordinator of Inter-American Affairs (an early U.S. intelligence agency led by Nelson Rockefeller and focusing on Latin America), of the World War II Office of War Information, and, in a later period, as an adviser to President Eisenhower on the psychological aspects of foreign policy. During the Kennedy administration, Cantril helped reorganize the U.S. Information Agency.[72]

According to the *New York Times,* the CIA provided Cantril and his colleague Lloyd Free with $1 million in 1956 to gather intelligence on popular attitudes in countries of interest to the agency.[73] The Rockefeller Foundation appears to have laundered the money for Cantril, because Cantril repeatedly claimed in print that the monies had come from that source.[74] However, the *Times* and Cantril's longtime partner, Lloyd Free, confirmed after Cantril's death that the true source of the funds had been the CIA.[75]

Cantril's first target was a study of the political potential of "protest" voters in France and Italy, who were regarded as hostile to U.S. foreign policy.[76] That was followed by a 1958 tour of the Soviet Union under private, academic cover, to gather information on the social psychology of the Soviet population and on "mass" relationships with the Soviet elite. Cantril's report on this topic went directly to then president Eisenhower; its thrust was that treating the Soviets firmly, but with greater respect—rather than openly ridiculing them, as had been Secretary of State John Foster Dulles' practice—could help improve East–West relations.[77] Later Cantril missions included studies of Castro's supporters in Cuba and reports on the social psychology of a series of countries that could serve as a checklist of CIA interventions of the period: Brazil, the Dominican Republic, Egypt, India, Nigeria, Philippines, Poland, and others.[78]

An important focus of Cantril's work under the CIA's contract were surveys of U.S. domestic public opinion on foreign policy and domestic political issues—a use of government funds many observers would argue was illegal.[79] There, Cantril introduced an important methodological innovation by breaking out political opinions by respondents' demographic characteristics and their place on a U.S. ideological spectrum he had devised—a forerunner of the political opinion analysis techniques that would revolutionize U.S. election campaigns during the 1980s.[80]

A second—and perhaps more important—example of the CIA's role in U.S. mass communication studies during the 1950s was the work of the Center for International Studies (CENIS) at MIT. The CIA became the principal funder of this institution throughout the 1950s, although neither the CENIS nor the CIA is known to have publicly provided details on their relationship. It has been widely reported, however, that the CIA financed the initial establishment of the CENIS; that the agency underwrote publication of certain CENIS studies in both classified and nonclassified editions; that CENIS served as a conduit for CIA funds for researchers at other institutions, particularly the Center for Russian Research at Harvard; that the director of CENIS, Max Millikan, had served as assistant director of the CIA immediately prior to his assumption of the CENIS post; and that Millikan served as a "consultant to the Central Intelligence Agency," as State Department records put it, during his tenure as director of CENIS.[81] In 1966, CENIS scholar Ithiel de Sola Pool acknowledged that CENIS "has in the past had contracts with the CIA," though he insisted the the CIA severed its links with CENIS following a bitter scandal in the early 1960s.[82]

CENIS emerged as one of the most important centers of communication studies midway through the 1950s, and it maintained that role for the remainder of the decade. According to CENIS's official account, the funding for its communications research was provided by a four-year, $850,000 grant from the Ford Foundation, which was distributed under the guidance of an appointed planning committee made up of Hans Speier (chair), Jerome Bruner, Wallace Carroll, Harold Lasswell, Paul Lazarsfeld, Edward Shils, and Ithiel de Sola Pool (secretary).[83] It is not known whether Ford's funds were in fact CIA monies. The Ford Foundation's archives make clear, however, that the foundation was at that time underwriting the costs of the CIA's principal propaganda project aimed at intellectuals, the Congress for Cultural Freedom, with a grant of $500,000 made at CIA request, and that the Ford Foundation's director, John McCloy (who will be remembered here for his World War II psychological warfare work), had established a regular liaison with the CIA for the specific purpose of managing Ford Foundation cover for CIA projects.[84] Of the men on CENIS's communication studies planning committee, Edward Shils was simultaneously a leading spokesman for the CIA-backed Congress for Cultural Freedom project; Hans Speier was the RAND Corporation's director of social science research; and Wallace Carroll was a journalist specializing in national security issues who had produced a series of classified reports on clandestine warfare against the Soviet Union for U.S. military intelligence agencies.[85] In short, CENIS communication studies were from their inception closely bound up with both overt and covert aspects of U.S. national security strategy of the day.

The CENIS program generated the large majority of articles on psychological warfare published by leading academic journals during the second half of the 1950s. CENIS's dominance in psychological warfare studies during this period was perhaps best illustrated by two special issues of *POQ* published in the spring of 1956 and the fall of 1958. Each was edited by CENIS scholars—by Ithiel de Sola Pool and Frank Bonilla and by Daniel Lerner, respectively—and each was responsible for the preponderance of *POQ* articles concerning psychological warfare published that year. The collective titles for the special issues were "Studies in Political Communications" and "Attitude Research in Modernizing Areas."[86]

CENIS scholars and members of the CENIS planning committee such as Harold Isaacs, Y. B. Damle, Claire Zimmerman, Raymond Bauer, and Suzanne Keller[87] and each of the special issue editors[88] provided most of the content. They drew other articles from studies that CENIS had contracted out to outside academics, such as a content analysis of U.S. and Soviet propaganda publications by Ivor Wayne of BSSR and a study of nationalism among the Egyptian elite by Patricia Kendall of BASR that was based on data gathered during the earlier Voice of America studies in the Mideast.[89]

The purported dangers to the United States of "modernization" or economic development in the Third World emerged as the most important theme of CENIS studies in international communication as the decade of the 1950s drew to a close. Practically without exception, CENIS studies coincided with those issues and geographic areas regarded as problems by U.S. intelligence agencies: "agitators" in Indonesia, student radicals in Chile, "change-prone" individuals in Puerto Rico, and the social impact of economic development in the Middle East.[90] CENIS also studied desegregation of schools in Little Rock, Arkansas, as an example of "modernization."[91]

In these reports, CENIS authors viewed social change in developing countries principally as a management problem for the United States. Daniel Lerner contended that "urbanization, industrialization, secularization [and] communications" were elements of a typology of modernization that could be measured and shaped in order to secure a desirable outcome from the point of view of the U.S. government.

"How can these modernizing societies-in-a-hurry maintain stability?" Lerner asked. "Whence will come the compulsions toward *responsible* formation and expression of opinion on which a free participant society depends?"[92]

In *The Passing of Traditional Society* and other texts, Lerner contended that public " 'participation' [in power] through opinion is spreading *before* genuine political and economic participation" in societies in developing countries[93]—a clear echo of Lippmann's earlier thesis. This created a substantial mass of people who were relatively informed through the mass media, yet who were socially and economically disenfranchised, and thus easily swayed by the appeals of radical nationalists, Communists, and other "extremists." As in Lippmann's analysis, mass communication played an important role in the creation of this explosive situation, as Lerner saw it, and in elite management of it. He proposed a strategy modeled in large part on the campaign in the Philippines that combined "white" and "black" propaganda, economic development aid, and U.S.-trained and financed counterinsurgency operations to manage these problems in a manner that was "responsible" from the point of view of the industrialized world.

This "development theory," which combined propaganda, counterinsurgency warfare, and selective economic development of targeted regions, was rapidly integrated into U.S. psychological warfare practice worldwide as the decade drew to a close. Classified U.S. programs employing "Green Beret" Special Forces troops trained in what was termed "nation building" and counterinsurgency began in the mountainous areas of Cambodia and Laos.[94] Similar projects intended to win the hearts and minds of Vietnam's peasant population through propaganda, creation of "strategic hamlets," and similar forms of controlled social development under the umbrella of U.S. Special Forces troops can also be traced in part to Lerner's work, which was in time elaborated by Wilbur Schramm, Lucian Pye, Ithiel de Sola Pool, and others.[95] Lerner himself became a fixture at Pentagon-sponsored conferences on U.S. psychological warfare in the Third World during the 1960s and 1970s, lecturing widely on the usefulness of social science data for the design of what has since come to be called U.S.-sponsored low-intensity warfare abroad.[96]

The Special Operations Research Office's 1962 volume *The U.S. Army's Limited-War Mission and Social Science Research* and the well-publicized controversy surrounding Project Camelot[97] show that the brutal U.S. counterinsurgency wars of the period grew out of earlier psychological warfare projects, and that their tactics were shaped in important part by the rising school of development theory.[98] Further, the promises integral to that theory—namely, that U.S. efforts to control development in the Third World, if skillfully handled, could benefit the targets of that intervention while simultaneously advancing U.S. interests—were often publicized by the USIA, by the Army's mass media, at various academic conferences, and in other propaganda outlets. In other words, as the government tested in the field the tactics advocated by Lerner, Pool, and others, the rationalizations offered by these same scholars became propaganda themes the government promoted to counter opposition to U.S. intervention abroad.[99]

The important point with regard to CENIS is the continuing, inbred relationship among a handful of leading mass communication scholars and the U.S. military and intelligence community. Substantially the same group of theoreticians who articulated the early cold war version of psychological warfare in the 1950s reappeared in the 1960s to articulate the Vietnam era adaptation of the same concepts. More than a half-dozen noted academics followed this track: Daniel Lerner, Harold Lasswell, Wilbur Schramm, John W. Riley, W. Phillips Davison, Leonard Cottrell, and Ithiel de Sola Pool, among others.[100]

This continuity of leading theoreticians became part of a broader pattern through which the "psychological warfare" of one generation became the "international communication" of the next. By about the mid-1950s, mass communication research was beginning to achieve some measure of scientific "professionalism" as a distinct discipline. Jesse Delia's history of the field captures one aspect of the shift well. Mainstream mass communication scholars'

> shared . . . commitment to pursue scientific understanding of mass communication's practical and policy aspects was transformed by the achieved professionalism of social scientists into pursuits defined within the questions and canons of established social science disciplines. Within many of the disciplines, the accepted canons of professionalism defined theoretical questions as of principal significance and sustained the bracketing of overtly value-centered questions. . . . By the end of the 1950s this attitude was firmly fixed as a core commitment among the majority of communications researchers.[101]

In other words, Delia argues, mass communications research became more "scientific," placed greater stress on theory, and took an increasingly objective view of the "values" (or social impact) of any given piece of applied research.

But Delia's insight should be stood on its head, so to speak, in order to more accurately reflect reality. Prominent mass communication researchers such as Lasswell, Lerner, Schramm, Pool, and Davison never abandoned the "practical and policy aspects of mass communications" (which is to say, psychological warfare and similar applied research projects for government and commercial customers), as Delia would seem to have it. Instead, they absorbed the values and many of the political attitudes of the psychological warfare projects into new, "scientificized" presentations of theory that tended to conceal the ethical and political presumptions of the early 1950s programs under a new coat of "objective" rhetoric.

The professionalization and institutionalization of the discipline brought with it a series of interesting rhetorical shifts that downplayed the relatively blatant convergence of interests between mainstream mass communication research and its funders that had characterized the first decade after 1945. A new rhetoric, one which was self-consciously "neutral" and "scientific," began to emerge. But the core conceptions about what communications "is" and what to do with it remained intact. This process of changing the labels while maintaining the core concept of employing communication principally as an instrument of domination can be clearly seen in some of those projects unfortunate enough to be caught on the cusp of the change.

At the Bureau of Social Science Research, for example, Chitra M. Smith prepared an extensive, annotated series of bibliographies for the RAND Corporation during 1951–54 entitled *International Propaganda and Psychological Warfare*.[102] This was clearly an "old"-style rhetorical presentation. It is useful from a historical point of view, however, because as an annotated bibliography, Chitra Smith's work provides a good indication of the scope of the concept of "psychological warfare" as it stood during the first half of the 1950s.

But by 1956 the rhetorical tide seems to have turned. That year, RAND compiled and published Smith's bibliographies with only two substantive changes: The title became *International Communication and Political Opinion,* and the author's credit was extended to both Bruce Lannes Smith and Chitra M. Smith.[103] The earlier acknowledgment of psychological warfare as the unifying theme of the collection—in fact, as its raison d'être—completely disappeared, without changing the content of the work.

A similar incident took place at Harvard's Russian Research Center. In 1954, Clyde Kluckhohn, Alex Inkeles, and Raymond Bauer prepared a psychological warfare study for the U.S. Air Force entitled "Strategic Psychological and Sociological Strengths and Vulnerabilities of the Soviet Social System."[104] Much of the work concerned the Soviet national communication system, which was Inkeles' speciality, including its technological, cultural, and political attributes. In 1956, the authors deleted about a dozen pages of recommendations concerning psychological operations during nuclear war then published the identical four-hundred-page text under the new title *How the Soviet System Works*.[105] That work, in turn, became a standard graduate reader in Soviet studies throughout the 1960s. The Kluckhohn, Inkeles, and Bauer text thus moved from its original incarnation as a relatively "naive" how-to manual for the exploitation of a rival communication system, to now make a much more sweeping—yet paradoxically more seemingly "objective" and "scientific"—claim concerning how Soviet reality "works."

These examples illustrate both the changes and the underlying continuity of mainstream mass communication research in the United States during the 1950s. Leonard Doob—author of the 1948 text *Public Opinion and Propaganda* and an activist in U.S. international propaganda projects until well into the 1980s—expressed the rhetorical shift well in an interview with J. M. Sproule:

> Doob indicates that the very term "propaganda" began to lose favor as the more objective [purportedly objective—author's note] concepts of communication, persuasion and public opinion replaced it in the lexicon of social science. Indeed, Doob reports he would not have dreamed of using propaganda as a significant theoretical term in his 1961 study of *Communication in Africa*.[106]

In truth, Doob's 1961 study was no less about "propaganda" in content or in the use to which it was put than had been his earlier work. What had changed was the rhetorical framework in which the concept of communication-as-domination was presented to the reader.

By the middle of the 1950s the process of stripping the social context from research and development in psychological warfare and recycling the remaining core concepts as simple "communication" research was well advanced. By then, several of the early claims made for the power that would flow from discovery of the "magic keys" to communication behavior had failed to prove out. Many mass communication experts had begun to regard the term "psychological warfare" as counterproductive, due to the hostility it generated among audiences targeted for persuasion. Discussing psychological warfare "in the public prints," as Leo Bogart wrote in a report to the U.S. Information Agency, "is like describing the technique of seduction, and how to make it look like wooing, in the presence of the girl you have seduced."[107] Further, as L. John Martin argued, openly acknowledging campaigns of psychological warfare during peacetime opens the sponsor to charges of violation of United Nations conventions and international law.[108]

As early as the American Association for Public Opinion Research convention of 1954, researchers under contract to the Voice of America and to an unidentified government agency publicly reported the failure of two forms of mass communication research that had been particularly popular with government clients.[109] Content analysis of foreign propaganda had been sold to the U.S. government on the basis of claims that careful monitoring of suspect publications could help predict shifts in the policies of rival regimes, and that it would reveal clandestine collaboration between Soviet propaganda agencies and ostensibly noncommunist publications around the world. Both claims had been based in large part on studies by Harold Lasswell, Nathan Leites, Ithiel de Sola Pool, and others in the World War II–era Library of Congress psychological warfare team. But researchers at the Bureau of Social Science Research, Harvard, and Rutgers reported in 1954 that they had failed to achieve the desired results.[110] Similarly, the VOA's Helen Kaufman indicated that VOA studies in Germany focusing on means for defusing Soviet claims of racial injustice in the United States had failed to support Hovland's widely accepted theories concerning audience responses to "one-sided" and "two-sided" propaganda.[111] Elsewhere that year, W. Phillips Davison wrote that "in general" he felt that "the role of agitation and propaganda in the communist equation has been exaggerated."[112] The myth of the "push-button millennium" in government propaganda had begun to unravel.

At the AAPOR conference of 1956, an analyst with the CIA's Radio

Free Europe decisively broke ranks. Gerald Streibel opened his presentation with a conventional acknowledgment that scholarly psychological warfare research was desirable, but he continued by saying that despite heavy government funding of applied mass communication research the "gap between the [psychological warfare] operator and the researcher is almost as wide as ever." Operators needed day-to-day information for "policy-making," he contended, and academics had failed to provide it. In the real world "psychological warfare is not so much anti-scientific as it is pre-scientific," he said. The magic keys sought by the state had simply not materialized, leading Radio Free Europe to turn to "journalists and other specialists" for their information and insights into propaganda techniques. "Psychological warfare is concerned with persuading people, not with studying them," he concluded.[113]

Streibel's comments created a minor crisis in the workshop. The session's reporter—the BASR's David Sills, who will be remembered from the Iranian "extremists" study mentioned earlier in this chapter—inserted a special note in the record stating that the Radio Free Europe paper "runs counter to many basic assumptions of applied research" and "represents a misunderstanding of both . . . policy-making and the potentialities of applied research." Each of the other speakers at the gathering attacked Streibel's conclusions.[114]

But the writing was on the wall. The problem with psychological warfare was but one aspect of a broader crisis in academic efforts to find Lowenthal's "push-button millennium." In the year that followed, prominent communication author William Albig reviewed the previous twenty years of communication studies and concluded that while output of papers in the field remained high, he was "not encouraged" by their depth. Little had been learned of "meaningful, theoretical significance about communications . . . [or] about the theory of public opinion." There had been a plethora of descriptive and empirical studies, but little useful synthesis about opinion formation and change, he contended.[115] Bernard Berelson was similarly pessimistic. The University of Chicago scholar concluded that the " 'great ideas' that gave the field of communications research so much vitality ten and twenty years ago have to a substantial extent worn out. No new ideas of comparable magnitude have appeared to take their place. We are on a plateau."[116] Even two of psychological warfare's most determined boosters, John Riley of Rutgers University and Leonard Cottrell of the Russell Sage Foundation, acknowledged at about that time that "disillusionment" had set in regarding the prospects for breakthroughs in the effectiveness of psychological warfare on the basis of existing concepts of applied communication research.[117]

Despite these discouraging words, what was in fact taking place was not the end of psychological warfare, but a shift in its targets and in some aspects of its rhetoric. The conceptualization of international conflict associated with MIT's Center for International Studies was coming to the fore. The early popularity of the "propaganda" aspects of psychological war—which is to say, those most directly tied to communication media—was in decline among government funders, while CENIS's vision of a broader, integrated strategy for "developing" entire nations was on the rise. The CENIS approach, it will be recalled, held that technological innovations in mass communication had helped create an explosive situation in developing countries by implicitly encouraging political participation by millions of people who remained economically and socially disenfranchised. The mass media were an important tool for managing that crisis CENIS argued; they could help educate people in new skills and make other positive contributions. But media alone were not enough. The United States should also organize suitable economic, political, and military institutions as part of the package. For those countries where the media and an aid package were not enough to stabilize the situation, CENIS said, the United States should provide arms, police, military advisers, and counterinsurgency support. Thus the CENIS approach came to be called "development theory" by communication specialists; among military planners it took the name "limited warfare."[118]

CENIS's work also became important in communication theory, narrowly defined. By the end of 1956, there was general agreement among CENIS specialists that audience effects played a substantial role in the communication process—the study of these effects, after all, was the basic rationale for the CENIS communication research program. Study of the "reception, comprehension and recall of political communications in underdeveloped or peasant societies" moved to center stage.[119] There was also tacit agreement that elite populations abroad should be the first targets of persuasive communication.

The "old style" of psychological warfare, and particularly its emphasis on Soviet and East European targets, seems to have come to be regarded as a slightly stagnant, albeit still important field. In the 1956 special CENIS issue of *Public Opinion Quarterly,* for example, editor Ithiel de Sola Pool limited articles concerning the Soviets to six out of forty-one published in the issue—a quite different balance from that found in the 1952 special issue on International Communications Research edited by Leo Lowenthal. Even Pool's introduction to the journal's section dealing with Soviet and Chinese Communist political communication has the feel of a backhanded compliment: The articles in the section, he wrote, show a sophistication of analysis that comes from "our constant concern with it for so long."[120]

There is no indication in the published writings that the CENIS authors still believed that magic keys to communication power could be easily located. Rather, the path to greater communication "effectiveness"—which is to say, the ability to manipulate an audience to a desired end—was now seen as incremental, with each new bit of insight contributing to a growing understanding of communication behavior. There also appears to have been general agreement among CENIS specialists concerning basic methodological issues such as sampling procedures and data analysis as well as consensus that rough-and-ready methodological shortcuts could be used when surveying hostile or "denied" populations.[121]

What all this meant as far as the pages of *Public Opinion Quarterly* were concerned was that the number of articles concerning Soviet communication behavior declined, while the number concerning contested countries in the Third World increased substantially. Leading scholars who had previously been frequent contributors of studies stressing cold war ideological struggles turned instead to a major debate within the profession over the failure of simple "cause-and-effect" models to predict communication behavior.

A 1959 article by W. Phillips Davison, "On the Effects of Communication," illustrates the dynamics of the new developments at the close of the period covered by this book. Davison was at that time at the RAND Corporation and had recently completed two books on Germany in the cold war, one of which was written with Hans Speier.[122]

Davison's essay provides one of the first extended articulations of what was to become the influential "uses and gratifications" approach to communication research. In it, he lays out a series of premises on the interplay between communication and human behavior, contending that all human actions are in some way directed toward the satisfaction of wants or needs. Because human attention is highly selective, individuals sort through the ocean of information that they encounter to find the messages that they believe (rightly or wrongly) will facilitate satisfaction of their needs. The individual's "habits, attitudes and an accumulated stock of knowledge" serve as "guides to action" during that sorting process. Davison goes on to argue that this framework permits a coherent explanation of a body of communication research data from the previous decade that would otherwise seem anomalous. Further research in psychology and sociology held the promise of revealing the specific mechanisms by which the sorting process works, he concluded.[123]

One intriguing aspect of Davison's paper is the conceptual link between this new analysis and the earlier body of psychological warfare research, particularly the unsuccessful search for magic keys to communication effects. Davison specifically rejects "passive audience" conceptions, then readapts the tactics for achieving domination over an audience to his new analysis. Here is how he concludes:

> The communicator's audience is not a passive recipient—it cannot be regarded as a lump of clay to be molded by the master propagandist. Rather . . . they must get something from the manipulator if he is to get something from them. A bargain is involved. Sometimes, it is true, the manipulator is able to lead his audience into a bad bargain. . . . But audiences, too, can drive a hard bargain. Many communicators who have been widely disregarded or misunderstood know that to their cost.[124]

The audience, then, is not passive; it might rather be seen as an unruly animal that must be tamed in order to extract a desired behavior. The underlying similarity of both the "old" and "new" constructions, however, is the urgency attached to discovering methods for the more effective subordination of the target audience to the will of the "communicator," and the absence of inquiry into the relationship between the communicator and political, economic, and military powers of his (or her) society. In both instances, the social context of communication is stripped away, not simply as a temporary measure to carry out a particular experiment in a controlled environment, but instead as a basic aspect of the theory itself. As Davison articulated it in 1959, communication again implicitly reduces to a collection of techniques for a "manipulator"—his word—this time explained with references to personal and social psychology.

Davison's reference points for his argument are drawn largely from the body of psychological warfare operations and studies that had played such a large role in the emergence and professionalization of the discipline. He gives three examples of means by which "communications can lead to adjustive behavior," two of which are illustrated with examples drawn from World War II psychological warfare.[125] Davison's other proofs in the study, each of which is footnoted, are drawn from the USIA propaganda campaigns in Greece, Lloyd Free and Hadley Cantril's overseas surveys for the CIA, Cooper and Jahoda's propaganda studies, debriefings of Soviet defectors, and Kecskemeti, Inkeles, and Bauer's studies of Soviet propaganda.[126]

No one can fault Davison for having read and used the literature. The point is that here again, the paradigm of domination in communication left a mark on later mass communication studies not generally remembered as having anything whatever to do with conceptions of U.S. national security, ideological struggles, or the cold war.

7

Internalization and Enforcement of the Paradigm of Domination

U.S. mass communication studies have never been as simple a matter as "funding = preconception," of course. True, sponsorship money usually flowed toward entrepreneurs promising innovations of greater utility to those who possess the wealth and influence necessary to set the research agenda. But social science has generated its preconceptions concerning communication in a way that is deeper and more complex than that. At any given moment, backers of the currently "dominant" preconceptions struggle both with colleagues who favor a variety of "alternative" constructions and with forces outside the field, in a fierce competition over the vision, methods, and formulations that will define the field. This rivalry, and the shifting alliances between leading social scientists and U.S. security agencies to which it gave rise, has remained much more tangled than the relatively straightforward economic relationships discussed in earlier chapters.

Leading mass communication researchers were not "bought off" in some simplistic sense during the 1950s; they instead internalized and reflected the values of the agencies they had been hired to assist for reasons that seemed to them to be proper, even noble. Interestingly, academic promotion of psychological warfare during the 1950s became one aspect of the field's defense against the nativist reaction known as McCarthyism. That defense reinforced the authority of political and academic centrists in communication studies at the expense of their rivals on both left and right.

Academic historians of mass communication studies generally agree that most social scientists of the 1930s and 1940s regarded themselves as social reformers, progressives, and even political radicals. At the National Opinion Research Center, to name only one example, founder and director Harry H. Field contended that NORC's main purpose was to permit "the voice of the common man to be heard by those in authority." That institution's founding documents stress that opinion polling should be seen as "a new means of making voters articulate, which in turn should increase public knowledge and public interest in political, social and economic questions." NORC's immediate predecessor organization, in fact, was Field's short-lived People's Research Corporation, whose name reflects the rhetoric and something of the spirit of much U.S. social science prior to 1940.[1]

The political-military crisis of World War II, however, forged a new harmony of purpose in most of U.S. society, and particularly between leading social scientists and the government, say Albert Biderman and Elisabeth Crawford in a little-known, but unusually frank study of academic–government relations prepared for the U.S. Air Force. Objectives such as restoring the economy, winning the war, defeating Nazism, and reestablishing world order after 1945 "rendered legitimate the tremendous increase of public and quasi-public intervention and planning called forth by [these] crises," they write. "Frequently, the only recognized sources of experience and expertise [for the government] for collecting these intelligence, planning and evaluational data were [*sic*] social scientists."[2] Soon a strong convergence of interests developed between existing elites seeking social engineering tools to manage crisis, on the one hand, and social scientists with reformist points of view concerning government policy, on the other. "The symbols of science often became as convenient for government clienteles of applied science as they were for social scientists who either sought government favor or justification for asserting their views concerning public policy," Biderman and Crawford contend.[3]

The strength of this national consensus, particularly during World War II, permitted social scientists to transform research projects that might otherwise have posed "fundamental value questions" for them into "purely instrumental" studies, Biderman and Crawford write.[4] In other words, study topics that might otherwise have seemed morally or politically suspect to reform-minded social scientists became acceptable, and even desirable, targets for academic inquiry.

The effects of bombing on the morale of [civilian] populations; the degree of democratization appropriate to the armed forces; the functions of true and false atrocity accounts in propaganda, domestic and foreign, all became not only important questions for research, but could be treated "objectively" as purely instrumental issues.[5]

Note that at least two, and arguably all three, of the examples Biderman and Crawford cite are studies widely accepted today as seminal documents in the emerging specialty of mass communication research. The study of the effects of bombing on civilians was the U.S. Strategic Bombing Survey, the survey work for which was organized by Rensis Likert. This was "the last important project in governmental [survey] research during the war. From the standpoint of design, it was also the most ambitious," writes Converse in her history of U.S. survey research. The Bombing Survey's published studies on German and Japanese morale were among the first genuinely systematic efforts to examine U.S. efforts at "persuasion"—albeit of a particularly violent sort—of foreign populations.[6] The "democratization" and "atrocity" studies they mention are the work of Stouffer, Hovland, and their colleagues in the *American Soldier* series, which employed U.S. troops as research subjects in some of the first large-scale, systematic tests of communication effects. The same studies are widely recognized as influential in the development of research methodologies for communication studies.[7]

Biderman and Crawford point to five basic factors that they believe made national security projects "professionally appropriate" among social scientists during the cold war years. Biderman can speak with some authority on this point, for his own early career was funded in substantial part by military and intelligence agencies, as was the project from which the material quoted here has been drawn.[8] Their typology includes:

"1. *Selective attention [among social scientists] to value-consonant elements of the military-political context.*" Scientists made common cause with the Pentagon in opposition to Stalinism, for example, while sidestepping the more problematic issues of U.S. imperial adventures abroad and the rise of the military-industrial complex at home.

"2. *Insulation [of social scientists] from the military's primary concern—violence.*"

"3. *Perceptions of asymmetrical relationships.*" Biderman and Crawford mean the belief among social scientists that they could use military money and resources to advance their own careers, while avoiding making a contribution to causes they disdained.

"4. *Organizational innovations which made participation [in military research] pose few threats to the autonomy of the profession.*" Military consulting fees and project funding often permitted social scientists to remain in universities and think tanks, rather than directly joining the government.

"5. *Fulfillment of scientific ambitions of sociologists.*" The funded projects were sometimes professionally rewarding or scientifically interesting.[9]

The second element, the "insulation" of academics from the effects of their activities, is particularly important. Biderman and Crawford and, separately, Morris Janowitz contend that the military's use of social science "has been limited chiefly to . . . political and psychological warfare, military government, and troop indoctrination," as Janowitz put it.[10] His comment illustrates two points simultaneously. First, that "militarized" communication studies enjoyed particular emphasis in government funding of social science; and second, that three of the more prominent recipients of such funding—Biderman, Crawford, and Janowitz—considered such work to be *nonviolent*. Biderman and Crawford further contend that many of their social science colleagues adopted the same rationale; namely, that U.S. psychological warfare (and troop morale studies, etc.) should be considered something fundamentally different from, say, development of improved warheads. One hint of the extent to which this conception permeated the U.S. social science establishment of the day can be found in their claim (in 1968) that of twenty postwar presidents of the American Sociological Association, "more than half are known to have had an involvement of some kind with defense research" during the cold war. Biderman and Crawford declined to name names, citing the "invidious connotation" that such work had gained in later years."

Their use of the term "insulation" here is adroit. By simply acknowledging that social scientists believed they were acting in good faith, Biderman and Crawford sidestep the more basic question of whether the academics' work actually increased social misery and violence. But the social scientists' beliefs are only part of what is at issue here. Equally relevant is the question of whether their beliefs were accurate, and most of the evidence shows that they were not.

The literal process of the military's social science research (including psychological warfare studies) only rarely involved front-line violence. But the various definitions of psychological warfare promulgated by the government, and most particularly the secret definitions designed for internal consumption, leave no doubt that violence was a consistent and often predominant characteristic of psychological warfare for those who were distributing the contracts. Many academics, too, must have understood on some level that their work was integral to overall U.S. national security tactics of the day. For one thing, scholars such as Wilbur Schramm, Ithiel de Sola Pool, and Leonard Cottrell had direct access to the internal government thinking on such matters through their service on elite advisory committees. Further, even a casual newspaper reader would have encountered information suggesting that there was some relationship between the widely reported U.S. role in violent coups or civil wars in Greece, Iran, Egypt, Guatemala, Laos, the Congo, and others, and the work of surveying public opinion and analyzing communication systems in those same countries. More generally, how else but through the shame associated with this knowledge can the pervasive secrecy and rationalization that continues to surround the social scientists' contribution to psychological warfare to this day be explained?

The conclusion is inescapable: The U.S. social scientists active in psychological warfare were not ignorant of their role, or of the violence that usually accompanied psychological operations. They were, rather, "insulated," just as Biderman and Crawford say, from consideration of the implications of their work.

Study of *Public Opinion Quarterly* and other prestigious academic journals of the period brings to light a number of indications why seemingly reform-minded academics participated in psychological warfare projects, and these reasons seem to roughly coincide with Biderman and Crawford's typology. There usually appears to have been a convergence of interests, rather than any single factor, that contributed to the strong support that efforts to dominate and manipulate other peoples enjoyed inside the academic communication research community. The motivations of particular individuals surely varied from case to case, but overall trends are clear.

First of all, psychological warfare work became a means of demonstrating patriotism, loyalty, and support for one's country. These sentiments were most often expressed in the texts of American Association for Public Opinion Research presidential addresses and similar ceremonial occasions. "Public opinion analysts are helping to combat the forces which currently threaten freedom and democracy," *POQ* told its readers in its summary of Samuel Stouffer's AAPOR presidential lecture of 1954. "To continue serving the needs of their society . . . social scientists must take a long-range view of history and work hard at improving their instruments of measurement."[12]

At least two elements seem to have undergirded Stouffer's inspirational message. He saw the United States as the protector of important attributes such as democracy, peace, humanitarianism, truthfulness, rationality, and Judeo-Christian values. U.S. social science was said by many advocates to be advancing these values worldwide through its research, thus turning back the tide of superstition and ignorance.[13] Meanwhile, many academics had the West's experience with Hitler and World War II fresh in their mind. As Stouffer's comment suggests, they regarded Stalinism and Third World nationalism as an integrated attack on Western culture generally, and that was seen as an important reason to close ranks to support the U.S. government's foreign policy initiatives.[14]

There is little reason to believe that money *alone* was an important motivating factor for these scholars, if only because there are considerably more lucrative fields than communication research open to talented, highly trained personnel. That having been said, however, it is clear that use of government funding facilitated certain types of research and the winning of professional prestige that might not otherwise have been available.

For example, some academics interested in quantitative methodology or in communication effects studies, who were also amenable to psychological warfare campaigns, sought government funding in an effort to pursue both goals simultaneously. Samuel Stouffer's program at Harvard's Laboratory of Social Relations illustrated this trend. On the one hand, Stouffer made clear his support for psychological warfare programs as a means of meeting the perceived challenge posed by "a handful of ruthless men in the Politboro who can press a fateful [atomic] button" unless convinced that the "might and determination of the free world will deter them."[15] On the other, Stouffer's publications and those of his staff appearing in *POQ* and the *American Journal of Sociology* focus almost entirely on narrowly drawn methodological issues involving the derivation of cumulative scales from unstructured interviews.[16] In this case, the U.S. Air Force, which was underwriting the research, was primarily interested in deriving strategic intelligence concerning the Soviet Union from interviews of Soviet refugees and defectors.[17] Stouffer facilitated both that goal and his own methodological interests by finding a means to adapt Guttman and Lazarsfeld's latent distance scales to the raw data from the interviews.[18] A similar phenomenon involving some of the same methodological questions can be seen in the work of Eric Marder of International Public Opinion Research on behalf of the U.S. Army's Human Resources Research Office[19] or in Stuart Dodd and Melvin DeFleur's Project Revere studies discussed earlier. This behavior fits well with the first and the fifth elements in Biderman and Crawford's typology.

Another important motivator among social scientists seems to have been a perceived need to "make a choice" between the United States and the Soviet Union, with failure to actively support U.S. government campaigns interpreted by leaders in the field as proof of "neutralism" or even of Stalinist sympathies. Daniel Lerner's work provides particularly vivid examples of these pressures. "The management of international consensus presents extremely complicated problems of symbolization," he wrote in a special *Public Opinion Quarterly* issue on International Communications Research at the height of the Korean War. "Neutralists" in the struggle with communism can be recognized by their claim that "the choice between the U.S. and USSR does not coincide with the choice between freedom and bondage," Lerner asserted, contending that those who favored the political symbols such as "peace, safety and relaxation [of tensions]" were promoting "Neutralist-Communist symbols" that had permitted the Free World to be "out-maneuvered in the world struggle for popular loyalties." Reserving judgment on the East–West ideological conflict should be viewed as an "evasion of political reality . . . based on inaccurate expectations which, at some point, [will be] rendered untenable by the course of actual events."[20]

It is worth noting that the campaign against "neutralism" was at that time the central focus of CIA propaganda among intellectuals within the United States and worldwide. Beginning in 1950, the CIA sponsored and financed the Congress for Cultural Freedom and a series of politically liberal, strongly anticommunist publications including *Encounter* (England), *Der Monat* (Germany), *Forum* (Austria), *Preuves* (France), and *Cuadernos* (Latin America) as a means of combating the perceived neutrality of intellectuals in the face of purported communist expansion. Sidney Hook, Melvin Lasky, Edward Shils, Daniel Bell, and Daniel Lerner, among others, emerged as prominent public spokesmen for this campaign, though they have insisted in later years that they were unaware of the CIA's sponsorship for their work. Either way, the point here is simply that fierce, social-democratic anticommunism became a genuinely powerful political movement in academe, in part because it enjoyed considerable covert government financing.[21]

Meanwhile, *POQ* and other prestigious journals presented academics who advocated rival communication paradigms, or who were not active supporters of U.S. foreign policy (the two were often intertwined), as persons possessed by mental diseases or personality disorders associated with totalitarian political systems.[22] Gabriel Almond's *Appeals of Communism* study (written with Herbert Krugman, Elsbeth Lewin, and Howard Wriggins of Princeton)[23] presented what is probably the most elaborate and ostensibly scientific version of this widely accepted analysis. Almond and his colleagues interviewed about 250 former communists who had resigned from parties in four Western countries, then concluded on the basis of this skewed sample that communism appealed mainly to "individuals who were confused and uncertain about their own identities." Leaders of communist organizations were said to be widely regarded by their own rank-and-file as "ruthless, cynical, remote, dogmatic, [and] opportunistic" individuals in whom "all values save power have been squeezed out."[24]

Whatever truth there may be in these characterizations, it is evident that the relentless publicity given to the conclusion that Marxists were (or might be) psychologically defective contributed to the sweeping delegitimization of critical perspectives during the 1950s. An alternative interpretation of Almond's data, which is in fact more consistent with basic social science than the Princeton conclusions, is that "individuals who were confused . . ." were more likely to *resign* from communist parties. But that was given short shrift by Almond and his colleagues and never seriously discussed at the time the work was published. Instead, contemporary academic journals presented the study's questionable methodology as a model of responsible research, and Almond himself went on to a prominent career in mainstream social psychology.

The social pressure on mass communication researchers to take a strong stand against any variety of critical thinking that sought to puncture widely held preconceptions about the role of the United States in the world was reinforced by another important factor: the growth of McCarthyism in U.S. society. During the early 1950s Senator McCarthy and his political allies launched a series of attacks on U.S. information programs and on the social sciences in general. These began with McCarthy's well-known campaign against the Voice of America, which led to the public purging of U.S. Information Service libraries, dismissal of Voice officials, and repeated congressional inquiries into alleged communists at the Voice.[25] Less well-known, but of equal importance in the present discussion, were congressional investigations into the major tax-exempt foundations led by Congressman Carroll Reece of Tennessee. Reece took as his theme that major U.S. foundations— including the Rockefeller Foundation, the Ford Foundation, the Carnegie Corporation, and the Social Science Research Council—were engaged in a campaign to promote socialism and "One World" government through funding social science studies Reece regarded as critical of the United States and the "free enterprise" economic system. He singled out John Dewey, Samuel Stouffer, and Bernard Berelson, among others, as purported ringleaders.[26]

The foundations' principal defense against these charges was that U.S. social science was a uniquely effective weapon in the cold war. Social Science Research Council president Pendleton Herring offered a report to the Reece committee contending that "in the eyes of communist leaders social science is regarded as one of the worst and most dangerous enemies of communist ideology and communist expansion. Indeed, so strong is the feeling against sociology that it is not permitted to teach it" in the Soviet Union. Herring went on to submit excerpts from two hostile reports published by the Soviets—"American Bourgeois Philosophy and Sociology in the Service of Imperialism" and "Contemporary American Bourgeois Sociology in the Service of Expansion"—as proof of the effectiveness of sociology's contribution to the cold war.[27]

The price tag for scholars who refused to support the cold war consensus could be quite high: shunning by colleagues, firing, loss of tenure or prospects for promotion, forced appearances before collegiate and state investigating boards, FBI inquiries, hostile newspaper stories, or worse.[28] Even very prominent academics were not exempt. The House Committee on Un-American Activities called Daniel Boorstin of the University of Chicago to testify in 1953, for example, because more than a decade earlier he had briefly joined the Communist party. (Boorstin cooperated with the investigation.)[29] FBI and U.S. military intelligence agents kept American Sociological Society conventions under surveillance in an effort to smoke out radicals;[30] Charles Beard, the longtime dean of American historians and former president of the American Historical Association, was drummed out of the profession when he refused to readjust his work to the new political realities;[31] and Harvard, MIT, Columbia, UCLA, and a score of other leading universities purged alleged Marxists and leftists from their faculties, often at the instigation of their ideological rivals among the professors.[32] Maryland became a trend-setter with regard to driving leftists from academe; in 1949 it passed the Ober Anti-Communist Act, which became a model statute for about a dozen other states.[33] (The law was eventually found to be unconstitutional.)

The FBI and other domestic security agencies hit institutions and scholars espousing Marxist interpretations of the social sciences particularly hard. The Jefferson School of Social Science—a thinly disguised, U.S. Communist party–sponsored institution that drew a remarkable five thousand students annually in the New York area during the early 1950s—was placed on the attorney general's list of subversive organizations, was denied tax-exempt status, had its student list subpoenaed, and was eventually harassed out of existence in 1955.[34] The House Un-American Activities Committee subpoenaed the officers and all of the records of the Jefferson School's sucessor, the Fund for Social Analysis, and soon drove that out of business as well. The Fund for Social Research had provided small grants to leftist scholars such as William Appleman Williams and Herbert Aptheker.[35] The Emergency Civil Liberties Committee attempted to organize a protest by U.S. social scientists against HUAC's actions, but with little success and, so far as can be determined, no support whatever from mainstream sociologists and communication researchers.[36]

This decade-long campaign of repression had a substantial chilling effect on the social sciences. Paul Lazarsfeld's 1955 study for the Fund for the Republic on the impact of political censorship on the social sciences found that 27 percent of a sample of 1,445 college teachers had begun to go out of their way ''to make it clear that they had no extreme leftist or rightist leanings.'' About 20 percent of the sample had altered the subjects they were willing to discuss in university classrooms, the reference material they assigned, or the research projects they undertook. Almost half of the teachers indicated that they were concerned that students might deliberately quote them out of context or otherwise garble the teacher's point of view in order to report them to school administrators or to the FBI. Some 394 respondents asserted that they believed their "point of view on a political subject [had been] reported unfavorably to higher authorities."[37]

Within this context, academic contributions to psychological warfare campaigns became in part a means of reaffirming one's political reliability. This is demonstrated by the foundations' testimony, cited earlier, where sociology's contribution to psychological warfare was presented as proof of its political legitimacy. The same trend can frequently be seen in *POQ*'s editorial introductions to its articles, where mildly controversial ideas are often prefaced with the claim that the author's intent has been to "draw neutrals into the American-centered coalition"[38] or to "improve America's effectiveness in the propaganda war."[39]

POQ provides an example of the paradoxical role that many academic institutions played during the McCarthy years. By continuing to publish scholars such as Stouffer and Berelson, the journal tacitly defended their legitimacy in the face of attacks from the radical right. At the same time, however, the act of defending their legitimacy necessarily carried with it some outline of what *illegitimacy* might be, if only by default, and the gradual construction of barriers separating "responsible" from "irresponsible" points of view.

In mass communication research and other fields, the academic community's shelter against McCarthyism consisted in important part of defining and defending paradigmatic theories, research methodologies, and standards of behavior around which the "center" or mainstream of the profession could consolidate—a circling of the wagons, so to speak.[40] This was not usually a battle for civil liberties or academic freedom per se, although there was no shortage of rhetoric along those lines. Academics who strayed too far from the safety of the center were for the most part abandoned to their fate, as the shunning of historian Charles Beard and of the Jefferson School of Social Science faculty illustrate.

This retreat to the center had important implications for mass communication research. It tended to reinforce the authority of the center of the profession, and of those academics who could draw on networks in the government and foundations for political support. It provided considerable incentive for scholars not to explore new approaches to understanding communication, as the results of the Lazarsfeld survey discussed earlier suggest. And it struck deeply at the academic legitimacy of both the "left" and "right" critiques of mainstream social science. The radical right's critique of U.S. social science in the 1950s, it may be recalled, was not so different in some ways from that of the radical left. Both protested the growing alliance between the state and elite scholars; both were suspicious of the obscurantism and exclusivity that often accompanied the evolution toward professionalism in the social sciences; and both believed (though for different reasons) that modern social engineering techniques posed serious threats to their constituencies.[41]

The delegitimizing of Marxist critiques of communication paradigms became one element of the field's defense against McCarthyism. At *Public Opinion Quarterly* and in major academic associations such as AAPOR, scholarly participation in psychological warfare projects was not viewed as an ethical problem, even when scholars concealed the sources of their funding[42] or employed questionable methodologies.[43] But pointed critiques of the inbreeding between social science and the state did pose problems for the center of the profession, and they were rarely published in academic journals or aired at professional meetings, regardless of whether the analysis came from the left or the right.

POQ, like other respectable journals, tended to ignore or even ridicule authors whose writings were outside of the mainstream of the field during the 1950s, while at the same time offering a steady flow of publicity and praise to academics who offered elegant elaborations of the commonly accepted assumptions about the character of communication. The journal published no articles by Theodor Adorno, Max Horkheimer or C. Wright Mills between 1950 and 1960, for example. It did offer three lukewarm book reviews: two for Mills (in fall 1954 and fall 1956) and one for Horkheimer (summer 1956)[44]—a gesture that tended to distance the journal from those authors, yet which tacitly conceded that they did have something to say to students of mass communication during this period. Meanwhile, the journal offered repeated articles, book excerpts, and guest editorial slots to academics in *POQ*'s favor, including Daniel Lerner, Harold Lasswell, and W. Phillips Davison.

The journal openly ridiculed writers who failed to use "scientific" formats for their ideas when offering heretical points of view on mass communication issues. Two examples of this can be found in Avery Leiserson's scathing review of George Seldes' *The People Don't Know* and Lloyd Barenblatt's commentary on Vance Packard's *Hidden Persuaders*.[45] Both Seldes and Packard argued that the mass media in the United States presented a monolithic, ideologically charged version of "reality" that had succeeded in shaping popular consciousness to a much greater degree than was generally recognized; *POQ* presented both authors to its readers as irresponsible crackpots.

The point here is not that *POQ* "should" have published more articles by Adorno, Horkheimer, and Mills, or that Seldes and Packard are above criticism. It is rather that *Public Opinion Quarterly* articulated and defended particular preconceptions about mass communication, and that more critical authors such as Adorno were tacitly defined by the journal as being largely outside the boundaries within which "responsible" dialog could be carried out.

In sum, there were both positive and negative reinforcements for academics participating in U.S. psychological warfare projects. Positive reinforcements included the perceived patriotism demonstrated by participating, the opportunity for rewards of money and academic prestige, and psychological warfare's usefulness as a means for legitimating oneself or one's profession in a society that was often suspicious of intellectuals or, indeed, of any sort of nonconformity. Negative inducements included the desire to avoid the consequences that would come with defeat at the hands of perceived enemies abroad, and the threat of punishments that could come with a failure to achieve political or social legitimacy. Particularly important in both instances was the phemonenon of "insulation," the ability of institutions and individuals to separate themselves from the effects of their work on others. Meanwhile, the profession's resistance against what has come to be known as McCarthyism carried with it a reinforcement of the political and scientific center at the expense of challenges from both the left and the right.

8

The Legacy of Psychological Warfare

Wilbur Schramm deserves special mention in any discussion of the evolution of ideas about communication among social scientists in the United States. Schramm's biographer, Steven Chaffee, has written that Schramm "towers above our field" and that communication studies between 1933 and 1973 might best be described as the "Age of Schramm." Schramm's specialty throughout his career was academic administration and the definition and dissemination of the mass communication "knowledge" of his day: Schramm was the "principal disseminator of that zeitgeist [of U.S. mass communication theory], those paradigms and the knowledge yielded by mass communication research," Chaffee contends.[1] James Tankard agrees that "Wilbur Schramm . . . probably did more to define and establish the field of communication research and theory than any other person."[2] Even when such comments are discounted for hyperbole, it is clear that Schramm was central to U.S. academic programs in mass communication studies between about 1948 and at least 1970.

Schramm's writings remain important today because of their continuing impact on later generations of scholars and as an illustration of the ideological and political preconceptions of the leadership of the communication education profession during the early cold war years. His writings between 1945 and 1960 reveal a distinctly black and white, Manichaean view of the world that pitted Schramm's enthusiastic Americanism against ideological rivals abroad and at home.[3]

Even Schramm's most vocal advocates concede that his work during his ascendancy to the peak of U.S. journalism education was characterized by "interpreting mass communication behavior in terms almost of 'good guys' and 'bad guys'" and by "a touch of ethnocentrism."[4] Though little remembered today, Schramm prepared his most influential writings, including the watershed text *The Process and Effects of Mass Communication,* as training materials for U.S. government propaganda programs.[5] Similarly, one of Schramm's most pervasive theoretical contributions, his still widely accepted distinction between "authoritarian" and "Soviet totalitarian" media systems, was developed under USIA contract and based largely on secondary sources concerning the Soviet Union that had themselves been prepared in U.S. psychological warfare programs during the early 1950s.[6]

There, Schramm contended that authoritarian, *anti*communist states should be seen as qualitatively better, more free, and more humane than the Khrushchev-era communist states in Eastern Europe, in part because of the structure of their communication systems. Schramm's schema lumped quite different societies together into "good" and "bad" categories, ignored the complex relationship between any society's claims and its actual behavior, and failed to account for elementary aspects of political life in both communist and noncommunist states. What his approach lacked in scientific rigor it more than made up for in political utility, however, for it provided a seemingly rational basis for democracies to underwrite extraordinarily corrupt and brutal governments as a means of facing down the purported totalitarian threat. Schramm's formulation has passed in and out of fashion in U.S. national security circles. Recently, it was particularly prominent during Jeane Kirkpatrick's tenure as U.S. ambassador the United Nations.[7]

Some important Schramm writings from the 1950s concerning communication remain inaccessable today, because they were prepared in connection with CIA- and military-sponsored psychological warfare projects that the government insists must remain secret more than thirty years later. Even so, it is possible to begin to trace the extent to which Schramm's career was bound up with U.S. psychological warfare campaigns. Examples of such work include:

1. U.S. Air Force studies of U.S. psychological operations during the Korean War, which were extensively recycled with government sponsorship in both scholarly and popular forms in several languages.[8]

2. Several major studies for the USIA, including an "evaluation" of that agency performed while Schramm was chair of a citizens' committee advocating expanded USIA operations.[9]

3. Analysis and consulting throughout the 1950s concerning the ostensibly private (but in reality CIA-directed) Radio Free Europe and Radio Liberation projects for the National Security Council and for Radio Liberation itself.[10]

4. Service as chair of the Secretary of Defense's Advisory Panel on Special Operations, which specialized in planning for propaganda, psychological warfare, and covert operations.[11]

5. A post on the highly influential Defense Science Board.[12]

6. USIA and Voice of America sponsorship for Schramm's *The Process and Effects of Mass Communication* (1954), *Four Working Papers on Propaganda Theory* (1955), *The Science of Human Communication* (1963), and perhaps of other general-circulation textbooks.[13]

7. Extensive contracting with the Office of Naval Research.[14]

8. Later in life, paid participation in a series of U.S. Agency for International Development (AID) programs seeking to define mass media development in El Salvador, Colombia, and other countries.[15]

Taken as a whole, the presently available portions of Schramm's writings establish that government psychological operations played a major role in his career at precisely the time that Schramm "almost single-handedly defin[ed] the paradigm widely used for decades in communication research," as Tankard puts it.[16]

Government-funded psychological warfare programs—and the concepts about communication and national security intrinsic to those projects—provided what has come to be called *positive feedback* in the social construction of scientific knowledge in communication studies. The term positive feedback, which is drawn from systems analysis, refers to the relationship between the overall behavior of so-called information industries, on the one hand, and the formats or technical standards adopted in those industries, on the other.

The problematic aspect of positive feedback, according to MIT's W. Brian Arthur, is that it can produce a phase lock that restricts the emergence of new knowledge, and which tends to confine intellectual innovation to established formats. "Early superiority [of an idea] is no guarantee of long-term fitness," Arthur writes. "Standards that are established early (such as the 1950s-vintage computer language FOR-

TRAN) can be hard for later ones to dislodge, no matter how superior the would-be successors may be.''[17] Well-entrenched formats or standards of knowledge can create closed systems of ideas that change only when they encounter more powerful external forces or collapse of their own weight, Arthur contends.

Such "formats" for ideas can be usefully understood as components of what Todd Gitlin calls the "dominant paradigm"[18] and Steven Chaffee terms the "zeitgeist" of mass communication studies.[19] Put briefly, any paradigm or zeitgeist embraces the professional consensus of knowledge concerning what a research subject "is," tools for examining it, a more-or-less defined research agenda, and a body of tacitly accepted rules for distinguishing "responsible" from "irresponsible" points of view on the subject at hand.[20]

The history of U.S. government spending on psychological warfare suggests that a positive feedback cycle existed in the "knowledge-based industry" of U.S. social science. Government spending on communication research stressed those aspects of the field that were regarded as of near-term value to the agencies paying the bills—agencies principally concerned with propaganda, intelligence, and military affairs. This restrictive tendency was reinforced by resource limitations, the necessity to justify federal agency budgets before a suspicious Congress, fear of McCarthyism, and the belief that immediate measures were necessary to confront the Soviet Union. Quantitative social science was particularly well suited to this government market. It conveyed the impression of being "hard" science and its stress on statistics often permitted reform-minded social scientists to sidestep political roadblocks created by Congress and by the powerful nativist lobbies in the United States. Government funding clearly had considerable impact on the development and testing of some of the most popular conceptual "formats" of mass communication research of the 1950s, such as Dodd's diffusion studies, Lerner's development studies, and others.

The path of scientific discovery in U.S. communication research was not decided in advance by the government or anyone else, of course. Although government funding did not determine what could be said by social scientists, it did play a major role in determining who would do the "authoritative" talking about communication and an indirect role in determining who would enjoy access to the academic media necessary to be heard by others in the field. This "positive feedback" for psychological warfare projects consisted initially of money, in the form of government contracts, which in turn brought other benefits: the opportunity to participate in a social network of academics with great influence within the profession (as Clausen's sociometric study establishes), ready access to scholarly journals for publication of results (as is seen in Dodd's Project Revere bibliography), invitations to participate in conference panels, university and professorial appointments, and similar opportunities for self-reinforcing status within the profession.[21]

Within this context, it is appropriate to review the scientific legacy left by government-funded psychological warfare research between 1945 and 1960. This inheritance can be seen in at least nine areas of mass communication studies:

1. Effects research.
2. Studies of the national communication systems of the Soviet Union and other countries regarded as problematic by U.S. policymakers.
3. Refinement of scaling techniques used in opinion questionnaires and in the algorithms employed to derive useful data from them.
4. Creation of opinion research and audience research techniques useful outside the United States, particularly in areas hostile to U.S. observers.
5. Early diffusion research.
6. Early development theory research.
7. Wilbur Schramm's articulation of the "zeitgeist" of the field of mass communication research and education.
8. Contributions to the refinement of "reference group" and "two-step" communication theories.
9. Contributions to "motivation" research and similar maintenance-of-morale techniques widely employed in commercial public relations.

The research into communication effects was particularly important, both for psychological warfare projects and for the development of communication studies as a distinct field of inquiry. The government played a crucial, albeit indirect role in the seminal *American Soldier* series of reports and in the related Yale studies led by Carl Hovland. All of the data collection for the *American Soldier* series, the costly data entry onto IBM punch cards, early theoretical development, salaries, and much of the overhead involved in the production of these reports were financed by the army during World War II in programs whose object was the maintenance of morale and discipline of the U.S.

armed forces.[22] The postwar analysis of the data by Hovland and his team—vitally important, yet the least expensive feature of the project—was underwritten by the Carnegie Corporation.[23] As discussed earlier, even the ostensibly "private" segment of the *American Soldier* project was carried out in coordination and with substantial overlap in personnel with contemporaneous psychological warfare projects. Data and conclusions derived from the Hovland experiments on issues such as source credibility, the effects of one-sided and two-sided propaganda on various audiences, the motivational impact of fear and atrocities, and the duration of opinion change, among others, became central to the elaboration of U.S. communication studies for most of the 1950s.[24]

Detailed studies of the national communication systems of countries regarded as targets for U.S. persuasion efforts also became an important focus of early mass communication studies. This led to detailed, relatively sophisticated studies of mass communication in the Soviet Union, its various constituent republics (Ukraine, Kazakhstan, etc.), the Eastern European satellite states, countries on the Soviet periphery (Iran, Turkey, etc.), and countries regarded as politically problematic by U.S. security agencies (France, Italy, Chile, Cuba, Indonesia, etc.). The studies of the Soviet communication system conducted in the mid-1950s by the Bureau of Social Science Research[25] appear to have been among the first reasonably comprehensive studies of a national communications *system* in the sense that phrase is used in the modern academic lexicon.[26]

Turning to methodological developments, psychological warfare programs underwrote the development of several quantitative methodologies that remain basic to mass communication studies and to what is euphemistically termed public communication research (i.e., public relations). These include much of the original work involved in the elaboration of content analysis as a quantitative research technique; contributions to the refinement of survey research via support of leading survey organizations; financing the development of experimental and quasi-experimental research techniques by Stouffer, Hovland, and others; underwriting the development of scaling techniques by Likert, Stouffer, and others; and financing several of the first efforts to employ computers in social science research.[27] Military and propaganda agencies also underwrote efforts by Ithiel de Sola Pool, Wilbur Schramm, and others to devise specialized research techniques suitable for deriving intelligence on public opinion and media usage from "denied" populations, particularly inside the Soviet Union.[28] These techniques have some broader applicability to the study of hostile subcultures generally—criminals, the very poor, the very rich, and so on—but have been most frequently employed in budget justifications for U.S. foreign propaganda programs.[29]

In the area of diffusion research, U.S. Air Force propaganda programs played a vital role in the diffusion studies by Dodd, DeFleur, and other sociologists at the University of Washington. Lowery and DeFleur conclude with some justification that these studies constitute one of several "milestones" in mass communication studies.[30] In this case, the air force underwrote virtually the entire cost of the program, selected air-dropped leaflets as the experimental stimulus, provided the means for delivery of the stimulus, and contributed significantly to the selection of those aspects of the "diffusion" phenomenon that would be subjected to study. It is evident that Dodd and his colleagues required the umbrella of authority provided by the air force in order to win permission to carry out the experiments in the first place.

The substantial role of psychological warfare programs observed in diffusion studies can also be seen in the early years of what is known as development theory. This aspect of communication theory has evolved considerably over the years,[31] but during the 1950s its intellectual center was the CENIS program at MIT. The central text for this trend was for years Lerner's *Passing of Traditional Society,* based on the Voice of America studies in the Middle East. Lerner and three other prominent development theorists, Ithiel de Sola Pool, Guy Pauker, and Everett Hagan, became CENIS staffers during the late 1950s.[32] Each was an active consultant and lecturer on communication issues as applied to U.S. counterinsurgency programs in the Third World.[33]

The work of Wilbur Schramm, who was clearly one of the single most influential articulators of the dominant paradigm of mass communication research of the 1950s, was so closely bound up with U.S. psychological warfare projects that it is often difficult to determine where Schramm's "educational" work began and his "national security" work left off. As noted a moment ago, Schramm's Manichaean vision of the U.S.–Soviet conflict was integral to his success as a government contractor and to his highly influential articulation of what Chaffee called the zeitgeist of modern mass communication research.[34]

Turning now to two of the most influential trends of mass communication research during the 1950s, it is possible to track a limited contribution of psychological warfare projects to the development of "two-step" and the related "reference group" communication theories. These schools—personified by Paul Lazarsfeld and Elihu Katz and by Robert Merton and Herbert Hyman, respectively—were primarily products of "civilian" research, so to speak, such as studies of communication and voting behavior in the United States.[35] Nevertheless, contemporary observers such as Bruce Lannes Smith concluded that government-funded psychological warfare studies also played an important role in the elaboration of both theories. Writing in early 1956, Smith paired Hans Speier's work in psychological warfare with Paul Lazarsfeld's election studies as the two most important intellectual sources of what would eventually come to be called "two-step" media theory. Both Speier and Lazarsfeld were concerned that "politically influential communications do not typically reach the broader strata of society through direct operation of the mass media," Smith wrote, "but are instead typically mediated through individuals or groups, whom Speier has named 'social relay points' and whom Lazarsfeld has called 'opinion leaders.'"[36] Smith credits the BASR's studies in the Middle East on behalf of the Voice of America as an important testbed for Lazarsfeld's studies of the two-step concept.[37] Similarly, he attributes most of the elaboration of "reference group" theory to Robert Merton and Herbert Hyman but then goes on to cite the Shils and Janowitz studies of World War II–era Wehrmacht disintegration and the CENIS program in international communications as influential contributors to the understanding of the reference group concept.[38] Stanley Bigman's studies for the USIA also contributed to the articulation of "personal influence" theories well before the publication of Katz and Lazarsfeld's pivotal *Personal Influence* in 1955.[39]

Finally, psychological warfare programs also made limited contributions to the development of "motivation" research and certain public relations techniques widely used in civilian commerce. The field of industrial motivation research has been largely commercial in its origin and financing. But there are obvious conceptual similarities between a government's efforts to maintain military and civilian morale and management programs for enforcing employee morale inside a major corporation. Stouffer's pioneering studies in this field had a military origin, it will be recalled. During the 1950s, corporate image advertising was also explicitly viewed as a form of "intra-societal psychological warfare," as *Public Opinion Quarterly* put it, borrowed from the government for use with U.S. audiences.[40] Similarly, Herbert Krugman, a prominent commentator on motivational research during the 1950s, cited the government's enthusiasm for psychological warfare as one of six contributors to advancing motivation research techniques—although Krugman was less than sanguine about some of the government's early claims for its effectiveness.[41]

Thus the U.S. government's psychological warfare programs between 1945 and 1960 played either direct or indirect roles in several of the most important initiatives in mass communication research of the period. Much of the foundation for effects research was a product of World War II psychological warfare. Several of the innovations in experimental and quasi-experimental research methodologies and in quantitative content analysis that proved to be fundamental to the crystallization of mass communication research into a distinct field of inquiry can be traced to research programs underwritten by U.S. military, intelligence, and propaganda agencies. Similarly, the substantial majority of cold war–era studies of foreign communication systems, message diffusion, and development theory were shaped by the perceived U.S. national security needs of the day.

There were at least three basic features to the relationship between government-funded psychological warfare programs and U.S. mass communication research between 1945 and 1960. First, U.S. psychological warfare was in part an applied form of mass communication theory. U.S. social science, including mass communication research, helped elaborate rationales for coercing groups targeted by the U.S. government and Western Industrial culture generally. It developed relatively sophisticated techniques used in attempts to exercise that dominion. As Wilbur Schramm noted in 1954, "propaganda"—that fixation of so much communication research of the day—"is an instrument of social control."[42]

Second, the government's psychological warfare programs provided a very large fraction of the funding available for mass communication research throughout the late 1940s and the 1950s. Key research centers such as the Bureau of Applied Social Research and the Institute for Social Research owed their survival to contracts with military, intelligence, and propaganda agencies, particularly during the crucial years of the early 1950s when communication studies emerged as a distinct discipline.

Next, the data show that the government projects did not determine what scientists could say—but they did strongly influence who would do the talking. The relative independence from direct interference with research results was a desirable aspect of military-funded social research from the point of view of the scientists,[43] and U.S. academics sometimes brought the contracting agency research results that were not welcome.[44] Having said that, though, it is also clear that government contracts helped organize and feed the informal networks of scientists who dominated the field of U.S. communication research throughout the decade, as Clausen's study showed.[45]

Despite its claims, communication studies in the United States have not typically been neutral, objective, or even held at arm's length from the political and economic powers of the day. Instead, communication studies entwined themselves with the existing institutions of power, just as have, say, the mainstream study of economics or atomic physics, whose inbreeding with the political and military establishment are so extensive as to have become common knowledge.

The claim of psychological warfare advocates has long been that this form of coercion would be cheaper, more flexible, and sometimes less brutal than conventional war, or that it could actually mitigate or avoid conflicts. They contended that U.S. use of these tactics abroad would be conducive to the emergence of the humanitarian and democratic values that the U.S. government, and most of the American academic community, professes to support.

The problem with such claims, however, is that the supposed beneficiaries of U.S.-sponsored psychological warfare in a long list of countries are worse off today than ever before. The majority of the people in many of the principal battlegrounds—Guatemala, Nicaragua, El Salvador, the Philippines, Turkey, Indonesia, and more recently Panama and the former Soviet Union come to mind—are in truth poorer today both materially and spiritually, less democratic, less free, and often living in worse health and greater terror than before this purportedly benign form of intervention began. Even some traditionally conservative leaders, notably Pope John Paul II, have concluded that the decades of superpower competition in the Third World—in which psychological warfare has been a central strategy—have left profound devastation in their wake.[46]

Discussion of psychological warfare remains controversial because reexamination of its record leads in short order to a heretical conclusion: The role of the United States in world affairs during our lifetimes has often been rapacious, destructive, tolerant of genocide, and willing to sacrifice countless people in the pursuit of a chimera of security that has grown ever more remote. Rethinking psychological warfare's role in communication studies, in turn, requires reconsideration of where contemporary Western ideology comes from, whose interests it serves, and the role that social scientists play in its propagation. Such discussions have always upset those who are content with the present order of things. For the rest of us, though, they permit a glimmer of hope.

Appendix

Dr. Stuart Dodd's List of "Revere-Connected Papers" (1958)

Bibliography of Revere-Connected Papers

1. Bowerman, Charles, with Stuart C. Dodd and Otto N. Larsen, "Testing Message Diffusion—Verbal vs. Graphic Symbols," *International Social Science Bulletin*, UNESCO, Vol. 5, September 1953.
2. Catton, William R., Jr., "Exploring Techniques for Measuring Human Values," *American Sociological Review*, Vol. 19, 1954, pp. 49–55.
3. ———, and Melvin L. DeFleur, "The Limits of Determinacy in Attitude Measurement," *Social Forces*, Vol. 35, 1957, pp. 295–300.
4. ———, and Stuart C. Dodd, "Symbolizing the Values of Others," in *Symbols and Values: An Initial Study*, Thirteenth Symposium of the Conference on Science, Philosophy, and Religion, New York, Harper, 1954, Chap. 34, pp. 485–496.
5. ———, and Richard J. Hill, "Predicting the Relative Effectiveness of Leaflets: A Study in Selective Perception with Some Implications for Sampling," *Research Studies of the State College of Washington*, Proceedings of the Pacific Coast Sociological Society, 1953, Vol. 21, pp. 247–251.
6. DeFleur, Melvin L., and Ørjar Øyen, "The Spatial Diffusion of an Air-

Stuart Dodd, "Formulas for Spreading Opinions," *Public Opinion Quarterly*, Winter 1958, p. 551.

borne Leaflet Message,'' *American Journal of Sociology,* Vol. 59, 1953, pp. 144–149.

7. Dodd, Stuart C., ''The Interactance Hypothesis—A Gravity Model Fitting Physical Masses and Human Groups,'' *American Sociological Review,* Vol. 15, 1950, pp. 245–256.

8. ———, ''Sociomatrices and Levels of Interaction—for Dealing with Plurels, Groups, and Organizations,'' *Sociometry,* Vol. 14, 1951, pp. 237–248.

9. ———, ''On Classifying Human Values—a Step in the Prediction of Human Valuing,'' *American Sociological Review,* Vol. 16, 1951, pp. 645–653.

10. ———, ''On All-or-None Elements and Mathematical Models for Sociologists,'' *American Sociological Review,* Vol. 17, 1952, pp. 167–177.

11. ——— and staff, ''Testing Message Diffusing in C-Ville,'' *Research Studies of the State College of Washington,* Proceedings of the Pacific Coast Sociological Society, 1952, Vol. 20, 1952, pp. 83–91.

12. ———, ''Testing Message Diffusion from Person to Person,'' *Public Opinion Quarterly,* Vol. 16, 1952, pp. 247–262.

13. ———, ''Controlled Experiments on Interacting—Testing the Interactance Hypothesis Factor by Factor,'' read at the Sociological Research Association Conference, Atlantic City, N.J., September 1952.

14. ———, ''Human Dimensions—a Re-search for Concepts to Integrate Thinking,'' *Main Currents in Modern Thought,* Vol. 9, 1953, pp. 106–113.

15. ———, ''Testing Message Diffusion in Controlled Experiments: Charting the Distance and Time Factors in the Interactance Hypothesis,'' *American Sociological Review,* Vol. 18, 1953, pp. 410–416.

16. ———, ''Can the Social Scientist Serve Two Masters—An Answer through Experimental Sociology,'' *Research Studies of the State College of Washington,* Proceedings of the Pacific Sociological Society, Vol. 21, 1953, pp. 195–213.

17. ———, ''Formulas for Spreading Opinion—a Report of Controlled Experiments on Leaflet Messages in Project Revere,'' read at A.A.P.O.R. meetings, Madison, Wis., Apr. 14, 1955.

18. ———, ''Diffusion Is Predictable: Testing Probability Models for Laws of Interaction,'' *American Sociological Review,* Vol. 20, 1955, pp. 392–401.

19. ———, ''Testing Message Diffusion by Chain Tags,'' *American Journal of Sociology,* Vol. 61, 1956, pp. 425–432.

20. ———, ''Testing Message Diffusion in Harmonic Logistic Curves,'' *Psychometrika,* Vol. 21, 1956, pp. 192–205.

21. ———, "A Predictive Theory of Public Opinion—Using Nine 'Mode' and 'Tense' Factors," *Public Opinion Quarterly,* Vol. 20, 1956, pp. 571–585.

22. ———, "Conditions for Motivating Men—the Valuance Theory for Motivating Behaviors in Any Culture," *Journal of Personality,* Vol. 25, 1957, pp. 489–504.

23. ———, "The Counteractance Model," *American Journal of Sociology,* Vol. 63, 1957, pp. 273–284.

24. ———, "A Power of Town Size Predicts Its Internal Interacting—a Controlled Experiment Relating the Amount of an Interaction to the Number of Potential Interactors," *Social Forces,* Vol. 36, 1957, pp. 132–137.

25. ———, with Edith D. Rainboth and Jiri Nehnevajsa, "Revere Studies on Interaction" (Volume ready for press).

26. Hill, Richard J., "A Note on Inconsistency in Paired Comparison Judgments," *American Sociological Review,* Vol. 18, 1953, pp. 564–566.

27. ———, "An Experimental Investigation of the Logistic Model of Message Diffusion," read at AAAS meeting, San Francisco, Calif., Dec. 27, 1954.

28. ———, with Stuart C. Dodd and Susan Huffaker, "Testing Message Diffusion—the Logistic Growth Curve in a School Population," read at the Biometrics Conference, Eugene, Ore., June 1952.

29. Larsen, Otto N., "The Comparative Validity of Telephone and Face-to-Face Interviews in the Measurement of Message Diffusion from Leaflets," *American Sociological Review,* Vol. 17, 1952, pp. 471–476.

30. ———, "Rumors in a Disaster," accepted for publication in *Journal of Communication.*

31. ———, and Melvin L. DeFleur, "The Comparative Role of Children and Adults in Propaganda Diffusion," *American Sociological Review,* Vol. 19, 1954, pp. 593–602.

32. ———, and Richard J. Hill, "Mass Media and Interpersonal Communication," *American Sociological Review,* Vol. 19, 1954, pp. 426–434.

33. Nehnevajsa, Jiri, and Stuart C. Dodd, "Physical Dimensions of Social Distance," *Sociology and Social Research,* Vol. 38, 1954, pp. 287–292.

34. Pence, Orville, and Dominic LaRusso, "A Study of Testimony: Content Distortion in Oral Person-to-Person Communication," submitted for publication.

35. Rainboth, Edith Dyer, and Melvin L. DeFleur, "Testing Message Diffusion in Four Communities: Some Factors in the Use of Airborne Leaflets as a Communication Medium," *American Sociological Review,* Vol. 17, 1952, pp. 734–737.

36. Rapoport, Anatol, "Nets with Distance Bias," *Bulletin of Mathematical Biophysics,* Vol. 13, 1951, pp. 85–91.

37. ——, "Connectivity of Random Nets," *Bulletin of Mathematical Biophysics,* Vol. 13, 1951, pp. 107–117.

38. ——, "The Probability Distribution of Distinct Hits on Closely Packed Targets," *Bulletin of Mathematical Biophysics,* Vol. 13, 1951, pp. 133–138.

39. ——, " 'Ignition' Phenomena in Random Nets," *Bulletin of Mathematical Biophysics,* Vol. 14, 1952, pp. 35–44.

40. ——, "Contribution to the Mathematical Theory of Mass Behavior: I. The Propagation of Single Acts," *Bulletin of Mathematical Biophysics,* Vol. 14, 1952, pp. 159–169.

41. ——, "Response Time and Threshold of a Random Net," *Bulletin of Mathematical Biophysics,* Vol. 14, 1952, pp. 351–363.

42. ——, and Lionel I. Rebhun, "On the Mathematical Theory of Rumor Spread," *Bulletin of Mathematical Biophysics,* Vol. 14, 1952, pp. 375–383.

43. ——, "Contribution to the Mathematical Theory of Contagion and Spread of Information: I. Spread through a Thoroughly Mixed Population," *Bulletin of Mathematical Biophysics,* Vol. 15, 1953, pp. 173–183.

44. ——, "Spread of Information through a Population with Socio-structural Bias: I. Assumption of Transitivity," *Bulletin of Mathematical Biophysics,* Vol. 15, 1953, pp. 523–533.

45. ——, "Spread of Information through a Population with Socio-structural Bias: II. Various Models with Partial Transitivity," *Bulletin of Mathematical Biophysics,* Vol. 15, 1953, pp. 535–546.

46. ——, "Spread of Information through a Population with Socio-structural Bias: III. Suggested Experimental Procedures," *Bulletin of Mathematical Biophysics,* Vol. 16, 1954, pp. 75–81.

47. Shaw, John G., "Testing Message Diffusion in Relation to Demographic Variables: an Analysis of Respondents to an Airborne Leaflet Message," submitted for publication.

48. Turabian, Chahin, and Stuart C. Dodd, "A Dimensional System of Human Values," Transactions Second World Congress of Sociology, International Sociology Association, 1954, pp. 100–105.

49. Winthrop, Henry, and Stuart C. Dodd, "A Dimensional Theory of Social Diffusion—an Analysis, Modeling and Partial Testing of One-way Interacting," *Sociometry,* Vol. 16, 1953, pp. 180–202.

Theses

50. M.A. Catton, William R., Jr., "The Sociological Study of Human Values," 1952.

51. M.A. Øyen, Ørjar, "The Relationship between Distances and Social Interaction—the Case of Message Diffusion," 1953.
52. Ph.D. Catton, William R., Jr., "Propaganda Effectiveness as a Function of Human Values," 1954.
53. Ph.D. DeFleur, Melvin Lawrence, "Experimental Studies of Stimulus Response Relationships in Leaflet Communication," 1954.
54. Ph.D. Hill, Richard J., "Temporal Aspects of Message Diffusion," 1955.
55. Ph.D. Larsen, Otto N., "Interpersonal Relations in the Social Diffusion of Messages," 1955.
56. Ph.D. Shaw, John G., Jr., "The Relationship of Selected Ecological Variables to Leaflet Message Response," 1954.
57. M.A. West, S.S., "Variation of Compliance to Airborne Leaflet Messages with Age and with Terminal Level of Education," 1956.

Monographs Published

58. DeFleur, Melvin L., and Otto N. Larsen, *The Flow of Information*, New York, Harper, 1958.

Bibliographic Essay

This book examined the interaction between U.S. psychological warfare and the development of mass communication theories and research methodologies between 1945 and 1960. The literature cited therefore centers on the following areas:

1. international events and the general sociopolitical context from 1945 through 1960, which are often referred to as the early cold war years;
2. U.S. psychological warfare operations during that period;
3. U.S. mass communication theory and research during that period;
4. writings of, and biographical data about, several major thinkers involved in both psychological warfare and mass communication research;
5. institutional histories of the major private organizations and government departments active in mass communication research and psychological warfare; and
6. Comparative data concerning Soviet and Western European work in psychological warfare and mass communication research.

In the following notes, discussion of the literature utilized in this study is divided into these six categories.

Sociopolitical Context, 1945–1960

There is an extensive literature concerning the events and politics of the early cold war years, and a complete review of that material is obviously beyond the scope of this project. A look at a handful of works concerning the general sociopolitical context of this period is useful, however, both for background on events of the day and for insight into how leading scholars and political figures interpreted those events.

Works that deal primarily with foreign affairs usually fall into one of four basic schools of thought concerning the cold war: orthodox, Soviet, revisionist, or postrevisionist. The rival orthodox and Soviet trends arose more or less contemporaneously during the 1940s and 1950s. These schools articulate what might be termed the "official" version of the cold war as viewed by the U.S. and Soviet political establishments, respectively.[1] Their basic features are their contention that the opposite side is responsible for the creation and escalation of the cold war,[2] a Manichaean dualism that views the rival camp as a powerful and evil enemy,[3] and a conviction that one's own side must wage a bitter or even desperate battle if it is to survive the aggression of the other.[4] A comparison of orthodox U.S. and Soviet writings strongly suggests that neither group accepted any substantial element of its rival's thinking as legitimate. These two trends were by far the dominant schools of thought during 1945–60.

The revisionist challenge to the orthodox school arose in the West during the late 1950s and early 1960s. There have been several revisionist variations, but the unifying tenet of this school has been the argument that the United States (rather than the Soviet Union) was the principal aggressor during the cold war.[5] The postrevisionist school emerged in the West during the 1970s as a means of reintegrating the revisionist rupture, so to speak; it concedes a number of factual arguments to the revisionists and plays down the Manichaean notions of the orthodox school while reasserting Soviet culpability for much of the cold war, particularly during 1945–60.[6]

General works that deal with domestic U.S. affairs during 1945–60 cannot be quite so easily divided into schools, in part because there has been a much richer and more complex range of published opinion. But a useful distinction can be made for the purposes of this study between those writers who regarded communism as a threat so imminent that it impelled a major domestic response (typically involving use of psychological warfare techniques against the U.S. population in order to secure national security and ideological unity)[7] and those who regarded that response as itself presenting greater practical danger to the United States than did communism.[8]

Taken as a whole, then, these general-context works both discuss and implicitly illustrate the continuing division within American society over the U.S. role in the cold war and in U.S.–Soviet relations generally. As has been seen, these divisions played an important role in the dynamics of psychological warfare's impact on mass communication theory during the study period.

Literature on Psychological Warfare

Literature concerning psychological warfare presents special problems not typically encountered in mass communication research. First, the substantial majority of U.S. psychological warfare policy writings and operational records since World War II were classified at the time they were created.[9] Many remain classified today or are accessible only in sanitized form through Freedom of Information Act requests.[10] In some cases, U.S. intelligence agencies deliberately destroyed all record of certain particularly sensitive operations—notably those involving biological warfare, chemical experimentation on humans, and murders—as a means of heading off congressional inquiries into psychological operations.[11]

Fortunately, however, the United States' comparatively open policies concerning government records have facilitated declassification of a substantial number of policy records concerning psychological warfare, as well as a more limited body of surviving operational records. Much of this material has not been published but is available to researchers at the National Archives, the Truman Presidential Library, and the Eisenhower Presidential Library. Highlights of these collections include the National Security Council's policy papers on psychological warfare,[12] the records of the Psychological Strategy Board,[13] and miscellaneous declassified U.S. Army, U.S. Air Force and U.S. State Department records.[14] Discussion and documentation concerning Central Intelligence Agency psychological operations can be found scattered throughout the collections just mentioned,[15] and fragmentary records concerning a number of CIA operations have been collected by the National Security Archive (a private archive),[16] the Center for National Security Studies,[17] and other organizations.

There is an extensive secondary literature concerning CIA psychological warfare operations. This includes histories written from several different points of view, memoirs of participants, and journalistic accounts. The reliability of this material runs from poor to excellent. Some sources include what appears to be intentional disinformation concerning U.S. psychological operations, but this problem can often be offset by cross-checking various authors' accounts against one another or against independently verifiable facts.[18] Recommended secondary sources on psychological warfare include definitions of the term "psychological warfare";[19] psychological warfare budgets and personnel;[20] clandestine CIA ownership and/or subsidies of newspapers, magazines, publishing houses, and radio stations;[21] suborning of reporters or media executives;[22] selective financing and/or manipulation of scholars in the United States and abroad;[23] clandestine radio broadcasting, including Radio Free Europe and Radio Liberty;[24] other clandestine communication techniques, such as use of propaganda balloons;[25] U.S. psychological operations during coups d'état in Guatemala, Iran, and elsewhere;[26] U.S. psychological operations during elections in Italy, France, and other countries in western Europe;[27] attempts to destabilize or encourage rebellion inside the Soviet bloc;[28] use of psychological warfare within the United States;[29] development and use of mind-altering drugs, including LSD;[30] replies to Soviet and/or Chinese propaganda;[31] impact of psychological warfare on intelligence estimates;[32] sociological and social-psychological studies of the Soviet Union;[33] and overviews of the role of social science research in the general intelligence mission.[34]

There is also an interesting literature published between 1945 and 1960 on the theory of psychological warfare that is often different in content and tone from the later histories and memoirs just mentioned. The work published during the early cold war years typically recounted World War II experiences with these techniques[35] or argued from an "orthodox" standpoint that psychological warfare was an essential weapon to use in the conflict with the Soviets.[36] As noted elsewhere, there was a considerable amount of writing concerning psychological warfare in *Public Opinion Quarterly* and other academic communication journals of the day.[37] Such writings were collected in several valuable casebooks and handbooks that offer accessible overviews of the public writings on psychological warfare by many of the authors, consultants, and political figures active in the field.[38]

There are a number of published and unpublished bibliographies concerning psychological warfare. The earliest of these date to the 1930s, before the term "psychological warfare" had entered English.[39]

Perhaps the most focused bibliographic compilation for the purposes of this book was prepared in 1951–52 by Chitra Smith for the Bureau of Social Science Research under contract with the RAND Corporation;[40] this was later published in slightly modified form by RAND and Princeton University Press.[41]

Myron Smith, Jr., prepared two relatively recent selected bibliographies on psychological warfare.[42] Smith's work includes 190 citations concerning such activities during World War II and a second collection of 668 citations covering 1945–80. The later collection is also broken out by subject area and by country. The Sociofile computerized data base includes a handful of citations to foreign-language works and to more current material.[43] Former State Department historian Neal Peterson recently prepared an annotated bibliography of writings concerning intelligence issues and the cold war that reviews much of the literature concerning the clandestine aspects of the cold war that has been published during the last decade.[44]

Also noteworthy is a recent annotated bibliography of commercial and scholarly communications studies regarded as useful for design of future psychological operations. The bibliography was prepared by Ronald McLaurin, L. John Martin, and Sriramesh Krishnamurthy for Abbott Associates, under contract to the undersecretary of defense for policy.[45]

These notes by no means means exhaust the list of literature on psychological warfare as it was conducted between 1945 and 1960, but they are indicative of its scope and general trends.

U.S. Mass Communication Theory and Research, 1945–1960

The history of mass communication theory and research has become a lively topic among academics during the past decade. Much of the present literature on the subject stresses the evolution of ideas that influenced the field, rather than the ways in which the social context of the day helped shape ideas. As a result, there has been relatively little inquiry into the sources of institutional and financial support for mass communication research during the years that it crystallized into a distinct field of inquiry. With the notable exception of Converse's[46] and Biderman and Crawford's[47] work, the role of U.S. psychological warfare programs in the evolution of post–World War II communication studies has largely escaped academic attention up to now. Indeed, a number of now standard texts that discuss the history of mass communication theory mention psychological warfare only in passing or not at all.[48]

This project has built on earlier studies on the history of communication research by Albig,[49] Barton,[50] Bennett,[51] Berelson,[52] Blumler,[53] Chaffee,[54] Chaffee and Hochheimer,[55] Converse,[56] Czitrom,[57] Delia,[58] Dennis,[59] Eulau,[60] Gitlin,[61] Hall,[62] Hardt,[63] Katz,[64] Lazarsfeld,[65] Lowery and DeFleur,[66] McLeod and Blumler,[67] Rogers,[68] Schramm,[69] Sproule,[70] Stouffer,[71] and Tankard,[72] among others, as well as earlier work in the relationship between the federal government and the social sciences by Beals,[73] Biderman and Crawford,[74] Crawford and Lyons,[75] Gendzier,[76] Horowitz,[77] Horowitz and Katz,[78] the Library of Congress,[79] Lyons,[80] McCartney,[81] Pool,[82] and others.

Although differing in emphasis, degree of detail, and political perspective, each of these accounts reflects a historical paradigm of more or less clearly defined "stages" of U.S. mass communication theory and research. While there is important evidence that the stages conception may itself be in part misleading,[83] it can nonetheless serve as a useful framework for discussion of how leading writers view the evolution of work in the field.

The stages are generally said to have begun with a period of early studies into the broad macrosocietal and ideological role of mass communications, which is usually dated from the late nineteenth century to around 1940. Thinkers widely regarded as exemplifying this trend include Durkheim, Tönnies, and Maine.[84] "Mass society" models with both "dark" and "light" overtones are widely associated with this work; the speakers in the discussion generally agreed that the mass media were playing a new, integrative role in modern society but often disagreed on the character of that society and quality of life that it could offer.[85]

In the United States, a strongly positivistic, quantitative approach to communications studies focusing on "middle range" communications effects supplanted most discussion of macrosocietal and ideological communications issues by about 1945. This approach continued to serve as the largely undisputed "dominant paradigm" for the field until well into the 1970s.[86] Most recent authors on the history of communication research agree that this post-1945 trend exhibited at least three characteristics. First, the funded research in the field centered on efforts to discover and quantify the "effects" of communication behavior. The social science tools applied to the task were for the most part surveys, content analysis, and experimental and quasi-experimental techniques borrowed from psychology and social psychology. Second, there was a rise of "two-step," "reference group," and eventually "limited effects" models of communications behavior. Each of these theories was based in large measure on the relatively limited and transitory impact of mass media messages on individual behavior that could be documented with the research methodologies then in favor. To the extent that these theories considered media's macrosocietal or ideological roles at all, they tended to extrapolate the minor quantifiable "micro" effects to a "macro" level. Third, communications research crystallized into a distinct field of scholarship after 1945, complete with professional cadre, institutional identity, a more-or-less defined research agenda, and a substantial body of agreed-upon knowledge. The date for this precipitation into a distinct field is necessarily arbitrary but is generally placed between 1949 and about 1955.[87]

Less common in the literature, but argued in this text and (in part) in work by Dewey,[88] Carey,[89] Hall,[90] Biderman and Crawford,[91] and others, are several corollary propositions. Commercial, political, and military groups seeking new techniques to preserve and advance their existing role in society provided the substantial majority of funds for the quantitative studies that elaborated narrowly positivistic models of communication behavior.[92] The U.S. government's psychological warfare programs were an important funder, particularly during the years in which mass communication research crystallized into a distinct field.[93] While the funders did not determine the results of mass communication studies, they did often determine which questions would receive attention, and they exerted considerable indirect influence on the selection of "leaders" and "authorities" in the field through the extension or withholding of the resources necessary for large-scale research. One result of this process was the virtual eclipse of conceptions of communication as a ritual or sharing behavior—which had been a prominent part of Dewey's thought,[94] for example—and its replacement by baroque elaborations of theories of communication as a highly instrumental process of persuasion and coercion.[95]

Biographical Data on Key Personalities

Four prominent mass communication researchers active in psychological warfare projects during 1945–60 provided the starting point for this book's examination of key personalities in this field. They are Hadley Cantril, Harold Lasswell, Daniel Lerner, and Wilbur Schramm, and each has left a substantial body of work concerning mass communication, psychological warfare, and political affairs.

Albert Hadley Cantril (generally known as Hadley Cantril) wrote or edited, alone or with colleagues, at least 24 book-length studies[96] and a reported 120 scholarly articles for professional journals.[97] Cantril published an intellectual memoir,[98] and biographical notes concerning his career are available in several standard sources.[99] Cantril is remembered primarily for the application of psychology to the study of political and social affairs and for his contributions to opinion research.[100] Particular note should be made of Cantril's longtime partner, Lloyd A. Free, who collaborated with Cantril in the Institute for International Social Research[101] and wrote several books with him.[102]

Harold Lasswell was probably the most prolific of the authors considered here, having written or edited some forty-seven identifiable book-length works between 1924 and 1980, several of which appeared in three and even four separate editions.[103] Lasswell is perhaps best remembered for his sloganlike formulations of political affairs and media dynamics, which became the foundation for many functionalist theories of the 1940s, 1950s, and 1960s.[104] Lasswell's *Propaganda Technique in the World War* (first issued in 1927 and subsequently reissued in three further editions) is widely regarded as one of the seminal works of modern mass communication theory.[105]

Daniel Lerner, a frequent collaborator of Lasswell's, wrote or coedited at least four texts with him,[106] each of which dealt in some manner with propaganda and psychological warfare. Lerner published at least eighteen book-length works during his career,[107] as well as numerous journal articles.[108] Lerner's work was somewhat more tightly focused than that of Cantril or Lasswell, with greater attention to psychological warfare, propaganda, and methodological issues in social science research.[109] Lerner either wrote, edited, or contributed to virtually every major collection of essays on psychological warfare published from 1945 to 1980.[110]

Wilbur Schramm is widely regarded as a pivotal figure in the crystallization of U.S. mass communications research into a distinct field of scientific inquiry.[111] Schramm's role as a psychological warfare contractor, operator, and promoter is less widely understood, however. During the 1950s, Schramm's personal income and professional prestige were to a significant degree dependent upon his work for the U.S. Air Force, U.S. Information Agency, Department of Defense, and the CIA-sponsored propaganda organization Radio Free Europe.[112]

The four authors discussed here—Cantril, Lasswell, Lerner, and Schramm—do not, of course, exhaust the list of noted social scientists and mass communication theorists active in psychological warfare projects during the early cold war years. Other prominent figures in mass communication research who participated in substantial, but varying, degrees include Kurt Back,[113] Edward Barrett,[114] Raymond Bauer,[115] Robert Bower,[116] Albert Biderman,[117] Stanley Bigman,[118] Leonard Cottrell,[119] Leo Crespi,[120] William Daugherty,[121] W. Phillips Davison,[122] Leonard Doob,[123] Murray Dyer,[124] Harry Eckstein,[125] Lloyd Free,[126] George Gallup,[127] Alexander George,[128] Robert Holt,[129] Carl Hovland,[130] Alex Inkeles,[131] Irving Janis,[132] Morris Janowitz,[133] Joseph Klapper,[134] Clyde Kluckhohn,[135] Klaus Knorr,[136] Hideya Kumata,[137] Paul Lazarsfeld,[138] Alexander Leighton,[139] Nathan Leites,[140] Paul M. Linebarger,[141] Leo Lowenthal,[142] L. John Martin,[143] Margaret Mead,[144] Jesse Orlansky,[145] Saul Padover,[146] Ithiel de Sola Pool,[147] DeWitt Poole,[148] Lucian Pye,[149] John W. Riley,[150] Carroll Shartle,[151] Chitra Smith,[152] Hans Speier,[153] Samuel Stouffer,[154] Ralph K. White,[155] and William R. Young.[156]

Institutional Histories

The institutional frameworks of U.S. mass communication research, on the one hand, and of U.S. psychological warfare operations, on the other, went through an intricate, interlocked evolution during 1945–60. Some familiarity with these shifts is necessary to understand the relationship between the two trends. Jean Converse[157] offers what is probably the best and most accessible institutional histories of the Bureau of Applied Social Research, National Opinion Research Center, and the University of Michigan's Institute for Social Research, each of which was a center of mass communication scholarship and a contractor for psychological warfare–related research at various points between 1945 and 1960. Additional institutional studies are available for the RAND Corporation,[158] BASR,[159] NORC,[160] ISR,[161] Massachusetts Institute of Technology's Center for International Studies,[162] and Harvard University's Russian Research Center.[163] The archives of the Bureau of Social

Science Research, an important center of both mass communication research and psychological warfare contracting during the 1950s, are now held by the University of Maryland Libraries' Special Collections unit and by American University. There is no history text, as such, concerning BSSR, but archivists have prepared a detailed finding aid to the Maryland record collection, which permits reconstruction of many BSSR activities.[164]

Institutional histories concerning psychological warfare operations are generally less accessible and less likely to be familiar to mass communication scholars. The sources cited in the "Psychological Warfare" section of this essay (above) cover much of this ground. Particularly noteworthy, however, are two histories of Radio Free Europe[165] and several recent studies of the U.S. Army's Special Forces.[166]

Soviet and European Psychological Warfare

This text focuses on the U.S. experience in psychological warfare without attempting to fully document the activities of U.S. rivals and allies in this field. Some comparative data are valuable nonetheless in order to place the U.S. efforts in context.

Internal documents concerning the development of psychological warfare strategy by the Soviet Union and its allies are not available at this writing, although there is testimony from East bloc defectors on the subject,[167] and some suggestion that relevant Soviet archives may open during the next decade.[168] There is also a substantial secondary literature from Western specialists concerning U.S.S.R. practices in this field.[169] For the most part, these writings reflect an "orthodox" conception of the cold war and a concern that Soviet propaganda has been effective in shaping the opinions of its target audiences.[170]

Original documentation concerning psychological warfare activities by U.S. allies in Europe is relatively sparse, but some secondary literature is available.[171] These works tend to be descriptive rather than theoretical in nature, but they suggest that Western European governmental thinking concerning propaganda and psychological warfare has followed roughly the same evolution seen in the United States.[172]

Notes

Chapter 1

1. Concerning ideological workers, today a substantial majority of employers of entry-level television and radio reporters, newspaper and magazine editors and writers, many types of advertising specialists, public relations personnel (or, to use the currently preferred term, "public communication" experts) require new hires to arrive with advanced degrees in one of several varieties of mass communication study. See W. W. Schwed, "Hiring, Promotion, Salary, Longevity Trends Charted at Dailies," *Newspaper Research Journal* (October 1981); Lee Becker, J. W. Fruit, and S. L. Caudill, *The Training and Hiring of Journalists* (Norwood, NJ: Ablex, 1987).

2. Albert Biderman and Elizabeth Crawford, *The Political Economics of Social Research: The Case of Sociology* (Springfield, VA: Clearinghouse for Federal Scientific and Technological Information, 1968).

3. On BASR, see Jean Converse, *Survey Research in the United States* (Berkeley: University of California Press, 1987), pp. 269, 275–76, 506–7 notes 37 and 42. On Cantril's IISR, see John Crewdson and Joseph Treaster, "The CIA's 3-Decade Effort to Mold the World's Views," *New York Times,* December 25, 26, and 27, 1977, with discussion of Cantril and the IISR on December 26. For Cantril's version, which conceals the true source of his funds, see Hadley Cantril, *The Human Dimension: Experiences in Policy Research* (New Brunswick, NJ: Rutgers University Press, 1967). On CENIS, see Massachusetts Institute of Technology, Center for International Studies, *The Center for International Studies: A Description,* (Cambridge: MIT, July 1955); U.S. Department of State, Foreign Service Institute, *Problems of Development and Internal Defense,* Report of a Country Team Seminar, June 11–July 13, 1962; (Washington, DC: Foreign Service Institute, 1962); and Ithiel de Sola

Pool, "The Necessity for Social Scientists Doing Research for Governments," *Background* 10, no. 2 (August 1966):111–22. Other major communication research projects that depended heavily on funding from U.S. government psychological warfare agencies included the National Opinion Research Center, the Survey Research Center (now named the Institute for Social Research), and the Bureau of Social Science Research. The text that follows discusses these in greater detail.

4. For details on the Department of State contracts, which produced a scandal when they were uncovered in 1957, see House Committee on Government Operations, *State Department Opinion Polls,* 85th Cong., 1st sess., June–July 1957 (Washington, DC: GPO, 1957).

5. Albert Biderman, "Social-Psychological Needs and 'Involuntary' Behavior as Illustrated by Compliance in Interrogation," *Sociometry* 23, no. 2 (June 1960):120–47; Louis Gottschalk, *The Use of Drugs in Information-Seeking Interviews,* Bureau of Social Science Research report 322, December 1958, BSSR Archives, series II, box 11, University of Maryland Libraries Special Collections, College Park; and Albert Biderman, Barbara Heller, and Paula Epstein, *A Selected Bibliography on Captivity Behavior,* Bureau of Social Science Research report 339-1, February 1961, BSSR Archives, series II, box 14, also at the University of Maryland. Biderman acknowledges the Human Ecology Fund—later revealed to have been a conduit for CIA funds—and U.S. Air Force contract no. AF 49 (638)727 as the source of his funding for this work. For more on the CIA's use of the Human Ecology Fund and of the related Society for the Investigation of Human Ecology, see John Marks, *The Search for the "Manchurian Candidate": The CIA and Mind Control* (New York: Times Books, 1979), pp. 147–63.

6. Jesse Delia, "Communication Research: A History," in Charles Berger and Steven Chaffee (eds.) *Handbook of Communication Science* (Newbury Park, CA: Sage, 1987), pp. 20–98.

7. Robert Merton, *Social Theory and Social Structure* (New York: Free Press, 1968), pp. 504–5, discusses Lazarsfeld's and Merton's own views. On this point see also Theodore Adorno, "Scientific Experiences of a European Scholar in America," in Donald Fleming and Bernard Bailyn (eds.), *The Intellectual Migration: Europe and America 1930–1960* (Cambridge, MA: Harvard University Press, 1969), p. 343; and Willard Rowland, *The Politics of TV Violence* (Beverly Hills, CA: Sage, 1983).

8. Thomas Kuhn, *The Structure of Scientific Revolutions,* 2nd ed. (Chicago: University of Chicago Press, 1972), p. 10.

9. Biderman and Elisabeth Crawford, *The Political Economics of Social Research.* For related texts concerning political and economic aspects of social science research, see Albert Biderman and Elisabeth Crawford, "The Basis of Allocation to Social Scientific Work," paper presented to American Sociological

Association, September 1969, now at BSSR Archives, series V, box 3, University of Maryland Libraries Special Collections, College Park; Albert Biderman and Elisabeth Crawford, "Paper Money: Trends of Research Sponsorship in American Sociology Journals," *Social Sciences Information* (Paris), 9, no. 1 (February 1970):51–77; Elisabeth Crawford and Gene Lyons, "Foreign Area Research: A Background Statement," *American Behavioral Scientist* 10 (June 1967):3–7; Elisabeth Crawford and Albert Biderman, *Social Science and International Affairs* (New York: Wiley, 1969); James McCartney, "On Being Scientific: Changing Styles of Presentation of Sociological Research," *American Sociologist* (February 1970):30–35; Pool, "The Necessity for Social Scientists Doing Research for Governments"; Gene M. Lyons, *The Uneasy Partnership; Social Science and the Federal Government in the Twentieth Century* (New York: Russell Sage Foundation, 1969); House Committee on Government Operations, *The Use of Social Research in Federal Domestic Programs,* 4 vols., 90th Cong. 1st sess. January–December 1967 (Washington, DC: GPO, 1967). For more recent analysis, see Richard Nathan, *Social Science in Government: Uses and Misuses* (New York: Basic Books, 1988); and Otto Larsen, *Milestones and Millstones: Social Science at the National Science Foundation, 1945–1991* (New Brunswick, NJ: Transaction, 1992). More critical texts on this issue include Ralph Beals, *Politics of Social Research* (Chicago: Aldine, 1969); Irving Louis Horowitz and James Everett Katz, *Social Science and Public Policy in the United States* (New York: Praeger, 1975); Irving Louis Horowitz (ed.), *The Use and Abuse of Social Science* (New Brunswick, NJ: Transaction, 1971); Irene Gendzier, *Managing Political Change: Social Scientists and the Third World* (Boulder, CO.: Westview Press, 1985).

10. Steven Chaffee and John Hochheimer, "The Beginnings of Political Communications Research in the United States: Origins of the 'Limited Effects' Model," in Michael Gurevitch and Mark Levy (eds.), *Mass Communications Yearbook,* Vol. 5 (Beverly Hills, CA: Sage, 1985), pp. 75–104, quote on p. 77.

11. Quoted in John Hughes, "'Free Radio' for China," *Christian Science Monitor,* July 30, 1992.

12. Pool, "The Necessity for Social Scientists Doing Research for Governments."

13. National Science Foundation, *Federal Funds for Science* (Washington, DC: GPO, 1953), pp. 35–48; and "The Federal Government in Behavioral Science," special issue of *The American Behavioral Scientist* 7, no. 9 (May 1964), William Ellis (study director).

14. James Burnham, *Containment or Liberation?* (New York: John Day, 1953), p. 188. For fragmentary, but supporting data see also Comptroller General of the United States (General Accounting Office), *U.S. Government Monies Provided to Radio Free Europe and Radio Liberty* (Washington, DC: GPO,

1972), with a classified annex obtained via the Freedom of Information Act; Sig Mikelson, *America's Other Voice: The Story of Radio Free Europe and Radio Liberty* (New York: Praeger, 1983); Larry D. Collins, ''The Free Europe Committee: American Weapon of the Cold War,'' Ph.D. diss., Carlton University, 1975, Canadian Thesis on Microfilm Service call no. TC20090; James R. Price, *Radio Free Europe: A Survey and Analysis* (Washington, DC: Congressional Research Service Document No. JX 1710 U.S. B, March 1972); and Joseph Whelan, *Radio Liberty: A Study of Its Origins, Structure, Policy, Programming and Effectiveness* (Washington, DC: Congressional Research Service, 1972).

15. National Science Foundation, *Federal Funds for Science,* and *American Behavioral Scientist*.

16. Biderman and Crawford, *Political Economics of Social Research,* pp. 20–26. For a detailed discussion of the role of the Ford Foundation and Carnegie Corporation, see Chapter 4.

17. See, for example, Paul Lazarsfeld and Wagner Thielens, *The Academic Mind: Social Scientists in a Time of Crisis* (Glencoe, IL: Free Press, 1958); or Ellen Schrecker, *No Ivory Tower: McCarthvism and the Universities* (New York: Oxford University Press, 1986).

18. Daniel Lerner with Lucille Pevsner, *The Passing of Traditional Society* (Glencoe, IL: Free Press, 1958).

19. William Daugherty and Morris Janowitz (eds.), *A Psychological Warfare Casebook* (Baltimore: Johns Hopkins [for U.S. Army Operations Research Office], 1958), p. 12; their reference is to Ladislas Farago, *German Psychological Warfare* (New York: Putnam, 1941).

20. Daugherty and Janowitz, *A Psychological Warfare Casebook,* pp. 12–35.

21. North Atlantic Treaty Organization, Military Agency for Standardization, *NATO Glossary of Terms and Definitions for Military Use* (unclassified) (Belgium: NATO, 1976), pp. 2–206 and Appendix J-1; on ''public diplomacy,'' see Robert Parry and Peter Kornbluh, ''Iran–Contra's Untold Story,'' *Foreign Policy* 72 (Fall 1988):3–30.

22. V. I. Lenin, *What Is to Be Done?* (1902; rpt. Peking: Foreign Languages Press, 1978), pp. 199–211; Mao Tse Tung (Mao Zedong), *Mao Tse Tung on Literature and Art* (Peking: Foreign Languages Press, 1967), pp. 1–44, 142–62.

23. The principal British psychological warfare agency during World War II, for example, was called the Political Warfare Executive; see Robert H. Bruce Lockhardt, ''Political Warfare,'' *Journal of the Royal United Service Institution* (London) (May 1950); Harold D. Lasswell, ''Political and Psychological Warfare,'' in Daniel Lerner (ed.), *Propaganda in War and Crisis* (New York: George Stewart, 1951), pp. 261–66.

24. Adolf Hitler, *Mein Kampf,* translated by John Chamberlain (New York: Reynal & Hitchcock, 1939); see also Arno Mayer, *Why Did the Heavens Not Darken? The Final Solution in History* (New York: Pantheon, 1988), pp. 95–103.

25. U.S. Department of the Army General Staff, Plans and Operations Division, *Psychological Warfare Study for Guidance in Strategic Planning* (originally top secret, now declassified), March 11, 1948, U.S. Army P&O 091.42 TS (section I, cases 1–7), RG 319, U.S. National Archives, Washington, DC. Emphasis in original.

26. U.S. Department of the Army, Joint Strategic Plans Committee, *JSPC 862/3* (originally top secret, now declassified), August 2, 1948, Appendix ''C,'' P&O 352 TS (section I, case 1), RG 319, U.S. National Archives, Washington, DC.

27. Ibid. Emphasis in original.

28. U.S. Department of the Army General Staff, *Psychological Warfare Study for Guidance in Strategic Planning.* Emphasis in original.

29. U.S. National Security Council, *NSC 10/2: Office of Special Projects* (originally top secret, now declassified), June 15, 1948, RG 273, U.S. National Archives, Washington, DC.

30. U.S. Department of the Army General Staff, *Psychological Warfare Study for Guidance in Strategic Planning.*

31. Ibid. For a more recent example of the same phenomena, see Parry and Kornbluh, ''Iran–Contra's Untold Story.''

Chapter 2

1. Margaret Mead, ''Continuities in Communication from Early Man to Modern Times,'' in Harold Lasswell, Daniel Lerner, and Hans Speier (eds.), *Propaganda and Communication in World History,* 3 vols. (Honolulu: University of Hawaii Press, 1980), Vol. 1, pp. 21–49.

2. Sun Tzu, *The Art of War,* translated by Samuel Griffith (London: Oxford University Press, 1971), pp. 63–84.

3. Josephina Oliva de Coll, *Resistencia Indigena ante la Conguista,* 4th ed. (Mexico City: Siglo Vientiuno Editores, 1983).

4. L. H. Butterfield, ''Psychological Warfare in 1776: The Jefferson–Franklin Plan,'' in William Daugherty and Morris Janowitz (eds.) *A Psychological Warfare Casebook* (Baltimore: Johns Hopkins [for U.S. Army Operations Research Office], 1958), pp. 62–72.

5. M. Andrews, ''Psychological Warfare in the Mexican War,'' in Daugherty and Janowitz, *Psychological Warfare Casebook,* pp. 72–73.

6. Morris Janowitz, ''The Emancipation Proclamation as an Instrument of Psychological Warfare,'' pp. 73–79, and B. J. Hendrick, ''Propaganda of the

Confederacy," pp. 79–84, both in Daugherty and Janowitz, *Psychological Warfare Casebook*.

7. Harold Lasswell, *Propaganda Technique in the World War* (1927; rpt. Cambridge: MIT Press, 1971), pp. 14–26, quote on p. 18.

8. Ibid., p. xxxi.

9. Alfred Paddock, *U.S. Army Special Warfare: Its Origins* (Washington, DC: National Defense University Press, 1982), p. 8.

10. Ibid.

11. Lasswell, *Propaganda Technique in the World War*, p. xxxii.

12. Walter Lippmann, *Public Opinion* (New York: Harcourt, Brace, 1922).

13. Walter Lippmann, *The Phantom Public* (New York: Harcourt, Brace, 1925).

14. Lasswell, *Propaganda Technique in the World War*, p. xxxii; D. Steven Blum, *Walter Lippmann* Ithaca, NY: Cornell University Press, 1984), pp. 49–64.

15. Lippmann, *Public Opinion*, p. 29.

16. Ibid., pp. 31, 32.

17. See, for example, book reviews by J. M. Lee, *Yale Review* 12 (January 23, 1922: 418; R. E. Park, *American Journal of Sociology* vol. 28 (September 1922):232; W. C. Ford, *Atlantic* (June 1922); or C. E. Merriam, *International Journal of Ethics* (January 1923):210. In contrast, John Dewey wrote that Lippmann's writing style was so accomplished that "one finishes the book almost without realizing that it is perhaps the most effective indictment of democracy as currently conceived ever penned." *New Republic* 30 (May 3, 1922):286. W. S. Myers commented that Lippmann "is essentially a propagandist, and his work is influenced by this characteristic attitude of approach toward any subject." 55 *Bookmark* (June 1922):418.

18. Harold Lasswell, Ralph Casey, and Bruce Lannes Smith, *Propaganda and Promotional Activities: An Annotated Bibliography* (1935; rpt. Chicago: University of Chicago Press, 1969), p. 43.

19. Harold Lasswell, "Propaganda," *Encyclopedia of the Social Sciences*, Vol. 11 (New York: Macmillan, 1937), pp. 524–25. See also Harold Lasswell, "Political and Psychological Warfare," in Daugherty and Janowitz, *Psychological Warfare Casebook*, pp. 21–40. Although Lasswell's importance as a theoretician of social control has been long recognized, it has been brought to renewed public attention in the United States in recent years largely through Noam Chomsky's media studies. See Noam Chomsky, *Intellectuals and the State* (Leiden, Netherlands: Johan Huizinga-lezing, 1977), pp. 9–10, and "Democracy and the Media," in *Necessary Illusions: Thought Control in Democratic Societies* (Boston: South End Press, 1989).

20. Robert Barnhart (ed.), *The Barnhart Dictionary of Etymology* (New York: Wilson, 1988), p. 195.

21. Willard Rowland, *Politics of TV Violence* (Beverly Hills, CA: Sage, 1983), pp. 53–59.

22. My thinking on this point was spurred by Oskar Negt's discussion of Horkheimer and Adorno in "Mass Media: Tools of Domination or Instruments of Liberation? Aspects of the Frankfurt School's Communications Analysis," *New German Critique* (Spring 1978): 61–79. 61ff.

23. Chomsky, *Intellectuals and the State,* pp. 9–10.

24. Joseph Goebbels, *Goebbels-Reden, 1932–1945,* 2 vols. (Düsseldorf: Drost, 1972); and Joseph Goebbels *Tagebuecher von Joseph Goebbels, Saemtliche Fragments,* 4 vols., edited by Elke Froehlich (Munich: K. G. Saur, 1987). For a guide to microfilmed collections of Goebbels' Reichministerium für Volksaufklärung und Propaganda, see U.S. National Archives, *Records of the Reich Ministry for Public Enlightenment and Propaganda,* No. 22 in the *Guide to German Records* series, Washington, DC: National Archives and Records Service, 1960.

25. L. D. Stokes, "The Sicherheitsdienst (SD) of the Reichsführer SS and German Public Opinion, 1939–1941," Ph.D. diss., Johns Hopkins University, 1972; Aryeh Unger, "The Public Opinion Reports of the Nazi Party," *POQ* 29, no. 4 (Winter 1965–66): 565–82; Arthur Smith, Jr., "Life in Wartime Germany: Colonel Ohlendorf's Opinion Service," *POQ* 36, no. 1 (Spring 1972): 72; Heinz Boberach, "Chancen eines Umsturzes in Spiegel der Berichte des Sicherheitsdienstes," in Juergen Schmaedeke and Peter Steinback (eds.), *Der Widerstand gegen den Nationalsozialismus* (Munich: Piper, 1989). For an extensive collection of captured reports from Ohlendorf's project, see Sicherheitspolizei des SD, *Meldungen aus dem Reich,* in U.S. National Archives microfilm of captured German records No. T-71, reel 5.

26. Carsten Klingemann, "Angewandte Soziologie im Nationalsozialismus," *1999: Zeischrift für Sozialgeshichte des 20. und 21. Jahrhunderts* (January 1989): 25; Christoph Cobet (ed.), *Einführung in Fragen an die Soziologie in Deutschland nach Hitler, 1945–1950* (Frankfurt am Main: Verlag Christoph Cobet, 1988). For an examination of interlocking problems concerning German geographical studies of the same period, which overlapped in certain respects with communication studies, see Mechtild Roessler, *Wissenschaft und Lebensraum: Geographische Ostforschung in Nationalsozialismus* (Berlin: Dietrich Reimer Verlag, 1990).

27. Chris Raymond, "Professor Is Accused of Promulgating Anti-Semitic Views as Journalist in Germany and U.S. in World War II," *Chronicle of Higher Education,* 38, no. 16, December 11, 1991, P.A–10. For Noelle's own 1939 description of her relationship with Nazism, see Elisabeth Noelle, "Fragebogen zur Bearbeitung des Ausnahmeantrages für die Reichsschrifttumskammer," May 15, 1939, in the collection of the Berlin Document Center.

28. Brett Gary, "Mass Communications Research, the Rockefeller Foun-

dation and the Imperatives of War 1939–1945,'' *Research Reports from the Rockefeller Archive Center* (North Tarrytown, NY, Spring 1991), p. 3; and Brett Gary, "American Liberalism and the Problem of Propaganda,'' Ph.D. diss., University of Pennsylvania, 1992. Gary's work is the first thorough study, so far as I am aware, of the important role of the Rockefeller Foundation in crystallizing paradigms for communication studies.

29. John Marshall (ed.), "Needed Research in Communication'' (1940), folder 2677, box 224, Rockefeller Archives, Pocantico Hills, NY, cited in Gary, *American Liberalism.*

30. Gary, "American Liberalism and the Problem of Propaganda.''

31. Ladislas Farago, *German Psychological Warfare* (New York: Putnam, 1941). For a history of the origin of the term, see William Daugherty, "Changing Concepts,'' in Daugherty and Janowitz, *Psychological Warfare Casebook,* p. 12.

32. Paddock, *U.S. Army Special Warfare,* pp. 5–8, 23–37.

33. Ibid., p. 6.

34. Anthony Cave Brown (ed.), *The Secret War Report of the OSS* (New York: Berkeley, 1976), pp. 42–63. There is a large literature on the OSS. For a reliable overview of the agency's activities, including basic data on its establishment and leadership, see Richard Harris Smith, *OSS* (Berkeley: University of California Press, 1972).

35. Paddock, *U.S. Army Special Warfare,* pp. 7–14; and Edward Lilly, "The Psychological Strategy Board and Its Predecessors: Foreign Policy Coordination 1938–1953,'' in Gaetano Vincitorio (ed.), *Studies in Modern History* (New York: St. Johns University Press, 1968), p. 346.

36. Kai Bird, *The Chairman: John J. McCloy* (New York: Simon & Schuster, 1992).

37. Paddock, *U.S. Army Special Warfare,* pp. 8–18; for an extended discussion, see Daniel Lerner, *Sykewar: Psychological Warfare Against Germany, D-Day to VE-Day* (New York: George Stewart, 1948).

38. On Poole's role in the establishment of *Public Opinion Quarterly,* see Harwood Childs, "The First Editor Looks Back,'' *POQ,* 21, no. 1 (Spring 1957): 7–13. On Poole's work at the Foreign Nationalities Branch of the OSS, see (Anthony Cave Brown (ed.), *Secret War Report of the OSS* (New York: Berkley, 1976), chapter 2. On Leighton, see Alexander Leighton, *Human Relations in a Changing World* (New York: Dutton, 1949). On Mead, see Carleton Mabee, "Margaret Mead and Behavioral Scientists in World War II: Problems of Responsibility, Truth and Effectiveness,'' *Journal of the History of the Behavioral Sciences* 23 (January 1987). On Stouffer, see note 49 below. On Cantril, see Hadley Cantril, "Evaluating the Probable Reactions to the Landing in North Africa in 1942: A Case Study,'' *POQ,* 29, no. 3 (Fall 1965): 400–410.

39. On Roper and on Elmo Wilson, also of the Roper organization, see Jean

Converse, *Survey Research in the United States* (Berkeley: University of California Press, 1987), pp. 171–72. On Doob and Leites, see Daniel Lerner (ed.), *Propaganda in War and Crisis* (New York: George Stewart, 1951), pp. vii–viii. On Kluckhohn, Leighton, Lowenthal, and Schramm, see Daugherty and Janowitz, *Psychological Warfare Casebook*, pp. xiii–xiv. On Speier, *Contemporary Authors*, Vol. 21–24, p. 829. On Barrett, Edward Barrett, *Truth Is Our Weapon* (New York: Funk & Wagnalls, 1953), pp. 31–32. After his death, the Associated Press identified Barrett as a former member of the OSS, though Barrett omitted that information from biographical statements published during his lifetime; see "Edward W. Barrett Dies; Started Columbia Journalism Review," *Washington Post,* October 26, 1989. For more on the OWI, see also Allan Winkler, *The Politics of Propaganda: The Office of War Information 1942–1945* (New Haven: Yale University Press, 1978); and Leonard Doob, "Utilization of Social Scientists in the Overseas Branch of the Office of War Information," *American Political Science Review,* 41, no. 4 (August 1947): 649–67.

40. Converse, *Survey Research in the United States,* pp. 163, 172.

41. Ibid., p. 309.

42. On Leites and Eulau, see Wilbur Schramm, "The Beginnings of Communication Study in the United States," in Everett Rogers and Francis Balle (eds.), *The Media Revolution in America and Western Europe* (Norwood, NJ: Ablex, 1985), p. 205; and Harold Lasswell and Nathan Leites, *Language of Politics* (New York: George Stewart, 1949), p. 298.

43. Nathan Leites and Ithiel de Sola Pool, "The Response of Communist Propaganda," in Lasswell and Leites, *Language of Politics,* pp. 153, 334.

44. Roger Wimmer and Joseph Dominick, *Mass Media Research* (Belmont, CA: Wadsworth, 1987), p. 165.

45. On Paley, Jackson, Padover, Riley, Janowitz, Lerner, and Gurfein, see Lerner, *Sykewar,* pp. 439–43. On Davison, see Daugherty and Janowitz, *Psychological Warfare Casebook,* p. xii. On Shils, see Lerner, *Propaganda in War,* p. viii.

46. On Davison and Padover, see Daugherty and Janowitz, *Psychological Warfare Casebook,* pp. xii–xiii. On Gurfein and Janowitz, see Smith, *OSS,* pp. 86, 217.

47. On Langer, Cater, and Marcuse, see Smith, *OSS,* pp. 17, 23, 25, 217. On Barrett, see "Edward W. Barrett Dies; Started Columbia Journalism Review." On Becker and Inkeles, see Daugherty and Janowitz, *Psychological Warfare Casebook,* pp. xi–xii. For a fascinating early memoir of the role of psychology and social psychology in OSS training and operations, see William Morgan, *The OSS and I* (New York: Norton, 1957).

48. Robin Winks, *Cloak and Gown: Scholars in the Secret War, 1939–1961* (New York: Morrow, 1987), pp. 43–44, 79.

49. On Samuel Stouffer's Morale Branch, see Samuel Stouffer, Arthur Lums-

daine, Marion Lumsdaine, Robin Williams, M. Brewster Smith, Irving Janis, Shirley Star, and Leonard Cottrell, *The American Soldier* (Princeton, NJ: Princeton University Press, 1949), pp. 3–53; and John Clausen, "Research on the American Soldier as a Career Contingency," *Social Psychology Quarterly* 47, no. 2 (1984): 207–13. On the OSS, see Barry Katz, *Foreign Intelligence: Research and Analysis in the Office of Strategic Services, 1952–1945* (Cambridge, MA: Harvard University Press, 1989): and Bernard David Rifkind, "OSS and Franco-American Relations 1942–1945" Ph.D. diss., George Washington University, 1983, pp. 318–36. On psychological operations in the Pacific theater, see Leighton, *Human Relations in a Changing World.*

50. Clausen, "Research on the American Soldier."

51. Ibid., p. 210.

52. Ibid., p. 212.

53. Barrett, *Truth,* p. 31fn.

54. "Edward W. Barrett Dies; Started Columbia Journalism Review."

55. Martin Jay, *The Dialectical Imagination: A History of the Frankfurt School and the Institute for Social Research, 1923–1950* (Boston: Little, Brown, 1973); and Katz, *Foreign Intelligence,* pp. 29ff.

Chapter 3

1. Senate Committee on Military Affairs, *Hearings on Science Legislation (S. 1297),* 79th Cong. 1st sess., October–November 1945, Part 4, pp. 899–902.

2. Ibid.

3. Ibid. On the continuum from hot war to cold war in the eyes of leaders of the U.S. intelligence community, particularly as it pertained to covert operations and psychological warfare, see testimony by Allen Dulles, John V. Grombach, Rear Adm. Thomas Inglis, Brig. Gen. Hayes Kroner, Lt. Gen. Hoyt S. Vandenberg, and Peter Vischer. House Committee on Expenditures in Executive Departments, *National Security Act of 1947.* June 27, 1947; published 1982 by the Permanent Select Committee on Intelligence (Washington, DC: GPO, 1982).

4. Anthony Cave Brown, *The Last Hero: Wild Bill Donovan* (New York: Vintage, 1982), pp. 775–84.

5. Jean Converse, *Survey Research in the United States* (Berkeley: University of California Press, 1987), pp. 180–82.

6. Ibid., pp. 175–85; Samuel Stouffer et al., *The American Soldier* (Princeton, NJ: Princeton University Press, 1949), pp. 28–29.

7. Alfred Paddock, *U.S. Army Special Warfare: Its Origins* (Washington, DC: National Defense University Press, 1982), p. 40.

8. John Prados, interview with author, December 12, 1989.

9. Maj. Gen. W. G. Wyman, letter to Asst. Chief of Staff G-2, War Department General Staff, "Project to Combat Subversive Activities [in the] United States," January 15, 1946, U.S. Army P&O 091.412 (section IA, case 7), RG 319, U.S. National Archives, Washington, DC; see also Paddock, *U.S. Army Special Warfare,* pp. 42–43.

10. Paddock, *U.S. Army Special Warfare,* 55–56.

11. Converse, *Survey Research in the United States,* p. 182. For background on Allied polling in occupied Germany, see Anna J. Merritt and Richard L. Merritt (eds.), *Public Opinion in Occupied Germany* (Urbana: University of Illinois Press, 1970); and Anna J. Merritt and Richard L. Merritt (eds.), *Public Opinion in Semisovereign Germany* (Urbana: University of Illinois Press, 1980).

12. Allan Robert Adler, *Litigation under the Federal Freedom of Information Act and Privacy Act* (Washington, DC: American Civil Liberties Foundation, 1990), pp. 42–44.

13. Paddock, *U.S. Army Special Warfare,* pp. 69–71.

14. Ibid., pp. 46–47.

15. John Prados, *Presidents' Secret Wars* (New York: Morrow, 1986), pp. 20–21.

16. Ibid., pp. 20, 27–29.

17. U.S. National Security Council, *NSC 4: Coordination of Foreign Information Measures* (confidential), December 9, 1947, RG 273, U.S. National Archives, Washington, DC.

18. Edward Barrett, *Truth Is Our Weapon* (New York: Funk & Wagnalls, 1953).

19. U.S. National Security Council, *NSC 4-A: Psychological Operations* (top secret), December 9, 1947, RG 273, U.S. National Archives, Washington, DC.

20. U.S. National Security Council, *NSC 10/2: Office of Special Projects* (originally top secret, now declassified), June 18, 1948, RG 273, U.S. National Archives, Washington, DC.

21. Intricate and seemingly contradictory conceptual structures of this type are far more common in affairs of state than is generally recognized; indeed, they are probably inherent in modern political communication systems. A particularly grotesque example of this can be seen in Nazi Germany's sublanguages used to manage the extermination of Jews. There, the state employed massive public information campaigns to mobilize the German bureaucracy and public for persecutory operations such as expropriation of Jewish property, "petty" (i.e., nonlethal) discrimination, and mass roundups of Jews for deportation. The truth—that the deportees were to be murdered—was aggressively denied by the Nazi information authorities, however, who claimed that the deportees were simply being relocated to work camps.

But despite the denials, small armies of personnel were required to actually manage the death camps, deliver the railroad shipments of Jews, make use of data derived from fatal experiments on work camp prisoners, and so on. These groups soon developed complex, specialized vocabularies of euphemisms and rationalizations in order to discuss their work without directly contradicting the official claim that deported persons were surviving and even prospering.

In time, knowledge of the exterminations seeped through German society, spread by rumors, jokes, foreign radio broadcasts, and the accidental revelations inherent in any large-scale program. The net result was both widespread knowledge of the genocidal efforts of Hitler's government and, simultaneously, an institutionalized and internalized denial of precisely the same knowledge. For many Germans, this belief structure proved to be quite ornate and resilient.

Roughly similar psychological and linguistic structures seem to have played a role in certain phases of Turkish *Ittyhad* efforts to exterminate Armenians during World War I, in atrocities during Stalin's rule in the Soviet Union, and in U.S. exploitation of former Nazis in intelligence operations. There are many obvious differences, of course, between the psychological and linguistic dynamics of atrocities and those of psychological warfare projects. Nonetheless, there are enough similarities to suggest that euphemistic "cover stories" are integral to much of modern political communication.

22. U.S. National Security Council, *NSC 10/2* On the importance of euphemism during mass crimes, see Raul Hilberg, *The Destruction of the European Jews* (New York: Harper, 1961), pp. 216, 566, 652.

23. Prados, *Presidents' Secret Wars*, p. 33.

24. Senate Select Committee to Study Governmental Operations with Respect to Intelligence Activities, *Supplementary Detailed Staff Reports on Foreign and Military Intelligence,* 94th Cong. 2nd sess., Part 4 Washington, DC: GPO, 1976), pp. 29–31. Hereinafter cited as Senate Select Committee.

25. Ibid., pp. 29–36; Prados, *Presidents' Secret Wars*, p. 81.

26. Col. S. F. Griffin, "Memorandum to the Record: NSC 10 (Psychological Warfare Organization)" (top secret), June 3, 1948; quote concerning mission from U.S. National Security Council, *NSC 10/2*.

27. Senate Select Committee, pp. 128–32.

28. Quoted in Paddock, *U.S. Army Special Warfare*, p. 75.

29. See, for example, "U.S. Rejects Charges of Anti-Polish Acts," *Department of State Bulletin* (February 23, 1953): 304–5.

Chapter 4

1. Examples of articles with this characteristic include John A. Pollard, "Words Are Cheaper Than Blood," *POQ* 9, no. 3 (Fall 1945): 283ff. (review of the work of the Office of War Information); Mrs. R. Hart Phillips, "The Future of American Propaganda in Latin America," *POQ* 9, no. 3 (Fall 1945):

305ff. (plea for expanded U.S. propaganda operations in the region); and Edward A. Shils and Morris Janowitz, "Cohesion and Disintegration in the Wehrmacht in World War II," *POQ* 12, no. 2 (Summer 1948): 280 (elaboration of reference group theory on the basis of evidence drawn from psychological operations against enemy military forces). *Public Opinion Quarterly*'s annual index typically appears as an unpaginated annex to the bound annual volumes of the journal. Unless otherwise noted, all unattributed articles in this chapter appeared in *POQ*.

For background on DeWitt Poole, see *Who Was Who,* Vol. 3, p. 692; and Sig Mickelson, *America's Other Voice: The Story of Radio Free Europe and Radio Liberty* (New York: Praeger, 1983), pp. 24, 41, 60, 259. Poole eventually became president of the Central Intelligence Agency–sponsored National Committee for a Free Europe.

2. See, for example, Warren B. Walsh's reviews of M. Sayers and A. Kahn's text *The Great Conspiracy: The Secret War against Russia,* 10, no. 4 (Winter 1946): 596–97, or of Henry Wallace's text *Soviet Asia Mission,* 11, no. 1 (Spring 1947): 135.

3. As used here, "financially dependent" upon psychological warfare contracting means deriving a substantial fraction of one's personal income or the backing for important professional projects from government efforts to apply social science to national security missions. Examples from *Public Opinion Quarterly*'s board of editors (later called its advisory board) include Hadley Cantril, Leonard Cottrell, W. Phillips Davison, George Gallup, Harold Lasswell, Paul Lazarsfeld, Rensis Likert, DeWitt Poole, Elmo Roper, Wilbur Schramm, Frank Stanton, Frederick Stephan, Samuel Stouffer, and Elmo Wilson. See the text and notes in Chapters 5, 6, and 8 of this book for specific projects and sources.

4. Major Paul C. Bosse, "Polling Civilian Japanese on Saipan," 9, no. 2 (Summer 1945): 176.

5. Pollard, "Words Are Cheaper Than Blood," p. 283.

6. Lt. Andie Knutson, "Japanese Opinion Surveys: The Special Need and the Special Difficulties," 9, no. 3, (Fall 1945): 313.

7. Phillips, "The Future of American Propaganda in Latin America," p. 305.

8. Nat Schmulowitz and Lloyd Luckmann, "Foreign Policy by Propaganda Leaflets," 9, no. 4 (Winter 1945): 428, and Jacob Freid, "The OWI's Moscow Desk," 10, no. 2 (Summer 1946): 156.

9. Ferdinand Hermens, "The Danger of Stereotypes in Viewing Germany," 9, no. 4 (Winter 1945): 418, M. I. Gurfein and Morris Janowitz, "Trends in Wehrmacht Morale," 10, no. 1 (Spring 1946): 78, Herbert von Strempel, "Confessions of a German Propagandist," 10, no. 2 (Summer 1946): 216, Elizabeth Zerner, "German Occupation and Anti-Semitism in France," 12, no.

2 (Summer 1948): 258, Edward Shils and Morris Janowitz, "Cohesion and Disintegration in the Wehrmacht in World War II," 12, no. 2 (Summer 1948): 280, Morris Janowitz (reviewer), "Attitudes of German Prisoners of War" and "Observations of the Characteristics and Distribution of German Nazis," 13, no. 2 (Summer 1949): 343, 346.

10. Nat Schmulowitz and Lloyd Luckmann, "Foreign Policy by Propaganda Leaflets," 9, no. 4 (Winter 1945): 428, Boris Joffe, "The Post Card—A Tool of Propaganda," 11, no. 4 (Winter 1947): 613, Marin Hertz, "Some Psychological Lessons from Leaflet Propaganda in World War II," 13, no. 3 (Fall 1949): 471.

11. Capt. John Jamieson, "Books and the Soldier," 9, no. 2 (Summer 1945): 320, Arnold Rose, "Bases of American Military Morale in World War II," 9, no. 4 (Winter 1945): 411, Karl Ettinger, "Foreign Propaganda in America" 10, no. 3 (Fall 1946): 329, Leo Crespi and G. Schofield Shapleigh, " 'The' Veteran—A Myth," 10, no. 3 (Fall 1946): 361, John Jamieson, "Censorship and the Soldier," 11, no. 3 (Fall 1947): 367, Paul Lazarsfeld, "The American Soldier: An Expository Review," 13, no. 3 (Fall 1949): 377.

12. Reviews of *The Great Conspiracy* 10, no. 4 (Winter 1946): 596, *Weapon of Silence*, 11, no. 1 (Spring 1947): 133, *Mass Persuasion: The Social Psychology of a War Bond Drive*, 11, no. 2 (Summer 1947): 266, *Paper Bullets: A Brief History of Psychological Warfare in World War II*, 11 no. 3 (Fall 1947) *Rebel at Large* [George Creel memoirs] 11, no. 4 (Winter 1947): 626, *Psychological Warfare*, 12, no. 2 (Summer 1948): 331, *Public Opinion and Propaganda* 12, no. 3 (Fall 1948): 496, *The Goebbels Diaries*, 12, no. 3 (Fall 1948): 500, *Persuade or Perish*, 12, no. 3 (Fall 1948): 511, *Overseas Information Service of the United States Government*, 13, no. 1 (Spring 1949): 136, *Strategic Intelligence for American World Policy*, 13, no. 3 (Fall 1949): 524, *Publizistik im Dritten Reich*, 13, no. 4 (Winter 1949): 692.

13. Jacob Freid, "The OWI's Moscow Desk," 10, no. 2 (Summer 1946): 156, George Counts, "Soviet Version of American History," 10, no. 3 (Fall 1946): 321, Martin Kriesberg, "Soviet News in the *New York Times*," 10, no. 4 (Winter 1946): 540, Dick Fitzpatrick, "Telling the World about America," 10, no. 4 (Winter 1946): 582; "Public Opinion Inside the USSR," 11, no. 1 (Spring 1947): 5, Alexander Dallin, "America Through Soviet Eyes," 11, no. 1 (Spring 1947): 26, W. Phillips Davison, "An Analysis of the Soviet-Controlled Berlin Press," 11, no. 1 (Spring 1947): 40, O. W. Riegel, "Hungary: Proving Ground for Soviet–American Relations," 11, no. 1 (Spring 1947): 58, H. M. Spitzer, "Presenting America in American Propaganda," 11, no. 2 (Summer 1947): 213, Richard Burkhardt, "The Soviet Union in American School Textbooks," 11, no. 4 (Winter 1947): 567, Hans Speier, "The Future of Psychological Warfare," 12, no. 1 (Spring 1948): 5, Jan Stapel and W. J. deJonge, "Why Vote Communist?" 12, no. 3 (Fall 1948): 390, Whitman

Bassow, "Izvestia Looks Inside USA," 12, no. 3 (Fall 1948): 430, Martin Kriesberg, "Cross Pressures and Attitudes: A Study of the Influence of Conflicting Propaganda on Opinions Regarding American–Soviet Relations," 13, no. 1 (Spring 1949): 5, Henry Halpern, "Soviet Attitudes Toward Public Opinion Research in Germany," 13, no. 1 (Spring 1949): 117, Louis Nemzer, "The Soviet Friendship Societies," 13, no. 2 (Summer 1949): 265, Kenneth Olson, "The Development of the Czechoslovak Propaganda Administration," 13, no. 4 (Winter 1949): 607, Leonard Doob, "The Strategies of Psychological Warfare," 13, no. 4 (Winter 1949): 635.

14. "Book Reviews," 10, no. 1 (Spring 1946): 99–103, with quotes drawn from p. 100.

15. Speier, "The Future of Psychological Warfare," pp. 5–18.

16. See index entries for "Propaganda" and "Psychological Warfare" in the unnumbered index pages appended to the bound volumes of *POQ*.

17. Donald McGranahan, "U.S. Psychological Warfare Policy," 10, no. 3 (Fall 1946): 446–50.

18. Ibid.

19. Ibid.

20. U.S. National Security Council, *NSC 4* and *NSC 4-A*. On Wisner's role in development of psychological warfare policy while serving as chief of the Occupied Areas Division at the Department of State, see SANACC Case No. 395, "Utilization of Refugees from the USSR in the US National Interest," March–July 1948 (top secret, now declassified and available on microfilm from Scholarly Resources, Wilmington, DE). On Speier's post at the Occupied Areas Division at the Department of State, see *Contemporary Authors,* Vol. 21–24, pp. 829–30, and *Contemporary Authors, New Revision Series,* Vol. 9, pp. 463–64.

21. Speier, "The Future of Psychological Warfare," pp. 5, 8.

22. Ibid., pp. 11, 14, 18.

23. U.S. National Security Council, *NSC 4* and *NSC 4-A;* see also House Select Committee on Intelligence, in *Village Voice,* "Special Supplement: The CIA Report the President Doesn't Want You to Read," February 16 and 22, 1976.

24. Warren B. Walsh's reviews include those of M. Sayers and A. Kahn's text *The Great Conspiracy: The Secret War Against Russia,* 10, no. 4 (Winter 1946): 596–97, of Henry Wallace's *Soviet Asia Mission,* 11, no. 1 (Spring 1947): 135, of William van Narvig's *East of the Iron Curtain,* 11, no. 2 (Summer 1947): 269, of John R. Deane's *The Strange Alliance,* 11, no. 3 (Fall 1947): 463, and of George Moorad's *Behind the Iron Curtain,* 11, no. 3 (Fall 1947): 463–64.

25. P. Luzzatto Fegiz, "Italian Public Opinion," 11, no. 1 (Spring 1947): 92–96.

26. Felix Oppenheim, "The Prospects of Italian Democracy," 11, no. 4 (Winter 1947): 572–580.

27. Charles A. H. Thompson, review, *Public Opinion and Foreign Policy,* 13, no. 2 (Summer 1949): 330; and C. Edda Martinez and Edward A. Suchman, "Letters from America and the 1948 Election in Italy," 14, no. 1 (Spring 1950): 111–25.

28. Psychological Strategy Board, Panel C. *Reduction of Communist Strength and Influence in France and Italy* (top secret), October 26, 1951, records of the Psychological Strategy Board, Harry S. Truman Library, Independence, MO; James Miller, "Taking Off the Gloves: The United States and the Italian Elections of 1948," *Diplomatic History,* 7, no. 1 (Winter 1983): 35–55; James Miller, *The United States and Italy, 1940–1950* (Chapel Hill: University of North Carolina Press, 1986); James Miller, "Roughhouse Diplomacy: The United States Confronts Italian Communism, 1945–58," *Storia della Relazioni Internazionali* 5, no. 2 (1989):279–311; Arnaldo Cortesi and "Observer," "Two Vital Case Histories," in Lester Markel (ed.), *Public Opinion and Foreign Policy* (New York: Harper Brothers/Council on Foreign Relations, 1949), pp. 197–212 (sanitized, but with contemporary Italian and French case studies).

29. Counts, "Soviet Version of American History," 321–28; and Alfred McClung Lee, "Are Only the Russians Guilty?" 11, no. 1 (Spring 1947): 173. Lee cites as evidence of his assertion data in Kriesberg's "Soviet News in the *New York Times,*" p. 540.

30. W. Phillips Davison, "Preferences of POQ Readers," 12, no. 3 (Fall 1948): 579–80.

31. Frederick W. Williams, "Regional Attitudes on International Cooperation," 9, no. 1 (Spring 1945): 38–50.

32. Ibid., p. 38.

33. Jean Converse, *Survey Research in the United States* (Berkeley: University of California Press, 1987), pp. 152–54, 165. Converse also notes an earlier example of the role of these confidential surveys in shaping the president's highly controversial strategy for promoting U.S. support for England in the years leading up to Pearl Harbor.

34. For background on Poole, see *Who Was Who,* Vol. 3, p. 692; Mickelson, *America's Other Voice,* pp. 24, 41, 60; and Christopher Simpson, *Blowback* (New York: Weidenfeld & Nicolson, 1988), pp. 134, 217–34 passim. See also Harwood Childs, "The First Editor Looks Back," 21, no. 1 (Spring 1957): 7, for Child's recollections on Poole's role in the founding of *Public Opinion Quarterly*.

35. For source material on Stanton's role with Radio Free Europe, see Mickelson, *America's Other Voice,* p. 124; and U.S. General Accounting Office,

U.S. Government Monies Provided to Radio Free Europe and Radio Liberty, report no. 173239, May 25, 1972, p. 79.

36. On Free's wartime career, see Converse, *Survey Research in the United States,* pp. 152–54; on his Central Intelligence Agency grant, see John Crewdson and Joseph Treaster, "Worldwide Propaganda Network Built by CIA," *New York Times,* December 26, 1977.

37. Association officers or editorial panel members who served with both groups included Samuel Stouffer, John W. Riley, and Leonard Cottrell.

38. Herbert Goldhamer, "Public Opinion and Personality" (p. 346), Hans Speier, "Historical Development of Public Opinion" (p. 376), Samuel Stouffer, "Some Observations on Study Design" (p. 355), and Leo Lowenthal, "Historical Perspectives of Popular Culture" (p. 323); each in *American Journal of Sociology* 56, no. 1 (January 1950). Lowenthal specifically cites his Voice of America work in support of his thesis; see p. 324.

39. Albert Biderman and Elizabeth Crawford, *Political Economics of Social Research: The Case of Sociology* (Springfield, VA: Clearinghouse for Federal Scientific and Technological Information, 1968), p. 5.

Chapter 5

1. Calculated from figures reported in National Science Foundation, *Federal Funds for Science* (Washington, DC: GPO, 1953), pp. 39–40.

2. National Science Foundation, *Federal Funds for Science* (Washington, DC: GPO, 1960), pp. 66–67. One 1962 survey of approximately two hundred sociologists and anthropologists found that 44 percent answered affirmatively when asked whether any part of their research, teaching, study, or consulting during the previous year had been underwritten by the government. Harold Orlans, *The Effects of Federal Programs on Higher Education* (Washington, DC: Brookings Institution Press, 1962), p. 98. By the 1960s, the federal government had become virtually the sole source of funding for large-scale social research in the $100,000 and over range. Albert Biderman and Elizabeth Crawford, *Political Economics of Social Research: The Case of Sociology* (Springfield, VA: Clearinghouse for Federal Scientific and Technological Information, 1968), p. 9.

3. Harry Alpert, "Opinion and Attitude Surveys in the U.S. Government," *POQ* 16, no. 1 (Spring 1952): 33–41. Alpert states in the introduction of this article that virtually all military intelligence–and propaganda-related studies have been excluded from the scope of his article. For data concerning military contracting, see Lyle Lanier, "The Psychological and Social Sciences in the National Military Establishment," *American Psychologist* 4, no. 5 (May 1949): 127–47. George Croker (U.S. Air Force Human Resources

Research Institute), "Some Principles Regarding the Utilization of Social Science Research Within the Military," pp. 112–25, and Howard E. Page (Psychological Sciences Division, Office of Naval Research), "Research Utilization," pp. 126–35, both in *Case Studies in Bringing Behavioral Science into Use* (Stanford: Institute for Communication Research, 1961), pp. 112–35; Erin Hubbert and Herbert Rosenberg, *Opportunities for Federally Sponsored Social Science Research* (Syracuse, NY: Syracuse University Maxwell Graduate School, 1951); Raymond Bowers, "The Military Establishment," in Paul Lazarsfeld, William Sewell, and Harold Wilensky (eds.), *The Uses of Sociology* (New York: Basic Books, 1967), pp. 234ff; Leonard Mead, "Psychology at the Special Devices Center, Office of Naval Research," *American Psychologist* 4, no. 4 (April 1949): 97ff (see pp. 98–100 for discussion of television-based experiments with "rapid mass learning"); Charles Bray, "The Effects of Government Contract Work on Psychology," and John T. Wilson, "Government Support of Research and Its Influence on Psychology," both in *American Psychologist* 7, no. 12 (December 1952): 710–18; Gene Lyons, "The Growth of National Security Research," *Journal of Politics* 25, no. 3 (1963): 489–508; Irving Louis Horowitz, "Why the DOD Is No. 1," *Trans-Action* 5, no. 6 (May 1968): 32.

4. Jean Converse, *Survey Research in the United States* (Berkeley: University of California Press, 1987), pp. 340–41.

5. Ibid., pp. 353, 357.

6. Clyde Kluckhohn, Alex Inkeles, and Raymond Bauer, *Strategic Psychological and Sociological Strengths and Vulnerabilities of the Soviet Social System* (Cambridge, MA: Russian Research Center, Harvard University, 1954; USAF contract no. 33 [038]-12909), pp. 20–22, and Annex 1 (on ISR role) and pp. 360–68 (on use in strategic air offensive on the Soviet Union). See also Tami Davis Biddle, "Handling the Soviet Threat: Arguments for Preventative War and Compellence in the Early Cold War Period," paper presented at the annual convention of the Society for Historians of American Foreign Relations, 1988; and Christopher Simpson, *Blowback* (New York: Weidenfeld & Nicolson, 1988), p. 138.

7. Quoted in Converse, *Survey Research in the United States,* pp. 353, 531 note 17.

8. Ibid., pp. 309, 327. See also National Opinion Research Center (Charles Mack), *Bibliography of Publications, 1941–1960* (Chicago: NORC, 1961), and *Supplement 1961–1971* (Chicago: NORC, 1972); James Davis, *Studies of Social Change Since 1948,* 2 vols. (Chicago: NORC, 1976).

9. Converse, *Survey Research in the United States,* pp. 321–22. For details on the Department of State affair, see House Committee on Government Operations, *State Department Opinion Polls,* 85th Cong., 1st sess., June–July 1957 (Washington, DC: GPO, 1957). For an example of the impact of these

studies, see the State Department's Policy Planning Staff internal discussion concerning U.S. public opinion on atomic warfare in the wake of the first Soviet atomic weapons test. Carlton Savage to George F. Kennan, untitled memo regarding first use of atomic bomb, December 21, 1949 (top secret), in Paul Nitze Papers, Policy Planning Staff files, box 50, RG 59, U.S. National Archives, Washington, DC.

10. Converse, *Survey Research in the United States,* pp. 309, 327.

11. Charles Fritz and Eli Marks, "The NORC Studies of Human Behavior in Disasters," *Journal of Social Issues* 10, no. 3 (1954): 26–41; Rue Bucher, "Blame and Hostility in Disaster" *American Journal of Sociology* 62, no. 5 (1957); Elihu Katz, "The Night the Sirens Wailed in Chicago," *Chicago Sun-Times,* April 24, 1960. For an example of BASR studies in the same area, see Fred Ikle, "The Social Versus the Physical Effects from Nuclear Bombing," *Scientific Monthly* 78, no. 3 (March 1954): 182–87.

12. For discussion of these studies as elements in nuclear war planning, see Jack Hirshleifer, *Disaster and Recovery: A Historical Survey* (Santa Monica, CA: RAND Corporation, RM-3079-PR, 1963).

13. Converse, *Survey Research in the United States,* pp. 269, 506–7 note 42.

14. Ibid., pp. 275–76, 506 note 37.

15. Ibid., p. 506 note 37.

16. Kluckhohn, Inkeles, and Bauer, *Strategic Psychological and Sociological Strengths and Vulnerabilities,* p. 402.

17. On VOA study history, see Daniel Lerner with Lucille Pevsner, *The Passing of Traditional Society* (Glencoe, IL: Free Press, 1958), pp. 79–80. On U.S. psychological warfare in the Middle East, see William Blum, *The CIA: A Forgotten History* (London: Zed, 1986), pp. 31–36, 67–76, 96–107; and Thomas Powers, *The Man Who Kept the Secrets: Richard Helms and the CIA* (New York: Pocket Books, 1979), pp. 106, 161, 431.

18. John Prados, *Presidents' Secret Wars* (New York: Morrow, 1986), pp. 94–98 (on Iran); Myron Smith, *The Secret Wars,* Vol. 2 (Santa Barbara, CA: ABC-Clio, 1981), pp. xxxiii, xxxv (on Egypt).

19. Converse, *Survey Research in the United States,* p. 290.

20. Lerner and Pevsner, *Passing of Traditional Society,* pp. 81, 449 notes 1–5.

21. Lanier, "The Psychological and Social Sciences," pp. 131–33; and "Psychological News and Notes," *American Psychologist* 3, no. 12 (December 1948): 559.

22. Lanier, "The Psychological and Social Sciences," pp. 131–32.

23. The precise figure apparently remains classified at this writing, and its size obviously depends in part on how broadly the Department of Defense defined "social science" in 1949. The figure reported here is calculated from

data presented by Lanier, who was at that time chair of the Committee on Human Resources' Panel on Human Engineering and Psychophysiology. Lanier's data were cleared by the Office of the Secretary of Defense prior to release (ibid., p. 131). Lanier's estimate is considerably higher than that offered by some other contemporary authors, notably Hubbert and Rosenberg, *Opportunities for Federally Sponsored Social Science Research*. It is, however, roughly consistent with figures offered by John Wilson of the National Science Foundation in "Government Support of Research," p. 715.

24. Lanier, "The Psychological and Social Sciences," p. 132.

25. On panel membership, see "Psychological News and Notes," p. 559. On Speier, see Hans Speier, "Psychological Warfare Reconsidered," RAND paper no. 196, February 5, 1951; Hans Speier, "International Political Communication: Elite and Mass," *World Politics* (April 1952 [RAND paper no. P-270]); Hans Speier and W. Phillips Davison, "Psychological Aspects of Foreign Policy," RAND paper no. P-615, December 15, 1954. On RAND's origins see Fred Kaplan, "Scientists at War: The Birth of the RAND Corporation," *American Heritage* 34 (June–July 1983): 49–64.

26. Alexander Leighton, *Human Relations in a Changing World* (New York: Dutton, 1949).

27. Carl Hovland, Arthur Lumsdaine, and Fred Sheffield, *Experiments in Mass Communication* (Princeton: Princeton University Press, 1949). This is the third volume in the *American Soldier* series.

28. "Psychological News and Notes."

29. Ibid.

30. On Dollard's and Gardner's roles with committee, ibid. On Gardner's role at Carnegie Corporation, see *Who's Who, 1974–1975*, p. 1099. On the Carnegie role in the *American Soldier* series, see Samuel Stouffer et al., *The American Soldier* (Princeton: Princeton University Press, 1949), p. 26.

31. Charles O'Connell, "Social Structure and Science: Soviet Studies at Harvard," Ph.D. diss. UCLA, 1990, pp. 178–79.

32. John Clausen, "Research on the American Soldier as a Career Contingency," *Social Psychology Quarterly* 47, no. 2 (1984): 212.

33. For Cantril's version, see Hadley Cantril, *The Human Dimension: Experiences in Policy Research* (New Brunswick, NJ: Rutgers University Press, 1967), pp. 131–32, 145. For the *New York Times* version, see John M. Crewdson and Joseph Treaster, "Worldwide Propaganda Network Built by the CIA," *New York Times,* December 26, 1977.

34. Thomas Sorenson, *The Word War: The Story of American Propaganda* (New York: Harper, 1968), p. 46.

35. Clausen, "Research on the American Soldier," p. 212.

36. "Cottrell, Leonard Slater," *Contemporary Authors,* Vol. 107, p. 100.

37. Leonard Cottrell, "Social Research and Psychological Warfare," *Sociometry* 23, no. 2 (June 1960): 103–19, with quote at p. 119.

38. See, for example, Wilbur Schramm's work for the National Security Council's highly secret Operations Coordinating Board, mentioned in Robert Holt, *Radio Free Europe* (Minneapolis: University of Minnesota Press, 1958), p. 236. For related material, see "Briefing Paper—Schramm Meeting," August 1, 1956 (formerly secret, declassified 1991), Wilbur Schramm files, USIA Library Historical Collection, Washington, D.C.

39. Robert Merton, *Social Theory and Social Structure* (New York: Free Press, 1968), pp. 504–5.

Chapter 6

1. John Riley and Wilbur Schramm, *The Reds Take a City: The Communist Occupation of Seoul* (New Brunswick, NJ: Rutgers University Press, 1951); John Riley, Wilbur Schramm, and Frederick Williams, "Flight from Communism: A Report on Korean Refugees," *POQ* 15, no. 2 (Summer 1951): 274 (unless otherwise noted, all unattributed articles in this chapter appeared in *POQ*); Wilbur Schramm, *F.E.C. Psychological Warfare Operations: Radio* (Washington and Baltimore: Operations Research Office, John Hopkins University, 1952, ORO-T-20 [FEC], secret security information). On USIA translation and distribution of the *Reds Take a City* text, see Raymond Bowers, "The Military Establishment," in Paul Lazarsfeld, William Sewell, and Harold Wilensky (eds.), *The Uses of Sociology* (New York: Basic Books, 1967), p. 245.

Several other prominent communication researchers drew on the same body of refugee interviews to prepare domestic propaganda during the Korean conflict. See W. Phillips Davison, "The Lesser Evil," *Reader's Digest* 58 (June 1951): 97–100. Davison's article was first prepared as RAND Corporation study no. P-194 (1951).

2. J. Mayone Stycos, "Patterns of Communications in a Rural Greek Village" 16, no. 1 (Spring 1952): 59–70, J. Mayone Stycos, "Interviewer Training in Another Culture" 17, no. 2 (Summer 1952): 236–46, Benjamin Ringer and David Sills, "Political Extremists in Iran: A Secondary Analysis of Communications Data" 17, no. 4 (Winter 1952–53): 689–702, J. Mayone Stycos, "Further Observations on the Recruitment and Training of Interviewers in Other Cultures" 19, no. 1 (Spring 1955): 68–78, Patricia Kendall, "The Ambivalent Character of Nationalism among Egyptian Professionals" 20, no. 1 (Spring 1956): 277, Morroe Berger (review), *The Passing of Traditional Society* 22, no. 3 (Fall 1958): 425.

3. For example, Eric Marder, "Linear Segments: A Technique for Scalogram

Analysis" 16, no. 3 (Fall 1952): 417–31, Samuel Stouffer, Edgar Borgatta, David Hays, and Andrew Henry, "A Technique for Improving Cumulative Scales" vol. 16, no. 2 (Summer 1952): 273–90, Andrew Henry, "A Method for Classifying Non-Scale Response Patterns in a Guttman Scale" 16, no. 1 (Spring 1952): 94–106, Edgar Borgatta and David Hays, "The Limitations on the Arbitrary Classification of Non-Scale Response Patterns in a Guttman Scale" 16, no. 3 (Fall 1952): 410–16, Edgar Borgotta, "An Error Ratio for Scalogram Analysis" 19, no. 1 (Spring 1955): 96–99.

4. See Brutus Coste, "Propaganda to Eastern Europe," 14, no. 4 (Winter 1950): 639–66. Coste was an employee of the National Committee for a Free Europe and later of the Assembly of Captive European Nations, both of which were financed almost exclusively by the CIA.

5. Sorenson, *The Word War*, pp. 21–30.

6. Denis McQuail, *Mass Communication Theory: An Introduction* (London and Beverly Hills: Sage, 1987), p. 5.

7. Edith Bjorklund, "Research and Evaluation Programs of the U.S. Information Agency and the Overseas Information Center Libraries," *Library Quarterly* (October 1968): 414; and Herbert Schiller, *The Mind Managers* (Boston: Beacon Press, 1973), pp. 140, 205.

8. "Proceedings of the American Association for Public Opinion Research at the Sixth Annual Conference on Public Opinion Research, Princeton, June 22–25, 1951," 15, no. 4 (Winter 1951–52): 768ff. For Davison panel, see AAPOR Conference Proceedings, "Contributions of Opinion Research to Psychological Warfare," 15, no. 4 (Winter 1951–52): 801–5. (Not to be confused with the Klapper and Lowenthal article with a very similar title elsewhere in the same issue.)

9. AAPOR Conference Proceedings, "Contributions of Opinion Research to Psychological Warfare," p. 802.

10. Joseph Klapper and Leo Lowenthal, "The Contributions of Opinion Research to the Evaluation of Psychological Warfare," 15, no. 4 (Winter 1951): 651.

11. AAPOR Conference Proceedings, "Contributions of Opinion Research to Psychological Warfare," p. 804.

12. AAPOR Conference Proceedings, "Opinion and Communications Research in National Defense," 15, no. 4 (Winter 1951–52): 794.

13. AAPOR Conference Proceedings, "Presidential Session," 15, no. 4 (Winter 1951–52): 795.

14. For overviews of Lowenthal's life and writings, see Martin Jay, *The Dialectical Imagination: History of the Frankfurt School and the Institute for Social Research 1923–1950* (Boston: Little, Brown, 1973), passim; Leo Lowenthal, *An Unmastered Past: Autobiographical Reflections of Leo Lowenthal* Martin Jay

(ed.), (Berkeley: University of California Press, 1987); Leo Lowenthal, *Literature and Mass Culture* (New Brunswick, NJ: Transaction, 1984); and Hanno Hardt, "The Conscience of Society: Leo Lowenthal and Communication Research," *Journal of Communication* 41, no. 3 (Summer 1991): 65–85.

15. Richard Crossman (ed.), *The God That Failed* (New York: Harper Brothers, 1949).

16. On disillusionment, see Crossman, *The God That Failed,* essays by Arthur Koestler, Richard Wright, Stephen Spender, etc.; John P. Diggins, *Up from Communism: Conservative Odysseys in American Intellectual History* (New York: Harper & Row, 1975), on Max Eastman, Sidney Hook, James Burnham, and others; Peter Coleman, *The Liberal Conspiracy: The Congress for Cultural Freedom and the Struggle for the Mind of Postwar Europe* (New York: Free Press, 1989), on Jay Lovestone and CIA-sponsored propaganda operations aimed at intellectuals.

17. Joseph Klapper and Leo Lowenthal, "Contributions of Opinion Research to Psychological Warfare," 15, no. 4 (Winter 1951) 651–62.

18. Lowenthal, *An Unmastered Past,* pp. 93–94.

19. *Ibid.,* pp. 81–110 passim.

20. Hardt, "The Conscience of Society."

21. Charles Glock, "The Comparative Study of Communication and Opinion Formation," 16, no. 4, (Winter 1952–53): 512–26.

22. Bureau of Social Science Research (Stanley Bigman, project director), "An Outline for the Study of National Communication Systems," prepared for the Office of Research and Evaluation, USIA, November 1953, BSSR Archives, series II, box 4, project no. 642, p. 1. University of Maryland Libraries Special Collections, College Park.

23. Glock, "The Comparative Study of Communication," p. 522.

24. Bureau of Social Science Research, "An Outline for the Study of National Communication Systems."

25. Bureau of Social Science Research, "Mass Communication in Eastern Europe," BSSR Archives, series II, box 10, project no. 303, University of Maryland Libraries Special Collections, College Park. See also BSSR, "Hungary," series II, box 11, project no. 303, in the same archive.

26. Bureau of Social Science Research, "Public Opinion in Philippines Survey," BSSR Archives, series II, box 3, project no. 627, University of Maryland Special Libraries Collections, College Park.

27. Bureau of Social Science Research (Lawrence Krader and Ivor Wayne, project directors), "The Kazakhs: A Background Study for Psychological Warfare" (Task KAZPO, technical report no. 23, November 1955), BSSR Archives, series II, box 4, project no. 649, University of Maryland Libraries Special Collections, College Park.

28. Ringer and Sills, "Political Extremists in Iran." On the coup d'état in Iran, see John Ranelagh, *The Agency: The Rise and Decline of the CIA* (New York: Simon & Schuster, 1987), pp. 260–64.

29. Alex Inkeles, "Soviet Reactions to the Voice of America," pp. 612–17; Paul Massing, "Communist References to the Voice of America," 618–22; Peter Rossi and Raymond Bauer, "Some Patterns of Soviet Communications Behavior," pp. 653–65—all in 16, no. 4 (Winter 1952–53).

30. Harold Mendelsohn and Werner Cahnman, "Communist Broadcasts to Italy," 16, no. 4 (Winter 1952–53): 671–80.

31. Richard Sheldon and John Dutkowski, "Are Soviet Satellite Refugee Interviews Projectable?" 16, no. 4 (Winter 1952–53): 579–94.

32. Daniel Lerner, "International Coalitions and Communication Content: The Case of Neutralism," 16, no. 4 (Winter 1952): 681–88, with quotes drawn from pp. 687, 684, 688, respectively.

33. Marjorie Fiske and Leo Lowenthal, "Some Problems in the Administration of International Communications Research," 16, no. 2 (Summer 1952): 149–59, with quote drawn from p. 150.

34. "Special Issue on International Communications Research; Leo Lowenthal, Guest Editor," 16, no. 4 (Winter 1952–53). *POQ*'s indexes are not paginated; for article counts see under "Propaganda." No index term for "Psychological Warfare" appears in the 1952 index, although the journal employs that term during both previous and later years.

35. Wilbur Schramm (ed.) *The Process and Effects of Mass Communication* (Urbana: University of Illinois Press, 1954).

36. Ibid., p. 469 (for Glock). See also chapters by Bruce Lannes Smith, Ralph White, and W. Philips Davison and Alexander George, each of which first appeared in the Lowenthal special issue of *POQ*.

37. University of Maryland, College Park Libraries, Historical Manuscripts and Archives Department, *Guide to the Archives of the Bureau of Social Science Research* (College Park: University of Maryland, n.d. [1987?]).

38. Account list cards, BSSR Archives, series I, box 13; Bureau of Social Science Research (Robert Bower), "Kazakhstan and the Kazakhs: Targets and Vulnerabilities in Psychological Warfare," working paper for Psychological Warfare Division, Human Resources Research Office, December 1954, BSSR Archives, series II, box 5, project 649; Lawrence Krader and Ivor Wayne, "The Kazakhs: A Background Study for Psychological Warfare."

On prisoner interrogation, see Albert Biderman, Barbara Heller, and Paula Epstein, *A Selected Bibliography on Captivity Behavior,* BSSR Research report 339-1, February 1961, U.S. Air Force contract no. AF 49(638)727, BSSR Archives, series II, box 14, project 339; Bureau of Social Science Research (Louis Gottschalk, MD). "The Use of Drugs in Information-Seeking Interviews," December 1958, BSSR Archives, series II, box 11, project 322, University of Maryland Libraries Special Collections, College Park.

39. Account list cards, BSSR Archives, series I, box 13; and Albert Biderman, "Social-Psychological Needs and 'Involuntary' Behavior as Illustrated by Compliance in Interrogation," 23, no. 2 *Sociometry* (June 1960): 120. For CIA role of Human Ecology Fund, see John Marks, *Search for the "Manchurian Candidate": The CIA and Mind Control* (New York: Times Books, 1979), pp. 147–63.

40. Account list cards, BSSR Archives, series I, box 13: Stanley Bigman, *Are We Hitting the Target?: A Manual of Evaluation Research Methods for USIE* (Washington, DC: U.S. Department of State [Official Use Only], 1951), BSSR Archives, series II, box 3, project no. 627; "Public Opinion in the Philippines," BSSR Archives, series II, box 3; "International Seminar to Be Held in Saigon," *Times of Vietnam*, December 13, 1958, p. 2, BSSR Archives, series I, box 13. The BSSR Archives is held by University of Maryland Libraries Special Collections, College Park.

41. Author's estimate based on BSSR Account list cards.

42. BSSR, *Are We Hitting the Target?* BSSR, "Public Opinion in the Philippines."

43. BSSR, *Are We Hitting the Target?* pp. 13–20.

44. Glock, "The Comparative Study of Communications and Opinion Formation," pp. 512–23. Bigman, in the BSSR proposal on national communication systems detailed in the next note, attributes this article jointly to Lazarsfeld and Glock, although only Glock's byline appears in *POQ*. Lazarsfeld had a second article on a closely related topic in the same issue of the journal.

45. Account list cards, BSSR Archives, series I, box 13; BSSR (Stanley Bigman), "An Outline for the Study of National Communication Systems."

46. Elihu Katz and Paul Lazarsfeld, *Personal Influence* (Glencoe, IL: Free Press, 1955).

47. BSSR, *Are We Hitting the Target?*

48. Daniel Lerner with Lucille Pevsner, *The Passing of Traditional Society* (Glencoe, IL: Free Press, 1958), p. 79; Bruce Lannes Smith, "Trends in Research in International Communication and Opinion, 1945–1955," 20, no. 1 (Spring 1956): 182–95.

49. BSSR (Stanley Bigman), "An Outline for the Study of National Communication Systems"; "Questionnaire for Opinion Leaders—Form B," BSSR Archives, series II, box 3, University of Maryland Libraries Special Collections, College Park.

50. Bernard Berelson, Paul Lazarsfeld, and William McPhee, *Voting* (Chicago: University of Chicago Press, 1954).

51. Katz and Lazarsfeld, *Personal Influence.*

52. Joseph Burkholder Smith, *Portrait of a Cold Warrior* (New York: Ballantine, 1976), p. 84. Smith was a CIA officer in the agency's Far Eastern division during the early 1950s, with responsibilities for political and psychological warfare in the Philippines. On counterinsurgency in the Philippines, see also Michael McClintock, *Instruments of Statecraft* (New York: Pantheon, 1992), pp. 85–120 passim; D. Michael Shafer, *Deadly Paradigms: The Failure of U.S. Counterinsurgency Policy* (Princeton: Princeton University Press, 1988); Walden Bello, "Counterinsurgency's Proving Ground: Low Intensity Warfare in the Philippines," in Michael Klare and Peter Kornbluh (eds.), *Low Intensity Warfare* (New York: Pantheon, 1988) 158–82.

53. William Blum, *The CIA: A Forgotten History* (London: Zed, 1986), pp. 40–43.

54. Smith, *Portrait*, pp. 74–104, concerning Paul Linebarger and the Philippines campaign.

55. Blum, *The CIA*, pp. 40–43.

56. Sorenson, *The Word War*, p. 65.

57. House Committee on Foreign Affairs, *The U.S. Ideological Effort: Government Agencies and Programs* 88th Comp., 1st Sess. (Washington, DC: GPO, 1964), pp. 62–63.

58. On country plans, see ibid., pp. 62–63; on coordination with NSC and CIA, see *NSC 10/2: Office of Special Projects,* June 15, 1948, and *NSC 5412/ 2: Covert Operations,* March 12, 1955, both in U.S. National Security Council Policy Papers File, RG 273, U.S. National Archives, Washington, DC; Sorenson, *The Word War*, p. 28; John Prados, *Presidents' Secret Wars* (New York: Morrow, 1986), pp. 84–87, 109.

59. Sorenson, *The Word War*, p. 46.

60. Shearon Lowery and Melvin De Fleur, *Milestones in Mass Communication Research* (New York: Longman, 1983), pp. 205–31.

61. Stuart Dodd, "Testing Message Diffusion from Person to Person," 16, no. 2 (Summer 1952): 247–62. Dodd does not acknowledge his sponsors here. Instead, he notes hypothetically, "Suppose that our Air Force wishes to drop leaflets on an enemy or a neutral population, whether civilian or military, or on our own population" (see p. 247).

62. Stuart Dodd, "Formulas for Spreading Opinions," 22, no. 4 (Winter 1958): 537, where Dodd notes that U.S. Air Force contract AF 13(038)-27522 underwrote the research. See also Lowery and De Fleur, *Milestones*, pp. 207–8.

63. Lowery and De Fleur, *Milestones*, p. 208.

64. Ibid.

65. On the U.S. Air Force interest, ibid., pp. 207–8; on the CIA interest, see Sig Mickelson, *America's Other Voice: The Story of Radio Free Europe*

and Radio Liberty (New York: Praeger, 1983), p. 56; on air-dropped leaflets' role in strategic war plans: author's interview with Fletcher Prouty, April 12, 1984.

66. Lowery and De Fleur, *Milestones,* pp. 205–31, with summary of important contributions at pp. 229–31; see also Dodd, "Formulas for Spreading Opinions," pp. 537–54.

67. Dodd, "Formulas for Spreading Opinions," pp. 551–54.

68. On the "bomber gap" affair, see John Prados, *The Soviet Estimate: U.S. Intelligence Analysis and Russian Military Strength* (New York: Dial, 1982), pp. 38–50.

69. Mikelson, *America's Other Voice,* p. 56.

70. Information on Cantril in this paragraph is from "Cantril, [Albert] Hadley," *National Cyclopedia of American Biography,* Vol. 55, pp. 211–12.

71. See, for example, William Buchanan and Hadley Cantril, *How Nations See Each Other* (Westport, CT: Greenwood, 1972), pp. 91–101; or Hadley Cantril, *The Politics of Despair* (New York: Basic Books, 1958).

72. "Cantril, [Albert] Hadley. See also collection of Psychological Strategy Board correspondence with Cantril, including Cantril's oblique reference to what appears to be clandestine CIA sponsorship and editing of his pamphlet *The Goals of the Individual and the Hopes of Humanity* (1951; published by Institute for Associated Research, Hanover, NH) in Cantril note of October 22, 1951; in Hadley Cantril correspondence, Psychological Strategy Board, Truman Library, Independence, MO.

73. John M. Crewdson and Joseph Treaster, "Worldwide Propaganda Network Built by the CIA" *New York Times,* December 26, 1977.

74. Hadley Cantril, *The Human Dimension: Experiences in Policy Research* (New Brunswick, NJ: Rutgers University Press, 1967), pp. 131–32, 145.

75. Crewdson and Treaster, "Worldwide Propaganda Network."

76. Hadley Cantril and David Rodnick, *Understanding the French Left* (Princeton: Institute for International Social Research, 1956).

77. Cantril, *The Human Dimension,* pp. 134–43.

78. Cantril, *The Politics of Despair;* Cantril, *The Human Dimension,* pp. 1–5, 144.

79. Lloyd Free and Hadley Cantril, *The Political Beliefs of Americans* (New Brunswick, NJ: Rutgers University Press, 1967). On the question of legality, note that the CIA's charter bars the agency from "police, subpoena, law-enforcement powers or internal security functions," a phrase that most observers contend prohibits the CIA from collecting intelligence on U.S. citizens inside the United States. On this point, see Thomas Powers, *The Man Who Kept the Secrets: Richard Helms and the CIA* (New York: Pocket Books, 1979), pp. 315–17, 367–70, concerning the CIA's Operation Chaos.

80. For an example of a similar, later technique, see "Redefining the Amer-

ican Electorate," *Washington Post,* October 1, 1987, p. A12, with data provided by the Times Mirror–Gallup Organization.

81. On CIA funding of CENIS, see Victor Marchetti and John Marks, *The CIA and the Cult of Intelligence* (New York: Dell, 1974), p. 181; and David Wise and Thomas Ross, *The Invisible Government* (New York: Vintage, 1974), p. 244. On CIA funding of studies, see Marchetti and Marks, *The CIA,* p. 181. For an example of a major study reported to have been underwritten by the CIA, see W. W. Rostow and Alfred Levin, *The Dynamics of Soviet Society* (New York: Norton, 1952). On CENIS as a conduit of CIA funds, see Wise and Ross, *The Invisible Government,* p. 244. On Millikan's role, see U.S. Department of State, Foreign Service Institute, "Problems of Development and Internal Defense" (Country Team Seminar, June 11, 1962).

82. Ithiel de Sola Pool, "The Necessity for Social Scientists Doing Research for Governments," *Background* 10, no. 2 (August 1966): 114–15.

83. Massachusetts Institute of Technology, Center for International Studies, *A Plan for Research in International Communications World Politics,* 6, no. 3 (April 1954): 358–77; MIT, CENIS, *The Center for International Studies: A Description* (Cambridge: MIT, July 1955).

84. Don Price Oral History, pp. 61–70, and Don Price memo, May 21, 1954 (appendix to oral history), Ford Foundation Archives, New York. The archival evidence concerning this aspect of the Ford Foundation's relationship with the CIA was first brought to light by Kai Bird.

85. On Shils, see Peter Coleman, *The Liberal Conspiracy* (New York: Free Press, 1989), pp. 98–209 passim. On Speier, see, Hans Speier, "Psychological Warfare Reconsidered," RAND paper no. 196, February 5, 1951; Hans Speier, "International Political Communication: Elite and Mass," *World Politics* (April 1952 [RAND paper no. P-270], Hans Speier and W. Phillips Davison, "Psychological Aspects of Foreign Policy," RAND paper no. P-615, December 15, 1954. Speier's other contemporary work that has since come to light includes several studies of Soviet response to West German rearmament, Soviet political tactics involving nuclear threats, a report on the *American Soldier* series, and a commentary on political applications of game theory. Speier died February 17, 1990, in Sarasota, Florida; see "Hans Speier, Sociologist," *Washington Post,* March 2, 1990. On Carroll, see Wallace Carroll, *The Army's Role in Current Psychological Warfare* (top secret, declassified following author's mandatory review request), February 24, 1949, box 10, tab 61, entry 154, RG 319, U.S. National Archives, Washington, DC; Wallace Carroll, "It Takes a Russian to Beat a Russian," *Life,* December 19, 1949, pp. 80–86; "CIA Trained Tibetans in Colorado, New Book Says," *New York Times,* April 19, 1973.

86. Ithiel de Sola Pool and Frank Bonilla (eds.), "A Special Issue on Studies in Political Communication," 20, no. 1 (Spring 1956); Daniel Lerner (ed.), "Special Issue: Attitude Research in Modernizing Areas," 22, no. 3 (Fall 1958).

87. In 20, no. 1 (Spring 1956): Harold Isaacs, "Scratches on Our Minds," p. 197; Y. B. Damle, "Communication of Modern Ideas and Knowledge in [East] Indian Villages," p. 257; Claire Zimmerman and Raymond Bauer, "The Effect of an Audience upon What Is Remembered," p. 238; Suzanne Keller, "Diplomacy and Communication," p. 176; and Harold Isaacs, "World Affairs and U.S. Race Relations: A Note on Little Rock," 22, no. 3 (Fall 1958): 364.

88. Ithiel de Sola Pool, Suzanne Keller, and Raymond Bauer, "The Influence of Foreign Travel on Political Attitudes of U.S. Businessmen," p. 161; Frank Bonilla, "When Is Petition 'Pressure'?" p. 39; Daniel Lerner, "French Business Leaders Look at EDC," p. 212—all in 20, no. 1 (Spring 1956); and Daniel Lerner, "Editors Introduction," p. 217; Ithiel de Sola Pool and Kali Prasad, "Indian Student Images of Foreign People," p. 292; Frank Bonilla, "Elites and Public Opinion in Areas of High Social Stratification," p. 349; all in 22, no. 3 (Fall 1958).

89. Ivor Wayne, "American and Soviet Themes and Values: A Content Analysis of Themes in Popular Picture Magazines," p. 314; Patricia Kendall, "The Ambivalent Character of Nationalism among Egyptian Professionals," p. 277—all in 20, no. 1 (Spring 1956).

90. Guy Pauker, "Indonesian Images of Their National Self," p. 305; Lucian Pye, "Administrators, Agitators and Brokers," p. 342; Alain Girard, "The First Opinion Research in Uruguay and Chile," p. 251; Kurt Back, "The Change-Prone Person in Puerto Rico," p. 330; Robert Carlson, "To Talk with Kings," p. 224; Herbert Hyman et al., "The Values of Turkish College Youth," p. 275; Raymond Gastil, "Middle Class Impediments to Iranian Modernization," p. 325; Gorden Hirabayashi and M. Fathalla El Khatib, "Communication and Political Awareness in the Villages of Egypt," p. 357; A. J. Meyer, "Entrepreneurship and Economic Development in the Middle East," p. 391; Richard Robinson, "Turkey's Agrarian Revolution and the Problem of Urbanization," p. 397; Lincoln Armstrong and Rashid Bashshur, "Ecological Patterns and Value Orientations in Lebanon," p. 406—all in 22, no. 3 (Fall 1958).

91. Isaacs, "World Affairs and U.S. Race Relations," p. 364.

92. Lerner, "Editor's Introduction," pp. 218, 219, 221.

93. Lerner and Pevsner, *The Passing of Traditional Society*, p. 396. Emphasis added.

94. Special Operations Research Office, *The U.S. Army's Limited-War Mission*, pp. 59–63, 69–77; Blum, *The CIA*, pp. 133–62.

95. On communications theorists' contributions to counterinsurgency, see Special Operations Research Office, *The U.S. Army's Limited-War Mission*, pp. 159–69 (Pye) and 199ff (Pool). See also Ithiel de Sola Pool (ed.), *Social Science Research and National Security* (Washington, DC: Smithsonian Institution [Office of Naval Research Project], 1963), pp. 1–25 (Pool), 46–74 (Schramm), 148–66 (Pye).

96. Special Operations Research Office, *The U.S. Army's Limited-War Mission*, pp. 282ff; see also U.S. Department of the Army, *Art and Science of Psychological Operations*, pp. xvii, 47–53.

97. The Camelot Affair precipitated the first genuinely public discussion of the collision between the professed humanitarian values of modern social science and the actual ends to which it had been put in the world political arena. In 1964, the U.S. Army hired private U.S. social scientists to conduct a series of long-term inquiries into the social structures, political and economic resources, ethnic rivalries, communication infrastructures, and similar basic data concerning developing countries considered likely to see strong revolutionary movements during the 1960s. The project exploded when nationalist and left-wing forces in Chile and other targeted countries protested, labeling Camelot a de facto espionage operation. Camelot contractors, notably sociologist Jesse Bernard of American University, replied that the criticism was "laughable" because Camelot's had been "designed as a scientific research project" in which the countries selected for study made "no difference." The argument escalated from there. See House Committee on Foreign Affairs, *Behavioral Sciences and the National Security*, Report No. 4, 89th Cong. 1st sess. (Washington, DC: GPO, 1965); Jesse Bernard, "Conflict as Research and Research as Conflict," in Irving Louis Horowitz, *The Rise and Fall of Project Camelot*, rev. ed. (Cambridge, MA: MIT Press, 1974), p. 129n.

98. Special Operations Research Office, *The U.S. Army's Limited-War Mission*, pp. 282ff; see also U.S. Department of the Army, *Art and Science of Psychological Operations*, pp. xvii, 47–53.

99. For example, Executive Office of the President, "NSAM No. 308: A Program to Promote Publicly U.S. Policies in Vietnam" (June 22, 1964); McGeorge Bundy, "NSAM No. 328: Military Actions in Vietnam" (April 6, 1965); "NSAM No. 329: Establishment of a Task Force on Southeast Asian Economic and Social Development" (April 9, 1965); and "NSAM No. 330: Expanded Psychological Operations in Vietnam" (April 9, 1965); each was obtained via the Freedom of Information Act from the U.S. Office of the Comptroller General.

100. On Lerner, Riley, Davison, Cottrell, and Pool, see Special Operations Research Office, *The U.S. Army's Limited-War Mission*, pp. xvi, 151–59, 199–202, 282–86. On Pool, Davison, and Schramm, see Pool, *Social Science Research and National Security*, pp. 1–74. On Lasswell, see Harold Lasswell, *World Revolutionary Elites: Studies in Coercive Ideological Movements* (Cambridge: MIT Press, 1966).

101. Jesse Delia, "Communication Research: A History," in Charles Berger and Steven Chaffee (eds.), *Handbook of Communication Science* (Newbury Park, CA: Sage, 1987), p. 59.

102. BSSR, Chitra Smith, *International Propaganda and Psychological War-*

fare: An Annotated Bibliography, BSSR Archives, series II, box 7, project 819, University of Maryland Libraries Special Collections, College Park.

103. Bruce Lannes Smith and Chitra Smith, *International Communication and Political Opinion* (Princeton: Princeton University Press, 1956).

104. Clyde Kluckhohn, Alex Inkeles, and Raymond Bauer, *Strategic Psychological and Sociological Strengths and Vulnerabilities of the Soviet System* (Cambridge, MA: Russian Research Center, Harvard University, 1954).

105. Raymond Bauer, Alex Inkeles, and Clyde Kluckhohn, *How the Soviet System Works* (1956; rpt. New York: Vintage, 1961).

106. Reported in Delia, "Communication Research," p. 59.

107. Leo Bogart, "Operating Assumptions of the U.S. Information Agency," 19, no. 4 (Winter 1955–56): 374.

108. L. John Martin, *International Propaganda: Its Legal and Diplomatic Control* (Minneapolis: University of Minnesota Press, 1958), pp. 205–6. See also: B.S. Murty, *The International Law of Propaganda* (New Haven: Yale University Press, 1989).

109. American Association for Public Opinion Research conference proceedings, "Propaganda Analysis," 18, no. 4 (Winter 1954–55): 445–46.

110. Ibid.

111. Ibid.

112. W. Phillips Davison, "A Review of Sven Rydenfelt's *Communism in Sweden,*" 18, no. 4 (Winter 1954–55): 375–88, with quote drawn from p. 377.

113. American Association for Public Opinion Research conference proceedings, "Propaganda and People in the Cold War," 20, no. 4 (Winter 1956–57): 757–60, with quote drawn from p. 757.

114. Ibid., p. 758.

115. William Albig, "Two Decades of Opinion Study: 1936–1956," 21, no. 1 (Spring 1957): 14–22.

116. Bernard Berelson, "The State of Communication Research," 23, no. 1 (Spring 1959): 1–6, with quote drawn from p. 6. Berelson's comments do not specify which "great ideas" he had in mind. The context of his comments suggests, however, that he was referring to use of interdisciplinary communication studies as a window on social behavior generally, Lippmann's concept of stereotype, the quantitative and methodological innovations associated with Lasswell's "who says what to whom" formulation, and similar basic concepts. Berelson's comments were delivered at the 1958 AAPOR conference. Wilbur Schramm, David Riesman, and Raymond Bauer, in comments on the Berelson analysis in the Spring 1959 issue, vigorously dissented; see pp. 6–17.

117. John Riley and Leonard Cottrell, "Research for Psychological Warfare," 21, no. 1 (Spring 1957): 147–58.

118. Irene Gendzier, *Managing Political Change: Social Scientists and the Third World* (Boulder, CO Westview Press, 1985); see also Special Operations

Research Office, *The U.S. Army's Limited-War Mission;* Rohan Samarajiva and Peter Shields, "Integration, Telecommunication and Development: Power in the Paradigms," *Journal of Communication* 40, no. 2 (Summer 1990): 84–105; Rohan Samarajiwa, "The Murky Beginnings of the Communication and Development Field," in N. Jayaweera and S. Amunugama (eds.), *Rethinking Development Communication* (Singapore: Asian Mass Communication Research and Information Centre, 1987).

119. "Images, Definitions and Audience Reactions in International Communications," 20, no. 1 (Spring 1956): 197.

120. Ithiel de Sola Pool, "Communication in the Global Conflict," 20, no. 1 (Spring 1956): 313.

121. These sentiments are implicit in the articles in the Spring 1956 special issue, but they are perhaps most concisely stated in the editor's introductions to each section of the issue; see pp. 2, 5, 49, 103, 143, 197, 249, 299.

122. W. Phillips Davison, "On the Effects of Communication," 23, no. 3 (Fall 1959): 343–60; and author's interview with W. Phillips Davison, November 14, 1990.

123. Davidson, "On the Effects of Communication," pp. 344–55, with quotes drawn from pp. 347, 349.

124. Ibid., p. 360.

125. Ibid., pp. 353–54.

126. Ibid., pp. 355, 348. Lloyd Free, *Six Allies and a Neutral* (Glencoe: Free Press, 1959), pp. 350, 357, 360.

Chapter 7

1. Jean Converse, *Survey Research in the United States* (Berkeley: University of California Press, 1987), pp. 305, 308. On reformist orientation of much social research prior to 1940, see also Albert Biderman and Elisabeth Crawford, *Political Economics of Social Research: The Case of Sociology* (Springfield, VA: Clearinghouse for Federal Scientific and Technological Information, 1968), p. 18.

2. Biderman and Crawford, *Political Economics of Social Research,* p. 30.

3. Ibid., p. 31.

4. Ibid.

5. Ibid., p. 32.

6. Converse, *Survey Research in the United States,* pp. 212, 484 notes 92–94. See Alexander Leighton, *Human Relations in a Changing World* (New York: Dutton, 1949), pp. 58–95, for an extended discussion of the measurement of the impact of conventional and atomic bombing on civilian morale in Japan.

7. See Edward Suchman, Samuel Stouffer, Leland DeVinney, and Irving Janis, "Attitudes Toward Leadership and Social Control," in Samuel Stouffer

et al., *The American Soldier*, Vol. 1, (Princeton: Princeton University Press, 1949), pp. 362–429. On propaganda effects, see Carl Hovland, Arthur Lumsdaine, and Fred Sheffield, *Experiments on Mass Communication* (Princeton: Princeton University Press, 1949). The same theme was later explored in considerable depth in studies by Irving Janis such as "Effects of Fear-Arousing Propaganda" (with Seymour Feshbach), *Journal of Abnormal Social Psychology* 48, no. 1 (1953): 78–92.

8. Biderman and Crawford, *Political Economics of Social Research*. See endpapers of study for contract data.

9. Ibid., pp. 46–47.

10. Morris Janowitz, *Sociology and the Military Establishment* (New York: Russell Sage Foundation, 1965), p. 121; cited in Biderman and Crawford, *Political Economics of Social Research,* cited in p. 46.

11. Quoted in Biderman and Crawford, *Political Economics of Social Research,* pp. 45–46.

12. Samuel Stouffer, "1665 and 1954" (AAPOR Presidential Address), *POQ* 18, no. 3 (Fall 1954): 233. Unless otherwise noted, all unattributed articles in this chapter appeared in *POQ*.

13. See, for example, Hadley Cantril, "Psychology Working for Peace," *American Psychologist* 4, no. 3 (March 1949): 69–73.

14. L. John Martin interview with the author, December 6, 1989.

15. Stouffer, "1665 and 1954."

16. Samuel Stouffer Edgar Borgatta, David Hays, and Andrew Henry, "A Technique for Improving Cumulative Scales," 16, no. 2 (Summer 1952): 273–91; Andrew Henry, "A Method for Classifying Non-Scale Response Patterns in a Guttman Scale," 16, no. 1 (Spring 1952): 94–106; Edgar Borgatta and David Hays, "The Limitations on the Arbitrary Classification of Non-Scale Response Patterns in a Guttman Scale," 16, no. 3 (Fall 1952): 410–16; Edgar Borgatta, "An Error Ratio for Scalogram Analysis," *POQ* 19, no. 1 (Spring 1955): 96–99. Each of these papers was underwritten by U.S. Air Force contract no. AF 33 (038)-12782 from the Human Resources Research Institute, Maxwell Air Force Base, Alabama; they constitute the basis of Stouffer's well-known "H-Technique."

17. Clyde Kluckhohn, Alex Inkeles, and Raymond Bauer, *Strategic Psychological and Sociological Strengths and Vulnerabilities of the Soviet System* (Cambridge, MA: Russian Research Center, Harvard University, 1954).

18. Stouffer et al., "A Technique for Improving Cumulative Scales."

19. Eric Marder, "Linear Segments: A Technique for Scalogram Analysis," 16, no. 3 (Fall 1952): 417–31.

20. Daniel Lerner, "International Coalitions and Communications Content: The Case of Neutralism," 16, no. 4 (Winter 1952): 681–88, with quotes drawn from pp. 682, 683, 685.

21. Christopher Lasch, "The Cultural Cold War: A Short History of the Congress for Cultural Freedom," in Barton Bernstein (ed.), *Towards a New Past* (New York: Pantheon, 1968), pp. 322–59; and Peter Coleman, *The Liberal Conspiracy* (New York: Free Press, 1989).

22. David Rodnick and Elizabeth Rodnick, "Notes on Communist Personality Types in Czechoslovakia," 14, no. 1 (Spring 1950): 81–88; Jean-Marie Domenach, "Leninist Propaganda," 15, no. 2 (Summer 1951): 265–73; Herbert Krugman, "The Appeal of Communism to American Middle Class Intellectuals and Trade Unionists," 16, no. 3 (Fall 1952): 331–55; Morris Janowitz and Dwaine Marvick, "Authoritarianism and Political Behavior," 17, no. 2 (Summer 1953): 185–201.

23. Gabriel Almond, with Herbert Krugman, Elsbeth Lewin, and Howard Wriggins, *The Appeals of Communism* (Princeton: Princeton University Press, 1954). See also Gabriel Almond correspondence file, Psychological Strategy Board, Truman Library, Independence, MO, in which Almond requests the Psychological Strategy Board to "monitor this study . . . and appraise the usefulness of the work we are doing here at Princeton from the point of view of the Psychological Strategy Board" (memo of April 16, 1952).

24. Almond, *The Appeals of Communism,* pp. 15, 18, 142.

25. On Voice of America hearings, see David M. Oshinsky, *A Conspiracy So Immense: The World of Joe McCarthy* (New York: Free Press, 1983), pp. 266–77 passim; and Robert William Pirsein, *The Voice of America* (New York: Arno, 1979), pp. 235ff.

26. House Special Committee to Investigate Tax-Exempt Foundations, *Tax Exempt Foundations* 83rd Cong. 2nd sess., (Washington, DC: GPO, 1954). For an overview of the committee's investigative thesis, see committee research director Norman Dodd's testimony (pp. 5–23) and that of his assistant Kathryn Casey (pp. 64–89). For Stouffer's defense, see Charles Dollard's (Carnegie Corporation) testimony (pp. 972–74). For Berelson's defense, see H. Rowan Gaither's (Ford Foundation) testimony (pp. 1035–36).

27. Ibid. Pendleton Herring testimony (pp. 794–865 passim, with quotes drawn from p. 838).

28. Ellen Schrecker, *No Ivory Tower: McCarthyism and the Universities* (New York: Oxford University Press, 1986); David Caute, *The Great Fear: The Anti-Communist Purge under Truman and Eisenhower* (New York: Simon & Schuster, 1978); Jane Sanders, *Cold War on the Campus: Academic Freedom at the University of Washington 1946–1964* (Seattle: University of Washington Press, 1979). Of related interest, see Philip Meranto, Oneida Meranto, and Matthew Lippman, *Guarding the Ivory Tower: Repression and Rebellion in Higher Education* (Denver: Lucha, 1985); Jonathan Feldman, *Universities in the Business of Repression* (Boston: South End Press, 1989); John Trumpbour (ed.), *How Harvard Rules: Reason in the Service of Empire* (Boston: South

End Press, 1989); Athena Theodore, *The Campus Troublemakers: Academic Women in Protest* (Houston: Cap and Gown Press, 1986).

29. Schrecker, *No Ivory Tower,* p. 42.

30. U.S. Federal Bureau of Investigation, "Daniel Lerner" FBI file no. 123-10557, correspondence from A. H. Belmont to V. P. Kay, August 3, 1953.

31. Peter Novick, *That Noble Dream: The "Objectivity Question" and the American Historical Profession* (Cambridge: Cambridge University Press, 1988). For a more concise presentation, see Peter Novick, "Historians, 'Objectivity' and the defense of the West," *Radical History,* No. 40 (January 1988): 7ff; and Jesse Lemisch, *On Active Service in War and Peace: Politics and Ideology in the American Historical Profession* (Toronto: Hogtown, 1975).

32. Schrecker, *No Ivory Tower;* Caute, *The Great Fear,* pp. 403–45.

33. Schrecker, *No Ivory Tower,* pp. 114–15. See *Laws of Maryland* (1949), Chapter 86, pp. 96ff, for legislative history.

34. Caute, *The Great Fear,* pp. 174–75.

35. House Committee on Un-American Activities, *Hearings Related to H.B. 4700, to Amend Section 11 of the Subversive Activities Control Act (The Fund for Social Analysis),* 87th Cong., 1st sess. (Washington, DC: GPO, 1961).

36. Emergency Civil Liberties Committee, "Petition to the Congress of the United States" (advertisement) *Washington Post,* May 31, 1961, p. A16. Note signatories on advertisement fail to include prominent U.S. social scientists.

37. Paul Lazarsfeld and Wagner Thielens, *The Academic Mind* (Glencoe, IL: Free Press, 1958), pp. 193, 194, 197–204, 218–22, 206, 382.

38. Lerner, "International Coalitions," p. 681.

39. William Glaser, "The Semantics of the Cold War," 20, no. 4 (Winter 1956): 691–716.

40. Schrecker, *No Ivory Tower,* pp. 219–338.

41. See, for example, testimony of A. H. Hobbs in House Committee to Investigate Tax Exempt Foundations, *Tax Exempt Foundations,* pp. 114–88.

42. As in Stuart Dodd, "Testing Message Diffusion from Person to Person," 16, no. 2 (Summer 1952): 247–62; or in the Bureau of Applied Social Research's practice of citing itself as a sponsor for research rather than the original source of the contract, e.g., Patricia Kendall, "The Ambivalent Character of Nationalism among Egyptian Professionals," 20, no. 1 (Spring 1956): 277.

43. Almond, *Appeals of Communism.* For an interesting recent critique of the research methodology originally used in Schramm's studies of broadcasting into eastern Europe, but more recently applied to U.S. propaganda broadcasting to Cuba, see U.S. General Accounting Office, *Broadcasts to Cuba: TV Marti Surveys Are Flawed* (GAO/NSIAD-90-252, August 1990).

44. Elliot Mishler, review, *Character and Social Structure,* by Hans Gerth and C. Wright Mills, 18, no. 3 (Fall 1954): 323; W. Philips Davison, review, *Sociologica: Aufsaetze, Max Horkheimer zum Sechzigsten Geburtstag Gewid-*

met, introduction by Horkheimer, 20, no. 2 (Summer 1956): 480; Arnold Rogow, review, *The Power Elite,* by C. Wright Mills, 20, no. 3 (Fall 1956): 613–15.

45. Avery Leiserson, review, *The People Don't Know,* by George Seldes, 14, no. 1 (Spring 1950): 156–57; Lloyd Barenblatt, review, *The Hidden Persuaders,* by Vance Packard, 22, no. 4 (Winter 1958): 579.

Chapter 8

1. Steven Chaffee (ed.), "The Contributions of Wilbur Schramm to Mass Communication Research," *Journalism Monographs,* No. 36 (October 1974): 1–8.

2. James Tankard, "Wilbur Schramm: Definer of a Field," *Journalism Educator* 43, no. 3 (Autumn 1988): 11. Schramm's impact as a definer of ideologically "responsible" analysis extended beyond communication research. See, for example, his role on the editorial board of the Center for Research in International Studies at Stanford University, a post he shared with Gabriel Almond.

3. See, for example, John Riley and Wilbur Schramm, *The Reds Take a City: The Communist Occupation of Seoul* (New Brunswick, NJ: Rutgers University Press, 1951); or Wilbur Schramm, "The Soviet Concept of 'Psychological' Warfare," in Hideya Kumata and Wilbur Schramm (eds.), *Four Working Papers on Propaganda Theory* (Urbana: Illinois Institute of Communications Research, 1955).

4. Chaffee, "The Contributions of Wilbur Schramm," pp. 4, 5.

5. Wilbur Schramm (ed.), *The Process and Effects of Mass Communication* (Urbana: University of Illinois Press, 1954), see Foreword for acknowledgment of USIA role. The influence of this text has been such that McLeod and Blumler, among others, date the emergence of communication research "as an autonomous academic discipline" from the publication of the 1954 Schramm text; see Jack McLeod and Jay G. Blumler, "The Macrosocial Level of Communication Science," in Charles Berger and Steven Chaffee (eds.), *Handbook of Communication Science* (Newbury Park, CA: Sage, 1987), p. 284.

6. Schramm on rival communications systems, see Schramm, "The Soviet Concept of Psychological Warfare," and Wilbur Schramm, "Soviet Communist Theory," in Fred Siebert, Theodore Peterson, and Wilbur Schramm, *Four Theories of the Press* (Urbana: University of Illinois Press, 1956), pp. 105–46. On Schramm's sources, Schramm's footnotes acknowledge his principal sources for his description of the Soviet communications systems are works by Frederick Barghoorn, Raymond Bauer, Merle Fainsod, Alex Inkeles, Paul Kecskemeti, Nathan Leites, and Philip Selznick, each of which was prepared in the Russian Research Project at Harvard; W. W. Rostow and Alfred Levin's *Dynamics of*

Soviet Society (New York: Norton, 1952), whose production and publication was sponsored by the CIA; a study by Sidney Hook prepared for the U.S. Air Force; and his own work for the USIA and the U.S. Air Force on propaganda in Korea. For a complete list, see Siebert, Peterson, and Schramm, *Four Theories,* pp. 152–53.

7. On Kirkpatrick, see Christopher Hitchens, "How Neoconservatives Perish: Good-bye to 'Totalitarianism' and All That," *Harpers* 281, No. 1682 (July 1990): 65. On Schramm's role in the origin and popularization of the "authoritarian" versus "totalitarian" concept, see Schramm, "Soviet Communist Theory." For an example of the persistence and gradual modification of this conceptual structure in today's communication theory, see Denis McQuail, *Mass Communication Theory: An Introduction* (London and Beverly Hills: Sage, 1987), pp. 111–19.

8. Riley and Schramm, *Reds;* John Riley, Wilbur Schramm, and Frederick Williams, "Flight from Communism: A Report on Korean Refugees," *POQ* 15, no. 2 (Summer 1951): 274 (unless otherwise noted, all unattributed articles in this chapter appeared in *POQ*); See also Wilbur Schramm and John Riley, "Communication in the Sovietized State, as Demonstrated in Korea," *American Sociological Review* 16 (1951): 757–66. See also Wilbur Schramm, *F.E.C. Psychological Warfare Operations: Radio* (Washington and Baltimore: Operations Research Office, Johns Hopkins University, 1952, ORO-T-20[FEC]).

9. Noted in Chaffee, "The Contributions of Wilbur Schramm," p. 34. Wilbur Schramm (chair), *U.S. Information Agency: A Program of Research and Evaluation for the International Information Administration* (Washington, DC: USIA, 1953).

10. Robert Holt, *Radio Free Europe* (Minneapolis: University of Minnesota Press, 1958), p. 236; Joseph Whelan, *Radio Liberty: A Study of Its Origins, Structure, Policy, Programming and Effectiveness* (Washington, DC: Congressional Research Service, 1972), pp. 299–301; see also Chaffee, "The Contributions of Wilbur Schramm," p. 31.

11. "Schramm, Wilbur Lang," *Contemporary Authors,* Vol. 105, p. 432; Chaffee, "The Contributions of Wilbur Schramm," p. 31.

12. Chaffee, "The Contributions of Wilbur Schramm," p. 31.

13. Schramm, *The Process and Effects of Mass Communication* (see Foreword for acknowledgment of USIA sponsorship). Kumata and Schramm, *Four Working Papers* (USIA contract 1A-W-362). Wilbur Schramm, *The Science of Human Communication* (New York: Basic Books, 1963); Chaffee, "The Contributions of Wilbur Schramm," p. 7.

14. *Contemporary Authors,* Vol. 105, p. 432.

15. Chaffee, "The Contributions of Wilbur Schramm," p. 17, 43–44.

16. Tankard, "Wilbur Schramm," p. 11.

17. W. Brian Arthur, "Positive Feedbacks in the Economy," *Scientific Amer-*

ican 262 (February 1990): 92–99, with quotes drawn from p. 99. For related and more detailed presentations, see W. Brian Arthur, "Self-Reinforcing Mechanisms in Economics," in Philip Anderson Kenneth Arrow and David Pines. (eds.), *The Economy as an Evolving Complex System* (Reading, MA: Addison-Wesley, 1988); Paul David, *Path Dependence: Putting the Past into the Future of Economics* (IMSSS Technical Report No. 533, Stanford University, November 1988); Elhanan Helpman and Paul Krugman, *Market Structure and Foreign Trade* (Cambridge: MIT Press, 1985).

18. Todd Gitlin, "Media Sociology: The Dominant Paradigm," *Theory and Society* 6, no. 2 (1978): 205–53.

19. Chaffee, "The Contributions of Wilbur Schramm," in Preface and p. 1.

20. Thomas Kuhn, *The Structure of Scientific Revolutions,* 2nd ed. (Chicago: University of Chicago Press, 1972).

21. John Clausen, "Research on the American Soldier as a Career Contingency," *Social Psychology Quarterly* 47, no. 2 (1984): 207–13. Stuart Dodd, "Formulas for Spreading Opinions," 22, no. 4 (Winter 1958): 537–54. Participation in panels is repeatedly demonstrated in the American Association for Public Opinion Research annual conferences throughout the 1950s, which regularly featured panels reporting on government-funded psychological warfare projects. Summaries of these panels typically appear in the winter issue of each year's *Public Opinion Quarterly*. On professional advancement, see, for example, Clausen, "Research," p. 212.

22. See Samuel Stouffer et al., *The American Soldier,* (Princeton: Princeton University Press, 1949), pp. 3–54, for an extended discussion of the origins and the financing of various stages of the project; p. viii for discussion of IBM punch cards.

23. Ibid. See also frontispiece of text for Carnegie Corporation acknowledgment. On Stouffer, Lumsdaine, and Hovland dependency on federal support, see, for example, Samuel Stouffer et al., "A Technique for Improving Cumulative Scales," 16, no. 2 (Summer 1952): 273–91; in which Stouffer acknowledges U.S. Air Force contract no. AF33 (038)-12782 as the principal underwriter of the development of his well-known "H-technique"; Arthur Lumsdaine and Irving Janis, "Resistance to 'Counterpropaganda' Produced by One-Sided and Two-Sided 'Propaganda' Presentations," 17, no. 3 (Fall 1953): 310. Note that Lumsdaine became the "monitor" for the U.S. Air Force contracts provided to Stouffer; and "Psychological News and Notes," *American Psychologist* 3, no. 12 (December 1948): 559.

24. See, for example, Lumsdaine and Janis, "Resistance to 'Counterpropaganda' "; W. Phillips Davison, "On the Effects of Communication," 23, no. 3 (Fall 1959): 343. Davison writes that Hovland's "laboratory experiments have made it possible to formulate an impressive number of propositions about

the effects of communications. . . . Attempts to systematize or derive propositions from the relatively small segment of qualitative experience that has been sifted [in this field] have been made largely in the literature of rhetoric, political communication, and psychological warfare.'' For examples of USIA application of Hovland's experimental data, see Ralph White, ''The New Resistance to International Propaganda,'' 16, no. 4 (Winter 1952–53): 541.

25. Bureau of Social Science Research, ''An Outline for the Study of National Communication Systems'' (November 1953), series II, box 4, project 642; ''Kazakhstan and the Kazakhs: Targets and Vulnerabilities in Psychological Warfare'' (December 1954), series II, box 5, project 649; ''The Kazakhs: A Background Study for Psychological Warfare'' (November 1955), series II, box 4, project 649; and ''Mass Communications in Eastern Europe'' (January 1958), series II, box 10–11, project 303; each is in the BSSR Archives, University of Maryland Libraries Special Collections, College Park.

26. Michael Gurevitch and Jay G. Blumler, ''Linkages Between Mass Media and Politics: A Model for Analysis of Political Communication Systems,'' in James Curran, Michael Gurovitch, and Janet Weellacott (eds.), *Mass Communications and Society* (Beverly Hills, CA: Sage, 1979).

27. On content analysis, see Harold Lasswell and Nathan Leites, *The Language of Politics* (New York: George Stewart, 1949), for a series of examples of wartime work by Lasswell, Leites, Janis, de Sola Pool, and others. On support of survey organizations and development of techniques, see Jean Converse, *Survey Research in the United States* (Berkeley: University of California Press, 1987), pp. 275–76, 340–41, 353, 357, 506–7 notes 37 and 42, 531 note 17; Carl Hovland, Arthur Lumsdaine, and Fred Sheffield, *Experiments in Mass Communication* (Princeton: Princeton University Press, 1949). On support for Likert and the Institute for Social Research, see Converse, *Survey Research in the United States,* pp. 340–41, 353, 537, 531 note 17; and Stouffer et al., *The American Soldier,* Vol. I, p. 26. On support for Stouffer, see Stouffer et al., ''A Technique for Improving Cumulative Scales.'' On financing the use of computers, see Stouffer et al., *The American Soldier.* Vol. I, p. 28.

28. On support for de Sola Pool, see Sig Mickelson, *America's Other Voice: The Story of Radio Free Europe and Radio Liberty* (New York: Praeger, 1983), p. 211. On support for Schramm, see Whelan, *Radio Liberty,* pp. 299–301.

29. Whelan, *Radio Liberty;* See also House Subcommittee on International Organizations and Movements, *Winning the Cold War: The U.S. Ideological Offensive* (Washington, DC: GPO, 1964), Part 6: ''US Government Agencies and Programs,'' and Part 7: ''Research Studies of the US Information Agency.''

30. Shearon Lowery and Melvin De Fleur, *Milestones in Mass Communication Research* (New York: Longman, 1983), pp. 204ff. U.S. Air Force contract no. 13(038)-27522 underwrote Dodd's Project Revere research. On financing, see pp. 207–8.

31. Everett Rogers, "The Passing of the Dominant Paradigm of Development," in *Diffusion of Innovations*, 3rd ed. (Glencoe, IL: Free Press, 1983), p. 121.

32. Ithiel de Sola Pool, "The Mass Media and Politics in the Modernization Process," in Lucien Pye (ed.), *Communications and Political Development* (Princeton: Princeton University Press, 1963), 234–53; Guy Pauker, "Indonesian Images of Their National Self," 22, No. 3 (Fall 1958): 305–24. Everett Hagen, *On the Theory of Social Change* (Homewood, IL: Dorsey Press, 1962). MIT, CENIS, *The Center for International Studies: A Description* (Cambridge: MIT, July 1955), pp. 59–60.

33. On Pool's, Pauker's, and Hagen's roles in counterinsurgency, see U.S. Department of State, Foreign Service Institute, *Problems of Development and Internal Defense*, Report of a Country Team Seminar (on counterinsurgency), June 11–July 13, 1962 (Washington, DC: Foreign Service Institute, 1962), Ithiel de Sola Pool (ed.), *Social Science Research and National Security* (Washington, DC: Smithsonian Institution [Office of Naval Research Project], 1963). For an elaboration of "development theory" as it applied to U.S. counterinsurgency in Third World countries, see remarks by Daniel Lerner, Ithiel de Sola Pool, Guy Pauker, Lucien Pye, Morris Janowitz, W. Phillips Davison, Hans Speier, and others in Special Operations Research Office, *The U.S. Army's Limited-War Mission*.

34. Chaffee, "The Contributions of Wilbur Schramm," p. 1.

35. On roots of "two-step" and "reference group" theories, see Elihu Katz and Paul Lazarsfeld, *Personal Influence* (Glencoe, IL: Free Press, 1955); Robert Merton, "Patterns of Influence" (1949) in Robert Merton, *Social Theory and Social Structure* (Glencoe, IL: Free Press, 1957); Herbert Hyman and Paul Sheatsley, "Some Reasons Why Information Campaigns Fail," 11, no. 3 (Fall 1947): 412–23.

36. Bruce Lannes Smith, "Trends in Research in International Communication and Opinion, 1945–1955," 20, no. 1 (Spring 1956): 182–96, with quotes drawn from p. 191.

37. Ibid.

38. Ibid.

39. Stanley Bigman, *Are We Hitting the Target? A Manual of Evaluation Research Methods for USIE* (Washington, DC: U.S. Department of State, 1951).

40. Leonard Pearlin and Morris Rosenberg, "Propaganda Techniques in Institutional Advertising," 16, no. 1 (Spring 1952): 5.

41. Herbert Krugman, "An Historical Note on Motivation Research," 20, no. 4 (Winter 1956): 719–23.

42. Hideya Kumata and Wilbur Schramm, "The Propaganda Theory of the German Nazis," in Kumata and Schramm, *Four Working Papers*, p. 37. In

Schramm's original conception, this attribute of propaganda applied simply to "totalitarian" societies. The Propaganda Theory project was prepared under USIA contract 1A-W-362.

43. Albert Biderman and Elisabeth Crawford, *The Political Economics of Social Research: The Case of Sociology* (Springfield, VA: Clearinghouse for Federal Scientific and Technological Information, 1968), pp. 46–47.

44. For example, Joseph Klapper (chair) "Propaganda and People in the Cold War" (AAPOR panel report), 20, no. 4 (Winter 1956): 757–60.

45. Clausen, "Research on the American Soldier."

46. Pope John Paul II, *Sollicitudo rei Socialis* (Encyclical Letter), February 19, 1988; Roberto Suro, "Papal Encyclical Says Superpowers Hurt Third World," Peter Steinfels, "An Unsparing View of Economic Ills," and "Excerpts from Papal Encyclical on Social Concerns of Church," each appearing in *New York Times,* February 20, 1988.

Bibliographic Essay

1. Among Western observers, see, for example, Dean Acheson, *Present at the Creation* (New York: New American Library, 1969), or James Forrestal, *The Forrestal Diaries,* edited by Walter Millis (New York: Viking, 1951). For an unusually candid "Soviet line" analysis of these issues, see Nikita Krushchev, *Krushchev Remembers,* edited and translated by Strobe Talbot (Boston: Little, Brown, 1970), pp. 361–62, 367–63, 392–93, 453–60; and Nikita Krushchev, *Krushchev Remembers: The Last Testament,* edited and translated by Strobe Talbot (Boston: Little, Brown, 1974), pp. 47–67.

2. John Foster Dulles, *War or Peace* (New York: Macmillan, 1950); or William Welch, *American Images of Soviet Foreign Policy* (New Haven: Yale University Press, 1970); and Vojtech Mastny, *Russia's Road to the Cold War* (New York: Columbia University Press, 1979).

3. Leaders of the People's Republic of China were particularly dramatic and consistent advocates of the Manichaean vision from 1949 until the death of Mao Zedong (Mao Tsetung) in 1976. See Mao Tsetung, *Selected Works of Mao Tsetung,* Vol. 5 (Beijing: Foreign Language Press, 1977): or two pamphlets from the Editorial Department of *Renmin Ribao* and *Honggi, Apologists of Neo-Colonialism* and *Peaceful Coexistence—Two Diametrically Opposed Policies* (Beijing: Foreign Languages Press, 1963). Among Western observers, see, for example, James Burnham, *The Coming Defeat of Communism* (New York: John Day, 1950); James Burnham, *Containment or Liberation?* (New York: John Day, 1953); or House Committee on Un-American Activities, *The Communist Conspiracy: Strategy and Tactics of World Communism* 84th Cong. 2nd sess. (Washington, DC: GPO, 1956).

4. Typical Western writings include Anthony Bouscaren, *A Guide to Anti-*

Communist Action (Chicago: Henry Regnery, 1958); American Security Council, *Guidelines for Cold War Victory* (Chicago: American Security Council Press, 1964); and Chamber of Commerce of the United States, *Communist Infiltration of the United States: Its Nature and How to Stop It* (Washington, DC: Chamber of Commerce of the United States, 1946). Soviet writings on this theme include L. Skvortsov, *The Ideology and Tactics of Anti-Communism,* translated by J. Turner (Moscow: Progress Publishers, 1969); and Nikolai Yakovlev, *CIA Target: The USSR,* translated by V. Schneierson and D. Belyavsky (Moscow: Progress Publishers, 1984); D. Volkogonov, *The Psychological War,* translated by Sergei Chulaki (Moscow: Progress Publishers, 1986). On Soviet tactics, see also Paul Lendvai, *The Bureaucracy of Truth: How Communist Governments Manage the News* (Boulder, CO: Westview Press, 1981).

5. Perhaps the most sophisticated example of this trend has been Daniel Yergin, *Shattered Peace: The Origins of the Cold War and the National Security State* (Boston: Houghton Mifflin, 1977). Earlier, widely cited "revisionist" writings include William Appleman Williams, *The Tragedy of American Diplomacy* (New York: Delta, 1961); Joyce Kolko and Gabriel Kolko, *The Limits of Power: The World and United States Foreign Policy, 1945–1954* (New York; Harper & Row, 1972); and David Horowitz (ed.), *Corporations and the Cold War* (New York: Monthly Review Press, 1969).

6. Walter Isaacson and Evan Thomas, *The Wise Men* (New York: Simon & Schuster, 1986); or John Lewis Gaddis, *The Long Peace: Inquiries into the History of the Cold War* (New York: Oxford University Press, 1987). For a sophisticated example of a "postrevisionist" interpretation of Soviet actions from a Western perspective, see Joseph L. Nogee and Robert Donaldson, *Soviet Foreign Policy Since World War II* (New York: Pergamon Press, 1981).

7. Bouscarin, *Guide;* American Security Council, *Guidelines for Cold War Victory.*

8. See, for example, David Caute, *The Great Fear: The Anti-Communist Purge under Truman and Eisenhower* (New York: Simon & Schuster, 1978); Richard Freeland, *The Truman Doctrine and the Origins of McCarthyism* (New York: Knopf, 1972); or Robert Griffith and Athan Theoharis (eds.), *The Specter: Original Essays on the Cold War and the Origins of McCarthyism* (New York: Franklin Watts, 1974).

9. For an overview, see Edward P. Lilly, "The Psychological Strategy Board and Its Predecessors: Foreign Policy Coordination 1938–1953," in Gaetano Vincitorio (ed.), *Studies in Modern History* (New York: St. Johns University Press, 1968), pp. 337–82.

10. For example, portions of the 1940s U.S. Army records known as the "Hot Files" (Record Group 319, entry 154, U.S. National Archives) have been declassified only since 1989 in response to my Freedom of Information Act request, and substantial numbers of these records remain classified. In 1989 the

Central Intelligence Agency intervened at the Truman Presidential Library to reseal records of the Psychological Strategy Board that had been declassified and open to the public for almost a decade.

11. John Marks, *The Search for the "Manchurian Candidate": The CIA and Mind Control* (New York: Times Books, 1979), pp. 204–5; Thomas Powers, *The Man Who Kept the Secrets: Richard Helms and the CIA.* (New York: Pocket Books, 1979); Senate Select Committee to Study Governmental Operations with Respect to Intelligence Activities, *Alleged Assassination Plots Involving Foreign Leaders: An Interim Report,* and *Final Report* 94th Cong. 2nd Sess. (Washington, DC: GPO, 1975 and 1976, respectively).

12. Basic policy papers include U.S. National Security Council, *NSC 4: Coordination of Foreign Information Measures,* December 9, 1947; *NSC 4-A: Psychological Operations,* December 9, 1947; *NSC 10/2: Office of Special Projects,* June 18, 1948; *NSC 43: Planning for Wartime Conduct of Overt Psychological Warfare,* March 9, 1949; *NSC 59: The Foreign Information Program and Psychological Warfare Planning,* December 20, 1949; *NSC 59/ 1: The Foreign Information Program and Psychological Warfare Planning.* (Report to President Truman), March 9, 1950; *NSC 59/1: Progress Reports,* March 9, 1950, December 26, 1950, July 31, 1952, October 30, 1952, and February 20, 1953; *Index to National Psychological Warfare Plan for General War,* April 9, 1951; *National Psychological Warfare Plan for General War,* May 8, 1951; *NSC 74: A Plan for National Psychological Warfare,* July 10, 1950; *NSC 127: Plan for Conducting Psychological Operations During General Hostilities,* February 21, 1952; *NSC 135, No 6: The National Psychological Warfare Effort; NSC 5412/2: Covert Operations,* December 28, 1955. The extent to which the case files associated with these decisions have been declassified varies from case to case. Each of these is held by the U.S. National Archives, Washington, DC.

13. An archival collection of Psychological Strategy Board records is available at the Truman Library, Independence, MO. See Dennis E. Bilger, "Records of the Psychological Strategy Board, 1951–1953, Shelf List," Truman Library, December 1981. For an overview of the board's activities, see Psychological Strategy Board, "Progress Report on the National Psychological Effort for the Period July 1, 1952, through September 30, 1952," President's Secretary's Files, Truman Library; see also Department of State, Office of the Assistant Secretary for Public Affairs, "Emergency Plan for Psychological Offensive (USSR)," April 11, 1951, President's Secretary's Files, subject file b. 188, Truman Library. In 1989 the Central Intelligence Agency intervened at the Truman Library to reclassify selected Psychological Strategy Board records that had been opened to the public for a decade or more.

14. See particularly Records of the U.S. Joint Chiefs of Staff, RG 218, CCS 385 (6-4-46), sections 7, 11, 16–17, 21–26, 31–47, 52–53, 71, 75–76, 79, 86;

and Records of U.S. Army Staff Organizations, RG 319, entry 154 "Hot Files" series, particularly P&O 091.412 TS, both of which are now available at the National Archives in Washington, DC. A finding aid exists for psychological warfare records in RG 331 (Records of Allied Operational and Occupation Headquarters) covering much of the 1945–60 study period, but unfortunately it remains classified at this writing.

15. Records of U.S. Army Staff Organizations, RG 319, entry 154 "Hot Files" series, particularly P&O 091.412 TS, National Archives, Washington, DC; Records of the Psychological Strategy Board, Truman Presidential Library, Independence, MO.

16. National Security Archive, 1755 Massachusetts Ave NW, Washington DC 20036.

17. Center for National Security Studies, 122 Maryland Ave NE, Washington DC 20002.

18. For an excellent, extended discussion of governmental use of secrecy and disinformation in the United States, see David Wise, *The Politics of Lying: Government Deception, Secrecy and Power* (New York: Vintage, 1973).

19. Lilly, "Foreign Policy Coordination"; Alfred Paddock, *U.S. Army Special Warfare: Its Origins* (Washington, DC: National Defense University Press, 1982); William Daugherty and Morris Janowitz (eds.), *A Psychological Warfare Casebook* (Baltimore: Johns Hopkins [for U.S. Army Operations Research Office], 1958), pp. 12–47. Archival material includes *Psychological Warfare Study for Guidance in Strategic Planning;* and State-Army-Navy-Air Force Coordinating Committee (SANACC) case file no. 304, "Psychological Warfare: Concepts and Organization" (May 1946–May 1949) available in declassified form via Scholarly Resources microfilm series of State-War-Navy Coordinating Committee (SWNCC) and State-Army-Navy-Air Force Coordinating Committee (SANACC) records (Wilmington DE: Scholarly Resources, 1978).

20. No comprehensive budget of U.S. psychological warfare activities is known to exist. CIA psychological warfare consultant James Burnham, however, put the overall figure at over $1 billion annually during its heyday in the early 1950s. See Burnham, *Containment or Liberation?*, p. 188; see also Comptroller General of the United States (General Accounting Office), *U.S. Government Monies Provided to Radio Free Europe and Radio Liberty* (Washington, DC: GPO, 1972) and Victor Marchetti and John Marks, *The CIA and the Cult of Intelligence* (New York: Dell, 1974), pp. 74–78, 174. On personnel, see Daniel Lerner, *Sykewar: Psychological Warfare Against Germany, D-Day to VE-Day* (New York: George Stewart, 1948), which includes an extensive (though not complete) list of U.S. and British personnel during World War II (pp. 438–49); Larry D. Collins, "The Free Europe Committee: American Weapon of the Cold War," Ph.D. diss., Carlton University, 1975; James R. Price, *Radio Free Europe: A Survey and Analysis* (Washington, DC:

Congressional Research Service Document No. JX 1710 U.S. B, March 1972); Joseph Whelan, *Radio Liberty: A Study of Its Origins, Structure, Policy, Programming and Effectiveness* (Washington, DC: Congressional Research Service, 1972).

21. John Crewdson and Joseph Treaster, "The CIA's 3-Decade Effort to Mold the World's Views, *New York Times,* December 25, 26, and 27, 1977; House Subcommittee on Oversight of the Permanent Select Committee on Intelligence, *Hearings: The CIA and the Media,* 95th Cong., 1st and 2nd sess. (Washington, DC: GPO, 1978); Peter Coleman, *The Liberal Conspiracy* (New York: Free Press, 1989), pp. 59–102. For Eastern European reportage, see Vitaly Petrusenko, *A Dangerous Game: The CIA and the Mass Media* (Prague: Interpress Prague, n.d. [1978?]).

22. Daniel Schorr, "Are CIA Assets a Press Liability?" [*More*] 8, no. 2 (February 1978). For useful overviews, see Arlene Sanderson, "The CIA–Media Connection," Freedom of Information Center Report No. 432, University of Missouri School of Journalism, 1981: Loch Johnson, *America's Secret Power: The CIA in a Democratic Society* (New York: Oxford University Press, 1989), pp. 183–203.

23. Robin W. Winks, *Cloak and Gown: Scholars in the Secret War, 1939–1961* (New York: Morrow, 1987); Coleman, *The Liberal Conspiracy,* pp. 1–12 (summary), 253–76 (tabular presentation of major activities); David Wise and Thomas Ross, *The Espionage Establishment* (New York: Bantam, 1968).

24. Marchetti and Marks, *The CIA,* p. 174; Sig Mikelson, *America's Other Voice: The Story of Radio Free Europe and Radio Liberty* (New York: Praeger, 1983).

25. "Company-Made Balloons Aid 'Winds of Freedom' Effort," *The Modern Millwheel* (General Mills employee publication), September 1951.

26. John Ranelagh, *The Agency: The Rise and Decline of the CIA* (New York: Simon & Schuster, 1987), pp. 260–69.

27. James Miller, *The United States and Italy 1940–1950: The Politics and Diplomacy of Stabilization* (Chapel Hill: University of North Carolina Press, 1986); William Blum, *The CIA: A Forgotten History* (London: Zed, 1986), pp. 23–31, 130–33, 166–70; Arnold Cortesi and "Observer," "Two Vital Case Histories," in Lester Markel (ed.), *Public Opinion and Foreign Policy* (New York: Harper & Brothers for the Council on Foreign Relations, 1949); Robert Holt and Robert van de Velde, *Strategic Psychological Operations and American Foreign Policy* (Chicago: University of Chicago Press, 1960), pp. 159–205. During 1975 the House Select Committee on Intelligence prepared a highly critical report on the CIA's clandestine efforts to manipulate elections in Italy and France. The CIA and the White House suceeded in halting official publication of the study, but a copy was leaked to the media and published in supplements to the *Village Voice* on February 15 and 22, 1976. See p. 86 of

the February 16 "Special Supplement: The CIA Report the President Doesn't Want You to Read," for discussion of agency intervention in Italian elections. Important original documentation can be found at the U.S. Psychological Strategy Board files, *Italy*. Truman Library, Independence, MO.

28. John Prados, *Presidents' Secret Wars* (New York: Morrow, 1986), pp. 40–60. See also Blum, *The CIA*, and Ranelagh, *The Agency*.

29. Jay Peterzell, "How U.S. Propaganda Has Fooled Congress," *First Principles* 8, no. 3 (1983) 1; Christopher Simpson, *Blowback* (New York: Weidenfeld & Nicolson, 1987), pp. 125–37, 218–19.

30. Martin Lee and Bruce Shlain, *Acid Dreams: The CIA, LSD and the Sixties Rebellion* (New York: Grove Press, 1985); and Marks, *The Search for the "Manchurian Candidate."*

31. Richard F. Staar (ed.), *Public Diplomacy: USA versus USSR* (Stanford, CA: Hoover Institution Press, 1986); and Mikelson, *America's Other Voice*. For Soviet commentary on this point, see A. Panfilov, *Broadcasting Pirates: Outline of External Radio Propaganda by the USA, Britain and FRG*, translated by Nicholas Bobrov (Moscow: Progress Publishers, 1981).

32. John Prados, *The Soviet Estimate, U.S. Intelligence Analysis and Russian Military Strength* (New York: Dial, 1982), pp. 38–50; Peterzell, How U.S. Propaganda Has Fooled Congress; Simpson, *Blowback;* Kurt Glaser, "Psychological Warfare's Policy Feedback," *Ukrainian Quarterly* 9 (1953).

33. Clyde Kluckhohn, Alex Inkeles, and Raymond Bauer, *Strategic Psychological and Sociological Strengths and Vulnerabilities of the Soviet Social System* (Cambridge, MA: Russian Research Center, Harvard University, 1954), U.S. Air Force contract no. 33(038)-12909; Alexander Dallin, Ralph Movrogordato, and Wilhelm Moll, *Partisan Psychological Warfare and Popular Attitudes under the German Occupation* (Washington, DC: U.S. Air Force, 1954 [published under the auspices of the War Documentation Project, Columbia University]). See also Tami Davis Biddle, "Handling the Soviet Threat: Arguments for Preventative War and Compellence in the Early Cold War Period," Paper presented at the annual convention of the Society for Historians of American Foreign Relations, Washington, DC, 1988.

34. Walter Laqueur, *A World of Secrets: The Uses and Limits of Intelligence* (New York: Basic Books, 1985); Carleton Mabee, "Margaret Mead and Behavioral Scientists in World War II: Problems of Responsibility, Truth and Effectiveness," *Journal of the History of the Behavioral Sciences* 23 (January 1987):3–13; see also Winks, *Cloak and Gown*.

35. Lerner, *Sykewar;* Daniel Lerner (ed.), *Propaganda in War and Crisis* (New York: George Stewart, 1951); Samuel Stouffer et al., *The American Soldier*, Vol. I (Princeton: Princeton University Press, 1949), pp. 3–53; see also the War Documentation Project studies cited in note 33 above.

36. Lerner, *Sykewar;* Kluckhohn, Inkeles, and Bauer, *Strategic Psychological and Sociological Strengths*.

37. See, for example, *Public Opinion Quarterly*'s special issue on international communications research (Winter 1952–53).

38. Major casebook-type texts (in chronological order) include Bruce Lannes Smith, Harold Lasswell, and Ralph Casey, *Propaganda, Communication and Public Opinion: A Comprehensive Reference Guide* (Princeton: Princeton University Press, 1946); Paul Linebarger, *Psychological Warfare* (1948; rpt. Washington, DC: Combat Forces Press, 1956); Lerner, *Propaganda;* Wilbur Schramm, FEC *Psychological Warfare Operations* (Baltimore: Operations Research Office, John Hopkins Press, 1952); Daugherty and Janowitz, *Psychological Warfare Casebook;* Ithiel de Sola Pool (ed.), *Social Science Research and National Security* (Washington, DC: Smithsonian Institution [Office of Naval Research Project], 1963). For more modern compilations, U.S. Department of the Army, *The Art and Science of Psychological Operations: Case Studies of Military Application,* 2 vols., edited by Ronald McLaurin (Washington, DC: Department of the Army contract no. 525-7-1, April 1976); a three-volume study edited by Harold Lasswell, Daniel Lerner, and Hans Speier, *Propaganda and Communication in World History* (Honolulu: University of Hawaii Press, 1980); Carnes Lord and Frank Barnett (eds.), *Political Warfare and Psychological Operations* (Washington, DC: National Defense University Press, 1989); Paul A. Smith, *On Political War* (Washington, DC: National Defense University Press, 1989).

39. Harold Lasswell, Ralph Casey, and Bruce Lannes Smith, *Propaganda and Promotional Activities: An Annotated Bibliography* (1935; rpt. Chicago: University of Chicago Press, 1969). This text goes well beyond strictly "media" conceptions of propaganda to consider applications of violence, social management, and the role of intelligence agencies; see pp. 43–49, 196–203, 230–34.

40. Bureau of Social Science Research, Chitra Smith, *International Propaganda and Psychological Warfare: An Annotated Bibliography,* BSSR Archives, series II, box 7, project 819, University of Maryland Libraries Special Collections, College Park. Of related interest is Vera Riley, *An Annotated Bibliography of Operations Research* (Chevy Chase, MD: Operations Research Office, Johns Hopkins University, 1953); and U.S. Department of State, Bureau of Intelligence and Research, Office of External Research, *Government Resources Available for Foreign Affairs Research* (Washington, DC: U.S. Department of State, 1965).

41. Bruce Lannes Smith and Chitra Smith, *International Communication and Political Opinion* (Princeton: Princeton University Press, 1956).

42. Myron J. Smith, *The Secret Wars: A Guide to Sources in English,* 2 vols. (Santa Barbara, CA: ABC-Clio, 1980, 1981).

43. My search of the Sociofile data base for citations concerning "psychological warfare" yielded three recent citations, including one examining the Chilean coup as a "prototype of counterrevolutionary psychological warfare";

see Silvia Molina-Vedia, "El Caso Chileno Como un Prototipo de Guerra Psicologica Contrarevolucionaria," *Revista Mexicana de Ciencias Politicas y Socioles* (October–March 1976–77).

44. Neal Peterson, "Recent Intelligence Literature and the History of the Cold War 1945–1960," paper presented at the annual conference of the Society of Historians of American Foreign Relations, June 1988.

45. Ronald McLaurin, L. John Martin, and Sriramesh Krishnamurthy, "Recent Developments in the Analysis of Audience Effects of Persuasive Communications, A Selected, Annotated Bibliography," Abbott Associates, Springfield, VA, July 1988 (Undersecretary of Defense for Policy contract no. MDA-903-88-C-0048).

46. Jean Converse, *Survey Research in the United States* (Berkeley: University of California Press, 1987).

47. Albert Biderman and Elisabeth Crawford, *Political Economics of Social Research: The Case of Sociology* (Springfield, VA: Clearinghouse for Federal Scientific and Technological Information, 1968).

48. See, for example, Denis McQuail, *Mass Communication Theory: An Introduction* (London and Beverly Hills: Sage, 1987), with no reference to psychological warfare and passing references to propaganda; or John C. Merrill, *Global Journalism: A Survey of the World's Mass Media* (White Plains, NY: Longman, 1983), with no references to either psychological warfare or propaganda. For a recent valuable exception to this trend, see Garth Jowett and Victoria O'Donnell, *Propaganda and Persuasion*, 2nd ed. (Newbury Park, CA: Sage, 1992).

49. William Albig, "Two Decades of Opinion Study: 1936–1956," *POQ* 21, no. 1 (Spring 1957): 14–22. Unless otherwise noted, all unattributed articles in this chapter appeared in *POQ*.

50. Allen Barton, "Paul Lazarsfeld and Applied Social Research," *Social Science History* (October 1979): 4–44.

51. Tony Bennett, "Theories of the Media, Theories of Society," in Michael Gurevitch and Tony Bennett (eds.), *Culture, Society and the Media* (London: Methuen, 1982), pp. 30–55.

52. Bernard Berelson, "The Present State of Communication Research," 22, no. 2 (Summer 1958): 178, and in more developed form, "The State of Communication Research," 23, no. 1 (Spring 1959): 1–5.

53. Jay Blumler, "European-American Differences in Communication Research," in Everett Rogers and Francis Balle (eds.), *The Media Revolution in America and in Western Europe* (Norwood, NJ: Ablex, 1985), pp. 185–99.

54. Steven Chaffee (ed.), "The Contributions of Wilbur Schramm to Mass Communication Research," *Journalism Monographs* No. 36 (October 1974).

55. Steven Chaffee and John Hochheimer, "The Beginnings of Political Communications Research in the United States: Origins of the 'Limited Effects'

Model,'' in Michael Gurevitch and Mark Levy (eds.), (*Mass Communications Yearbook,* vol. 5 (Beverly Hills: Sage, 1985).

56. Converse, *Survey Research.*

57. Daniel Czitrom, *Media and the American Mind* (Chapel Hill: University of North Carolina Press, 1982), pp. 122–46.

58. Jesse Delia, ''Communication Research: A History,'' in Charles Berger and Steven Chaffee (eds.), *Handbook of Communication Science* (Newbury Park, CA: Sage, 1987), pp. 20–98.

59. Everette Dennis, ''Whence We Came: Discovering the History of Mass Communication Research,'' in Nancy Weatherly Sharp (ed.), *Communication Research: The Challenge of the Information Age* (Syracuse, NY: Syracuse University Press, 1988), pp. 3–20.

60. Heinz Eulau, ''The Columbia Studies of Personal Influence,'' *Social Science History* 2, no. 4 (May 1980): 207–28.

61. Todd Gitlin, ''Media Sociology: The Dominant Paradigm,'' *Theory and Society* 6, no. 2 (1978): 205–53.

62. Stuart Hall, ''The Rediscovery of 'Ideology': Return of the Repressed in Media Studies,'' in Gurevitch and Bennett *Cultures, Society and the Media,* pp. 56–90.

63. Hanno Hardt, ''Comparative Media Research: The World According to America,'' *Critical Studies in Mass Communication* 5 (June 1988): 129–46.

64. Elihu Katz, ''Communication Research Since Lazarsfeld,'' 51 (1987): 525–45.

65. Paul Lazarsfeld, ''Historical Notes on the Empirical Study of Action: An Intellectual Odyssey [1958],'' in *Qualitative Analysis: Historical and Critical Essays* (Boston: Allyn and Bacon, 1972).

66. Shearon Lowery and Melvin DeFleur, *Milestones in Mass Communication Research* (New York: Longman, 1983).

67. Jack McLeod and Jay Blumler, ''The Macrosocial Level of Communication Science,'' in Charles Berger and Steven Chaffee (eds.), *Handbook of Communication Science* (Newbury Park, CA: Sage, 1987), pp. 271–322.

68. Everett Rogers, ''Contributions and Criticisms of Diffusion Research,'' in *Diffusion of Innovations*, 3rd ed. (Glencoe, IL: Free Press, 1983).

69. Wilbur Schramm, ''The Unique Perspective of Communication: A Retrospective View,'' *Journal of Communication* 33, no. 3 (Summer 1983); and Wilbur Schramm, ''The Beginnings of Communication Study in the United States,'' in Everett Rogers and Francis Balle (eds.), *The Media Revolution in America and in Western Europe* (Norwood, NJ: Ablex, 1985), pp. 200–211.

70. J. Michael Sproule, ''Progressive Propaganda Critics and the Magic Bullet Myth,'' *Critical Studies in Mass Communication* 6 (September 1989): 225–46.

71. Stouffer et al., *The American Soldier,* Vol. 1, pp. 3–54, for an extended discussion of Stouffer's highly influential Research Branch of the U.S. Army.

72. James Tankard, "Wilbur Schramm: Definer of a Field," *Journalism Educator* 43, no. 3 (Autumn 1988): 11–16.

73. Ralph Beals, *Politics of Social Research* (Chicago: Aldine, 1969).

74. Biderman and Crawford, *The Political Economics of Social Research;* Albert Biderman and Elisabeth Crawford, "The Basis of Allocation to Social Scientific Work," paper presented to American Sociological Association, September 1969, now at BSSR Archives, series V, box 3, University of Maryland Libraries Special Collections, College Park: Albert Biderman and Elisabeth Crawford, "Paper Money: Trends of Research Sponsorship in American Sociology Journals," *Social Sciences Information* (Paris), (February 1970): 51–77.

75. Elisabeth Crawford and Gene Lyons, "Foreign Area Research: A Background Statement," *American Behavioral Scientist* (June 1967). See also Elisabeth Crawford and Albert Biderman, *Social Science and International Affairs* (New York: Wiley, 1969).

76. Irene Gendzier, *Managing Political Change: Social Scientists and the Third World* (Boulder, CO: Westview Press, 1985).

77. Irving Louis Horowitz (ed.), *The Use and Abuse of Social Science* (New Brunswick, NJ: Transaction, 1971); Irving Louis Horowitz (ed.), *The Rise and Fall of Project Camelot* (Cambridge: MIT Press, 1974).

78. Irving Louis Horowitz and James Everett Katz, *Social Science and Public Policy in the United States* (New York: Praeger, 1975).

79. Legislative Reference Service, Library of Congress, *The U.S. Ideological Effort: Government Agencies and Programs,* published as a committee print by the House Committee on Foreign Affairs, 88th Cong., 1st sess. (Washington, DC: GPO, January 1964).

80. Gene M. Lyons, *The Uneasy Partnership: Social Science and the Federal Government in the Twentieth Century* (New York: Russell Sage Foundation, 1969). For a more recent analysis, see Richard Nathan, *Social Science in Government: Uses and Misuses,* (New York: Basic Books, 1988).

81. James McCartney, "On Being Scientific: Changing Styles of Presentation of Sociological Research," *American Sociologist* 5 (February 1970): 30–35.

82. Ithiel de Sola Pool, "The Necessity for Social Scientists Doing Research for Governments," *Background* 10, no. 2 (August 1966): 111–22.

83. The most important social dynamic of theoretical development in social sciences appears to be one of *integration* and *acceptance* of theories, rather than "discovery" or simple articulation of new ideas. The distinction is important, in part because the former processes depend to a much greater extent on recognition by established authorities in the field. The "stages" conception tends to downplay the often politicized process involved in the acceptance of

theories in favor of assumptions about a normative process of scientific advance on the basis of "truths." Several examples of the importance of acceptance (rather than simple articulation) can be readily identified. Lowery and De Fleur contend that Lazarsfeld's famous "1955" theory of the role of primary groups in mass communication was in truth a rediscovery of earlier—but not yet fully integrated—work by Rothlisberger and Dixon and by others. Lowery and Defleur, *Milestones*, pp. 180–82. Similarly, McLeod and Blumler point out that "mass society" as a term and a theoretical category was never adopted by those theorists who are most often tagged with that name. "Mass society" was in fact a 1959 categorization of earlier theorists with substantially different perspectives, and one that was constructed at least in part for polemical purposes. McLeod and Blumler, "The Macrosocial Level," p. 282. The category of "mass society" theorists nevertheless remains in wide use in construction of the "stages" of mass communication theory.

84. McLeod and Blumler, "The Macrosocial Level," p. 282.

85. Ibid.

86. Gitlin, "Media Sociology."

87. Czitrom, *Media and the American Mind*, pp. 131–39; Delia, "Communication Research," pp. 54–73; McLeod and Blumler, "The Macrosocial Level," p. 284.

88. John Dewey cited in James Carey, *Communication as Culture* (Boston: Unwin Hyman, 1989), p. 22.

89. Ibid., pp. 13–68.

90. Hall, "The Rediscovery of 'Ideology,' " pp. 59–65.

91. Biderman and Crawford, *Political Economics of Social Research*, pp. 29–55.

92. Hall, "The Rediscovery of 'Ideology,' " pp. 59–62.

93. Biderman and Crawford, *Political Economics of Social Research*, pp. 32–38, 45–46; National Science Foundation, *Federal Funds 1953*, pp. 37–40.

94. Cited in Carey, *Communication*, p. 22.

95. *Ibid.*, and, from a different perspective, Hall, "The Rediscovery of 'Ideology,' " pp. 59–62.

96. This total is derived from listings of Cantril's works in *Who Was Who*, Vol. 5, p. 113, in *National Cyclopedia of American Biography*, Vol. 55, pp. 211–12, and the University of Maryland's GEAC computerized bibliographic reference system. Texts that focus substantially on questions of psychological warfare, propaganda, or mass media theory include *The Psychology of Radio* (with Gorden Allport, 1935); *The Invasion from Mars* (1940); *The Psychology of Social Movements* (1941); *Gauging Public Opinion* (contributing editor, 1944); *Understanding Man's Social Behavior* (1947); *The "Why" of Man's Experience* (1950); *Public Opinion, 1935–1946* (1951); *How Nations See Each Other: A Study in Public Opinion* (with William Buchanan, 1953); *The French*

Left (with David Rodnick, 1956); *The Politics of Despair* (1958); *Soviet Leaders and Mastery over Man* (1960); *Human Nature and Political Systems* (1961); *The Pattern of Human Concerns* (1965); *The Human Dimension: Experiences in Policy Research* (1967); and *The Political Beliefs of Americans* (with Lloyd Free, 1967).

97. "Cantril, [Albert] Hadley," *National Cyclopedia of American Biography*, Vol. 55, p. 212.

98. Hadley Cantril, *The Human Dimension: Experiences in Policy Research* (New Brunswick, NJ: Rutgers University Press, 1967).

99. *Obituaries on File* (1979), Vol. 1, p. 93; *Who Was Who*, Vol. 5, p. 113; *National Cyclopedia of American Biography*, Vol. 55, pp. 211–12.

100. Converse, *Survey Research*.

101. Ibid. See also Howland Sargeant, "Oral History Interview, December 15, 1970," Columbia University Library.

102. Free and Cantril *The Political Beliefs of Americans*. Lloyd Free also was a joint author or credited by Cantril as a major contributor to a number of Institute for International Social Research studies, including *Attitudes, Hopes and Fears of Nigerians* (Princeton: Princeton University Press, 1964) and *Six Allies and a Neutral* (Glencoe, IL: Free Press, 1959), as well as Cantril's own *The French Left* (1956), *The Politics of Despair* (1958), and *Soviet Leaders and Mastery over Man* (1960).

103. The total of works reported here is derived from listings of Lasswell's works in *Current Biography* (1947), pp. 75–77, *Who's Who* (1976–77), pp. 1833–34, and the University of Maryland's GEAC computerized bibliographic reference system. Texts that focus substantially on questions of psychological warfare, propaganda, or mass media theory include *Propaganda Technique in the World War* (1927); *Psychopathology and Politics* (1930); *Propaganda and Promotional Activities: An Annotated Bibliography* (with Bruce Lannes Smith and Ralph Casey, 1935); *Politics: Who Gets What, When, How* (1936); *Propaganda, Communication and Public Opinion* (with Bruce Lannes Smith and Ralph Casey, 1946); *Study of Power* (1950); *World Revolution in Our Time* (1951); *National Security and Individual Freedom* (1951); *Comparative Studies of Elites* (1952); *Comparative Studies of Symbols* (with Ithiel de Sola Pool and Daniel Lerner, 1952); *The Policy Sciences: Recent Developments in Scope and Method* (with Daniel Lerner, 1951); *World Revolutionary Elites: Studies in Coercive Ideological Movements* (with Daniel Lerner, 1966); *World Revolutionary Propaganda* (1970); *Propaganda and Communication in World History*, 3 vols. (edited, with Daniel Lerner and Hans Speier, 1980). Books that appeared in multiple editions include *Propaganda Technique in the World War* (1927, 1938, 1971, 1972); *Psychopathology and Politics* (1930, 1934, 1960, 1969); and *Politics: Who Gets What, When, How* (1936, 1950, 1958).

104. For example, "Politics: Who Gets What, When, and How" and "Mass

communication research is the study of who says what through what channel to whom, with what effect" (a formulation Lasswell continued to favor at least as late as 1980). Note also Lasswell's contribution to the classic functionalist description of the "tasks," or functions, of the media noted in McQuail, *Mass Communication Theory*, pp. 70, 191. For a concise summary of Lasswellian media theory, see *Propaganda and Communication in World History*, Vol. I, "Introduction."

105. McQuail, *Mass Communication Theory*, pp. 70, 191; Roger Wimmer and Joseph Dominick, *Mass Media Research* (Belmont, CA: Wadsworth, 1987), pp. 6, 16; *Current Biography* (1947), pp. 375–77.

106. Lerner's work with Lasswell includes *Comparative Studies of Symbols* (with Ithiel de Sola Pool, 1952); *The Policy Sciences: Recent Developments in Scope and Method* (1951); *World Revolutionary Elites: Studies in Coercive Ideological Movements* (1966); and *Propaganda and Communication in World History*, 3 vols. (edited, with Hans Speier, 1980).

107. This figure derived from listings in *Contemporary Authors* (New Revision Series), Vol. 6, p. 292, and the University of Maryland's GEAC computerized bibliographic reference system.

108. *Contemporary Authors*. Vol. 6, p. 292.

109. Ibid.

110. Examples include *Sykewar: Psychological Warfare Against Germany* (1949, reissued 1971); *Propaganda in War and Crisis* (editor, 1951); *Passing of Traditional Society: Modernizing the Middle East* (with Lucille Pevsner, 1958).

111. Tankard, "Wilbur Schramm," pp. 11–16; Chaffee, "Contributions of Wilbur Schramm."

112. For the U.S. Air Force: John W. Riley and Wilbur Schramm, *The Reds Take a City: The Communist Occupation of Seoul* (New Brunswick, NJ: Rutgers University Press, 1951); John Riley, Wilbur Schramm, and Frederick Williams, "Flight from Communism: A Report on Korean Refugees," 15, no. 2 (Summer 1951): 274–86; and Wilbur Schramm and John Riley, "Communication in the Sovietized State, as Demonstrated in Korea," *American Sociological Review* 16 (1951): 757–66. The *POQ* text (p. 274) acknowledges sponsorship by the Human Resources Research Institute of the U.S. Air Force's Air University. For the USIA: Wilbur Schramm, "The Soviet Concept of 'Psychological' Warfare," in Hideya Kumata and Wilbur Schramm, *Four Working Papers on Propaganda Theory* (Urbana, IL: Institute of Communication Research, 1955). See cover statement for acknowledgment of USIA contract 1A-W-362 as sponsor; Wilbur Schramm (chair), *U.S. Information Agency: A Program of Research and Evaluation for the International Information Administration* (Washington, DC: USIA, 1953); Wilbur Schramm (ed.), *The Process and Effects of Mass Communication* (Urbana: University of Illinois Press, 1954); see Foreword for

acknowledgment of USIA sponsorship of this text. The influence of this text has been such that McLeod and Blumler, among others, date the emergence of communication research "as an autonomous academic discipline" from the publication of the 1954 Schramm text ("The Macrosocial Level," p. 284). Wilbur Schramm, *The Science of Human Communication* (New York: Basic Books, 1963) (Voice of America lecture series); see also Chaffee, "The Contributions of Wilbur Schramm," p. 34.

For the Department of Defense: Schramm, *FEC Psychological Operations;* see also Chaffee, "The Contributions of Wilbur Schramm," p. 31.

For Radio Free Europe: Robert Holt, *Radio Free Europe* (Minneapolis: University of Minnesota Press, 1958), p. 236; Whelan, *Radio Liberty,* pp. 299–301.

113. Bureau of Social Science Research (Kurt Back), *Information Transmission and Interpersonal Relations,* Technical Report No. 1, U.S. Air Force contract no. AF 18(600)1797; now in BSSR Archives, series II, project 322, University of Maryland Libraries Special Collections, College Park.

114. Edward Barrett, *Truth Is Our Weapon* (New York: Funk & Wagnalls, 1953). Barrett was an OSS veteran, assistant secretary of state for U.S. foreign propaganda programs, founder of the *Columbia Journalism Review,* and dean of Columbia Graduate School of Journalism; see "Edward W. Barrett Dies; Started Columbia Journalism Review," *Washington Post,* October 26, 1989.

115. Kluckhohn, Inkeles, and Bauer, *Strategic Psychological and Sociological Strengths,* U.S. Air Force contract no. 33(038)-12909. This text was eventually published with an expurgated title as Raymond Bauer, Alex Inkeles, and Clyde Kluckhohn, *How the Soviet System Works: Cultural, Psychological and Social Themes* (New York: Vintage, 1956), and has been widely used as a college text.

116. Bureau of Social Science Research (Robert Bower), "Kazakhstan and the Kazakhs: Targets and Vulnerabilities in Psychological Warfare," working paper for Psychological Warfare Division, Human Resources Research Office, December 1954, BSSR Archives, series II, box 5, project 649, University of Maryland Libraries Special Collections, College Park.

117. Albert Biderman, "Social-Psychological Needs and 'Involuntary' Behavior as Illustrated by Compliance in Interrogation," *Sociometry* (June 1960): 120–47 (U.S. Air Force contract no. AF 18 [600]1797). Biderman acknowledges this study was also supported in part by the Society for the Investigation of Human Ecology, which has been reported to have served as a conduit for Central Intelligence Agency–funded psychological research; see Marks, *The Search for the "Manchurian Candidate,"* pp. 133n, 137, 139n, 147–67. On Biderman, see also Bureau of Social Science Research (Albert Biderman et al.), *A Selected Bibliography on Captivity Behavior,* BSSR Research Report 339-1 (U.S. Air Force contract no. AF 49[638]727), now at BSSR Archives,

series II, box 14, project 339, University of Maryland Libraries Special Collections, College Park.

118. Bureau of Social Science Research (Stanley Bigman, project director), "An Outline for the Study of National Communications Systems," prepared for the Office of Research and Evaluation, USIA, November 1953, BSSR Archives, series II, box 4, project no. 642, University of Maryland Special Collections, College Park.

119. Leonard Cottrell served as 1952–53 chair of the Advisory Committee on Psychological and Unconventional Warfare, U.S. Department of Defense (see Daugherty and Janowitz, *Psychological Warfare Casebook,* p. xi). See also John Riley and Leonard Cottrell, "Research for Psychological Warfare," 27, no. 1 (Spring 1957): 147–58; and Leonard Cottrell, "Social Research and Psychological Warfare," *Sociometry* 23, no. 2 (June 1960): 103–19.

120. Leo Crespi, "Some Social Science Research Activities in the USIA (Unclassified Abstract)," in Special Operations Research Office, *The U.S. Army's Limited-War Mission and Social Science Research* (symposium proceedings, March 1962), pp. 317–18; Crespi served as chief of the USIA survey research division.

121. Daugherty and Janowtiz, *Casebook.* For a fuller biography of Daugherty's extensive psychological warfare experience, see U.S. Department of the Army, *The Art and Science of Psychological Operations,* p. xi.

122. Special Operations Research Office, *The U.S. Army's Limited-War Mission,* pp. xvi, 157ff. See also W. Phillips Davison, "Alliances," in Ithiel deSola Pool (ed.), *Social Science Research and National Security* (Washington, DC: Smithsonian Institution, 1963), pp. 26–44; Office of Naval Research contract no. 1354(08). Davison was employed throughout the 1950s by the RAND Corporation; see, for example, "Some Observations on the Role of Research in Political Warfare" (RAND P-226); "Psychological Aspects of Foreign Policy" (with Hans Speier, P-615); "The Role of Mass Communications During the Berlin Blockade" (P-665); "A Note on the Political Role of Mass Meetings in a Mass Communications Society" (P-812): and "Power—The Idea and Its Communication" (P-1869). Also: author's interview with W. Phillips Davison, November 14, 1990.

123. Leonard Doob, "The Utilization of Social Scientists in the Overseas Branch of the Office of War Information," *American Political Science Review,* 41, no. 4 (August 1947): 649–67; Leonard Doob, "The Strategies of Psychological Warfare," *POQ* 13, no. 4 (Winter 1949): 635–44.

124. Murray Dyer, *The Weapon on the Wall: Rethinking Psychological Warfare* (Baltimore: Johns Hopkins Press, 1959). Dyer was an employee of the Operations Research Office at Johns Hopkins University.

125. Harry Eckstein, "The Internal War: Problem of Anticipation," in Ithiel deSola Pool (ed.), *Social Science Research and National Security* (Washington,

DC: Smithsonian Institution, 1963), pp. 102–47. Eckstein was a specialist in counterinsurgency warfare employed by the Center for International Studies at MIT.

126. Lloyd Free "General Premises for VOA," in U.S. Department of the Army, *The Art and Science of Psychological Operations*, pp. 364–68. See p. xiii for biographical details concerning Free's work.

127. George Gallup, "The Challenge of Ideological Warfare," in John Boardman Whitton (ed.), *Propaganda and the Cold War* (Washington, DC: Public Affairs Press, 1963), pp. 54–56.

128. Alexander George, *Propaganda Analysis: A Study of the Inferences Made from Nazi Propaganda in World War II* (Evanston, IL: Row, Peterson, 1959).

129. Holt, *Radio Free Europe;* Holt and van de Velde, *Strategic Psychological Operations;* Robert Holt, "A New Approach to Political Communication," in John Boardman Whitton (ed.), *Propaganda and the Cold War* (Washington, DC: Public Affairs Press, 1963), pp. 41–53.

130. For Hovland's role in the oversight of military psychological warfare contracting, see "Psychological News and Notes," *American Psychologist* 3, no. 12 (December 1948): 559; for more detail on the Committee on Human Resources, see Lyle Lanier, "The Psychological and Social Sciences in the National Military Establishment," *American Psychologist* 4, no. 5 (May 1949): 127ff, 131–33.

131. Alex Inkeles, *Public Opinion in Soviet Russia: A Study in Mass Persuasion* (Cambridge, MA: Harvard University Press, 1950). See also Kluckhohn, Inkeles, and Bauer, *Strategic Psychological and Sociological Strengths;* Daugherty and Janowitz, *Psychological Warfare Casebook,* p. xii.

132. Irving Janis, "Persuasion," in U.S. Department of the Army, *The Art and Science of Psychological Operations*, pp. 609–24. See p. xvi for biographical details.

133. Daugherty and Janowitz, *Psychological Warfare Casebook*.

134. Joseph Klapper and Leo Lowenthal, "Contributions of Opinion Research to Evaluation of Psychological Warfare," 15, no. 4 (Winter 1951–52): 651–62. Klapper was an employee of the USIA Research and Evaluation staff under Lowenthal.

135. Kluckhohn, Inkeles, and Bauer, *Strategic Psychological and Sociological Strengths*. For discussion of the psychological warfare role of the Russian Research Center that Kluckhohn directed, see Biddle, "Handling the Soviet Threat."

136. Klaus Knorr, "The Intelligence Function," in Ithiel deSola Pool (ed.), *Social Science Research and National Security* (Washington, DC: Smithsonian Institution, 1963), pp. 75–101, Knorr was a nuclear weapons specialist with the Center for International Studies at MIT.

137. Kumata and Schramm, *Four Working Papers on Propaganda Theory*.

See cover statement for acknowledgment of USIA contract 1A-W-362 as sponsor. Kumata also served as an instructor at the Green Berets' Psychological Warfare School at Fort Bragg, NC; see Daugherty and Janowitz, *Psychological Warfare Casebook*, p. xiii.

138. On Lazarsfeld's role in USIA and Office of Naval Research Projects projects, see Converse, *Survey Research*, p. 290; Bruce Lannes Smith, "Trends in Research in International Communication and Opinion," 20, no. 1 (Spring 1956): 191; Bureau of Social Science Research (Stanley Bigman), "An Outline for the Study of National Communications Systems"; Robert Merton and Paul Lazarsfeld, "Studies in Radio and Film Propaganda," in Robert Merton (ed.), *Social Theory and Social Structure* (Glencoe, IL: Free Press, 1957), pp. 509–28; Paul Lazarsfeld, "An Episode in the History of Social Research: A Memoir," in Donald Fleming and Bernard Bailyn, *The Intellectual Migration: Europe and America 1930–1960* (Cambridge, MA: Harvard University Press, 1969), pp. 270ff; Paul Lazarsfeld, "The Policy Science Movement (An Outsiders View)," *Policy Sciences* 6 (September 1975): 211–22; Paul Lazarsfeld Oral History, Columbia University Library, recorded November 1961–August 1962. See also Inkeles, *Public Opinion in Soviet Russia*, p. xiii.

139. Alexander Leighton, *Human Relations in a Changing World* (New York: Dutton, 1949).

140. Nathan Leites, "The Third International on Its Change of Policy" and Nathan Leites and Ithiel de Sola Pool, "The Response of Communist Propaganda to Frustration," both in Harold Lasswell and Nathan Leites, *The Language of Politics* (New York: George Stewart, 1949). Nathan Leites and Ernst Kris, "Trends in Twentieth Century Propaganda," in Lerner, *Propaganda in War*, pp. 39–54; and Nathan Leites, *A Study of Bolshevism* (Glencoe, IL: Free Press, 1953). Leites was on the social science staff of the RAND Corporation.

141. Paul Linebarger, *Psychological Warfare*, 2nd ed. (Washington, DC: Combat Forces Press, 1954); Paul Linebarger, "Warfare Psychologically Waged" in Lerner, *Propaganda in War*, pp. 267–73; Special Operations Research Office, *The U.S. Army's Limited-War Mission*, pp. xvi, 79. Linebarger became professor of Asiatic studies at the School of Advanced International Studies, Princeton; see Lerner, *Propaganda in War*, p. viii. See Joseph B. Smith, *Portrait of a Cold Warrior* (New York: Ballentine, 1976), pp. 74–103, concerning Linebarger's psychological warfare training projects for CIA agents.

142. Leo Lowenthal (guest editor), "Special Issue on International Communications Research," 16, no. 4 (Winter 1952–53); Joseph Klapper and Leo Lowenthal, "Contributions of Opinion Research to Evaluation of Psychological Warfare," 15, no. 4 (Winter 1951–52): 651–62. For Lowenthal's own version, see Leo Lowenthal, *An Unmastered Past: Autobiographical Reflections of Leo Lowenthal*, edited by Martin Jay (Berkeley: University of California Press, 1987), pp. 81–110.

143. L. John Martin, *International Propaganda* (Minneapolis: University of

Minnesota Press, 1969); L. John Martin (ed.), "Propaganda in International Affairs," *Annals of the American Academy of Political and Social Science* (special issue) 398 (1971); L. John Martin, Ronald D. McLaurin, and Sriramesh Krishnamurthy, *Psychological Operations Program Evaluation,* and Ronald D. McLaurin, L. John Martin, Sriramesh Krishnamurthy, et al., *Recent Developments in the Analysis of Audience Effects of Persuasive Communications: A Selected Annotated Bibliography,* both prepared for the Undersecretary of Defense (Policy), contract no. MDA-903-88-C-0048, 1988. See also Martin's contributions to Lasswell, Lerner, and Speier, *Propaganda,* Vol. 3 pp. 249–94. Martin served in a number of posts at USIA, including coordinator of overseas research and chief of the Program Analysis Division; see U.S. Department of the Army, *The Art and Science of Psychological Operations,* p. xix, for biographical data.

144. Mabee, "Margaret Mead," pp. 3–13.

145. Special Operations Research Office, *The U.S. Army's Limited-War Mission,* p. xvi.

146. Saul Padover and Harold Lasswell, *Psychological Warfare and the Strategy of Soviet Propaganda* (New York: Foreign Policy Association, 1951); Saul K. Padover, "Psychological Warfare in an Age of World Revolution," *Columbia Journal of International Affairs* 5 (1951): 3–12. Padover served as an Office of Strategic Services officer assigned to psychological warfare duty in Europe during World War II and subsequently became a professor and dean of the School of Politics at the New School for Social Research in New York: see Daugherty and Janowitz, *Psychological Warfare Casebook,* p. xiii.

147. Nathan Lietes and Ithiel de Sola Pool, "The Response of Communist Propaganda to Frustration," in Harold Lasswell and Nathan Leites (eds.), *Language of Politics* (New York: George Stewart, 1949), p. 334; Special Operations Research Office, *The U.S. Army's Limited-War Mission,* pp. xvi, 199ff; Ithiel de Sola Pool, "Social Science in the Nuclear Age," in Ithiel de Sola Pool (ed.), *Social Science Research and National Security;* pp. 1–25; Ithiel de Sola Pool, "The Changing Soviet Union," in U.S. Department of the Army, *The Art and Science of Psychological Operations,* pp. 1043–50, (see p. xxi for biographic data); and Ithiel de Sola Pool, "The Necessity for Social Scientists."

148. Mikelson, *America's Other Voice,* pp. 24, 41, 60, 259; see also "Poole, Dewitt Clinton," *Current Biography 1950,* pp. 461–63.

149. Lucian Pye, *Guerrilla Communism in Malaya* (Princeton: Princeton University Press, 1956). Pye was a professor at the Center for International Studies at MIT, a frequent consultant to government agencies concerning psychological warfare aimed at Asians, and the beneficiary of a number of government contracts designed to gather intelligence concerning the appeal of communism to Asians in Malaya, Burma, and Southeast Asia; on these points see Pye's biography in U.S. Department of State, Foreign Service Institute, *Problems of Development and Internal Defense.* Report of a Country Team

Seminar, June 11–July 13, 1962 (Washington, DC: 1962) Foreign Service Institute.

150. Riley and Schramm, *Reds;* John Riley, Wilbur Schramm, and Frederick Williams, "Flight from Communism: A Report on Korean Refugees," *POQ* (Summer 1951): 274; Schramm and Riley, "Communication in the Sovietized State"; Riley and Cottrell, "Research for Psychological Warfare." Riley also served as vice chair of the secretary of defense's advisory panel on special operations; see *Who's Who* (1974–75), p. 2589.

151. Director of research, Human Resources Research Institute of the U.S. Air Force Air University (1952–53); consultant and contractor to military services (1954–59); chief of psychology and social science division of the Office of Director of Defense Research and Engineering of the Department of Defense (1961–64); other posts; see *Who's Who* (1974–75), p. 2792. See also Carroll Shartle, "Selected Department of Defense Programs in Social Science," in Special Operations Research Office, *The U.S. Army's Limited-War Mission,* pp. xvi, 322ff.

152. Bureau of Social Science Research, Chitra M. Smith, *International Propaganda and Psychological Warfare.*

153. Hans Speier and Ernst Kris, *German Radio Propaganda* (London: Oxford University Press, 1944); Hans Speier, "The Future of Psychological Warfare," 12, no. 1 12 (1948): 5–18; Hans Speier, "Morale and Propaganda," "War Aims in Political Warfare," and "Psychological Warfare Reconsidered" in Lerner, *Propaganda in War* pp. 3–25, 69–89, 463–91; Hans Speier, *Psychological Aspects of Global Conflict* (Industrial College of the Armed Forces, 1955); Lasswell, Lerner, and Speier, *Propaganda and Communication.* Speier's RAND Corporation studies pertaining to psychological aspects of international conflict include "Psychological Warfare Reconsidered" (1951, P-196); "International Political Communication: Elite vs. Mass" (1951, P-270); and "Psychological Aspects of Foreign Policy" (with W. Phillips Davison, 1954, P-615). Speier was a founder and eventually director of the U.S. Foreign Broadcast Information Service during World War II, then a senior officer of the Overseas Branch of the Office of War Information: he served as director of social science at the RAND Corporation from 1948 to 1960 and as a member of its research council from 1960 to 1969; see *Contemporary Authors,* New Revision Series, Vol. 9, pp. 463–64; Vol. 2, p. 530.

154. Stouffer et al., *The American Soldier;* Stouffer, "A Technique for Improving Cumulative Scales," Samuel Stouffer, "1665 and 1954," 18, no. 3 (Fall 1954): 233–38.

155. Ralph K. White, "The New Resistance to International Propaganda," 16, no. 4 (Winter 1952) 539–50. White later served with the USIA Special Projects Division; see Special Operations Research Office, *The U.S. Army's Limited-War Mission,* p. 338.

156. U.S. Army Operations Research Office psychological warfare research

team in Korea (1951–52); William R. Young, "GULAG Slavery Inc.: The Use of an Illustrated Map in Printed Propaganda," in Daugherty and Janowitz, *Psychological Warfare Casebook,* pp. xiv, 597–602.

157. Converse, *Survey Research,* pp. 162–415 passim.

158. RAND Corporation, *RAND: 25th Anniversary Volume* (Santa Monica, CA: RAND Corp., n.d. [1974?]); Bruce L. R. Smith, *The RAND Corporation* (Cambridge, MA: Harvard University Press, 1966); RAND Corporation, *Index of Selected Publications of The RAND Corporation,* Vol. 1 (Santa Monica, CA: author, 1962); and RAND's quarterly periodical, *Selected Abstracts.*

159. Barton, "Paul Lazarsfeld"; Eulau, "The Columbia Studies"; Merton and Lazarsfeld, "Studies in Radio and Film Propaganda"; Judith Barton (ed.), *Guide to the Bureau of Applied Social Research* (New York: Clearwater, 1984).

160. Charles Fritz and Eli Marks, "The NORC Studies of Human Behavior in Disaster," *Journal of Social Issues* 10, no. 3 (1954): 26–41. Charles Mack, *National Opinion Research Center Bibliography of Publications 1941–1960* and *Supplement 1961–1971* (Chicago: NORC, 1961 and 1972, respectively); Paul Sheatsley, "NORC: The First Forty Years" (Chicago: National Opinion Research Center, 1987); *NORC Report 1985–1986* (Chicago: National Opinion Research Center, 1987).

161. Charles Cannell and Robert Kahn, "Some Factors in the Origins and Development of the Institute for Social Research, the University of Michigan," Institute for Social Research Working Papers Series No. 8034, January 1984.

162. Massachusetts Institute of Technology, Center for International Studies, *The Center for International Studies: A Description* (Cambridge: MIT, July 1955). See also Massachusetts Institute of Technology, Center for International Studies, "A Plan of Research for International Communication: A Report," *World Politics* 6, no. 3 (April 1954): 358–77.

163. Biddle, "Handling the Soviet Threat"; Charles O'Connell, "Social Structure and Science: Soviet Studies at Harvard," Ph.D. diss., University of California at Los Angeles, 1990; Harvard University, Russian Research Center, *The Harvard Project on the Soviet Social System: Survey of Research Objectives* (Cambridge, MA: Russian Research Project, 1951); Russian Research Center, *Five Year Report and Current Projects* and *Ten Year Report and Current Projects 1948–1958* (Cambridge, MA: Russian Research Center, 1953 and 1958, respectively).

164. University of Maryland, College Park Libraries, Historical Manuscripts and Archives Department, *Guide to the Archives of the Bureau of Social Science Research* (College Park: University of Maryland, n.d. [1987?]).

165. Mikelson, *America's Other Voice;* Holt, *Radio Free Europe.*

166. Paddock, *U.S. Army Special Warfare,* offers perhaps the best available reconstruction of the evolution of U.S. psychological warfare, special warfare, and covert operations capabilities. See also Aaron Bank, *From OSS to Green*

Berets: The Birth of the Special Forces (Novato, CA: Presidio Press, 1986); Charles Simpson, *Inside the Green Berets: The First Thirty Years* (Novato, CA: Presidio Press, 1983). For an excellent recent text that includes considerable historical material, see Michael McClintock, *Instruments of Statecraft* (New York: Pantheon, 1992). Of related interest, see Edward Herman and Gerry O'Sullivan, *The "Terrorism" Industry: The Experts and Institutions that Shape Our View of Terror* (New York: Pantheon, 1989).

167. "Testimony of Ladislav Bittman, former Deputy Chief of the Disinformation Department of the Czechoslovak Intelligence Service" and Central Intelligence Agency, "Soviet Covert Action and Propaganda," both in House Subcommittee on Oversight of the Permanent Select Committee on Intelligence, *Hearings: Soviet Covert Action,* 96th Cong., 2nd sess. (Washington, DC: GPO, 1980).

168. For a useful summary of developments concerning access to East bloc archives, see *Cold War International History Project Bulletin,* No. 1 (Washington, DC: Woodrow Wilson International Center for Scholars, Spring 1992).

169. Selected examples include Leites and Pool, "Response of Communist Propaganda"; Lendvai, *Bureaucracy of Truth;* Roger Beaumont, "Soviet Psychological Warfare and Propaganda," *Signal* 42, no. 3 (1987):75–84.

170. Harold Lasswell, "The Strategy of Soviet Propaganda," Headline Series Pamphlet 86 (New York: Foreign Policy Association, 1951); Brutus Coste, "Propaganda in Eastern Europe," 14 (Winter 1950):639–66; Evron Kirkpatrick, *Target—The World: Communist Propaganda Activities in 1955* (New York: Macmillan, 1956); John C. Clews, *Communist Propaganda Techniques* (New York: Praeger, 1964); or Lawrence Eagleburger, "Unacceptable Intervention: Soviet Active Measures," *NATO Review* (April 1983).

171. Cyril Barclay, *The New Warfare* (London: Clowes, 1953); Peter Watson, *The War on the Mind: The Military Uses and Abuses of Psychology* (New York: Penguin, 1980); and McClintock, *Instruments of Statecraft.*

172. Michael McClintock, "Emulating the Europeans: American Counterinsurgency and Unconventional Warfare" (unpublished paper, written in May 1990, in author's possession); Jacques Ellul, *Propaganda* (New York: Knopf, 1971); Bennett Clark, "The BBC's External Services," *International Affairs* (London) 35 (April 1959):170–80; or Carey McWilliams, "Knights in Shining Buicks," *Nation* 172 (January 6, 1951).

Index

Academic censorship, 103–4
Adorno, Theodor, 105
Advertising, 44, 114
Advisory Panel on Special Operations
  (Department of Defense), 109
Agitation, 11
Agriculture, Department of, 26, 53
Aguinaldo, Emilio, 75
Air Force, 53, 54, 56, 61, 67, 100, 125,
  131; Crawford and Biderman's study
  for, 95–98; diffusion studies, 113 (*see
  also* Project Revere); and Harvard's
  Russian Research Center, 59, 60, 87;
  The Reds Take a City study, 163–64
Airborne Reconnaissance Units, 37
Albig, William, 89, 128
Allport, Gordon, 80
Almond, Gabriel, 101
Alpert, Harry, 53, 59
Alumni networks, 27–30, 57–60. *See
  also individual agencies*
Ambition, professional, sociologists', 97
"America House" cultural centers, 38
American Association for Public Opinion
  Research, 65–67, 88–89, 98–99, 105
"American Bourgeois Philosophy and
  Sociology in the Service of
  Imperialism," 102
American Institute of Public Opinion, 49
American Journal of Sociology, 50–51,
  53, 65
American Psychologist, 53, 59

American Sociological Association, 50,
  97, 103
American Sociological Review, 50
American Sociological Society. *See*
  American Sociological Association
American Soldier project, 51, 59, 60, 96,
  111–12
American University, 72, 132
Anti-sabotage, 40
Appeals of Communism (Almond et al.),
  101
Aptheker, Herbert, 103
Are We Hitting the Target? (Bigman),
  73, 74
Armed forces: democratization in, 96;
  morale and training programs, *Public
  Opinion Quarterly* articles on, 43;
  Public Opinion Quarterly authors' and
  editors' ties to, 48–51; sponsors
  diffusion research, 75–79. *See also* Air
  Force; Army; Navy, U.S., Office of
  Naval Research
Army, 53; Air Corps (*see* Air Force);
  Chemical Corps, 55; Civil Affairs
  Division, 35; declassified records on
  psychological warfare, 125; defines
  psychological warfare, 11–12; Division
  of Morale Research Branch, 26, 27–
  28, 29, 34, 35, 58, 60; Psychological
  Warfare Division, 25, 26, 27, 29, 35;
  scientific advisory panel, 61; Special
  Forces, 84, 132

Arthur, Brian, 107
Assassinations, 11, 40
Asymmetrical relationships, perceived,
    between sociologists and armed forces,
    97
Atomic physics, economics of, 115
Atomic war, threat of, 54, 55, 87; posed
    by U.S., 7
Atrocity accounts, false, 96
Audience: elite versus mass, 73; passive,
    92
Autonomy, sociologists, perceived, 97

Back, Kurt, 72, 131
Balloons, 79, 126
Barenblatt, Lloyd, 106
Barrett, Edward, 26, 28–29, 38, 131
Barton, Allen, 128
Bauer, Raymond, 59, 83, 87, 93, 131
Beals, Ralph, 128
Beard, Charles, 103, 104
Becker, Howard, 27
Bell, Daniel, 101
Bennett, John W., 36
Berelson, Bernard, 74, 89, 102, 128
Berlin Crisis of 1948, 45, 64
Biderman, Albert, 51, 72, 95–98, 127,
    128, 129, 131
Bigman, Stanley, 73–74, 114, 131
Blum, William, 74
Blumler, Jay, 128
Bogart, Leo, 88
Bolshevik revolution of 1917, 16
Bombing, 58, 79, 96
Bonilla, Frank, 83
Boorstin, Daniel, 102–3
Bower, Robert, 72, 131
Bowers, Raymond, 57
Brazil, CIA intervention in, 81
Broadcasting, 126; to eastern Europe, 6–
    7, 35, 64–65. *See also* Radio Free
    Europe; Voice of America
Brosin, Henry, 57
Bruner, Jerome, 82
Bureau of Applied Social Research
    (Columbia University), 4, 53, 55–57,
    64, 69, 70, 72, 73, 114, 131
Bureau of Social Science Research
    (BASR), 4, 51, 53, 69, 70, 72–75,
    88, 112, 127, 131–32
Burnham, James, 67, 68

Cambodia, 84
Campbell, Angus, 54
Cantril, (Albert) Hadley, 4, 20, 22, 26,
    49, 50, 61, 80–81, 93, 130
Carey, James, 129
Carnegie Corporation, 58, 59–60, 102,
    112
Carnegie Foundation, 9
Carroll, Wallace, 82
Casey, Ralph, 43
Cater, Douglas, 27
Catton, William, 75
Censorship: academic, 103–4; postal, 36
Center for International Studies (CENIS)
    (MIT), 4, 53–54, 81–84, 89–90, 113,
    114, 131
Center for National Security Studies,
    125
Center for Russian Research (Harvard
    University), 59, 60, 82, 87, 131
Central Intelligence Agency. *See* CIA
Central Intelligence Group (CIG), 34,
    37. *See also* CIA
Chaffee, Steven, 6, 107, 108, 113, 128
Chapman, Dwight, 57–58
Chemical Corps, U.S. Army, 55
Chicago, University of, Waples'
    newspaper and reading studies at, 22
Chile, 83, 112
China, 7, 64, 68
Christianity, evangelical propaganda and,
    44
CIA (Central Intelligence Agency), 4, 9,
    50, 53, 53, 72, 75, 100; documents on
    psychological warfare, 125–26;
    established, 34, 37; funding of
    publications, 100–101, 126; funds
    communication theorists, 79–93; and
    Harvard's Russian Research Center,
    59, 60; Office of Policy Coordination,
    39–41, 45; in the Philippines, 74–75;
    Public Opinion Quarterly's ties to, 43,
    48–51; radio broadcasts, 6–7 (*see also*
    Radio Free Europe; Voice of America)
Civil Affairs Division, U.S. Army, 35
Civil Defense Administration, Federal,
    52
Civil wars, 98
Clausen, John A., 27, 111, 115
Cold war, 7, 10, 34, 39, 102; U.S. and
    Soviet "official" version of, 124

Columbia University purges alleged Marxists, 103. *See also* Bureau of Applied Social Research
Commando raids, 24
Commercial advertising, 44
Commercial application of communication theory, 19–20, 44. *See also* Advertising
Committee on Human Resources, Department of Defense, 57–59
Commodities, 20
Communication, social order maintained through, 17–19
Communication in Africa (Doob), 87
Communication theory and research, 3, 115; commercial applications, 5, 19–20; content analysis, 22, 88, 112; and development theory, 84–85, 90, 110, 113; diffusion studies, 75–79, 110, 112; early, 8–9, 16–18; institutional histories, 131–32; "limited effects," 129; literature, 127–29; methods and dominant ideology, 107–15; Nazi, 21–22; opinion leaders, 71, 73, 114; personal influence model, 73–74; personalities, bibliography on, 129–31; and psychological warfare literature, 125–27; reference groups, 71, 111, 113, 129; sociopolitical context, bibliography of, 123–25; "two-step," 79, 111, 113, 129
Communist Party, Italy, 47–48
"Comparative Study of Communications and Opinion Formation, The" (Glock), 69–70
Conant, James B., 60
"Confidential" classification, 38
Congo, the (Zaire), 98
Congress for Cultural Freedom, 82, 100
Consumer democracy, 20–21
"Contemporary American Bourgeois Sociology in the Service of Expansion," 102
Content analysis, 22, 88, 112
"Contributions of Public Opinion Research to Psychological Warfare" (AAOPR session), 66
Converse, Jean, 54, 96, 127, 128, 131
Corson, William, 40–41
Cottrell, Leonard, 28, 59, 61, 85, 89–90, 98, 131

Counterinsurgency, 11, 74, 84–85
Counts, George, 48
Coups d'etat, 56, 98, 126
Crawford, Elizabeth, 51, 72, 95–98, 127, 128, 129
Creel, George, 15
Crespi, Leo, 36, 43–44, 131
Crisis management, 95
Cuadernos (periodical), 100
Cuba, 81, 112
Cultural centers, 36, 38
Czechoslovakia, 64
Czitrom, Daniel, 128

Damle, Y. B., 83
Daugherty, William, 131
Davis, Elmer, 26
Davis, Kingsley, 56, 59
Davison, W. Phillips, 27, 66, 85, 86, 88, 91–93, 105, 131
Defectors and refugees from Soviet Union, studies of, 54, 59, 100
Defense, Department of, 4, 6, 9, 52, 57–59, 125, 131
Defense Science Board, 109
DeFleur, Melvin, 75, 76, 100, 113, 128
Delia, Jesse, 62, 85–86, 128
Demobilization, after World War II, 35, 36
Democratization, within armed forces, 96
Demolition, 40
Deniability, 39
Dennis, Everette, 128
Denver, University of, 27
Deutsche Lebensgebiete, 21
Development theory, 84–85, 90, 110, 113
DeVinney, Leland, 28, 60
Dewey, John, 102, 129
Diffusion research, 75–79, 110, 112
Diplomacy, as psychological operation, 11
Division of Program Surveys (Department of Agriculture), 26
Document forgery, 12
Documentary films, as propaganda, 35
Dodd, Stuart, 76, 100, 110, 113
Dollard, Charles, 58, 59, 60
Dollard, John, 60
Dominican Republic, 81
Donovan, William, 24, 26
Doob, Leonard, 26, 87, 131

Double agents, 40
Drugs, mind-altering, 126
Dulles, John Foster, 81
Durkheim, Émile, 128
Dyer, Murray, 131

Eastern Europe: broadcasting to, 6–7, 35,
    64–65 (*see also* Radio Free Europe;
    Voice of America); leafletting of, 79;
    vulnerability to psychological warfare
    studied by BSSR, 72
Eastman, Max, 67
Eckstein, Harry, 131
Effects research, 111
Egypt, 56, 81, 83, 98
Eisenhower, Dwight D., 75
Eisenhower Presidential Library, 125
El Salvador, 115
Emergency Civil Liberties Committee,
    103
Encounter (periodical), 100
Espionage, 12
Eulau, Heinz, 27, 128
Europe, psychological warfare by U.S.
    allies in, 131. *See also* Eastern
    Europe; Western Europe
Evacuation, 40
Evangelical Christian propaganda, 44
Exchange programs, scholarly, 38
Experiments in Mass Communications
    (Hovland), 58

FBI (Federal Bureau of Investigation), 9,
    103, 104
Federal Reserve Board, 54
Feedback, positive, 109–10
Fegiz, P. Luzzato, 47
Field, Harry H., 95
Fink, Ray, 72
Ford Foundation, 9, 28, 82, 102
Foreign Broadcast Information Service,
    80
"Foreign Information Measures," 39.
    See also Psychological warfare
Forgery of enemy documents, 12
Forum (periodical), 100
*Four Working Papers on Propaganda
    Theory* (Schramm), 109
France, 37, 81, 112, 126
Free, Lloyd A., 49, 50, 81, 93, 130, 131
Free Europe Fund, 50
Freedom of Information Act, 12, 36, 125

Fund for Social Analysis, 103
Fund for Social Research, 103
Fund for the Republic study,
    Lazarsfeld's, 103–4
"Future of Psychological Warfare, The"
    (Speier), 44, 45–46

Gallup, George, 26, 131
Gardner, John, 59
Gary, Brett, 22
Gendzier, Irene, 128
Genocide, and mass communication, 20,
    22
George, Alexander, 131
Gitlin, Todd, 110, 128
Glock, Charles, 56, 69–70, 71–72, 73
Goebbels, Paul Josef, 21
Goldhamer, Herbert, 51
Gottschalk, Louis, 72
Greece, 45, 93, 98
Guatemala, 98, 115, 126
Guerilla warfare, 7, 11, 12, 15, 24, 40
Gurfein, Murray, 27
Guttmann, Louis, 28, 100

Hagan, Everett, 113
Hall, Stuart, 128, 129
Hardt, Hanno, 128
Harvard University, 88; Laboratory of
    Social Relations, 99; purges alleged
    Marxists, 103; Russian Research
    Center, 59, 60, 82, 87, 131
Health, Education and Welfare,
    Department of, 53
Herring, Pendleton, 60, 102
Hidden Persuaders, The (Packard), 106
Hill, Richard, 75
Hillenkoetter, Roscoe, 37
Hitler-Stalin pact of 1939, 67
Hochheimer, John, 6, 128
Hoehn, Reinhard, 22
Holt, Robert, 131
Hook, Sidney, 67, 101
Horowitz, Irving Louis, 128
House Committee on Un-American
    Activities (HUAC), 102, 103
Houston, Lawrence, 37
Hovland, Carl, 28, 58, 59, 88, 96, 111–
    12
How the Soviet System Works
    (Kluckhohn et al.), 87
Huk guerillas, Philippines, 7

Human Ecology Fund, 72
Human Relations and Morale panel,
Committee on Human Resources, 58–
59
Hunter, Walter, 57

India, 81
Indonesia, 83, 112, 115
Inkeles, Alex, 27, 59, 87, 93, 131
Inquiry, The (intelligence agency), 16
Institute for International Social
Research, 4, 61, 130
Institute for Social Research (University
of Michigan), 53, 54, 115, 131
Institute of Human Relations (Yale
University), 27
Insulation of social science research, 96,
97, 106
Insurrection, 11
Integration, racial, 34, 83
Interior, Department of the, 52
*International Communication and
Political Opinion* (Smith & Smith),
86–87
International Communications Research
issue of *Public Opinion Quarterly*, 67,
91, 100
*International Propaganda and
Psychological Warfare* (Smith &
Smith), 86–87
International Public Opinion Research,
100
Iran, 7, 56, 70, 98, 126
Isaacs, Harold, 83
"Italian Public Opinion" (Fegiz), 47
Italy, 47–48, 69, 81, 112, 126

Jackson, C. D., 27, 75
Janis, Irving, 27, 131
Janowitz, Morris, 27, 97, 114, 131
Japan, U.S. Strategic Bombing Survey,
58
Jefferson School of Social Science, 103,
104
John Paul II, Pope, 116
Josephs, Devereaux, 60

Katz, Elihu, 57, 73, 113, 128
Katz, James Everett, 128
Kaufman, Helen, 88
Kazakhstan, 72, 112
Keller, Suzanne, 83

Kendall, Patricia, 57, 83
Kennan, George, 40
Keppel, Frank, 60
Kidnapping, 12, 40
Kirkpatrick, Jeane, 7, 108
Klapper, Joseph, 66, 131
Kluckhohn, Clyde, 26, 60, 87, 131
Knorr, Klaus, 131
Knowledge, sociology of, 4–5
Kohler, Foy, 67
Korean War, 7, 63, 64, 65
Krishnamurthy, Sriramesh, 127
Krugman, Herbert, 101, 114–15
Kumata, Hideya, 131

Labor Department, 52
Labor rebellions, post-World War I, 16
Laboratory of Social Relations (Harvard),
99
Lambert, Gerard, 49
Landsdale, Edward, 74
Langer, Walter, 27
Lanier, Lyle, 58
Laos, 84, 98
Larsen, Otto, 75
Lasky, Melvin, anti-neutralism of, 101
Lasswell, Harold, 13, 15, 16, 22–23, 29,
43, 50, 59, 85, 86, 105; on
communication and social order, 17–
19, 21; heads War Communications
Division, 26, 27; at Library of
Congress, 22, 88; *Propaganda
Technique in the World War*, 16, 130;
serves on Ford Foundation granting
committee, 82
Latent distance scales, 100
Latin America, 81
Lazarsfeld, Paul, 4, 19–20, 22, 26, 28,
50, 55–56, 67, 73, 74, 82, 113, 114,
128, 131; on commercial
communications research, 5, 62; Fund
for the Republic study, 103–4;
Personal Influence, 73, 74
Leafletting, 43, 67, 76–79
Leaks, 38
Lee, Alfred McClung, 48
Leighton, Alexander, 26, 58, 60, 131
Leiserson, Avery, 105–6
Leites, Nathan, 26–27, 88, 131
Lerner, Daniel, 10, 27, 64, 66, 70–71,
83–84, 85, 86, 100, 101, 105, 110,
113, 130

Lewin, Elsbeth, 101
Library of Congress, 22, 26, 88, 128
Likert, Rensis, 26, 50, 54, 59, 96, 112
"Limited effects" theory, 129
Linebarger, Paul M., 74, 131
Lippmann, Walter, 13, 16, 17, 18, 21, 84
Lovestone, Jay, 67, 68
Lowenthal, Leo, 51, 66, 67, 68–69, 71, 91, 131
Lowery, Shearon, 76, 113, 128
LSD, experimental use of, 126
Lyons, Gene, 128

Maccoby, Nathan, 27–28
MacMillan, John, 66
Magazines, control of, 36
Magruder, John, 32
Magsaysay, Raymond, 74
Maine, Henry, 128
Manpower panel, Committee on Human Resources, 58
Mao Zedong, 7
Marcuse, Herbert, 27, 29, 68
Marder, Eric, 100
Marquis, Donald, 57
Marshall, John, 22–23
Martial law, proposed for United States, 46
Martin, L. John, 88, 127, 131
Marxism, 35
Marxists: alleged, purged from universities, 103; reformed, 67–68; thought to be deranged, 101
Massachusetts Institute of Technology. *See* MIT
Mauldin, W. Parker, 28
McCarthy, Joseph, 65, 102
McCarthyism, 10, 65, 94, 102–4
McCartney, James, 128
McCloy, John, 25, 82
McClure, Robert, 26, 35–36
McGranahan, Donald, 44–45, 46
McLaurin, Ronald, 127
McLeod, Jack, 128
McPeak, William, 28
McPhee, William, 74
McQuail, Denis, 64
Mead, Margaret, 131
Menninger, William C., 57
Merton, Robert, 5, 28, 62, 114

Michigan, University of: Institute for Social Research, 53, 54, 131; Survey Research Center, 54
Middle East: economic development in, 83; psychological operations targeting, 69; Voice of America survey in, 56, 64, 83
Millikan, Max, 82
Mills, C. Wright, 105
Mind-altering drugs, 126
MIT: Center for International Studies (CENIS), 4, 53–54, 81–84, 89–90, 113, 114, 131; purges alleged Marxists, 103
"Modernization," 83
Monat, Der (periodical), 100
Money laundering, 50, 81
Morale, armed forces, and training programs, *Public Opinion Quarterly* articles on, 43
Morale, civilian: and bombing, 96; World War II German and U.S., *Public Opinion Quarterly* articles on, 43
Mossadegh, Mohammed, 70
Motivation research, 111, 114
Motivations, social scientists', for psychological warfare work, 110–11; negative, 102–6; positive, 98–102
Murder, 11; of double agents, 40

National Advisory Committee on Aeronautics, 53
National Archives, 125
National Committee for a Free Europe, 50
National Opinion Research Center (NORC), 4, 26, 27, 54–55, 95, 131
National Science Foundation, 52, 53
National Security Act of 1947, 37
National Security Archive, 125
National Security Council, 13, 37–40, 45, 46, 48, 64, 75, 109, 125
Navy, U.S., Office of Naval Research, 53, 54, 56, 66
Near East. *See* Middle East
Networks, "old boy/girl," 27–30, 57–60. *See also individual agencies*
Neutralism, campaign against, 100
New School for Social Research, 45
Newsreels, 35
Nicaragua, 115

Nigeria, CIA intervention in, 81
Noelle, Neumann, Elisabeth, 22
NSC 4, 38, 45, 48
NSC 4-A, 38–39, 45, 48
NSC 10/2, 39–41
Nuclear threat, 54, 55, 87; posed by U.S., 7

Ober Anti-Communist Act, 103
Occupied Areas Division, State Department, 49
O'Connell, Charles, 60
Odbert, Henry, 58
Office for Special Projects (CIA), 39. *See also* Office of Policy Coordination
Office of Intelligence and Research (State Department), 52
Office of International Information, 64
Office of Naval Research, 53, 54, 56, 66
Office of Policy Coordination (CIA), 39–41, 45
Office of Public Opinion Research (Princeton University), 49, 80
Office of Radio Research (Columbia University), 22
Office of Strategic Services. *See* OSS
Office of the Coordinator of Information, 24
Office of the Coordinator of Inter-American Affairs, 80–81
Office of War Information. *See* OWI
Ohlendorf, Otto, 21–22
Old boy/girl networks, 27–30, 57–60. *See also individual agencies*
"On the Effects of Communication" (Davison), 91–93
"Opinion and Communications Research in National Defense" (AAOPR session), 66–67
Opinion leaders, 71, 73, 114
Opinion polls, 21, 43, 53, 54, 111; techniques for, 36, 43, 73
Oppenheim, Felix, 47
Order, social, and mass communication, 17–19
Orlansky, Jesse, 131
Osborn, Frederick, 60
OSS (Office of Strategic Services), 24, 25–26, 27, 32–33, 37, 68
OWI (Office of War Information), 24, 26, 28–29, 34, 43, 55, 81
Øyen, Ørjar, 79

Packard, Vance, 106
Paddock, Alfred, 24
Padover, Saul, 27, 131
Paley, William S., 27
Panama, 115
Paramilitary operations, 37
Passin, Herbert, 36
Passing of Traditional Society, The (Lerner), 10, 84, 113
Patterson, Robert, 37
Pauker, Guy, 113
People Don't Know, The (Seldes), reviewed in *Public Opinion Quarterly*, 105–6
People's Research Corporation, 95
Personal Influence (Katz & Lazarsfeld), 73, 74, 114
Personal influence model, 73–74
Personnel and Training panel, Committee on Human Resources, 58
Peterson, Neal, 127
Phantom Public, The (Lippmann), 16
Philippines, 7, 73–75, 81, 115
Poland, CIA, 81
"Political Extremists in Iran" (Ringer & Sills), 57, 70
"Political warfare," 11
Polling, 21, 43, 53, 54, 111; techniques, 36, 43, 73
Pool, Ithiel de Sola, 4, 8, 27, 83, 84, 85, 86, 88, 91, 98, 112, 113, 128, 131
Poole, DeWitt, 25–26, 42, 50, 51, 131
Population Council, 28
Positive feedback, 109–10
Positivism, 19, 128
Postal censorship, 36
Postcards, 43
Preuves (periodical), 100
Princeton Listening Center, 80
Princeton Radio Project, 80
Princeton University: Institute for International Social Research, 4, 61, 130; Office of Public Opinion Research, 22, 49, 80; *Public Opinion Quarterly* founded at, 22
Process and Effects of Mass Communication, The (Schramm), 71, 108
Program Surveys operation, World War II, 54
Project Camelot, 85

Project Revere, 75, 79, 100, 111, 118–22
Propaganda, 11, 15, 40, 43–44, 45, 83, 115; black, 12–13, 24–25, 34, 84; gray, 12, 13, 36; white (overt), 12, 24, 38, 84
Propaganda, Communication and Public Opinion (Smith et al.), reviewed in *Public Opinion Quarterly*, 43
Propaganda Technique in the World War (Lasswell), 16, 130
"Prospects of Italian Democracy, The" (Oppenheim), 47
Psychological operations, 31, 34; covert, 38; and the Korean War, 63–64, 65
Psychological Strategy Board, Truman's, 75
Psychological warfare, 3, 8; compared with propaganda, 43–44; contractual ties to *Public Opinion Quarterly* board, 43; definitions of, 11–13, 43–44, 115; literature on, 125–27; *Public Opinion Quarterly* articles about, 43; redefined after World War II, 31–41; research in, as patriotism, 98–102; researchers, bibliography on, 129–31; sociopolitical context, bibliography of, 123–25; Soviet, 7; vulnerability studies, BSSR's, 72; in World War II, 23–30
Psychological Warfare Division (U.S. Army), 25, 26, 27, 29, 35
Psychology of Radio, The (Cantril & Allport), 80
Psychophysiology panel, Committee on Human Resources, 58
Public Opinion (Lippmann), 16, 17
Public Opinion and Propaganda (Doob), 87
Public Opinion Quarterly, 13, 53, 57, 126; authors' and editors' ties to CIA, armed forces, and State Department, 48–51; CENIS issues, 83, 91; CIA, armed forces and State Department ties to, 42–43; content and editorial line, during Korean War, 65, 67, 69–72; explicit psychological warfare articles, 43–46; founded, 22, 25, 42; on image advertising, 114; International Communications Research issue, 67, 91, 100; in McCarthy era, 104; Project Revere reports, 76, 79; publishes Stouffer group, 99–100; *Reds Take a*

City, The, findings in, 63; suppresses alternative paradigms, 101, 105–6; and U.S. government "internationalists," 46–48
Public Opinion Research Project (Princeton University), 22, 49, 80
Public relations, 44, 112
Puerto Rico, "change-prone" individuals in, 83
Pye, Lucian, 84, 131

Racial integration, 34, 83
Radio broadcasts into Eastern Europe, 6–7, 35, 64–65. *See also* Radio Free Europe; Voice of America
Radio Free Europe, 50, 88–89, 109, 126, 131, 132
Radio Liberation, 109
Radio Liberty, 126
RAND Corporation, 51, 53, 58, 66, 82, 86, 91, 127, 131
Reds Take a City, The (Schramm, Riley, & Williams), 63–64
Reece, Carroll, 102
Reference groups, 71, 111, 113, 129
Refugee studies, 54, 59, 100
"Regional Attitudes on International Cooperation" (Williams), 49
Reich, Das (journal), 22
"Relay points," social, 114. *See also* Opinion leaders
Research Branch, Division of Moral, U.S. Army, 26, 27–28, 29, 34, 35, 58, 60
RIAS radio, 35
Riley, John W., 27, 63, 85, 89–90, 131
Ringer, Benjamin, 57, 70
Rockefeller, Nelson, 61, 75, 81
Rockefeller Foundation, 13, 22–23, 28, 55, 60–61, 81, 102
Rogers, Everett, 128
Roosevelt, Franklin D., 24
Roper, Elmo, 26
Russell Sage Foundation, 60, 61
Russian Research Center (Harvard University), 59, 60, 82, 87, 131
Rutgers University, 88

Sabotage, 11, 12, 24, 37, 40, 45
Saipan, military intelligence-gathering on, 43
Scaling techniques, 111, 112
Scholarly exchange programs, 38

Schramm, Wilbur, 26, 54, 71, 84, 85, 86, 98, 107–09, 112, 113, 115, 128, 130–31; *The Reds Take a City*, 63–64
Science of Human Communication, the (Schramm), 109
Seldes, George, 105–6
Selective attention, and social science research, 96
Shartle, Carroll, 57, 131
Shaw, John G., 75
Shils, Edward, 82, 101, 114
Sills, David, 57, 70, 89
Slesinger, Donald, 23
Smith, Bruce Lannes, 43, 86, 114
Smith, Chitra M., 86, 127, 131
Smith, Joseph B., 74
Smith, Myron, Jr., 127
Smith-Mundt Act, 64
Social order, and mass communication, 18–19
"Social relay points," 114. *See also* Opinion leaders
Social Science Research Council, 28, 61, 102
Sociofile data base, 127
Sociology of knowledge, 4–5
Sociometry, 57
South Vietnam, 72. *See also* Vietnam
Soviet Union, 7, 43, 68, 81, 83, 112, 115, 126, 131; surveys of refugees and defectors from, 54, 59, 100
"Soviet Version of American History, The" (Counts), reviewed in *Public Opinion Quarterly*, 48
Special operations, 12, 24
Special Operations Research Office, 84
Special Studies and Evaluation Subcommittee of SANACC, 37
Speier, Hans, 26, 44, 45–46, 49, 51, 58, 82, 91, 114, 131
Spencer, Lyle, 28
Sproule, J. Michael, 87, 128
Sputnik launch, 53
Stalin, Josef, 7, 67
Stanford University, 27
Stanton, Frank, 19, 26, 50
State Department, 4, 36, 45, 52, 55, 70, 125; and *Public Opinion Quarterly*, 42–43, 48–51
State-Army-Navy-Air Force Coordinating Committee (SANACC), 37
Stephan, Frederick, 57
Stereotype, 17, 80

Stouffer, Samuel, 57, 99–100, 102, 112, 114, 128, 131; *American Soldier* project, 51, 59, 60, 96, 111–12; and the Research Branch, 26, 27–28, 29, 34, 35, 58, 60
Strategic bombing surveys, 58, 79, 96
Strategic hamlets, 84
Streibel, Gary, 89
Stycos, Joseph, 66
Subversion, 12, 24, 40, 45, 46
Sun Tzu, 15
Survey Research Center (University of Michigan). *See* Institute for Social Research
Survey Research in the United States (Converse), 54

Tankard, James, 107, 109, 128
"Target capture," 12
Tennessee Valley Authority, 53
Terror, 15
Think tanks, 97
Third World: "modernization," 83; nationalism, 68
Time and *Life*, BASR's readership surveys for, 55
Tonnies, Ferdinand, 128
"Top secret" classification, 38
Torture, 4, 72
Treasury Department, 26
Truman, Harry S., 34, 45, 75
Truman Presidential Library, 125
Turkey, 45, 56, 115
"Two-step" communications theory, 79, 111, 113, 129

Ukraine, 112
United States Information Service (USIS), 64. *See also* USIA
United States International Information and Educational Exchange Project, 73
University of California at Los Angeles (UCLA) purges alleged Marxists, 103
University of Maryland, 131
U.S. Army's Limited-War Mission and Social Science Research, The, 84
"U.S. Psychological Warfare Policy" (McGranahan), 45–45
USIA (U.S. Information Agency), 9, 52, 53, 64, 72, 73, 74, 81, 85, 93; Bigman's studies for, 114; Schramm's studies for, 109, 131
U.S.S.R.. *See* Soviet Union

Vandenberg, Hoyt, 34
Vietnam, 7, 74, 84. *See also* South
    Vietnam
Voice of America (VOA), 12, 35, 38,
    51, 56, 57, 64–69, 71, 83, 88, 102,
    109
Voicelessness, subverted to
    consumerism, 20
Voting (Berelson, Lazarsfeld, &
    McPhee), 74

Walsh, Warren, 47
Waples, Douglas, 22
War Communications Division (Library
    of Congress), 26, 27
War Department, U.S.: Psychologic
    Branch, 25; psychological warfare and
    propaganda in World War I, 16. *See
    also* Defense, Department of
Warfare: civil, 98; clandestine or
    convert, 12, 34, 36, 37, 39, 40;
    economic, 40; limited, 90; undeclared,
    31. *See also* Psychological warfare
Watergate investigation, congressional,
    37
Wayne, Ivor, 72, 83

Weltanschauungskrieg, 11, 24
Western Europe, radio broadcasting to
    and surveys of, 64
White, Ralph K., 131
Wiggins, Lee, 56
Williams, Appleman, 103
Williams, Frederick W., 36, 49, 63
Willits, Joseph, 23
Wilson, Elmo, 26, 59, 66
Wilson, Woodrow, 15–16
Wisner, Frank, 39–40, 45, 49
World War I, psychological warfare in,
    15–16
Worldviews, seduction of rival, 20. *See
    also Weltanschauungskrieg*
Wriggins, Howard, 101
Wyman, W. G., 34–35

Yale University Institute of Human
    Relations, 27
Young, Donald, 28
Young, William R., 131
Yugoslavia, occupied, 37

Zaire. *See* Congo, the
Zimmerman, Claire, 83